IN-DEPTH INTERVIEWING

Principles, Techniques, Analysis

Second edition

For Boris and Terrence;
to Hannah and to the memory of the grandparents
I never had the chance to know;
to the memory of the late
Carl Reinganum;
and the Rechter family.

IN-DEPTH INTERVIEWING

Principles, Techniques, Analysis

Second edition

VICTOR MINICHIELLO
ROSALIE ARONI
ERIC TIMEWELL
LORIS ALEXANDER

 LONGMAN

Addison Wesley Longman Australia Pty Limited
95 Coventry Street
South Melbourne 3205 Australia

Offices in Sydney, Brisbane and Perth,
and associated companies throughout the world.

Produced by Addison Wesley Longman Australia Pty Ltd
Printed in Malaysia through Longman Malaysia, GPS
Set in Sabon

National Library of Australia
Cataloguing-in-Publication data

In-depth interviewing : principles, techniques, analysis.

2nd ed.
Bibliography.
Includes index.
ISBN 0 582 80101 X.

1. Interviewing. I. Minichiello, Victor

158.39

The
publisher's
policy is to use
paper manufactured
from sustainable forests

Contents

Preface

In-depth Interviewing: Principles, Techniques, Analysis was originally published as *In-depth Interviewing: Researching People*. It provides a discussion of the use of in-depth interviewing as a method for understanding people. The book is written for undergraduate and postgraduate social science and health science students who are studying research methods; for researchers who want a thorough exposition of the value of in-depth interviewing; and for clinical practitioners who wish to hone their skills in the clinical and research interview.

This book was written at the request of our students who kept threatening to publish our lecture notes because they were unable to find an adequate Australian text. In some texts, in-depth interviewing is treated superficially as one among many research methods. In other texts, it is discussed as one of a number of ways of doing qualitative research and given second place to participant observation. A third type of book is the 'learned monograph' which attempts to put forward original and methodologically critical ideas, but does not aid the novice and often uses language understood only by the initiated. Finally, there are manuals which provide prescriptive guidelines for the doing of 'good' in-depth interviewing. We believe that the intrinsic nature of in-depth interviewing does not lend itself to the manual or prescriptive text approach.

We have concentrated on one method—in-depth interviewing—by providing a systematic account of it. The book, written by a multi-disciplinary team, goes beyond simply providing a description of collecting data by this method. It shows the reader the relationship between theory and research; the connections between data collection, analysis and report writing; and the field strategies one might develop in order to cope with the social and political context of qualitative research.

This new edition incorporates a number of major changes in response to constructive comments provided by colleagues and students through their reviews of *In-depth Interviewing: Researching People,* our own conceptual shifts over the years and recent developments in qualitative methodology. The changes include:

- an expanded discussion on the theoretical background to qualitative research and sampling;
- a more cohesive section on the theoretical underpinning of interpretative research;
- a new section on computer applications in qualitative research;
- a more explanatory chapter on data analysis which now illustrates, through research examples, the basic principles involved in organising and identifying themes from the on-going data;
- a more explicit conceptualisation of the ethics and politics surrounding the research process; and
- an expanded discussion of the clinical and research interview.

Our aim for the second edition has been to refine our discussion of the methodology of in-depth interviewing. We have changed the sub-title of the book to *Principles, Techniques, Analysis* to more fully capture the range of issues associated with this method.

This book has been a joint effort throughout, with no senior or junior authorship. Victor Minichiello, in conjunction with Damien Ridge and Rosemarie Stynes, took primary responsibility for the chapters on data organisation and analysis, and writing about theoretical sampling, and jointly with Rosalie Aroni, in setting the context for qualitative research; Rosalie Aroni for the chapters on the nature and forms of in-depth interviewing, life history, ethics and the pragmatics of doing in-depth interviewing; Eric Timewell for writing the chapter on the philosophical underpinning of interpretative research, and Loris Alexander, with Eric Timewell, the chapter on clinical interviewing.

For students

The text was not written to be read like a novel. Some chapters contain more complex material than others. Digesting the information involves hard work and persistence. For this reason, we suggest that the student reads the book in the following way. First, skim the entire book to obtain a general understanding and appreciation of the scope, uses and issues surrounding the method. Do not get held up by difficult details but come back to them. Do not panic if you find chapter 2 difficult to grasp at first. The material presented here is a summation of many complex philosophical debates.

Second, re-read the book, this time reading each chapter carefully and taking notes. Underline key issues and summarise these in your own words. Then you might wish to study selected chapters that pertain to your research project (for example, life histories, clinical in-depth interviewing). Of course, as our own teachers have told us, learning how to do research ultimately rests on the experience of trial and error in the field. However, even this type of apprenticeship works more efficiently when the apprentice has a firm foundation. This book will provide you with that foundation so you can confidently enter the field with a level of competence.

You will notice that we have highlighted words which are explained in a glossary. This will allow you to quickly check on new terms and their meanings. Students often complain about interferring jargon with learning. However, jargon is necessary because it enables the author to be more specific in defining the real world. Unfortunately, this specialised usage is not part of everyone's vocabulary. If the student wishes to participate in more advanced discourse then it is necessary to learn the language. Glossaries are there to be used as a means of understanding and demystifying the subject matter.

For the instructor

This text is not intended to be all things to all people. The aim of the book is to act as a guide rather than to be seen as a 'cookbook'. It does not cover all the special circumstances that may arise from the doing of in-depth interviewing. We believe that it would be inappropriate, if not impossible, to provide a recipe because each project will inevitably lead to different circumstances. We invite instructors to draw on their own research experience and knowledge to provide more detailed guidelines and illustrations to help students. We also hope that instructors take a critical approach and further discuss the definitions provided in the glossaries. We have found that the most useful and easily understood examples are those drawn from the disciplines and professions in which the student is engaged. It is for this reason that we have purposely *not* set assignments at the end of each chapter.

Acknowledgements

The ideas for this book have evolved over a number of years through our teaching experience and conversations with students and colleagues. The need for such a book was first identified by participants of the Australian Consortium for Social and Political Research Incorporated *(ACSPRI)'s Summer Program in Social Research Methods and Research Technology* who provided us with the impetus to write a textbook for teaching purposes. In writing the book, we have learned a great deal and have come to appreciate the insights and achievements of the growing number of researchers using qualitative research in their work. We would like to acknowledge our intellectual debt to them.

Three colleagues require special mention for their significant contribution in the writing of this second edition and its production. The revised and expanded data analysis chapters have been written jointly with Damien Ridge (chapter 10) and Rosemarie Stynes (chapter 11 and the appendix)—members of the Sexual Health Research Group, School of Behavioural Health Sciences at La Trobe University. Bruce Cairns was responsible for typesetting, proofreading and formatting the entire manuscript. His professionalism, patience and public relation and computer skills became an integral and invaluable part of this project.

Chapter 2 has new material which owes a great deal to the talk and teaching of Michael Dutton, Anthony Elliott and, above all, John Cash. The appendix on computers in qualitative research received extensive comments from Lyn Richards—and we are most grateful for her generous and valuable contribution.

We are also grateful for the support and encouragement given to us by our students and colleagues at the Faculty of Health Sciences at La Trobe University, and, in particular, Heather Gardner, Jack James and Hal Kendig. We would also like to thank Felicity Allen, Ian Anderson, Jan

Browne, Louise Farnworth, the Reverend David Hodges, Paul Komesaroff, Ian McDonald, Mike McGartland, Alison Page, Steve Polgar, Shane Thomas and Yoland Wadsworth, who offered many useful ideas and criticism, and to the reviewers of the first edition, whose comments clarified our thinking. We are grateful to Louisa Ring Rolfe at Longman Australia for her editorial support. Our thanks to Carlo Golin for his graphic illustrations. However, only we are responsible for any weaknesses the book may have.

Finally, a note on non-sexist language. In writing this book we have attempted to exclude any suggestion of gender bias. There is nothing gender-specific or gender-intrinsic about any of the interpersonal or research roles we describe. However, where we have quoted authors and interviewees, rather than pepper their words with *sics*, we have preferred to let them speak their minds in their own way, however prejudiced it may seem today.

VM, RA, ET, LA
Melbourne
January 1995

List of figures

Chapter 1

Introduction

This text was written because of our concerns regarding frequent misapprehensions about the use of in-depth interviewing as a method for understanding people. The following quotation drawn from a conversation with one of our students illustrates this concern:

> I always thought that in-depth interviewing would be really easy until I got there. I bungled the first two interviews completely. It was only after I re-read my lecture notes and spoke to people who had done it before that I had some idea of what to do next (undergraduate student at La Trobe University commenting on a qualitative research methods assignment).

Most people assume that in-depth interviewing is not difficult to carry out because they have been exposed to journalistic interviewing. However, the *interview* is a complex and involved procedure when used as a social science research tool. Media presentations which rely on interviewing generally follow a pattern of interrogation rather than conversation. In-depth interviewing when used in social science research is more subtle in order to give access to knowledge—a knowledge of meanings and interpretations that individuals give to their lives and events.

We also discovered an imbalance in research texts which are currently available in Australia. The large majority of these books have been written about what has come to be known as quantitative research, that is, those methods based on positivist understandings of social reality. Such understandings rely on looking for the causes of social phenomena apart from the subjective states of individuals (a more detailed discussion can be found in chapter 2). What is often labelled qualitative research was simply glossed over as being an alternative way of collecting data. This relatively minor mention suggests the low esteem in which such methods were held by authors and by implication, how readers should view this approach.

Qualitative methodology was seen not to conform to the canons of scientific method as described in such texts. In-depth interviewing as a qualitative research method is either not mentioned at all or it is briefly discussed in single paragraphs only. More recently, it has been presented in the context of 'asking questions' in chapters of books which deal predominantly with survey-style research (de Vaus 1990; Kidder & Judd 1986; Polgar & Thomas 1991). Such chapters focus largely on question-naires and refer to interviewing as a complementary activity. However, when they use the term interviewing they are usually referring to structured interviews used in survey research. In-depth interviewing is called unstructured interviewing and is presented as an alternative to standardised or structured interviewing. These descriptions were usually restricted to less than a page of text in books of three hundred or more pages.

In the 1960s and 1970s, there was a change in the way that social science was conceptualised by many of its practitioners. The writing of this book is tied to these theoretical and methodological shifts which also became apparent in the social and health sciences in Australia. The approach taken by these academics and researchers was anti-positivist, whether it was called interpretivist, *symbolic interactionist* or *social actionist*. Irrespective of label, these perspectives followed the writings of certain German philosophers of the nineteenth century who saw social reality as the product of meaningful social interaction. Holding such views binds one to understanding social phenomena from the actor's perspective. This led to the use of alternative research methods. As Bryman points out:

> The pivotal point for much of the controversy was the appropriateness of a natural science model to the social sciences ... Much of the argument levelled against the orthodoxy of quantitative research derived from the growing influence of phenomenological ideas which gained considerable following in the 1960s ... Research methods were required which reflected and capitalized upon the special character of people as objects of inquiry.
> A qualitative research strategy in which *participant observation* and un-structured interviewing were seen as the central data-gathering planks, was proposed (1988, pp. 2–3).

Theoretical background

Let us briefly examine the theoretical historical background of in-depth interviewing. Since the beginning of the Romantic movement there has been widespread hostility to the tendency of the Enlightenment and its successors—positivism, utilitarianism, scientism—to flatten out or rationalise away the meaning of life, both individual and social. This hostility was voiced from many quarters: the advocates of cultural individuality reaching from Herder to Said (Berlin 1976; Said 1978); the philosophers of consciousness from Hegel to Husserl (Hegel 1931; Steiner 1994); the theorists of the unconscious from Schopenhauer to Freud (Schopenhauer 1966; Freud 1988b); the methodologists of human understanding from Dilthey to Weber (Habermas 1987a; Weber 1949); and the historians of lost mentalities from Friedrich Schlegel to Febvre (Schlegel 1979; Burke 1973). These voices and those who heeded them contributed to a number of theoretical and methodological developments occurring in such diverse intellectual endeavours as *hermeneutics*, psychology, and *ethnography* (drawn from anthropology), which were ultimately incorporated into the research culture of the social and behavioural sciences. More recently, the overt questioning of social relations in the 1960s and 1970s (often referred to in the mass media as the 'Vietnam' or 'protest' era) combined with the impact of 'second wave' feminism also contributed to the development of a research ethos which was very much more concerned with the politics and *ethics* of research. The debate here centred around the ways in which research was conducted and the uses to which the findings were put. In-depth interviewing was and is viewed as an inheritor and, at the same time, the inheritance of these diverse theoretical and political underpinnings.

As chapter 2 will show, understanding theory when learning to interview is important because research methods used in social research are ultimately based on the assumptions inherent in the different theoretical and methodological approaches. By choosing the technique of in-depth interviewing you are inevitably making a theoretical and methodological choice. A conscious and critical awareness of your theoretical and methodological position will enable you to recognise choices in the research process which are consistent with such a position.

When you undertake social research, the choice of method signals to other researchers and readers that you hold a particular methodological and theoretical approach which influences what you are trying to accomplish in your research. This will be taken into account in any assessment, evaluation or utilisation of your work. For instance, if you choose to do research using surveys or psychometric testing and proceed to statistical analysis of your data, it could reasonably be assumed that you hold positivist assumptions about the nature of social reality. You probably also believe that the only way to gain reliable knowledge of the social world is to measure it by quantifying it. It is unlikely, then, that you would have gained the opinions of your 'subjects' on the accuracy of your findings before publication of the research report or that they had been involved as co-researchers. Other researchers and readers of your research report assume that these choices are consistent with the stance indicated by your choice of method.

So what choices are we making when we choose in-depth interviewing? Irrespective of the intellectual and academic disciplines involved and their boundaries, the theoretical antecedents of in-depth interviewing coalesce in what is known as the interpretive tradition. What is this interpretive tradition? And why is in-depth interviewing associated with it? Interpretation as an approach to social and historical phenomena has a complex history that can only be partially sketched here (for a detailed discussion see Hammersley 1989). Hermeneutics, a method of interpreting meaning, was developed many centuries ago in the context of literary and religious exegesis in order to try to understand authoritative texts in which meaning was disputed or hidden. Although it is indirectly influenced by this older hermeneutic tradition, the more recent modern *interpretive approach* to the social sciences and history can be traced to the nineteenth- and early twentieth-century German intellectuals such as Dilthey and Husserl and their reactions to positivistic approaches to social and historical phenomena (Dilthey 1976; Steiner 1994). *Positivism* at this point refers to the belief that the study of social phenomena should employ the same scientific techniques as the natural sciences.

Phenomenology, especially through the work of Husserl and his interpreter Alfred Schütz, has had an impact on the contemporary interpretive approaches in sociology, by emphasising the forms and varieties of consciousness and the ways in which humans can apprehend the world in which they live (Husserl 1928; Schütz 1962). Weber (1949) with his notion of *Verstehen* (empathic *understanding*) and Simmel (1894) with his belief that the focus of social research should be social interaction among conscious actors, provided alternative ways not only of conceiving of the world but also the means by which to investigate it. In sociology and social psychology the inheritors and developers of this tradition were and are the symbolic interactionists (of the Chicago, Iowa and Californian Schools), ethnomethodologists, critical theorists (the Frankfurt School), action researchers and certain feminist. It is not possible to detail the influence of the symbolic interactionists and ethnomethodologists in this text. It has been considerable, in theoretical and pragmatic terms. (For an intellectual, intelligent and critical examination of their impact see Hammersley 1989.)

In the mid 1800s journalists in England also responded to the idea of the time about respecting the point of view of those whose experiences you wished to comment on. They began doing *in-depth interviews* as a means of providing accurate interpretations of social life. For example, Mayhew's interviews with the poor of London, published as a series in the *Chronicle*, provided a full and detailed description of the moral, intellectual, material, and physical condition of the industrial poor. His work dealt with poverty, exploitation and the precarious lives led by the London poor, specifically from their perception of the situation and in their own words. His record of human experience rather than the statistics, which he also included, was applauded and emulated by fellow journalists and social scientists over the next 100 years (Mahew 1985). His influence extended as far as Terkel's (1977) study of workers. Mahew's study was highly regarded in anthropological circles of the day, and, as a consequence, field-based studies were recognised as a legitimate form of 'scientific investigation'.

Concurrent developments occurred in anthropology with the introduction and use of ethnography as an acceptable research method. This was signalled as acceptable and useful in the 1920s when Malinowski carried out fieldwork among the Trobiand Islanders in order to gain access to their perceptions of everyday practices and the meanings they attached to them (Malinowski 1948). This tradition was carried on and developed by anthropological interpretivists such as Clifford Geertz (1973). For them the goal of theorising in research is seen to be the development of understanding of direct lived experience rather than construction of abstract generalisations. Theory building in the social sciences is described as proceeding by 'thick description' defined as description that goes beyond simply reporting of an act (thin description), and describes and probes the intentions, motives, meanings, contexts, situations and circumstances of action (Denzin 1992). In psychology, contemporary inheritors of interpretive theory have been called 'social constructionists' (MacGartland & Polgar 1994). A significant influence on their outlook was the work of the sociologists Berger and Luckmann (1967), who argued for the social construction of reality and its 'knowability' through interpretive methods. Cushman (1990) follows in this tradition by arguing that the subject matter of psychology should involve the socially constructed and historically situated self. Some psychologists have also drawn on Freud's use of in-depth interviewing as one of the tools for the interpretation of the unconscious (Freud 1988a).

Bridging the personal and social

Many social, behavioural and clinical researchers and practitioners have been brought up within the tradition of *positivism*, without exposure to the basic tenets of German idealism. However, over the last seventy years or so, increasing theoretical and methodological dissatisfaction with the gulf between these two traditions has resulted in a new generation of theorists who have begun to outline alternative points of view about the nature and practice of social science. For example, Bourdieu and Giddens focus on social practice when questioning the old divisions in social theory in their writings on *methodology* (Bourdieu 1990b, 1991; Giddens 1984, 1990). Bourdieu argues that social life is to be examined in relation to what he calls the 'habitus'. This refers to the active dispositions which social agents (individual human beings) employ in the course of social life. In Bourdieu's view, social organisation neither expresses 'subjective meaning' nor is it just 'given'. Rather, social forms are actively created and re-created in the course of day-to-day social activity.

Giddens focuses on what he calls 'the duality of structure'. Groups, be they small collectives or large societies, have definite structural character-istics and these appear 'objective' to the individual actor. Yet their structural characteristics are not like objects in nature in that they exist only in and through human action. He argues that social agents draw on the structural properties of the social whole in the conduct of their everyday behaviour, and that behaviour at the same time constitutes or gives form to those structural qualities or aspects. Both Bourdieu and Giddens focus on the idea that when individuals act, they do so in contexts or settings which are structured in certain ways and are continually being restructured. They suggest that these actions are brought about by the social actor's knowledgeable use of 'rules' (the tacit conventions of everyday life). Both regard the in-depth interview as a useful way to learn about such knowledge. Their theories provided a means of incorporating the structural features of social life into social and *interpretive research*.

Habermas (1987b) is a major proponent of what has come to be called critical theory. This approach is drawn from Marx and Freud. Habermas sees it as what he calls 'the critical sciences' as opposed to the natural or interpretative sciences. The primary concern of critical science is not prediction or interpretation, but criticism. It is designed to aid the emancipatory interests of exploited or oppressed people by offering them a critique of their political and/or economic condition. In terms of methods, critical theorists 'privilege' their 'subjects' by giving them 'a say'—much in the same way as interpretive theorists—by using methods such as in-depth interviewing. However, the interview in this context is meant (through the social interaction process itself) to enlighten and thereby 'cure' the social ills that the individual or group is experiencing. Nevertheless, in this theory the authority and expertise still lie with the researcher who in the process of the interview is to lead the *informant* to true knowledge of their oppressed condition which would, by being exposed, lead to its alleviation.

Other approaches, which are known as *'action research'* or 'partici-patory research', also favour an openly partisan position. This is the position adopted by researchers such as Wadsworth (1991). According to the ideals of participatory research, the primary beneficiaries of the research should be the participants who have also played a significant role in 'doing' the research (co-researching) as well as providing the data for it. Qualitative methods, such as in-depth interviewing, have played a significant role in the development of such research models because they are intended to get at the meanings that participants ascribe. In this form of research, the research act should make the participant wiser, both through the process engaged in and through knowledge of the outcome. This means that the aim, form, and content of the research be defined in terms of their interests and understandings and that they be given authority over how the research is conducted. If anything, the researcher acts as a facilitator or just another member of the research team.

Recent feminist research is similar in its approach, in that it attempts to erase the distinction and power differential between researcher and researched. Although there are a variety of feminisms, it has been pointed out by a number of feminist theorists that research should promote the shared ends of some community of women (Harding 1986, 1991; Oakley 1988). It has been suggested that the fundamental focus for feminist researchers is the validation of women's subjective experiences as women and as people. Therefore, there is (contrary to most textbook advice) personal meaning invested for both researcher and researched in the social interaction of the interview. There is a different power relationship between the participants implied by the politics of choosing to engage in feminist research—which, in effect, is a form of action or participatory research. Until the publication of Oakley's analysis of the failure of textbook versions of interviewing, it was often assumed that the *structured* or *semi-structured interview* was the most useful method for gaining access to women's perceptions of their lives. However, she and other researchers pointed out that in-depth interviewing (working in much the way that we describe it) can operate as a means of political action in promoting social change, as well as a form of investigation (Harding 1991; Roberts 1988). This form of in-depth interviewing empowers participants in the same way as other forms of participatory research.

Debate within and outside feminist circles which focuses on the issue of what constitutes good science, necessitates asking what science is for and who it is for. This is essentially a political and social question. It is not just a question of method, but a question of method being intrinsically a question of value. What is the political and ethical goal of such activity? And how do we best utilise our research in keeping faith with these goals and maintain personal and professional integrity? Harding (1991) argues that in democratic societies science must be able to distinguish between how people want the world and how the world is meant to be.

Action research and some forms of feminist research oppose the common distinction between researcher and researched. In action research those who do the research and the people 'on whom the research is done' are the same. In traditional science models one separates pure from applied research and the findings of research (often labelled the 'results') from their use. It is argued that research should precede and be kept separate from any education program or political action that might use or apply the findings. However, in action and feminist approaches, findings and use are designed to combine together and research becomes part of education programmes and political action.

Changes in research methods teaching

The teaching of research methods occurred in tandem with the publication of texts. In reviewing research methods courses offered to undergraduate students in Britain between 1960 and 1980, Wakeford (1981) notes that 'methods' often meant teaching students about survey research. While some mention of participant observation and unstructured interviewing was included in the curriculum, the emphasis was on drilling competence in quantitative techniques. Students in these courses were taught about the principles of *sampling*, how to conduct surveys, how to calculate means, significance tests and so on. What was often omitted from the curriculum was the development of a broader understanding of research and the relationship between theory and method; how research questions develop in the social and political context in which the researcher lives and works; and how the research questions to be asked influence the choice of method. The Australian scene was no different.

During the 1970s and 1980s, just as there had been change in the type of texts published, so there was an attendant change in curriculum and teaching practices. It is a chicken-and-egg argument as to which situation came first. More courses in Australian tertiary institutions included discussions of qualitative methods and integration of methods. Courses were being oriented to research practice rather than simply methods, and students were beginning to examine research practices not just in terms of the ethics of the individual researcher but in relation to the political and social context of the research process itself.

In the USA, Britain and Australia there were a number of texts produced which dealt with two areas—qualitative research methods in entirety (Bogdan & Biklen 1992; Jorgensen 1989; Lofland & Lofland 1984; Schwartz & Jacobs 1979; Taylor & Bogdan 1984) and accounts of the experience of social research in progress (Bell & Encel 1978; Bell & Newby 1977; Shaffir & Stebbins 1991; Shaffir, Stebbins & Turowetz 1980). Most of the former texts centred on participant observation as the preferred and most useful model of doing qualitative research. In-depth interviewing was included in these texts as a second choice and its unique and special features were not highlighted. The latter texts provided a realistic account of doing social research which contrasted with the sanitised process described in traditional texts. This mission of showing social research realistically, with all its difficulties, was important and useful for intending researchers. However, when in-depth interviewing was discussed, it was mostly in terms of difficulties and failures. We felt that the advantages of using in-depth interviewing needed specific clarification. This book provides social and health researchers with not only possible recipes for using in-depth interviewing but also a political legitimation for its use. After all, if you can point to a textbook in the area, then the method must be worthwhile and acceptable within the scientific domain!

Let us point out at this stage that we regard in-depth interviewing as a method which can be categorised as a qualitative research method because it is drawn from that tradition. Although we recognise the inadequate and frequently inappropriate use of the terms quantitative and qualitative to describe and label methodologies, they are the ones that are most frequently used in the other texts (Bryman 1988). It is important for the reader to be aware of such usage for two reasons: firstly, so that there is less confusion in interpreting the jargon and secondly, so that the reader is aware of the underlying assumptions made when referring to in-depth interviewing as a qualitative method. To this end, we feel it is necessary to provide the reader with a brief account of the traditionally ascribed characteristics of quantitative and qualitative research.

Understanding qualitative and quantitative research

As was discussed earlier, qualitative research attempts to capture people's meanings, definitions and descriptions of events. In contrast, quantitative research aims to count and measure things (Berg 1989). As shown in figure 1.1, the characteristics distinguishing qualitative and quantitative approaches to research can be divided into two major categories: conceptual—the nature of the phenomena studied; and methodological—the handling of data (Parse, Coyne & Smith 1985).

Researchers adopt a given method because they have been trained to believe that their preferred method is superior to, or more scientific than, others (Banks 1979; Goodwin & Goodwin 1984). However, a number of scholars have argued that whether researchers choose to use qualitative or quantitative methods is a matter of training, ideology and the research question asked (Denzin 1989; Sieber 1973; Strauss 1987). While there can be no doubt that training influences our methodological practice, this argument loses sight of the interrelationship between theory and method. As chapter 2 will discuss further, the choice of method is also influenced by the assumptions that the researcher makes about science, people and the social world. In turn, the method used will influence what the researcher will see.

Figure 1.1 Traditional characteristics of qualitative and quantitative research approaches

	Qualitative	*Quantitative*
Conceptual	• Concerned with understanding human behaviour from the informant's perspective. • Assumes dynamic and negotiated reality.	• Concerned with discovering facts about social phenomena. • Assumes a fixed and measurable reality.
Methodological	• Data are collected through participant observation, unstructured interviews. • Data are analysed by themes from descriptions by informants. • Data are reported in the language of the informant.	• Data are collected through measuring things. • Data are analysed through numerical comparisons and statistical inferences. • Data are reported through statistical analyses.

Conceptual

A major distinguishing characteristic between qualitative and quantitative approaches is the way in which the research phenomenon is identified for inquiry. As discussed earlier, qualitative researchers challenge the assumption that human beings can be studied by a social scientist in the same way as a natural scientist would study things. They argue that human behaviour is different in kind from the actions of inanimate objects. People are uniquely conscious of their own behaviour. Smith et al. explain:

> ... inanimate objects do not react differently because a theory has been advanced or a prediction made, but human beings can alter their behaviour precisely because social scientists have proffered a theory or made a prediction (1976, p. 59).

For this reason, qualitative researchers seek to uncover the thoughts, perceptions and feelings experienced by informants. They are most interested in studying how people attach meaning to and organise their lives, and how this in turn influences their actions.

Qualitative methods, such as in-depth interviewing and participant observation, are said to allow the researcher to gain access to the motives, meanings, actions and reactions of people in the context of their daily lives. This methodological approach, without relying on the predetermined and fixed application of the predictive and prescriptive requirements of the quantitative methodologies, facilitates an understanding of the informants' perceptions. The focus of qualitative research is not to reveal causal relationships, but rather to discover the nature of phenomena as humanly experienced. It is a deliberate move away from quantification and testing of hypotheses. As chapter 2 will show, in-depth interviewing is more than a specific data-collection technique.

Quantitative researchers are said to take a different view of the role informants play in the research process. Informants are usually treated as *subjects* who supply data that have been pre-ordered by the researcher. Many quantitative researchers argue that informants hold a blurry understanding of their social world. It is up to social scientists to provide accurate accounts of 'what is really going on out there' by using the tools of science. The researcher borrows familiar lay concepts, such as family support, caregiving, discrimination, gives them precise definitions and develops measurement procedures that allow him or her to uncover regularities among the subject's observable characteristics. Of particular interest to the quantitative researcher are explanations that offer causes.

Social facts, it is argued, can only be explained by other social facts and in terms which are quite different from those employed by the informants themselves. The individual's interpretation of his or her situation stands outside the analysis or play only a very small part in it.

As Babbie comments:

> One of the chief goals of the scientist, social or other, is to explain why things are the way they are. Typically, we do that by specifying the causes for the way things are: some things are caused by other things (1979, p. 423).

Methodological

Another way to distinguish between qualitative and quantitative research is in terms of the notation system used to handle the data. Qualitative researchers are not primarily concerned with assigning numbers to their observations or transcripts. Data from participant observation, *unstructured interviews* and oral accounts are studied for themes in the natural language of the participants. The classification system used to code the data is not usually numerical. The data are transformed by using the language of scientific knowledge to make the participants' descriptions and experiences of their social world accessible to those who have not participated in it. The handling of data in quantitative studies, by contrast, is predominantly through statistical analyses, where the data are produced by counting and measuring. These are assigned numerical scores.

Three examples of in-depth interviewing

Having described the characteristics of qualitative and quantitative approaches, we now turn our attention to presenting three studies which illustrate in-depth interviewing as a form of qualitative research. These studies provide illustrations which help us to understand the nature and purpose of qualitative research.

As stated previously, a primary focus of in-depth interviewing is to understand the significance of human experiences as described from the actor's perspective and interpreted by the researcher. This requires that the researcher has personal interaction with the individuals and their context so that he or she can hear people's language and observe behaviour *in situ*. Face-to-face interaction and careful observation enable the researcher to discover contradictions and ambivalences within what 'on the surface' may seem to be a simple reality (Reinharz & Rowles 1988). For example, many gerontology studies report that caregivers often discussed giving care to a parent who is 'like a child' (Day 1985). However, Bowers' (1987) study shows that caregivers do not really perform these tasks in ways which would reinforce this description of their parents. Rather, these tasks are performed in a manner which protects the parent's self-image and is not a threat to the biological parent–child relationship.

Studies using in-depth interviewing attempt to tap into people's experiences by presenting analyses based on empirically and theoretically grounded descriptions. The aim is to understand the interpretations people attach to their situations. In the words of Clifford Geertz:

> Believing, with Max Weber, that man is an animal suspended in webs of significance he himself has spun, I take culture to be those webs, and the analysis of it to be therefore not an experimental science in search of law but an interpretative one in search of meaning (1973, p. 5).

For example, the authors of the studies described below state the purpose of their research in the following ways:

> In order to understand the invisible aspects of care-giving and the associated stress, it is necessary to understand the world of care-giving from the perspective of the care-givers ... grounding a study in the experiential world of the subjects can indicate where researchers have incorporated assumptions that are inconsistent with that world and, consequently, how those theories need to be altered (Bowers 1987, p. 22).

> To address the issue of what physicians actually tell patients and how they arrive at that decision, this study focuses on a single episode in breast cancer treatment—the event of telling the patient for the first time that she has cancer. This study is a participant observation and interview account of the episode, framed from the physicians' perspective (Taylor 1988, p. 110).

> This study explores the contextual conditions under which condoms are/are not used, emphasising personal accounts and views relating to condom usage/non-usage. Specifically the study examines sex as communication—the dyadic coming together of two individuals where aspects of person are challenged by interconnection with another, and behaviour is determined by a complex mix of

biography and interaction. The study, through its emphasis on the dyadic context of sexual interactions, aims to move away from the previous focus on knowledge and attitudes towards an account of the social conditions which promote and inhibit condom usage. [T]he emphasis is to understand the process of sexual interaction between people. Issues such as power, safety, pleasure, danger, love, desire and trust are negotiated and expressed not as static features but as a dynamic process in which the participant's emotions, feelings and intentions are affected by time, personal interpretations and social context (Browne & Minichiello 1994, pp. 232–3).

The accounts derived from the interviews are studied for themes. These themes are reported in the language of the researcher. This represents a shift in discourse from the original text; from the informant's language to the language of the researcher.

All three articles report their data in a narrative as opposed to a numerical format. Each report contains illustrations derived from quotes from informants, field-note excerpts from the researcher's note book or from case studies. Sometimes these illustrative data are used to give a sense of reality to the account and portray the viewpoint of the informant, as in the case studies reported in the Browne and Minichiello study. Or the illustrative data can be used to give credibility to and evidence for the author's theoretical argument, as in the Bowers study.

The three studies reported here are examples of proposition-building, rather than descriptive, studies. They are selected for discussion because many researchers equate excellence with conceptualisation research. However, because researchers may have different purposes in mind, not all qualitative studies result in 'theory' building. The main point to remember here is that while authors may use identical data-gathering techniques, they may be researching and writing with different ends in mind. It is important for the reader to understand that evaluation of the quality and usefulness of a study should be placed within the context of the author's purpose. We discuss this issue in more detail in chapters 8 and 9.

Analytical induction and theoretical sampling are two essential features underlying qualitative studies (Rose 1982). More will be said on these topics later. Suffice to say, these two processes aid the researcher in building, expanding and testing *propositions* while collecting data. Analytical induction requires that analysis and data collection are conducted concurrently, allowing the research question to evolve in response to emerging conceptual insights. A common feature of qualitative studies is that the initial research question is often revised during the research process, moving from a very general to a very focused question. For this reason, sampling decisions are dependent on analysis of the incoming data in relation to the developing theory. Sampling is guided by the search for contrasts which are needed to clarify the analysis and achieve the *saturation* of emergent categories (Glaser & Strauss 1967). The aim is not to strive for a representative sample but to identify purposive cases that represent specific types of a given phenomenon. This sampling strategy allows the researcher to study the range of types rather than determine their distribution or frequency (Trost 1986). For example, once the typology of decision-making situations was constructed, Minichiello and his colleagues (1990) searched for nursing home residents who were classified as being in one of four decision-making situations. Residents with different characteristics (for example, marital status, living arrangement) were selected to test and expand the explanations being offered to account for why residents varied in their involvement in decision making.

Two of the three studies described below show how in-depth interviewing, as a data-gathering technique, can be used with other methods. While the Bowers (1987) and Browne and Minichiello (1994) studies relied solely on in-depth interviews, the Taylor (1988) study combined in-depth interviews with other data-collection techniques, such as participant observation and questionnaires. It is important for readers to realise that the world of qualitative methodology extends beyond the in-depth interviewing technique. Methods should be selected and utilised according to the research question. Sometimes this means relying solely on one method; at other times a *multi-method approach* is useful (Jick 1979). The multi-methods approach could involve the use of participant observation, survey questionnaires, in-depth interviewing and the *content analysis* of documents. The integration of a multi-method approach is referred to as triangulation (Denzin 1989). This involves combining different methods in the same study to highlight different dimensions of the same phenomena, to compensate for shortcomings of each method or to validate the findings by examining them from several vantage points (Reinharz & Rowles 1988). Chapter 8 discusses the utility and legitimacy of using a multi-method approach.

Study 1

'Intergenerational caregiving: adult caregivers and their ageing parents' by Barbara Bowers. This study was published in *Advances in Nursing Research*, 1987, vol. 9, no. 2, pp. 20–31. The focus of Bowers' investigation is to understand the world of caregiving from the perspective of the caregivers. While there has been much research conducted on family caregiving in the past decade, Bowers notes that most studies have focused on describing caregiving in terms of which tasks are being performed by whom, how often, and with what consequences for the person receiving care as well as the person giving care. This information has been largely collected by administering a questionnaire which asks people to report on the specific tasks involved in providing care. The tasks were often defined in terms of activities of daily living, such as bathing, transporting, grooming, preparing meals, giving financial assistance, etc. This information provided a rich data base of the characteristics of those in need of care and their caregivers; the content of caregiving; and the impact of caregiving on caregivers. An underlying assumption behind these studies is that caregiving is solely a task activity. However, Bowers argues that caregiving is an activity which includes plans and decisions made by caregivers, and that while these are not observable tasks, they may have important consequences for the lives of caregivers. In an attempt to reconceptualise caregiving as a purpose activity, Bowers undertook a study which focused on the caregivers' experiences and the strategies used to provide care for frail parents. The aim of the study was to discover a conceptual model of different types of caregiving based on the purpose for providing such care.

In-depth interviews with a sample of sixty caregivers were conducted. Most of the interviews were carried out in the homes of the informants and were taped, transcribed and coded by the researcher. Bowers ensured that the sample included caregivers who found themselves in different types of situations. She included pairs of parents and offspring living together and those living in separate residences, as well as caregivers who were providing support to parents with different levels of cognitive and physical impairment. This sampling strategy (known as theoretical sampling, see chapter 8) allowed her to examine the caregiving role as it is experienced in a number of situations, and to compare and contrast how adults in different situations were providing care to their parents. The interviews were carried out in the form of a conversation (see chapter 4). That is, the researcher allowed the questions to arise as she was talking with her informant. Earlier questions centred around understanding 'How does one become a caregiver?', 'What is most stressful about being a caregiver?' and 'What is it like to be a caregiver of one's parent?'. As Bowers gained a better understanding of the topic, she paid more attention to the consequences of 'failed caregiving' and strategies for providing 'invisible caregiving'.

Bowers' analysis centres around identifying and describing the characteristics of different categories of family caregiving based on purpose, and the caregiving work involved in each of these categories. Five categories of caregiving are discussed. Bowers documents the features surrounding different types of caregiving activities and provides support for her findings with case excerpts from her analysis file. The five categories of caregiving are: anticipatory, preventative, supervisory, instrumental and protective care. Each of these are highlighted with case studies. For example, the following case excerpt is used to illustrate an example of protecting the parent from awareness of the situation:

A 57-year-old woman, Anne, described how her elderly mother took great pride in having dinner prepared for her each night when Anne came home from work. The mother's ability to cook was seriously affected by her mild cognitive as well as sensory impairment. This meant that Anne was frequently given meals she described as inedible (for example, salt was substituted for sugar). Rather than confront her mother with the situation she ate what was put in front of her (p. 27).

The study demonstrates how in-depth interviewing can be used to generate data which provide an understanding of how families care for their elderly relatives. The findings of this study have implications for health professionals. While health professionals often think of caregiving in terms of the 'hands-on' tasks which maintain the person's physical integrity and health status, family members place greater emphasis on emotional well-being and protection of parental identity. Successful intervention is partly dependent on it being congruent with the experiences of clients. Lack of an adequate assessment of family caregiving experience may preclude effective intervention.

Study 2

'Telling bad news: physicians and the disclosure of undesirable information' by Kathryn Taylor. This study was published in *Sociology of Health and Illness*, 1988, vol. 10, no. 2, pp. 109–32. Taylor provides an account of how physicians deliver 'bad news' to patients who have been diagnosed as having breast cancer. The purpose of the paper is to describe how physicians organise the event of telling patients their diagnosis and the strategies developed for routinising the task.

The research is based on observation of 118 events of surgeon disclosure to women who had breast cancer, and in-depth interviews with seventeen surgeons. While the observations of the patient/client interaction allowed her to see and hear how physicians stage the event of telling the patient for the first time that she had cancer, the interviews provided further information on physicians' rationale for their disclosure tactics. It also gave the researcher the opportunity to test out whether the conclusions she had reached from the observations were consistent with the physician's account.

Taylor conducted the study over four years in a breast cancer clinic at a general hospital in Canada. She remained in the room while surgeons talked to their patients. She explains:

> I sat facing the doctor, so that the patient had her back to me. In this way I was able to observe the physicians' facial expressions and gestures, and could clearly hear the conversation. I was introduced to each patient, and all women were asked if they preferred that I leave the room—none did. I made brief notes during the event, and dictated the details immediately after (p. 112).

Taylor presents data which illustrate that the disclosure contains three phases designed to facilitate the surgeons' task of initiating 'a status change in women they did not know, from healthy female to breast-cancer patient with a life-threatening illness requiring immediate, but not always effective surgical intervention' (p. 115). The three phases discussed are preamble, confrontation and diffusion. In each of these stages, the physician uses a number of strategies to reduce the impact of the disclosure and maintain control over a situation they see as stressful. However, Taylor illustrates that while each surgeon developed a predictable, rigid approach in order to routinise the disclosure process, how the event was staged varied in relation to whether the surgeon was an 'experimenter' or 'therapist'. Taylor labelled surgeons as experi-menters if they emphasised the scientific-experimental approach to treatment. In contrast, the therapists were those surgeons who operated on the individuality of each case and saw their primary responsibility as recommending a particular treatment for each patient.

Taylor combined her participant observation and interview data to show the different approaches and strategies used by experimenters and therapists to disclose the bad news. Excerpts from her observation of surgeon/patient interaction are used to reconstruct situations which typify the disclosure policies. The following episode of a doctor-patient interaction is used to illustrate the experimenter's disclosure policy:

> Experimenter: 'Enormous strides have been made in cancer research. We are making terrific headway. You know, if you had had this diagnosis a few years ago, there would not have been a whole lot that could have been done. We now have techniques for conquering all sorts of problems we could not have touched, even ten years ago ...'
> Patient: 'Did you get my report back?'
> Experimenter: 'Yes, as a matter of fact, I have the [pathology] report here somewhere on my desk. Let me see [reaching over to pick up a slip of paper from a pile]. Ah yes, it says, 'infiltrating and intraductal lobular carcinoma, well encapsulated in ...'
> Patient: 'You mean—it is—I've got cancer?'
> Experimenter: 'Yes.'
> Patient: 'Are you sure?'
> Experimenter: 'Yes, I went down and checked in the lab and ...'
> Patient: 'Am I going to die?'
> Experimenter: 'We have a lot of tools to fight with. Let's talk about the options. You see there is no real 'best therapy' as I am sure you are aware. As a matter of fact in the latest issue of the Journal [New England Journal of Medicine], there was an interesting article this week ...'
> Patient: 'You mean I am going to die? [Patient cries and shakes].'
> Experimenter: 'Now listen, I was saying there is a lot we can do. We have to make some serious decisions. Pull yourself together ... please.'
> Patient: 'You mean I am going to die ... my God ... my kids ... what was that you were saying about surgery? I know I don't have to lose my breast ... right? ... right? ... Oh my God.'
> Experimenter: 'We really don't know which surgery is best. We do not have any real answers. We are collecting data to help us with these questions. Let me tell you about this clinical trial ...'
> Patient: 'Doctor, I am asking YOU what you think is best for me. For God's sake you are a doctor ... I don't want my breast off ... but then ... I want to live ... I've got three kids you know ...'

> Experimenter: *'You know many women have breast disease. Why I was reading somewhere that the new figures show one out of every 11 women in North America will have some trouble during her lifetime. A lot of them will do well ... and of course, some won't. But as they know, unfortunately, medicine has not always been considered an exact science ... All those women who develop breast cancer now have a unique opportunity to help us get scientific answers to very old questions ... to help their daughters somewhere down the road. YOU can really help us get more accurate information about the disease, and help us test the ammunition we are now using. We can't be sure of anything, until we have hard proof, and you can be very important in helping us do that. Entering a clinical trial, is one positive step patients can take in a very unfortunate situation' (pp. 118–19).*

After presenting this illustration, the author conducted an analysis of how the surgeon introduced the topic, arranged the discussion, handled stressful confrontation with the patient and diffused the impact of the diagnosis. A comparison between the strategies used by experimenters is contrasted with those used by therapists. For example, while experimenters gave exact and detailed information, whether the patients wished it or not, the therapists defined their role as selecting and interpreting information in a manner they thought the patient wanted to hear it. The author draws the readers' attention to ways of improving the doctor–patient communication and highlights the role of medical education training to teach physicians what and how to tell their patients bad news.

Study 3

'The condom: why more people don't put it on' by Jan Browne and Victor Minichiello. This qualitative study was published in *Sociology of Health and Illness*, 1994, vol. 16, no. 2, pp. 229–51. Browne and Minichiello provide an account which explains the circumstances under which heterosexual men and women use, or decide not to use, condoms. The study sheds light on the social processes of sexual interaction between people to understand how issues such as power, safety, pleasure, danger, love, desire and trust are negotiated. The research question is phrased within a framework which conceptualises sex as interactive, whereby sexual encounters are seen to be partly based on participants taking into account, and being influenced by, each others' actions and intentions. Within this context, the interaction with 'the other' may restrict the autonomy of the individual and result in the suspension of his or her usual sexual practices, preferences and attitudes towards sex.

A qualitative approach was selected because the researchers were collecting data on the meaning and interpretations people give to their sexual encounters. In-depth interviews with twenty-nine informants were conducted using a multi-stage data collection design. Stage one consisted of eighteen unstructured interviews. The second stage included more focused interviews with eleven informants who were purposively selected to provide clarification on issues arising from the first set of interviews. The sample included self-identified middle-class Australian heterosexual men and women, aged between 23 to 40 years, who provided contrasts on the following sampling categories: age, gender, sexual experience, marital status and experience in long- or short-term and/or casual sexual relationships.

A *recursive model of interviewing* was used, whereby the informants were encouraged to offer relevant data using a conversation format. The *interview guide* included the following broad categories: sexual history and the perceived influence of socialisation on their sexual expression; content and format of condom-related conversations with sexual partners; perceived ability to broach the subject of condoms and to engage in sexual negotiation; differences between situations when condoms were/were not used and content of thoughts about these sexual encounters; attitudes towards the condom and about condom sex as opposed to non-condom sex; perceptions and meanings given to partner's responses and reactions to condoms within the encounter; and perception of personal risk.

The authors present data which tease out the informants' perceptions and interpretations of condom sex using the following categories: condom sex as 'other' sex, condom 'embarrassments', 'stop-station' and condom 'desensitiser'. The discussion highlights that condom sex is seen as 'different sex' in that it involves some adjustment and action not previously required during sex. Two types of condom experience emerge from the data—'being practised at using condoms' and 'condom memories'—both of which have some influence on condom usage. For example, being practised at condom use made it less difficult to use condoms through improved adeptness of application and the diminution, but never eradication, of the 'stop-station' effect. Condom memories centred around the quality of condom sex, usually described as inferior sex, and partner reactions to condoms. The influence of condom memories on the meaning informants give to their sexual encounters is documented and substantiated through quotes from informants.

In analysing condom 'dialogues', the researchers show that these occur at two levels—the interpersonal condom dialogue between two or more people, and the discursive dialogue which occurs in the minds of people. Interpersonal condom dialogues represent 'negotiations' in sexual encounters. These negotiations include asking questions such as 'Are you on the pill?', 'Do you want to/will you use a condom?', 'Where is it?', 'I don't like them'. Sometimes the dialogues are often limited in scope, form and content and are non-verbal and reliant on shared, pre-existent set understandings. The researchers show how sexual urgency, emotional arousal, embarrassment and not wanting to seem too knowledgeable about sexual issues ensure that people hold back on lengthy discussions about condoms. Data are presented in the form of quotes from informants to highlight the personal and social issues made explicit through these sex conversations.

The discursive dialogue provides a frame of reference against which people can judge and understand their experience and test out how they can best engage in sexual encounters. The analysis shows how such 'internal' dialogues revolve around trying to make sense of and resolve conflicts of interest between self/other protection, relationship maintenance and partner receptivity to condoms. A comparison of gender differences in condom dialogues is also presented. Finally, the researchers provide an analysis of condom decisions which support the proposition that the decision to use condoms is dependent upon a process of internalisation and personalisation of intention to use it.

The significance of the results are discussed in terms of promoting sex education campaigns which empower individuals to engage in sexual safety. Safe sex educators must become more aware that using a condom means something different to informants. Individuals enter into sexual relations with a dislike of condoms and a vision of condom sex as 'other sex'. Education must therefore promote safe sex as pleasurable in order to be effective and change public attitudes towards condoms. Safe sex campaigns must also address issues related to gender inequalities in relationships and move the focus away from promoting female responsibility to creating a balanced strategy which recognises the impact of male sexuality and shared responsibility on condom use in heterosexual encounters.

How this book is organised

The chapters in this book follow traditional divisions of subject matter, not because we believe that is how the research process occurs but simply for ease of writing about such processes in an accessible manner. Thus, chapter 2 examines how we conceive understanding other human beings, and how we perceive and define science when we wish to understand people as individuals or as members of groups. Chapter 3 covers the preparation work involved in doing a research project using in-depth interviewing. This aspect of research is very rarely examined in the literature and it is most often at this stage that research falls down.

Chapter 4 outlines in-depth interviewing as a social science method which is used to understand people. It provides an account of how in-depth interviewing has been done by workers in the field and highlights some of the advantages and the problems encountered in employing this method. Chapter 5 outlines some of the skills and strategies employed in asking questions. Chapters 6 and 7 provide the reader with discussions of two distinct models of in-depth interviewing—the *life history* and the clinical interview.

Chapter 8 considers the pragmatic and methodological issues that confront researchers in the field. Chapter 9 raises the political and ethical concerns that the researcher might encounter in doing in-depth interviewing.

Chapter 10 documents and formalises some of the ways in which data organisation and analysis can be approached by researchers using in-depth interviewing and chapter 11 offers the reader suggestions for making sense of and interpreting the data, and for the encapsulation of the research project in a written form for dissemination purposes.

We have also included in the appendix an application of how qualitative computer software can be used to assist the researcher with data storing and analysis. In addition, a glossary and a list of references is included at the end of the book.

Chapter 2

Understanding people

This chapter gives the basis for our approach to doing in-depth interviews. Following on from the historical outline we gave in chapter 1, our approach is grounded in the theory of *understanding* first given classical form by Weber last century and refined and elaborated since. The theory holds that the way to understand people differs from the scientific way of explaining nature. To understand people, we must discover the contents of their minds—their beliefs, wishes, feelings, desires, fears, intentions. These contents make up a system which can only be known by inference. To grasp the way such a system works is to be able to interpret the meaning of someone's actions. One of the best forms of evidence for such inferences is the in-depth interview.

The details of this argument are controversial, but it is enough for our purposes that a consensus has emerged in the social sciences, a consensus that an interpretive approach is a valid means, perhaps the only one we have, of understanding one another. This chapter gives the elements of that consensus (Davidson 1980a; Quine 1960; Rorty 1991; Searle 1983).

Reasons and causes

Most of the attempts to define what it is to be scientific have focused on explaining events in terms of their antecedent causes. That probably is an excellent place to start if by being scientific we mean the natural sciences. But social science is usually based on a different kind of explanation. Explaining people often means explaining their behaviour not in terms of causes but of their reasons. Reasons here are quite different from causes. A *causal explanation* looks for an antecedent event or state which can, in principle, be manipulated to produce a certain effect. For instance, an explanation of why your skin has turned yellow (the effect) might look for an infection in your liver (the potential cause). But a social science explanation attributes the person's behaviour (gambling a fortune on the roulette tables) to their reasons, to some of the contents of the person's mind (perhaps a belief that a particular betting system is bound to win). These contents have a technical name: they are said to be *Intentions*.

An Intention (with a capital 'I' to distinguish it from an ordinary intention) is any of those mental attributes showing 'aboutness'—beliefs, for example, are all *about* some state of affairs. They are about the world outside our minds. So, for instance, when one believes that it is cold outside, the proposition that it is cold outside has added to it the mental attitude of belief. To specify the whole Intention, we must give both the attitude (here, the belief) and the proposition (here, the sentence about it being cold outside). Examples of Intentions are belief, fear, hope, desire, love, hate, aversion, liking, disliking, doubting, wondering whether, elation, depression, anxiety, pride, remorse, sorrow, acceptance, intention, amusement and disappointment (Searle 1983). Many, but not all, Intentions are described using the grammatical form of the so-called *propositional attitudes*:

subject + verb + 'that' + sentence

e.g. *I hope that it is cold outside.*

Intentions include such propositional attitudes, as well as other mental states. These Intentions are unobservable theoretical entities similar to the viruses and atoms which occur in the sciences of nature. Like viruses or atoms, a particular Intention cannot be seen with the naked eye; its existence has to be *inferred*. That is not to say, of course, that the *way* we infer its existence is the same. Indeed, the way we make inferences about Intentions is very different.

The hope that it would be cold outside is quite a different Intention to wanting an ice-cream, and so is the hope that it is hot outside. If one believes that it is cold outside, that is not to say that one's mind is cold (nor in this case that the world outside that mind is cold either) but that the Intention refers outside the mind itself. In that way, it is like other aspects of language. Any meaningful sentence refers beyond itself; and this gives us a hint of the important role played in Intentional explanation by language generally. When we give an Intentional explanation we not only attribute a mind to the person whose behaviour we are explaining, but we are specifying the Intentions which are the contents of his or her mind; and those contents have to be specified in a language.

Of course, any explanation has to be given in a language. But when we give an Intentional explanation, we are implying also that the language is either the language of the person or a translation of his or her language. So we are implying that the person thinks, and that he or she thinks in some language. Intentional explanation is for and about language-understanders and language-users.

This partly explains why we are very reluctant to attribute very complex Intentions to animals who cannot give an account of themselves. We could say that a cat is waiting at the back door to go out because it believes it is a warm day outside. But it is going too far to say that the cat is going outside to read *The Mayor of Casterbridge* in the sun. That is attributing to the cat a whole range of beliefs and experiences for which there is little or no evidence. Similar borderline status is allotted to newborn babies and to the very sick. There are endemic doubts about these cases which suggests that assessing them is indeed a matter of elaborate inference. More aspects of such borderline cases will be discussed further when we come to consider the concept of the person. All these Intentions together form an interlocking linguistic whole which constitutes each person's mind. Knowing the person's mind is the precondition to understanding and explaining behaviour.

Interpretation of texts

If Intentional explanation is for language-users and language understanders, what does it mean to say that we have a language? What is a language? At the very least, a language is an ordered arrangement of signs. When a sentence is used to state a truth about the world (rather than to ask a question or make a joke), then we say we have a statement. When these statements are formed into a tissue of interconnected sentences, then we have a text, and the science of interpreting texts is called *hermeneutics*. Many thinkers have suggested that in explaining human behaviour, what we need is a hermeneutic approach, not a causal one (Gadamer 1975). Human beings, according to these thinkers, are text-like, and should be read as texts: human behaviour has meaning in the way that a text has meaning, and to give a causal explanation of human behaviour is to erase its essential meaning. What, then, is this business of interpreting texts which is being proposed as the way for us to understand one another?

The essential feature of hermeneutics that we are concerned with is this: the only way we have to interpret a text is to give it an overall, global, holistic meaning. This implies that the individual parts of a text cannot be given definitive meaning by themselves, although we can allow them provisional meaning while we go ahead with the interpretation of the whole from which they come. This alternation between the parts and the whole of a text is known as the *hermeneutic circle*. To understand the parts we must understand the whole: to understand the whole we must understand the parts. But there is no doubt that the definitive interpretation rests on the coherence of the whole interpretation of the whole text.

This, in turn, implies that the more of a complete text we have available to us for interpretation the better. Conversely, the more parts of the text that are missing, the more difficult it becomes to put the whole text together—to supply the missing pieces of the jigsaw, so to speak.

In practice, however, we do not always know the limits of the text or how many parts of it are missing. If a book or a handout looks complete and there seem to be no numbered pages missing, for example, then we can be reasonably sure that we have the whole text. But when the text in question is the narrative given to us by a client, there is no clear sign or indication that the story is complete or that it has come to an end. Often our clients tell us that the story has come to an end—'I guess that is about it', they say—but that is just precisely where we should be suspicious of premature closure. This problem of when to stop is one which is chronic in this kind of research, because there can rarely be found any reliable internal cue which signals 'The End' to a discourse. We are doing an archaeology of fragments without knowing when we are to stop digging.

Other researchers have looked to the intentions of the author of the text. A novel is written to amuse us, and will have in mind the sort of experiences and the sort of vocabulary which its readers could be expected to understand. In other words, one group of cues to understanding a text will be provided by a set of assumptions about what the author wanted to do with his or her communication.

While it is important to point to the existence of these, we should remind ourselves that looking for these intentions can present a minefield of disagreement among rival interpreters. For one thing, any piece of behaviour is open to rival interpretation, and writing a text is just one more piece of behaviour; for another thing, every text will have, in addition to its official intentions, a shadow set of unofficial intentions, a sub-text. For instance, a friend might officially write to tell you what a good time she is having in Nepal, but unofficially giving a big hint that she is perfectly capable of living independently of you; and your friend might unconsciously be letting you know that this display of independence is something of a fraud, because reading between the lines it is quite obvious that she is missing you dreadfully. (We will see later that recent thinkers have given other reasons to doubt whether talking about the intentions of text-producers has any value at all.)

Text-like behaviour

These text-like properties are relevant to human behaviour for two basic reasons: firstly, human beings use and produce texts all the time, that is, they give an account of themselves in their speech and writing; secondly, even when they are not obviously producing text, their behaviour still has some of the characteristics of text.

The most important of these characteristics is something we have already mentioned in passing: no piece of human (or, for that matter, most animal) behaviour guarantees its own interpretation. Conversely, every piece of behaviour has a potentially infinite number of possible interpretations which could be placed on it. That is not to say that all such interpretations would be equally good, valid or true; we usually have good reason to prefer one or two to the others; but nothing definitively rules the others out. Sometimes we want people to believe that our behaviour means just exactly what we say it means; and we get very annoyed when they seem to doubt our sincerity. But no act can proclaim itself to mean what it says.

Others have wanted to by-pass what people say in order to look at the natural state of people's bodies. What people say may be open to doubt, but what their bodies say cannot be doubted, or so goes this line of reasoning. But this cannot be right. Our bodies can show a certain level of arousal, but others cannot tell us definitively what form of arousal is occurring and why. That is the problem of telling the difference between a blink and a wink; between a sigh and a simple exhalation. In context, we do make up our minds which is which, but this is an interpretation made on the balance of evidence. We can never directly read the meaning of the behaviour. Sometimes, though, the unintended by-products of people's actions, including the state of their bodies, can provide give-away clues to their hidden intentions. Leaving fingerprints behind at the scene of a crime is an outstanding example of an unintended clue to one's Intentions. But these will still take their place in an overall interpretation of the person's reasons for leaving the clues.

When we make this interpretation, it turns out to be similar to the way we interpret texts. We give the behaviour of the person an overall meaning, and the meaning of the particular parts of their behaviour falls into place within the context of the whole. The same problem of closure which we mentioned earlier occurs here too: we can never be absolutely sure that we have seen all the evidence necessary to assess someone's behaviour; nevertheless, we make such judgements every day.

When we were interpreting a text, we tried to give the text as much overall consistency and intelligibility as we could. When it comes to assessing overall behaviour, including the 'texts' that people utter, we try to give a global interpretation of both their behaviour and their speech. This interpretation attributes to them, of course, Intentions. That is, we explain them and their behaviour by postulating theoretical entities, abstract things which cannot be directly seen. We know these theoretical entities only by their effects: they have a place in our theories of how the world works.

The theoretical entities involved in explaining people, then, are Intentions. And when we offer a global or holistic assessment of people's behaviour we look at both their beliefs and their desires, among the whole range of their Intentions. We construe these to make the people we are explaining seem as rational as possible. Notice that rationality is not·a property of individual beliefs alone, but depends on the place of an individual belief in an overall belief system. If there are two competing theories as to why someone does something, we will prefer the theory which represents the person as rational to the one which does not. In this way, our understanding of people confers a status on them. Explaining people takes an effort, an effort in which we can fail. The risk of failing is to take away that status, allowing the person to be regarded by ourselves and others as somewhat less human. This is one of the many ways in which Intentional explanation has an inescapable moral and political quality that causal explanation does not.

Rationality

So we set out to understand people (and ourselves) by making them as rational as possible. Most of this rationality comes down to various types of consistency. We try to see the person's words and aims today as meaning much the same as they did yesterday. These are various kinds of self-consistency.

Then there is the kind of consistency which relates us to our culture. We prefer to make a person seem to share and co-operate in the beliefs and goals of his or her society. Again, this is not to assume that people are nothing but ciphers for their social setting; but it is to see conventionality as more acceptable then eccentricity. Seeing everyone as eccentric is incoherent.

This bias against eccentricity extends to a bias against conceptual schemes radically different from our own. If a person from Mars has a very different way of seeing the world, how would we know this? To understand this person would be to see the points of similarity to ourselves, that is, not all that radically different. On the other hand, if this person were radically different we may not know it. To begin to be different, in a word, is to begin to be unintelligible. Disagreement must be seen against a background of fundamental agreement. Alas, this is not an idea that appeals to those who prefer exoticism to clear thinking.

These kinds of rationality have to do, then, with consistency of various kinds, with *thin rationality* (Elster 1983). But there is another kind of rationality which goes further than consistency.

If we think about it, we can easily imagine someone who was perfectly consistent but at the same time perfectly mad, because their (consistent) beliefs or desires did not seem those which a member of our society should entertain. Someone, for example, who believed that the ultimate goal of human life was to weep as much as possible in our allotted lifespan would seem to lack this extra kind of *broad rationality*. Perhaps this broad kind of rationality comes down in the end to consistency too—consistency with the purposes of those around us. But, nevertheless, it goes beyond the simpler qualities of thin rationality. Notice that thin rationality is the rationality which the interpretation of people shares with the interpretation of texts: the meaning of the whole text we referred to before is largely a matter of overall consistency.

Intentional explanation overlaps other kinds of explanation. It is important not to be mislead by the overlap into thinking that Intentional explanation has almost universal scope. For example, in biology we sometimes explain physical features, perhaps the shape of a bird's beak, as having a 'purpose' in furthering the survival of the species. But notice that the purpose in this kind of functional explanation is neither that of the beak nor the bird, but of the species as a whole or of its gene pool, which are given no choice in the matter. In that sense, biological explanation is only superficially 'mentalistic'.

Likewise attributing a purpose to a tool like a washing machine. The purpose of a washing machine is to wash clothes, that is, the purpose here is that of the maker or the owner, who has a mind, not that of the washing machine, which does not. The washing machine's purpose is derivative, not original, not its own.

Animals themselves (rather than animal species) are a more complex case. We attribute original purposes to animals, and fully propositional attitudes, for example, we say that the cat wants to go outside to sit in the sun. And this implies that they can have some sort of belief system expressible in a language, for example, that it is sunny outside, that this door is the way outside, that the cat wants to be in the sun, etc. But we are not prepared to attribute complex or reflexive Intentions to animals—their goals have been laid down by their biology, and do not include their attempting to make themselves more tolerant, or to explain the difference between Italian and English forms of the sonnet. Even if they were able to give us an account of themselves, it would not be a very complicated account.

Computers, or computer programs, can give an account of themselves. For instance, they can report on their current amount of memory, or list their available files. They also have elaborate linguistic contents and can, to some extent, define and refine their own goals. Perhaps it is just to the extent that they can be self-defining that we might some day be inclined to allow them full personhood.

The concept of the person

The discussion of *functionalism* and the earlier discussion of reasons lead on to discussing the concept of the person. So far we have only suggested indirectly what it is to be a person, by contrast with what it is not to be one. Persons act for reasons, not because of causes. In this sense their behaviour can be voluntary (although this is not to say that all the person's behaviour will be voluntary). Some of these reasons will be desires and wishes, not just beliefs; and in that sense a person is someone who has goals. Not only that, these goals will be original—they will be the purposes of the person himself or herself, not the purposes of some other being.

Something further distinguishes the full concept of the person. A person's goals may include plans to alter himself or herself, perhaps in quite novel ways. Say, for example, that you set out to be the first person in Melbourne to skate-board to Sydney while simultaneously reciting the Polish national anthem backwards; there would be no question of your simply doing that without reflection or practice. Your biological inheritance would not equip you to do so, because in itself such behaviour has no obvious survival value.

Moreover, it is certain that you would have to practice and rehearse such behaviour in order to turn yourself into the sort of person who could do such a thing. Part of your goal would therefore include changing certain aspects of yourself. More elaborately and more conventionally, you might set out at another time to be a saint or to tell the funniest jokes in your family. All such goals imply self-modification: in that sense they are reflexive, they turn back on ourselves.

If, then, we say that persons are beings who have original goals, some of which are reflexive, then it becomes clear that persons are not exactly identical with human beings. Some human beings will lack these qualities if they are new-born or very sick; and some non-human beings will also have the attributes of persons: gods, ghosts, gremlins and angels will have complex novel plans of their own, freely chosen.

Parts of the mind

Being fully a person therefore implies that to some extent our minds have parts. At the very least there is the part which wants to alter the other parts. *Reflexivity* entails some minimal specialisation of our minds, and to that extent our minds have compartments. Some thinkers—Freud for instance—have taken this compartmentalisation to far greater lengths. Maybe they are right, maybe not. We do not need to commit ourselves either way. But notice that if we say that there is an unconscious mind, then it must be an unconscious mind, and it must have Intentions for its contents: unconscious wishes, beliefs, whims, doubts, intentions etc.

A separate question is whether there can be causal antecedents for parts of our minds. We argued before that Intentions and physical causes are incompatible forms of explanation. But it is possible that certain groups of ideas we have might seem to have a rational framework, but, in fact, depend on the physical state of our stomachs, or glands in our heads, or the presence of someone with whom we are madly in love. In these cases, we say that our reasons are not real reasons, but *rationalisations*, and that we are in the grip of an addiction or a drive which deprives us of our freedom. These addictions or drives, then, are causes of our beliefs and our behaviour; but they are not reasons for them. That is why we ignore their rationality when we use them to explain the addict's behaviour. If all our behaviour were determined by drives and addictions, then we could say that our behaviour was wholly caused, and that all our reasons were really rationalisations. But we have no good scientific grounds to believe that any such cynical possibility is true.

Reductionism

There is a variant cynicism that we must consider though. Some philosophers have argued that Intentional explanation is only causal explanation in disguise: Intentional explanation can be reduced to causal explanation. Intentional explanation may look different, but we can treat them as the same, and use the same methods for investigating claims about mental phenomena as we do when investigating causal phenomena. The appearance of difference between them is an illusion.

According to these philosophers, the reduction is to be achieved by saying that events in our minds are only events in our brains, but under different labels. When a person comes to believe that it is cold outside, this is the same as particular neurons firing or chemical changes taking place in his or her brain. What takes place is the same event, but in the first instance the event is seen by an outside observer; in the second, the event is seen from within. However, it is nevertheless the same single event (Dennett 1987; Quine 1960).

Other philosophers have replied that this equivalence may be right, in the sense that we do think with our brains, and there is no reason to believe that there is an independent mental realm which needs to be postulated to accommodate our mental attributes. But causation requires us to fit the events it describes into a pattern of laws; the pattern has to repeat itself, or, in principle, to be repeatable, for the causal explanation to hold true. But this is exactly what is not possible with mental events like beliefs, because there have never been any such laws discovered. And even if there were, it would be an extra step to fit mental events and physical (brain) events into the same universal laws, because mental events have to be assessed under different holistic criteria to those affecting our assessment of physical events. The laws could never be confirmed because the grounds for assessing them would always be shifting. So causal explanation cannot, in practice, be applied; *reductionism* does not work (Davidson 1980b).

Treating people as things

Reductionism of the kind we have been discussing has a long history, itself part of the history of nineteenth-century *positivism*. Positivism in its original form was part of an attempt to replace religion by science as the foundation of knowledge and society (Comte 1864). This attempt was often allied to the contemporary boom in technology and the resulting increase that technology gave power—power over nature and, in the case of firearms or of factories for example, power over other people. Such programs naturally laid great emphasis on distinguishing science from non-science. This distinction was sought in the *form* of scientific ideas, the *methods* by which they were found to be true and in the *reasoning* by which the ideas and methods were connected. For a number of historical reasons, all these ways of distinguishing science from non-science were modelled on the most prestigious sciences of the nineteenth century, especially Newtonian physics: science on this model was *natural* science. The form of its ideas was that of laws explaining the natural causes of things; the method by which they were found was that of experiment; the reasoning by which such laws were derived from experiments was induction or deduction, both forms of logic known since the Greeks. Experiment came by definition to be tied to the idea of control of what happens in the natural world. And the very meaning of scientific terms came to be defined as their role in explaining experiments, logic and laws.

Unavoidably, a program which gave such preferential treatment to natural science made other forms of knowledge seem second rate or even illegitimate. Not only did religion or poetry seem doubtful forms of knowledge; history, our view of other cultures and their languages, even our insight into the people around us seemed remote from experiment and never likely to lead to universally true general laws (although the thought of the nineteenth and twentieth centuries is littered with failed attempts to unearth laws of behaviour or history from beneath the ground of human society). Our insight into the people around us seems instead to be a form of *understanding* (in German, *Verstehen*). The meaning of the talk and the actions of people seems partly local to themselves, and constantly adjusted to make sense of their behaviour *on their terms*. Moreover, the meaning we give them implies that they have considerable freedom of action, and can therefore be moral agents, praised or blamed for what they say and do—this is the field not of natural science but of the social or the moral sciences, a field which the writers we have discussed in chapter 1 were especially anxious to stake out. It makes no sense to attribute plans and intentions to people if they have no freedom to carry them out (and hence the freedom to carry out alternative plans). And likewise it makes no sense to blame or praise people for acts they had no choice in executing. And any attempt to understand people by experimenting on them must coerce them away from their status as free human beings towards treating them as mere things—things in this sense, that they can be acted on but cannot themselves act. People have reasons, things have causes.

Yet if, according to the positivist program, everything people do is governed by universal laws (of which they are, of course, mostly ignorant) then our sense that people are free to take some responsibility for themselves would be an illusion. The positivist program seemed to give support to determinism at the expense of human free will, and could be expected to view non-experimental explanations of human behaviour as wilfully obscurantist. An anti-positivist program could be expected to reply that positivism was not only simplistic and erroneous—rubbing out any distinction between involuntarily following a law and voluntarily following a rule—but manipulative and evil too. Certainly, it would be wrong for us to pretend to the reader that this subject has no history, or that its history is uncontroversial. Indeed, our personal experience has been that these matters were debated with great bitterness in Western institutions of learning until the 1980s.

Why is this no longer the case? Probably because the positivist program collapsed from within. Its appeal depended on its seeming more coherent than other ways of seeing the world. But no-one could succeed in showing exactly how the logic of scientists differed from the logic of other people, or how experiments provided them with a basis of evidence unavailable to other people (Lakatos 1970). Rather, it emerged that scientists behaved like any other social group protecting its beliefs against hostile views of the world. Experiments were seen to play a part-ritual, part-confirming role within a richly elaborated tradition of prejudice (Kuhn 1970). In other words, science came to look rather like a form of religion. And as a kind of religion in a multicultural world science had undoubted claims to respect but not to hegemony.

Doing and saying

Of course, saying something is a particular sort of act—doing something with words. Like any act it has its associated intentions, for example to inform or deceive, and it has unintended consequences. But there is another way in which doing and saying are opposed.

Saying you are going to do something is not the same as doing it, alas, and the fact that we are aware of many forms of rationalisation and being cheap with words shows that we use this opposition all the time in explaining human behaviour. We have discussed earlier the many forms of consistency we look for in attributing rationality to people; perhaps one of the most important forms is consistency of talk with action: we have to reconcile what people say with what they do in order to make sense of them.

This point connects with an important limitation on in-depth interviewing as a way of understanding people. If you undertake in-depth interviews of such a pure kind that you only get people's verbal account of what they think and do, then you are, by definition, excluding any check on how what they say squares with what they do. It becomes very hard to exclude the possibility that what you are hearing is self-deception, or interviewer-deception perhaps. Luckily, very few in-depth interviews are really pure in this way, and life provides many means of cross-checking our interviewee's story against his or her behaviour.

In a comparable way, pure observation of behaviour using *a participant observation* model has built-in limitations as an approach, usually because there are far too many possible stories consistent with what we manage to see of others' actions. But in practice, most researchers, like most people who are not researchers, ask people what they are doing, and so conduct informal in-depth interviews as they go along. Often we overhear what people have to say for themselves too, as if we were listening in on in-depth interviews conducted by other people on our behalf.

Can understanding people be a method?

These points about human action are not made to strike despair into your heart, or to make you feel hopeless about this kind of explanation. After all, we all do it successfully every day. The sociologist Garfinkel (1967) has made the point that our understanding of other people and our dealing with them depends on an enormous range of interpretive skills which we learn and exercise unconsciously but which are implicit in our social practice. We develop a natural mastery which is untaught and only examined when there is a clash of interpretation—just as we tend to think about grammar only when we or someone else notices that we have made a mistake. As with grammar, the fact that social interpretation is not formalised and is not taught does not prevent us exercising a remarkable level of skill: most of us would find it difficult to *write* a novel but we can *understand* what the novelist is saying about his or her characters.

The fact that this kind of explanation is holistic, theoretical and indeterminate allows us to answer a question we set ourselves above: does social science allow us any greater certainty than natural science that our theories are right and our opponents are wrong? No. In social science we must be even more humble before the possibility that our understanding is provisional and local. Neither natural nor social science offers a 'logic of discovery' or a 'logic of justification' (Lakatos 1970; Popper 1959). We can adhere to certain basic principles, but there can be no guarantee that these principles will provide a correct answer.

Nevertheless, it is highly desirable that a scientific explanation be *valid* (based on sound reasoning) and *reliable* (based on sound examples). These two desirable attributes are sharply at issue in interpretive explanation, and now we are in a position to see why. The overall rationality attributed to an individual's mind is, of course, just what validity amounts to in this kind of explanation; in fact, it is impossible to consistently imagine what could possibly be *more* valid than that.

So far so good. The complications set in when we try to imagine what would be the equivalent in mentalistic explanation of scientific *reliability*. You could not independently value an interpretation for consistency over time or over different aspects of someone's behaviour, because that is exactly why we prefer the explanations we do in the first place: interpretations have a kind of built-in reliability and they are constantly being updated to provide it. But they could never be found independently to be reliable; that would be cheating.

Remember, too, that there is reason to believe that there may be no good way of choosing between certain competing explanations of someone's behaviour and talk. This itself places limits on what we can mean here by *validity*. It certainly does *not* mean that if one explanation is valid then all others must be invalid. Perhaps it would be better to speak about *degrees* of 'goodness' for explanations, rather than the extremes of acceptable or unacceptable, which is what a term like valid implies.

The next complication is that interpretive explanations are hard to *generalise*. All along we assume that all minds are more or less subtly different from one another, and, if this is so, then it follows directly that we can only make inexact or partial generalisations about more than one mind at a time. By contrast, the 'units' we explain in natural science are assumed to be mostly the same; that, after all, is why we choose the units we do. For instance, sycamore trees are classified as a maple because they are, in most respects, the same as maples; and one maple is the same as any other. This is why discussing maples (the 'unit' of explanation here) is worth doing. So the problem now looks like this: we can have one explanation for all maples, but for people we need as many explanations as there are people to be explained. This induces nightmare visions of endless explanation, visions which have lead some people into reductionist despair.

Some theorists have said that natural science explanations are *nomothetic*—leading us to explain things by virtue of class membership—while social science explanations are *idiographic*—explaining each individual on his or her own terms (Allport 1942). This distinction fits in more or less with what we have just said, but we dislike the distinction because we believe there is more to it than that. Remember that we said earlier that part of attributing rationality to someone implies an assumption that they have more or less the same conceptual scheme as ourselves: eccentricity can only be partial to be intelligible. Remember also that society goes to great lengths to make us intelligible to one another, at least when we are waiting at the traffic lights or submitting an essay to be marked. So there are good grounds, philosophical and sociological, for assuming that people's minds are largely the same. Their bodies, also, are mostly the same; and in a given society it is likely that their material setting—street lighting, shape of front garden—will also be comparable. Putting all this together means we can, with some confidence, expect to be offered tea or coffee when visiting an Australian suburban house, but not betel nut. So generalisation is possible; it is just a matter of finding what features of people's beliefs can be generalised and which ones cannot. Not, in the end, all that different from maple trees.

Some principles of understanding people

This is a list of principles used in giving the best possible Intentional explanation of a given person's behaviour. These principles have been extracted from the philosophical literature in an attempt to find some kind of interpretive bedrock; without them, we would hardly have Intentional explanation at all. In this, they are more basic than such tricks of the trade as getting people drunk to make them talk—tricks which have empirically been found to produce useful results.

Notice that we have no reason to assume that the following principles are a complete set, or that there is no overlap between them. Also, it may be that some of them should not be on the list: all are somewhat controversial. Nor can we assume that any two of these principles will always favour a particular interpretation of a given action. Indeed, when they conflict, we have not, as yet, any means of giving one principle precedence or dominance over another.

Therefore we cannot assume that perfect application of these principles is possible, or that there will ever be one best explanation. Nor can we assume that there is any favoured place to start our investigations, or any right place to complete them: interpretation is in a constant state of revision and the only reason we put up with such an unreliable mode of explanation is that, practically, it is all we have. Here, then, are the principles, together with references to some classic texts, in which they have been defined:

Rationality. Construe the person's behaviour so as to maximise the rationality of his or her beliefs, desires and actions (Davidson 1984). Maximise the mutual consistency of beliefs, desires and actions; and maximise their compatibility with what is known and valued in the surrounding culture (Elster 1968, 1983).

Centrality. Assume that some of the person's beliefs are more central than others, that is, more firmly held and adhered to in the face of contrary evidence (Quine 1960).

Cultural Commonality. Assume as much overlap as possible between the person's beliefs and those of his or her culture.

Methodological Commonality. Attribute as much commonality as possible between the person's beliefs and your own (Davidson 1984).

Cultural Semantics. Translate or interpret the person's words so as to give maximum fit between the person's language and the person's culture (Quine 1960).

Methodological Semantics. Translate or interpret the person's words so as to give maximum fit between his or her language and your own .

Intentionality. Construe the person's behaviour as far as possible as intentional, meaningful and voluntary (Elster 1968, 1983).

Truth-telling. Maximise the person's truth-telling, both to you and to others.

Social Context. Assume that the person's behaviour, both verbal and non-verbal, is given meaning by his or her social context.

Ideals. Maximise the similarity between the person's underlying aims or ideals and those of his or her culture.

Self-directedness. Maximise the person's responsibility for being the sort of person he or she is—his or her self-directedness (Taylor 1985).

Selfishness. Maximise the selfishness of the person's behaviour (Elster 1968, 1983).

Creativity. Minimise the originality of thought and action attributed to the person.

Levels of analysis

So far we have discussed principles of understanding. These should not be understood as *theories* of why people think and act as they do. Theories are of primary importance to understanding people but giving our theories about people is not the aim of this book. Here, we are attempting only to provide a framework into which other people's theories can be placed. It is important to provide a strong framework because theorists have often been hampered by a framework which restricts them to a narrow class of theories. For instance, if you believe that the only good form of scientific explanation of people is to show what events are causing their behaviour, it will be almost impossible for you to refer to their thinking, for thoughts have an internal structure but events do not. Choosing to analyse data at the event-level excludes almost any possibility of theorising about people's thinking.

There are many other ways in which choosing the wrong level of analysis can similarly limit theorising. Many researchers focus on *patterns of speech sounds* in the discourse of interviewees. This can be a valuable indicator of social class, for example, or of anxiety levels. At the same time, such a focus could never reveal that an interviewee was obsessed with the idea of, say, being a mother, because the concept of motherhood can only be revealed when speech is analysed into units of *meaning*, especially words and phrases. Other analyses require full *sentences*, particularly if the beliefs (rather than salient concepts) of the interviewee are being investigated. In such analyses we must look at patterns of sentences; conceptually, you can only express a belief in a full sentence, and rationality (or irrationality) as a *relationship* between multiple sentences:

> Stephen won't go into the centre of Richmond.
> There are power lines running through the centre of Richmond.
> Stephen believes that being near power lines causes cancer.

To convey Stephen's state of mind, in this example, requires something like these three sentences, not just one of them and not just their constituent themes or phrases.

Sometimes the relations between sentences are very complex ones, and the level of analysis may need to work on whole *narratives* or *scenarios*. For instance, an interviewee may see most people's life stories, including his own, as ending in betrayal and disappointment. If he is very self-aware he may just say so, providing one or two sentences as evidence. But more likely his pessimism will operate beneath his awareness. In that case, it will be evidenced in whole families of sentences, ordered into narratives. Unless the researcher is willing to look at the narrative level of discourse, the pattern cannot disclose itself. (All narratives are checked for consistency, like any text, and made to conform to the laws of common-sense physics: except, perhaps, in South American novels, Stephen is not allowed to appear in two places at once. In themselves, narratives have a kind of explanatory power which even astrophysics cannot do without— laws of physics cannot by themselves explain how the universe came to be precisely as it is. But when we talk of narrative levels of analysis, we need something extra: *types* of narrative. Narratives are discussed further in chapter 7.)

Problems with levels are not always due to excessively wide or narrow units of analysis. They can be caused instead by the depth of analysis imposed on a text or an interview. By this we mean the interpretive significance that the researcher places on what is said. When, for instance, Stephen says that there are 'power lines running through the centre of Richmond', he may be saying that, in some sense, his life has been split in two. The powerlines in that case are a metaphor or symbol. To see such a symbol is to load the phrase 'power lines', or perhaps the whole sentence, with a complex inference. This is an inference which may easily be disputed. It is also an inference which could not mechanically be performed by a computer program set to analyse a text: there is no certain way—no algorithm—to make the inference. This is just the reason why such interpretations are often regarded as disreputable, the resort of charlatans; but we need to keep sight of forms of interpretation which have a vague or complex relationship to the words that people say—the surface of discourse—or we will find ourselves wrongly assuming that people's meaning is always transparent. As you might expect, these issues arise again when we come to evaluate computer packages for research in chapter 11.

The position of the speaker

Finally, parts of interviewees' discourse do not mean the same at all times. The meaning of the words they say shifts with the context in which they are uttered. The whereabouts of the speaker gives important cues to what he or she is referring to. Social context, for our purposes, is even more important. What social role is the speaker enacting and what social role is the listener enacting? What the words mean is altered or framed by the intentions, social position and power of the speaker and the speaker's relation to the listener. There is an account of the Russian poet Pasternak being telephoned in the middle of the night by Stalin, who supposedly asked, 'What do you think of Mandelstam as a poet?'. When thousands of people were being sent to the Gulag, these simple words took on a horrible meaning they would not have had if uttered on other lips. Their meaning shifts again when the reader learns that the account is being given by Mandelstam's widow thirty years later (Mandelstam 1970).

The *speaking position* of the interviewer and interviewee, then, is an important element in the analysis of the interview. In the nature of things, clues to the speaking position may best be found 'off the record', outside the visible or audible traces of the interview itself (another blow to those who would like all the materials of analysis close to the surface of what people actually say). In the clinical interview especially, the power of the clinician can transpose the meaning of everything said.

An interview, then, will be a dialogue, an exchange of speeches between speakers. Their speeches will be *intertextual*; that is, they will refer to and comment on one another's material. Each speaker will speak from a sequence of positions: maker of statements, answerer of questions, endorser of truths, critic of assumptions, and so on. Some of these positions will be positions of relative power, to some extent socially endowed from beyond the dialogue, to some extent negotiated within the fleeting circumstances of the direction it takes. In some circumstances, one speaker may have the power to suppress or invoke whole areas of knowledge from the exchange between them or to impose a 'reality' on the meanings expressed by the other.

Perhaps human reality consists entirely in those statements that can be communicated (Habermas 1987b). Perhaps there can be no sense given to what is 'real' beyond what people have the power to impose on dialogue (Foucault 1972). In any case, an interview will be, like any human interaction, an exchange of symbolic verbal and non-verbal gestures drawn from a repertoire of known meanings—meanings of words, meanings of 'speech acts' (Searle 1969). Therefore, what interviewees say can often be understood only within the context of an unfolding extemporised drama (or comedy). This idea of a symbolic interaction (Garfinkel 1967) is described in more detail in chapter 6.

Decentred subjects

Another feature of the way we explain people is implicit in what we have discussed so far. The fundamental unit of interpretive explanation is the individual person. That is, people are explained, at least to begin with, on their own terms, rather than by being classified as a member of a larger group or class. Of course, once we have explained them, then we can classify them with the class of (literally) like-minded people. And even in explaining them, we take into account from the beginning their probable membership of social groups. Nevertheless, it is individuals not families, classes or societies who are rational, consistent and meaningful; and, in that sense, explanation begins therefore with individuals. The name of this assumption is *methodological individualism*.

Methodological individualism has been discussed by John Elster (1968, 1983). We believe it to be a valid approach up to a certain point. We have outlined a theory of the rational person. If that were all there was to it, then there would be clear and simple implications for the in-depth interview. If the person is reasonably consistent, then a straightforward hermeneutic interpretation of the person's discourse in the interview largely represents what the person is. On this approach, people are what they say and think. But what if the person were only a dummy speaking for a hidden ventriloquist? In that case, we would not be interested in construing the speech of the doll, but in interpreting the motives of the ventriloquist. There is a large group of theorists who hold that, in very varied ways, people are ciphers for external agencies (Foucault 1984; Freud 1921; Bourdieu 1990a). Naturally, their view of the in-depth interview is more complex than the one we have outlined. They want to interview the ventriloquist who speaks only through the dummy. Interpretation for them will therefore be complex, suspicious, tentative, and racked with doubt. The role of the in-depth interview in their project will be necessarily different from someone who holds that personal meaning is close to the surface of individual consciousness. Their project will need to make much more elaborate inferences about the structures of thought and feeling under study than, for instance, a common sense theorist.

This is not to say that all theorists of ventriloquism agree with one another. There are many differing approaches which hold in common that the presentation of the person's self is an illusory or uninteresting front for more important entities. Since most of those who have thought in this way use a European vocabulary of 'subject' for the person and 'object' for the world he or she interacts with, we can adopt their vocabulary to summarise the underlying point of agreement. The person whom we have said should be construed to be as self-consistent and socially intelligible as possible is, to these theorists, an illusion, and the autonomous and self-determining 'self' of which he or she is aware is an illusory unit too. In the eyes of these theorists, people's beliefs and actions, including their beliefs about themselves, are determined elsewhere. That is why they choose to talk of the person as a *'decentred subject'*.

So this section of our chapter is not about a special category of person who has somehow become decentred. It is about whether all people are decentred in some sense. And obviously, since this book aims to show how we can understand people by interviewing them, it is important for us to acknowledge that the value and meaning of the interview will be different for those who believe in the decentred subject. Hence our metaphor of ventriloquist and doll. In-depth interviews with dolls should not pretend to be in-depth interviews with ventriloquists.

We have said that there is no agreement among critics of the unitary person. To summarise all the ways in which they differ would be an enormous task beyond the scope of this book. Instead, we concentrate on certain significant ways in which their views bear on our argument, and try to assimilate them as well as we can to our purposes.

The alienated person

Many of these views are those of people who believe in a role for the unconscious in affecting human beliefs and behaviour. But theorists of the unconscious themselves take radically different views of just what the unconscious is and does. Some writers like Lyotard (1989) and (sometimes) Freud (1988b) himself see the unconscious as a quasi-physical process of drives and their regulation which distorts our conscious thinking. Others like Jaspers (Healy 1990) hold that such distortion is just what marks out those mental illnesses which are due to physical causes. Yet others, particularly 'ego-psychologists', hold that human maturity consists precisely in achieving an integrated self and that the appearance of disunity is a sign of relative immaturity (Erikson 1963; Sullivan 1955). Allowing for the crude level of summary on which we are operating, it is possible to say that for all this group of theorists the person, including the person being interviewed, is a rational being whose rationality is being undermined, like a sane person under the intermittent influence of a drug or someone knocked sideways off a straight road. Whether the influence comes from within or without, it works to deflect the person from the ways of reason. It follows that interpretation consists in these cases in allowing for the distortion in order to restore the underlying rationality of the subject. Sometimes this will be possible only in the abstract; at other times it will imply waiting until natural processes have restored rationality to the person, or perhaps until a medical treatment has taken effect. Natural processes have turned signal into noise: interpretation consists in restoring the signal.

The philosopher Habermas (1987b) sees these processes of distortion as social, not natural, and the work of interpretation as the restoration of human autonomy. But his view for our purposes is otherwise the same as the others'. Human beings for Habermas are autonomous unities whose rationality has often been dethroned and awaits restoration.

The person as tool of an external rationality

A group of recent French writers see matters otherwise. Lacan, Foucault and Bourdieu are writers who differ radically on many matters but whose view of the person's agency is fundamentally similar (Bourdieu 1990b; Bowie 1991; Foucault 1970, 1972, 1979). This view is that there is a unified rationality which we can discover and interpret, but it is not to be found in the individual (hence not directly in the in-depth interview). For Lacan, for instance, the actions of each person are governed by his or her unconscious. This unconscious has little individuality; it is mainly the insertion into the individual mind of external social values built into the structure of language (Bowie 1991).

For Foucault, the terms of explanation are not language itself, but the explanatory discourses which seek power not for people but for themselves:

> Power relations are both intentional and nonsubjective. If in fact they are intelligible, this is ... because they are imbued, through and through, with calculation: there is no power which is exercised without a series of aims and objectives. But this does not mean that it results from the choice or decision of an individual subject; let us not look for the headquarters that presides over its rationality ... the logic is perfectly clear, the aims decipherable, and yet it is often the case that no one is there to have invented them ... (1979, pp. 94–5).

This is ventriloquism with a vengeance. The discourse itself almost has a personality and unity; but we can investigate it only through the actions of people. Foucault's work consisted almost entirely in the examination of historical documents, but it has been taken up with great energy by researchers basing their work on the in-depth interview. Wendy Hollway (1984), for instance, charts the ways in which men and women's individual histories and social positions lead them to select and to alternate available self-validating discourses of gender and sexual relations—discourses of male natural urges, of female emotionality, and so on.

Bourdieu (1984) is a master of the in-depth sociological interview who sees his interviewees as agents with complex motives. But implicit in their words—their words constitute the evidential base of all Bourdieu's work—is a system of social structure and motivation of which they are almost entirely unaware and which stretches far beyond their intentions. Bourdieu shares with Foucault a conviction that the centres of action are mainly beyond or alien to the self. The main action takes place off-screen.

The person as chaos

The views we have sketched so far seek some form of rational meaning to study, whether within the person or intruded from without. But others see this quest for an intelligible rationality as fundamentally mistaken. Therefore they are the writers most completely opposed to the attempt we have made to construe our interviewees as being as rational as possible. For these writers, any rationality we discover is likely to be imposed on our interviewees by our own quest for meaning, or perhaps by our covert demands that the interviewee present to us a coherent personality for our consumption (much like someone lying in court because they think the magistrate will not understand the real, confused, reasons). Perhaps the most famous of these writers are those literary critics who have attacked the *idea* of an author (Foucault 1984). In their eyes, the authors who receive prizes, have their collected works published, and whose influence can be seen in the work of other (equally dubious?) authors are themselves fictions. These fictions have been created by a consumer need for neat explanation: the neat explanation which needs to believe that all Jeanette Winterson's novels form a coherent *œuvre* because they have been created by Winterson's personality, itself a coherent whole. On the contrary, these critics say, any writer's work may be fundamentally split or dispersed in its meaning, as though written by numerous different hands (or impulses), some of them deceitful, some positively amnesic. Looking for unity in an author's work can blind us to the ways in which it has been produced by contrary impulses, or by language itself, or by the time or society in which they work. It is easy to imagine what these critics would make of a mere *interview* with Winterson.

We have spoken about the text-like qualities of people's speech. Now it seems that texts themselves have been radically criticised as incoherent. These criticisms extend of course to the interpretation of an interview. Maybe we think we are interviewing Jeanette Winterson but actually we are interviewing several people. Maybe we are interviewing her readers. Maybe we are interviewing the *Zeitgeist*.

Then there is rather different view of Lyotard in *The Postmodern Condition* (1984). People have been intelligible in traditional terms, but times have changed. In the world of post-capitalism, with the rapid exchange of information world-wide, people have a shallow emotional investment in traditional structures like the family, but an intense investment in the information-loaded, fluctuating, ambiguous media present. The implications for the researching interviewer are the same: do not look for too much consistency or too much coherence; and what coherence is found cannot be relied on to be there next week, or to be seen by another interviewer in another setting.

What difference does the theory of the decentred subject make to our approach?

This survey is by no means meant to be an introduction to the work of the thinkers we have mentioned. Rather, it is meant to indicate a broad and influential movement of ideas which could be taken to endanger the foundations on which we have built this book. That is, we think it is important for the reader to realise that the concept of the unified person has been radically criticised in the last twenty years. We have no intention in this book of indirectly supporting an idealised (and hence false) picture of just what human beings are. On the other hand, we think there are good reasons for believing that the make-the-most-of-it approach we advocate stands up. For one thing, many of the attacks on the idea of the autonomous person bears on the interpretation of interviews: the criticism works at the level of social and historical theory. We do not dissent from these criticisms; but this is a book about the practicalities of the interview and the theory *we* need is a theory, in the end, about what happens in the interview and how best to conduct ourselves in such a setting.

Furthermore, many of these criticisms actually work to support what we have said. What people say can only be seen to be self-contradictory, for instance, if delimited parts of what they say make isolated sense. To find a contradiction, rather than just an unintelligible mess, in people's discourse, we need a provisional apparatus for hearing what they have to say. *That* is what we have set out to provide. Our stance is always one of provisionally maximising the rationality of our interviewees; but that is no guarantee that what they say will have any overall rationality at all; or that our interpretation must be the right one. Indeed, we have emphasised that there can never be any one canonically correct way of reading other people's minds. Bourdieu, just like us, has to postulate that his interviewees are speaking ordinary French and saying rather ordinary things in it. It is from just such banal beginnings that his remarkable conclusions are drawn.

Finally, there is an ethical implication which we have already hinted at. Interviewers are social actors. One of their acts may be to endow the interviewee with an easy intelligibility unknown beyond the notepad and the tape-recorder. Sometimes between us and the interviewee we can discover meanings which will be of long-lasting value to the interviewee. But that very possibility alerts us to another one: however relative the truths we uncover together might be, we want them to have a value beyond that of a one-off illusion for two. We will discuss this further in our chapter on ethics.

Chapter 3

Preparation work

The first step in conducting any research is to formulate a specific research problem and related research questions. The research problem posed at the beginning of any project is often very general. The research question needs to be focused. For example, to simply state that you want to conduct a study of older people living in nursing homes is not very specific. What aspects of the institutionalisation process do you want to learn about? Do you want to study why older people are admitted into nursing homes, or what happens to them once they are admitted? Are you interested in examining issues which are associated with the pre- or post-admission stage, or both? Do you want to study the views of older men, older women, or both? The physically or mentally disabled? What conceptual framework will you be adopting? For example, will you apply a sociological or psychological perspective to study the admission process? These questions need to be answered prior to entering the field. Answers to these questions assist researchers to clarify and narrow their research focus. Researchers rarely enter the field on the day that they think of a research problem. Time is set aside to reflect on the question being asked. The question is posed in the context of previous work on the topic.

There are two types of preparation work that researchers engage in prior to entering the field. One type of preparation work, as discussed in chapter 8, relates to developing strategies for getting in, learning the ropes, maintaining relations, leaving the field and developing sampling and other method procedures. Preparation work discussed in this chapter relates to the conceptualisation of the research statement and research question. Although details of the researchers' preparation work are seldom reported in their final report, a considerable amount of time is spent on this activity. For example, Lopata (1980) reports spending a full year reviewing the literature on ageing, grief, divorce, ethnicity, and attending support group meetings for widows prior to undertaking her study on the support system of American widows. As a result of this work, Lopata developed a better understanding of issues associated with widowhood, such as changes in role involvements, social networks, types of loneliness and methods of coping with them, emotional support systems and forms of social interaction. Lopata's time spent 'researching' her research topic is not atypical of the experiences of other researchers or doctoral students (Shaffir & Stebbins 1991; Shaffir, Stebbins & Turowetz 1980).

Preparation work involves spending time in the library and locating and reading literature which will assist the researcher to further focus the question being asked. It may also involve documentary research and use of tools such as biographical dictionaries, membership directories of professional associations, newspapers, and *Who's Who in Australia* to learn more about specific individuals, places or situations.

Preparation work can also influence the researcher's success in gaining entry and *establishing rapport* with subjects once in the field. For example, Spector (1980) reports how he used documentary research to identify the central figures involved in the debate to demedicalise homosexuality. He developed a file on each of the public figures involved in the debate. This preparation work, before the interview, Spector argues, was crucial in influencing his entry into the field and getting public officials to take his work seriously. He notes:

> Well-known people tend to expect this work—in fact, [they expect] a mastery of what is in the public record. They may grow impatient with questions that could be easily answered by a look at public documents or their writings (1980, p. 100).

Sampling procedures can also be shaped by such preparation work. Spector identified his sample by examining who the media reported as being key figures in the debate. On the basis of this information, he contacted individuals for interviews. He also used public statements reported in the media to cross-check information he received while interviewing the informants.

This chapter will discuss why the review of the literature is an essential aspect of the research process, and will describe how to use the library to locate pertinent information from different sources. As alluded to earlier, we are including in the *review of literature* both the technical literature and the non-professional, popular literature. The technical literature includes research, theoretical and philosophical reports and papers which characterise the formal knowledge base of the professions and disciplines, while the non-professional, popular literature includes material such as biographies, diaries, fiction writing and catalogues.

While all researchers recognise the contribution a review of literature plays in the research process, there is some debate among qualitative researchers on the role it should play in assisting researchers to formulate their research questions. Quantitative researchers identify the hypotheses that will be tested in their studies prior to entering the field. The purpose of conducting a review of the literature is to ensure that all relevant assumptions are incorporated into the study design. Hypotheses are spelled out, variables identified and questionnaires constructed on the basis of this knowledge. For example, there is little opportunity for the researcher to change or add new questions once the data-collection stage has begun.

Qualitative researchers, however, do not have to identify their propositions prior to entering the field. The methodological thrust of qualitative research is the possibility of the development of theory without any particular commitment to specific prior knowledge. They do not search out data to prove or disprove hypotheses they hold before entering the field. Rather, as Glaser and Strauss (1967) argue, propositions and theories are developed from the many pieces of evidence which are interconnected concurrently with the data-collection process. For this reason, the review of the literature plays a different role in qualitative studies. The literature acts as a stimulus for thinking.

Qualitative researchers, however, disagree about whether the review of the literature should be conducted before or after the fieldwork (Glaser 1992; Strauss & Corbin 1990). We suggest that the literature review should be conducted *throughout* the qualitative research process. There are several reasons for this. First, the literature may sensitise you to crucial issues which others have identified, as well as to examine what has been neglected in the literature. Second, the literature may spark off ideas about how to proceed with the research or even identify questions which can be included in the analysis. It is not uncommon for researchers to provide insights into further lines of investigations in their published reports. Third, reading the literature for ideas, as suggested by Glaser (1992), may generate theoretical sensitivity to concepts. Fourth, the literature can identify sampling categories which you may want to include in the research design (see chapter 8). And finally, the researcher, by being aware of what has been published on the topic, is better placed to examine, for example, reasons for discrepancies between what is reported in the literature and what the data suggests, and pursue this line of inquiry while in the field.

There is a point, however, which we must make clear. When doing a search for a qualitative study the literature should be viewed as a sounding board for ideas and that its suggestions and interpretations should not be taken for granted (Denzin 1968). In line with the theoretical principles underlying qualitative methodology (see chapter 2), the researcher measures his or her achievement by calling into question prior knowledge and discovering new ideas. We agree with Glaser (1992, p. 31) that the major challenge when conducting a review of the literature within a *qualitative research design* is contending with 'rich derailments provided by the relevant literature in the form of conscious or unrecognised assumptions of what ought to be found in the data'. For this reason, it is important that you do not enter the field with a fixed framework that will automatically interpret what you see or hear. As Bogdan and Biklen note:

> The danger in reading literature while you are conducting your study is that you may read and find concepts, ideas or models that are so compelling they blind you to other ways of looking at your data. Try to avoid jamming your data into pre-formed conceptual schemes ... [It] is perfectly honorable to do research that illustrates others' analytical schemes, but try to distance yourself enough to formulate concepts of your own or to expand the work of others (1992, pp. 161–2).

If the data fit the concepts from the literature, do not be afraid to borrow them. If they do not, it is an error to force the data to fit the concepts.

Why conduct a review of literature?

There are many reasons for conducting a review of the literature. The most obvious one is to find out what is already known about the topic chosen for study. If you decide to investigate what younger people think about safe sex, then a good starting point is to find out if other researchers have asked this question and what they have reported. There is no point asking a question which has been the topic of extensive investigation unless your sole aim is to replicate the study on a different population (for example, Aboriginal youths/Australian youths). Research should never be conducted in ignorance of previous knowledge. The accumulation of knowledge depends on its being connected to current ideas. There are very few topics that do not have *some* published material.

For example, if you were to conduct a literature search on the topic of acoustic neuroma, a tumour found in the brain, you would discover that there are few publications on this subject. The nomenclature, acoustic neuroma, has only been used in the last ten years. However, this does not mean that there is no literature which is pertinent to a study that examines illness careers of people who have had an operation for acoustic neuroma. There is a rich sociological literature on the meaning of illness.

Kaufman's (1988) study on the strategies stroke patients use to renegotiate their identity after the operation provides an interesting analysis of how people's actions can be influenced by their perceptions of illness. The issues which he describes as characterising the experience of recovering from a stroke, such as *stigmatisation*, the redefined self and attempt to return to normal, can provide a useful framework for understanding how individuals reconstruct their experiences in the pre- and post-operation acoustic neuroma stages.

An important aspect of the researcher's work is to place his or her study in the context of current knowledge and to broaden scientific knowledge. Researchers conduct a search of the literature not only to find what others have written on the topic but to justify the contribution their study will make to current knowledge. For example, Minichiello and his colleagues (1990) address the issue of decision making for entry to nursing homes. They reviewed the literature on decision making and ageing and posed their question in the context of the psychosocial research on control and ageing. The contribution of the study to current knowledge of the topic is that it examines the different levels of engagement in the process of entry. Few studies have examined the actual processes by which older people are included or excluded in decision making to enter nursing homes. Research reports are often evaluated in terms of their contribution to knowledge. A study might be methodologically flawless but considered a failure by a critical reviewer if the study is not conceptually sound and advances knowledge.

The review of the literature also assists researchers to locate conceptual schemes which can act as a guide to raising questions and making sense of data. For example, Bowers (1987; see also chapter 1) develops a model of family caregiving centred on the purpose for the type of care that caregivers are providing. Based on these findings, several other researchers have contributed to the development of theory about family caregiving by examining how staff and family members share the responsibility of providing care to nursing home residents (see Bowers 1988). Researchers can also follow up an idea that has been mentioned in a report. Often research reports identify additional questions which can be investigated by other researchers.

Finally, a review of the literature can provide useful suggestions on how to plan the method design of your study. Much can be learnt from the experience of other researchers regarding issues of locating and gaining access to subjects. In recent years, a rich literature has been published on researchers' personal accounts of their fieldwork experiences (Punch 1986; Shaffir, Stebbins & Turowetz 1980; Shaffir & Stebbins 1991; Sprinivas, Shah & Ramaswamy 1979; van Maanen 1988). The researcher can learn many lessons from both the successes and failures of other researchers (Dempsey & Dempsey 1986; Shaffir, Stebbins & Turowetz 1980). For example, the ethical question of *confidentiality* which Laud Humphreys (1970) confronted after publishing the results of his study on impersonal sex in public places, draws our attention to the difficulties researchers can face when conducting disguised research.

Becoming familiar with the library

A library can look intimidating to someone who does not know how to access the wealth of information it contains. The novice user entering the library is confronted with hundreds of journals, thousands of books, and computer terminals. Searching for the right book may be like looking for a needle in a haystack. The difference between a successful and unsuccessful library expedition will depend on your knowledge of the library. A lot of valuable time and energy can be saved by acquainting yourself with the library facilities and holdings. Anyone who has spent time doing library work can tell you how easy it is to be flooded with literature on a topic, and spend a great deal of time locating journals and books. These two factors probably account for why many people feel anxious about using the library. Librarians can, however, reduce such anxieties.

All libraries have a 'Reference and Enquiries' desk. Sitting behind this desk is a librarian able to acquaint you with the use of the *card catalogue*, the various *indices* (or indexes as they are referred to in some libraries), abstracts and *computer-assisted searches*. Librarians also offer guidance on the most appropriate reference works to be consulted for specific purposes. They can inform you about such things as conditions of borrowing, copyright, costs for interlibrary loans, photocopy services and loan materials available from co-operating libraries. The library offers a range of instructional programmes for users, including a tour of the library, instructions on catalogue use and sessions on information resources for particular subject areas. These orientation sessions are useful to both the novice and experienced users. Libraries vary in terms of the type of cataloguing system they use. It is advisable to consult the librarian to find out what classification system has been adopted in your particular library. Some libraries, for example, use the Dewey Decimal Classification System while others use the Library of Congress System. Depending on which system is used, the books will be given a different set of code numbers.

The range and volume of literature contained in the library is enormous and always growing. Researchers continue to write, publishers continue to publish and libraries continue to purchase. This creates a problem for those of us who have to locate material within this growing collection. The problem we often face is not that the library does not hold information on our topic but how we locate the information. Fortunately, reference material is available to assist us to locate the pertinent literature.

It is important to remember that a library's resources are not restricted to the collection contained in it. Interlibrary loan allows you to borrow books and journals which are not available in your library. Librarians can assist you to locate literature available in other libraries. It is advisable that you plan interlibrary loan requests well ahead as the item may take as long as three weeks before you receive it. The next section will provide a brief discussion on how these library resources can be used for this purpose.

Resource material in the library

There are a number of useful sources that can be consulted to locate books and articles. These include: the card catalogue, indices, abstracts and computer-assisted literature-search programmes. The card catalogue is mainly used to locate books in the library. The information contained in the card catalogue includes an alphabetical listing of books classified under the categories of the title of the book, the name of the author or the subject heading. Card catalogues in many libraries are now in microfiche format or stored on a computer. All books, audiovisual items and journals in the library are listed in the computer catalogue (Online Public Access Catalogue or OPAC). These computer terminals are often located just inside the library entrance or close to the reference desk. OPAC is easy to use. You simply select the author, title or subject menu program and then type the required information. The computer will list the information on the screen and inform you whether the item is located in the library.

While the card catalogue is a useful place for researchers to begin their literature search it does not provide access to all published material on the topic. Excluded from the card catalogue are articles in journals. Unlike books, articles in journals are written and published much more rapidly and frequently. These often represent the most recent literature on the topic. For this reason, journals are an excellent starting point to trace the literature. While articles can be found through a manual search of journals, a much more reliable way to locate the articles is by consulting indices or abstracts. Indices and abstracts are used to obtain information to periodicals and other literature which is not contained in the card catalogue. Most disciplines publish indices and abstracts which summarise the literature published in journals relevant to the field. Some indices and abstracts are interdisciplinary and cover published material from a number of disciplines.

Indices include reference materials on books and periodicals. Identification of relevant material is by means of subject terms in the form of keywords or thesaurus terms. An index does not reproduce the article but provides the information required to locate the article: name of author(s), title of article, name of journal, volume, year and page numbers. Abstracts provide similar information, but in addition include a short summary on the purpose, methods and major findings of the research studies, rarely exceeding 150 words. This information is useful when the content of the article cannot be determined simply by reading the title.

In addition to manual searches of the card catalogue, indices and abstracts, computer-assisted literature searches can also be used to identify relevant publications. Most libraries have access to computer-based bibliographic processing systems which contain a database of hundreds of thousands of articles published in journals and other literature. The information held in the computer database is similar to that found in the indices and abstracts. There are a number of computer-search programs available. Some of these are listed in figure 3.1. The *Directory of Online Information Resources* provides an exhaustive list of databases programs and a description of their contents.

Most of the computer-search programs provide access to journals only. The system is programmed by subjects and not authors. For this reason, it is important that users provide precise information on the topic to be searched. Most libraries will conduct a computer literature search at a charge. Cost is determined by the particular database that is searched and the time it takes to complete the work requested. Time spent on selecting appropriate descriptors can save money in online searching time.

The term institutionalisation is too broad for describing a study which specifically focuses on the processes of admitting older people into nursing homes. The usage of this term will not allow the computer to distinguish literature written on older people admitted into nursing homes from the more general studies which include a wide range of people admitted into different types of institutions (for example, hospitals, hostels). If we want to locate information which is specific to our topic then we must construct a set of terms which will produce relevant information on older people living in nursing homes. We might therefore give the librarian the following set of words—aged, nursing home admission.

There are a number of indexing vocabulary manuals that assist the user to narrow topics which do not have headings specific enough for online searching. These reference sources provide a vocabulary of subject headings (for a detailed list see Haselbauer 1987).

Indices and abstracts

Indices and abstracts are published in many professional fields. Figure 3.1 provides a list of the major social and health sciences indexing and abstracting services and their equivalent computerised databases. Some of these will be briefly discussed below. (For a description of a comprehensive listing of indices and abstracts see Haselbauer 1987.) It is important for researchers to become familiar with, and consult, the range of sources available to them. Too often, researchers restrict their literature search to sources within their discipline. For example, because health science is a broad subject area, there are many sources from other disciplines which include health science as subject matters. Given the title, *Sociological Abstracts*, a health-science researcher might not think to consult this source. However, a quick glance at *Sociological Abstracts* reveals that it contains references to numerous articles on the ethical and social aspects of health practice, and on policy-making issues related to public health.

Index Medicus is the major index to medical periodical literature and can be computer searched through MEDLINE (Medlars Online), the earliest online database. It is published monthly by the National Library of Medicine. The first volume was published in 1879 and an annual cumulation began in 1960. *Index Medicus* covers an international collection of over 3000 periodicals including life sciences, medicine and allied health topics. The index is arranged by subject headings. The subject headings are assigned by indexers using a controlled vocabulary, MeSH (Medical Subject Headings). It is important for users to consult MeSH for the appropriate subject heading before using the index itself. It may be frustrating to find nothing under the term cancer; however, looking it up in MeSH produces the information that neoplasms is the preferred term.

Indices/Abstracts	*Computer searching databases*
Arts and Humanities Citation Index	AHCI
Australian Public Affairs Information	AUSINET
Cumulative Index to Nursing &	
* Allied Health Literature*	CINAHL
Current Index to Journals in Education	ERIC
International Nursing Index	MEDLINE
Index Medicus	MEDLINE
Occupational Safety and Health	DIALOG
Science Citation Index	SCISEARCH
Social Science Citation Index	SOCIAL SCISEARCH
Physical Fitness and Sport Medicine	SPORT DATABASE
Public Affairs and Public Policy Index	PAIS
Biological Abstracts	BIOSIS
Clinical Abstracts	CLINICAL ABSTRACTS
Excerpta Medica	EMBASE
Mental Health Abstracts	NIMH
Nursing Abstracts	NURSING ABSTRACTS
Sociological Abstracts	SOCIOLOGICAL ABSTRACTS
Psychological Abstracts	PSYCHINFO

Figure 3.1 Indices, abstracts and computer searching databases in health sciences and related literature

The *Cumulative Index to Nursing and Allied Health Literature* is a comprehensive index designed to meet the specific needs of nursing and allied health professionals. Some of the allied health fields included are occupational therapy, physiotherapy, medical records and health education. The index was first published in 1956. The index covers over 300 nursing and allied health journals and can be computer searched through the NURSING AND ALLIED HEALTH database.

The *Science Citation Index* and the *Social Science Citation Index* are useful reference sources for science and social science researchers. The *Science Citation Index* is a multidisciplinary science index and covers citations in over 3000 major journals of science. The index has been published since 1961. It covers the pure and applied science such as biology, chemistry, physics and zoology. Approximately 54 per cent of its coverage is literature in the life sciences and clinical practice. A library survey on the use of reference sources in biomedical libraries found the *Science Citation Index* to be the most heavily used reference tool (Haselbauer 1987). The Institute for Scientific Information offers portions of its database for direct online searching through SCISEARCH.

The *Social Science Citation Index* provides indexing for some 2000 periodicals in such fields as anthropology, economics, political science, psychology and sociology. The index has been published quarterly since 1962 and can be searched through SOCIAL SCISEARCH computer database.

While the above describe indices, a number of useful abstracts are also published, for example, in the fields of biology, psychology, medicine and sociology. As was mentioned earlier, the additional information contained in abstracts is a statement on the research question, the specific method(s) of data collection, sample details, type of analysis used and results.

The most widely used medical abstracting service is *Excerpta Medica* which includes content coverage of over 3500 international journals in human medicine and biology. The annual abstract service was first published in 1947 and can be searched through the EMBASE computerised database. Abstracts are in English, regardless of the language of the original article. Journal literature represents ninety-five per cent of the citation; monographs, dissertations, conference papers and reports comprise the remaining five per cent. The *Guide to Excerpta Medica Classification and Indexing System* provides detailed notes on how to use the abstract service.

Biological Abstracts provides a comprehensive coverage of the worldwide life-sciences literature and includes a wide range of topics from the medical, physiological and pharmaceutical literature. It was first published in 1926. *Biological Abstracts* scans 9000 journals, and abstracts only articles and other original papers published in periodicals. It consists of three sections: content summaries of research reports, with a subject-specific headings index at the beginning of the section; names of books, with complete bibliographic information and a brief synopsis; and scientific conferences, with bibliographic information on the conference plus names and addresses of speakers and the titles of their papers. The *Guide to the Use of Biological Abstracts* provides useful material for the beginning researcher to locate literature contained in the abstract. It can be searched through the BIOSIS online.

Psychological Abstracts has been published by the American Psychological Association since 1927. It covers the world's literature in psychology and related disciplines such as anthropology, education, linguistics, pharmacology, physiology, psychiatry and sociology. This source scans approximately 1000 periodicals and 1509 books, technical reports and monographs each year. This abstract can be searched through PSYCHINFO computer database. Because *Psychological Abstracts*, like many other abstract services, uses a controlled vocabulary of subject headings, searchers are advised to begin their work by consulting the *Thesaurus of Psychological Index Terms*. For each entry, the *Thesaurus* supplies broader, narrower and related terms, and cross-references from terms not used.

Sociological Abstracts covers journals published by sociological associations and periodicals containing the word sociology in their title. It includes journals from the fields of anthropology, community development, economics, education, medicine, philosophy, political science and statistics. This source first began publication in 1953 and can be searched through SOCIOLOGICAL ABSTRACTS computer database.

A useful Australian abstract source is the *Australian Public Affairs Information* (APAIS). APAIS is a comprehensive abstract service for Australian scholarly journals in the social sciences, humanities and public affairs fields. The APAIS Thesaurus lists the vocabulary of subject terms used to index articles. The first edition was published in 1981 and the most recent edition (third) in 1986. APAIS has been available as a computer-searchable database on AUSINET since 1978.

An index-card system to record information

Once you have located pertinent literature material on a topic, the next task is to read and extract the relevant information from these sources. However, this poses a problem. The issue to be faced is, how do you retain this information given the fact that you may have read hundreds of articles? One strategy is to photocopy all these articles and to consult each original article when you are doing the analysis of the literature. However, this can be both time consuming and expensive. A more effective way of summarising and studying the information found in the literature is to store relevant information on an *index card* as you read the articles. A number of researchers have developed systematic card index storing procedures for recording a critical review of the literature (Seaman 1987). This section will discuss strategies for recording the content of literature reviewed.

What information to collect

The first step in reviewing the literature involves reading the report. Reports often follow a logical progression of ideas and arguments. The reader is provided with information about the:

1 statement of the problem;
2 general question(s) asked;
3 theoretical position;
4 choice of research design and method;
5 choice of sample;
6 presentation of findings; and
7 a discussion of the implications of the results.

When you read the report, it is helpful if you keep notes on each of these categories. These should be summarised in your own words rather than those of the authors. If direct quotes will be used make sure you copy the information and the reference details (for example, page number) accurately. If you do not record this information, you will find yourself making another trip to the library. Use quotation marks to indicate the quoted material.

Using a computer database can be a highly efficient way of developing an index system since information can be readily found and accessed. Database software includes programs such as FilemakerPro (for Macintosh/Windows), DBase (for MS-DOS), and Superbase (Windows). As an example, FilemakerPro software allows you to design records on the screen just as you would design an index system on cards. You can flick through these records on the screen much like cards and automatically search for information contained in your records. This means that if you adopt an index system as outlined in this chapter, you will be able to quickly find records on a certain subject or combination of subjects. For instance, you can compile records by author(s), publication date, or topic area, for example you could find all records which contain information about gender and AIDS published after 1990. The ability to quickly find records and information that you are looking for while reviewing the literature saves time and is a clerical advantage. The drawbacks include the initial costs in purchasing the software and the time invested in learning how to use it.

When designing a database you need to include all the information that you would include if you were designing a manual card system. Each entry on a record is called a 'field'. For instance, 'publication date', 'author name(s)', 'title of report', 'research question', 'main findings and conclusion' should all be separate fields. Additionally, you need to design the layout of the record on the screen so that there is enough room on each record to record all the information. You will need to consult the software manuals accompanying the database software for details about how to set up the database.

Below are a number of hints for managing a computer index system:

- always make back-ups of your database file and store these in several locations since electronic information can be lost, erased or damaged;
- give each record a unique identification number (this helps for example in sorting cards into the order that they were entered);
- include a 'comments' field so that when you are browsing through a retrieval of records, you can note ideas which emerge from comparing and contrasting records;
- include a field called 'keywords' and use a consistent list of keywords in this field so that you can easily recall all records related to a topic, for example 'youth' could be a keyword for a range of words (adolescent, young person, teenager) that appear in the report;
- ensure that the layout for a field is no larger than your computer screen so that you can read the entire entry without having to scroll.

An example of the type of information which can be included on an index card is presented in figure 3.2. This example provides general format guidelines of how the information can be organised. Some researchers prefer to record their information in a spiral notebook because in this way the references are contained in one source rather than on separate cards (Nieswiadony 1987). The reader is encouraged to design a recording system that he or she finds most appealing and useful, as long as its content covers the information described below and the same format is used each time.

Each index card should begin with the full reference details of the report. The call number of the journal or book and the library where it can be located should also be recorded. This information is valuable because it can save you considerable time if you have to consult the book or journal again. There are several systems prescribing the style of writing and referencing of literature, such as the Oxford and the Harvard. (For a detailed discussion on the presentation of reference material and guidelines on writing research papers, see Gelford & Walker 1991 and Walker 1987.)

Most libraries hold the manuals describing these reference systems. We suggest that you adopt the commonly used Harvard system. The following information is included: the surname of the author or authors, followed by their first initials; the year of publication; the complete title of the book or article; the journal in which the article appears; the details of the volume and pages of the article, or if a book, the name of the publishing company and the city of publication.

Writers often describe the statement of the problem and the question(s) asked in the first page of the report. You should note the focus of the study and the theoretical perspective used by the author in a paragraph or two. Although most research reports provide a theoretical perspective that serves as a basis for the study, not every researcher makes it clear which perspective they have used in the study. Finding and analysing the theoretical perspective of a study can be tricky. Researchers often include a discussion of the theoretical perspective for a study among other information in the introductory materials. It is important that you try to decipher the theoretical basis of the study by examining and identifying underlying assumptions to the study and how these link to the broader universe of knowledge.

You should also note the substantive literature which is reviewed. Although references will appear throughout the text, particular attention should be paid to the literature that is used to substantiate the conceptual or content area of the study. This literature is easy to find because most reports begin with a substantive literature review. It is part of the background information of the report. Some substantive literature can also be found in the Discussion or Implications sections of the report. Your task is to note what material has been included, and assess how the literature presented has been used to provide a rationale for the problem statement.

Most reports include a separate section on methods. The index card should include a few sentences which summarise the methodological design of the study. This includes assessing the appropriateness of the research design to the question asked and evaluating sampling, data analysis and ethical issues. Did the study use a qualitative or quantitative design? A longitudinal or cross-sectional approach? Were structured or unstructured interviews conducted? Was the research design descriptive, exploratory or experimental? What sampling framework was used? What ethical issues were raised?

The final paragraphs of the index card can be used to briefly summarise the main findings, and the conclusions and/or implications of the study. You might also include reflections on how the report has influenced your thoughts on the topic. These comments can be included under the category of Ideas.

The main purpose of the literature review is to examine how your proposed study can fit into a broader knowledge base. In order to achieve this goal, you will need to identify the strengths and gaps in the current knowledge base. This requires an understanding of what was studied and how it was done. It was mentioned at the beginning of the chapter that, as a critic, you can learn much from the success and failure of other researchers' efforts. The main objectives are to identify theoretical, methodological and substantive contributions of a study so that these can be incorporated into your work, and to note the gaps in existing knowledge so that you legitimate your planned work. This analysis can assist you to identify productive avenues for further investigations, to place your study in context of existing knowledge, and to ask questions which have not been addressed in the literature.

Source: Minichiello, V. (1987) 'Someone's decision: that is how I got here', *Australian Journal of Social Issues,* vol. 22, pp. 345–56. (Abbotsford Campus, La Trobe University NURS J: 62)   (1 of 4)

Research question: The study sheds light on the role older people, family members and health professionals play in the decision to seek nursing home care. The article also examines how the resident's living arrangement affects his/her perception of his/her situation, the options available to them, and who becomes involved in the decision-making process.

The author notes that there have been few studies (he cites two studies—which we will follow up) which have paid systematic empirical attention to these questions. While there is no explicit reference to theory, the author is clearly working within a sociological framework and using a functionalist perspective. He argues that as family members turn to formal agencies to meet the daily needs of their aged relatives, they adopt an advocate role. For this reason, family members collaborate with gatekeepers of nursing homes and are influential actors in the decision-making process.

Minichiello article   (2 of 4)

Much of the literature cited to substantiate this position is written by authors using a functionalist perspective.**Method:** The author collected data by interviewing ninety aged residents and their next-of-kin. A semi-structured questionnaire was used. Qualitative data were collected on the residents' feelings about moving to a nursing home. All the interviews were tape-recorded and conducted at the nursing home. The sample is not representative and includes only those residents assessed by the professional nursing home staff as capable of hearing and comprehending questions. This places limits on the generality of the results.

Main findings and conclusions: The study found that people play different roles in the decision-making process. Most older people were minor participants in the decision to enter a nursing home. The qualitative data highlight the processes by which family members and health professionals exclude the older person from the decision-making process. Residents recognised that the person who first raised the topic of moving to a nursing home is not necessarily the most influential actor in the decision-making process.

Minichiello article   (3 of 4)

While most residents identified the physician as the person who first raised the topic of moving into a nursing home, family members were seen as the most influential actors, although there were differences in which actors were identified as influential depending upon living arrangement.

Ideas: There are a number of issues that the author does not address: is there an association between level of disability, marital status, gender and involvement in the decision-making process? The author does not tell us very much about the characteristics of people who make decisions for themselves. Who are they? What distinguishes this group from those people who find themselves in situations where others have acted on their behalf? Are there different levels of decision making? Of course there is the decision to move into a nursing home. But what about the decision of selecting a nursing home? Is it possible for some residents not to be involved in making the decision to move in a nursing home but to be involved in selecting the nursing home they will move to?

Minichiello article   (4 of 4)

The concepts of power and conflict are all applicable to this study. The author has decided not to apply these concepts to understand the topic of decision making.

The study has brought to my attention the difficulty of interviewing the more disabled residents. If I want to include this group in my sample, how do I collect data about them? Maybe through family members?

The Minichiello article does not discuss whether there were similarities or differences between the stories of the older person and the stories provided by their relatives about the decision-making process. If the two stories were similar, then family members can be used as a proxy interview in those cases where it is not possible to directly talk with the older person. I need to examine the literature specifically dealing with methodological issues in studying the institutionalised aged. This may give me ideas about data-collection strategies.

Figure 3.2 An example of a review of the literature index card

Chapter 4

In-depth interviewing

'Prime Minister, are you going to call an early election?'
'What sort of question is that? You know I have promised to run to full term.'
'Yes but ... '
'There are no buts. When we make a promise to the electorate then we keep it!'
'You might wish to keep it Prime Minister, but your party might want a new leader at the helm. What is to stop them forcing you into an election situation where ... '

'Mr Woolley, are you worried about the rise in crime among teenagers?'
'"Yes", I said.'
'Do you think there is a lack of discipline and vigorous training in our comprehensive schools?'
'Yes.'
'Do you think young people welcome some structure and leadership in their lives?'
'Yes.'
'Do they respond to a challenge?'
'Yes.'
'Might you be in favour of reintroducing National Service?'
'Yes.'

—*Yes, Prime Minister* (Lynn & Jay 1987, p. 106)

When we think of *interviews*, it is usually journalistic interviews as in the first quotation, or survey-style interviews as in the second, that come to mind. We rarely categorise interviews as conversations. Nevertheless, *in-depth interviewing* is conversation with a specific purpose—a conversation between researcher and informant focusing on the informant's perception of self, life and experience, and expressed in his or her own words. It is the means by which the researcher can gain access to, and subsequently understand, the private interpretations of social reality that individuals hold. This is made public in the interview process.

Chapter 2 discussed how we understand science and people. This chapter examines interviewing and the different methods of carrying out interviews. It then focuses on in-depth interviewing, what it is, how it differs from other forms of interviewing and why and when it can be used. Chapter 5 examines the skills used in doing interviewing as a research method.

What is an interview?

There are a number of definitions of interviewing, each tied to the particular form or type of interview. The common elements of these definitions are:

> a face-to-face verbal interchange in which one person, the interviewer, attempts to elicit information or expressions of opinion or belief from another person or persons (Maccoby & Maccoby 1954, p. 499).

Essentially, interviewing is a means of gaining access to information of different kinds. It is done by asking questions in direct face-to-face interaction. For example, the researcher may ask you questions which range from the trivial (for example, what brand of toilet paper do you use?) to the serious and/or disturbing (for example, what is your attitude to compulsory AIDS testing?; do you believe certain ethnic groups should reside in Australia?; or what do you think of having exams?). One frequently used method for finding out about such things is the interview, where one can directly ask the person or group what they do, or what they think, about a particular subject. In-depth interviewing is one form of interviewing. But before we discuss in-depth interviewing, we examine other forms of interviewing that are available.

Interview models

Interviewing can take a variety of forms. Most texts say that along a continuum you will find structured interviews at one end, and in-depth interviewing at the other (Babbie 1989; Bailey 1982; Kidder & Judd 1986; Taylor & Bogdan 1984). Other forms of interviewing lie somewhere between the two extremes.

Structured interviews	*Focused or semi-structured interviews*	*Unstructured interviews*
Standardised interviews Survey interviews Clinical history taking	In-depth interviews Survey interviews Group interviews	In-depth interviews Clinical interviews Group interviews Oral or life-history interviews

Figure 4.1 Interviewing methods: the continuum model

Figure 4.1 gives us the traditional image of interviewing found in most methods textbooks. The following descriptions are given so that readers can differentiate between methods as they are practised, and not simply as they are written about in reports of research. The terms *structured*, *semi-structured* and *unstructured* refer to the process of the interview.

There are debates about whether it is correct or necessary to make such distinctions. For our purpose, it is important to understand what these terms refer to. Armed with knowledge of the terminology, you can decide whether the debate is meaningful and whether you want to join in.

Structured interviews

In social research, structured interviews (also known as standardised or survey interviews) are predominantly used in surveys or opinion polls. Writers of research methods texts which focus primarily on structured interviewing as the model that social scientists use tend to neglect or devalue the in-depth interview. They assume that 'the asking of questions' is the main source of social scientific information about everyday behaviour and that the method of asking questions and receiving answers should not follow the usual patterns of informal conversation (Shipman 1972).

In structured interviews, standardised questions are carefully ordered and worded in a detailed *interview schedule*. Each research subject is asked exactly the same question, in exactly the same order as all other subjects. This is done to ensure comparability with other studies and to try to prevent differences or bias between interviews. The schedule consists predominantly of *closed-ended questions* asked in a pre-determined order. Open-ended questions may be included and are also asked in a predetermined order.

Closed-ended questions are those questions in which the informant is asked to choose between several predetermined answers, for example, 'Will you vote Labor in the next election?'. 'Yes/ No/Don't know' are the options provided for the response. Such questions are inflexible, but enable the researcher to code responses more easily and therefore cost less than open-ended questions. The underlying assumption made by the researcher using structured interviewing is that the questions he or she is asking are relevant to the area of inquiry. The primary criticism of closed-ended questions is that they do not allow the researcher to find out from the informant what is relevant to them or allow them to express different views. This shortcoming leads many researchers to consider alternative interviewing strategies such as in-depth interviewing.

Open-ended questions or free-answer questions are sometimes used in structured interviews. These are questions in which the researcher asks the informant how he or she feels or thinks about the topic under scrutiny; for example, 'How do you feel (or, what do you think) about the introduction of the dying with dignity legislation?'. The researcher then takes note of whatever the informant says in response to the question. These responses often lead to further questions which some authors argue increase datacoding difficulties and therefore research costs (Kidder & Judd 1986). However, we claim that when such questions are used in in-depth, focused or unstructured interviewing, the richness of the data obtained is worth the cost.

Another factor in structured or survey interviewing is the relationship between interviewer and informant and the respective roles they play. The assumption is that the researcher controls the flow of the conversation by asking questions and recording the responses of the 'subordinate' informant. In fact, the informant is usually referred to as the '*subject*' or '*respondent*', because he or she is expected to respond to set questions rather than to inform through participation in a conversation. The interviewing situation is regarded as 'a one-way process in which the interviewer elicits and receives, but does not give information' (Roberts 1988, p. 30).

Face-to-face interaction may have its positive side in providing higher response rates than other survey methods, but in many texts, prospective researchers are warned of the dangers inherent in the interview process (Bailey 1982). The researcher may gain access by establishing trust and developing rapport with the informant, but is cautioned against over-involvement or getting 'too close' as this might influence objectivity and introduce bias into the research. As Roberts points out:

> ... textbooks advise interviewers to adopt an attitude toward interviewees which allocates the latter a narrow and objectified function as data ... interviews are seen as having no personal meaning in terms of social interaction, so that their meaning tends to be confined to their statistical comparability with other interviews and the data obtained from them ... (1988, p. 30).

To summarise, researchers using structured interviewing assume that they know what sort of information they are after. Therefore, the role of the interviewer is to facilitate responses to the questions, that is, to be 'a neutral medium through which questions and answers are transmitted' (Babbie 1989, p. 245). The social interaction between the participants is formalised and highly structured to enhance reliability (that is, the extent to which the research can be replicated and tested for possible researcher influence or error). The underlying assumption is that objectivity is desirable and achievable.

Criticisms of the structured approach. There have been a number of criticisms of the structured approach to interviewing. Two of these criticisms are relevant to our discussion. Many researchers (Bell & Roberts 1984; Finch 1984; Oakley 1988; Wakeford 1981) recognised that the idealised descriptions of structured interviewing in textbooks and research reports did not describe the social reality of interviewing. They illustrated how real research happens by publicly acknowledging this in accounts which accurately detailed the vagaries of structured interviewing.

In addition, in the 1970s, there was much discussion about the philosophical and political issues of research, particularly the question of the appropriateness or otherwise of the natural science model to the social sciences. It was argued (Taylor & Bogdan 1984) that experimental and survey methods did not adequately deal with the differences between objects and people, and that there were more valid ways in which to study social reality. In-depth interviewing was said to be one of these ways.

Focused or semi-structured interviews

Focused or semi-structured interviews are used either as part of the more quantitatively-oriented structured interview model, or of the qualitatively-oriented in-depth interviewing model. This is because researchers on either side of the two 'poles' of this arbitrary continuum use this strategy when it helps to answer their research questions. Essentially, this process entails researchers using the broad topic in which they are interested to guide the interview. An interview guide or schedule is developed around a list of topics *without* fixed wording or fixed ordering of questions. The content of the interview is focused on the issues that are central to the research question, but the type of questioning and discussion allow for greater flexibility than does the survey-style interview. As with in-depth interviewing, this may reduce the comparability of interviews within the study but provides a more valid explication of the informant's perception of reality.

Semi-structured or focused interviews are modelled more closely on the unstructured than the structured model of interviewing. This means that the topic area guides the questions asked, but the mode of asking follows the unstructured interview process. Both unstructured and semi-structured (or focused) interviews involve an in-depth examination of people and topics.

Unstructured interviews

Unstructured interviews refer to interviews which dispense with formal interview schedules and ordering of questions and rely on the social interaction between interviewer and informant to elicit information. The *recursive model of interviewing* is often used in this method.

The unstructured interview takes on the appearance of a normal everyday conversation. However, it is always a controlled conversation which is geared to the interviewer's research interests. The element of control is regarded as minimal, but nevertheless present in order to keep the informant 'relating experiences and attitudes that are relevant to the problem' (Burgess 1982a, p. 107).

Group interviews

Group interviews are those interviews in which the interviewer gathers together a group of informants in order to engage them in conversation for the purpose of research. This is carried out using either focused or semi-structured interviews, or in-depth interviews. There are a number of different types of group interview. These include focus groups, memory work groups and reference groups. The purpose for doing a group interview is usually tied to not only the research question, but also the pragmatic exigencies of the research process, such as restricted access to a particular sample, funding restrictions or time constraints. Others (for example Fontana & Frey 1994) suggest that the group interview can be used for several purposes, ranging from exploratory and phenomenological through to pre-testing other research tools. More recently, the purpose for engaging in this style of interviewing has been tied to explicit political goals underpinning the research project—such as in some types of feminist research, action research and research conducted by members of minority ethnic groups studying their own group.

Focus groups are usually focused interviews operating in a group format. They were developed in the 1940s in order to facilitate advertising and market research by gathering consumer opinions of products, service delivery or advertising effectiveness. They involve discussions amongst small groups of people (6–12) with the researcher acting as a moderator or facilitator. The researcher usually introduces the topics for discussion and then facilitates the conversation process or encourages participation without his or her own input.

Why use focus groups? Apart from all the reasons you would cite for using any interview process, focus groups provide the advantages of gathering data more quickly and more economically than individual interviews; and more importantly, they allow informants to 'react to and build upon the responses of other group members' (Stewart & Shamdasani 1991, p. 16). This is obviously important when you wish to examine the processes of social interaction or group dynamics as they happen (almost in the role of participant observer). What are labelled as the three most obvious disadvantages of using focus groups are, in some ways, typical of social interaction in groups and may not really be disadvantages at all if you are actually studying group processes. However, if you are looking for individual responses then the following issues are of concern. First, due to the nature of the group setting the responses of the participants are not independent. 'Group think' may be an outcome due to this, be it in a formal or informal setting. Second, the evolving discussion and views expressed may come to be directed by a dominant group member. Third, and concomitantly, some of the participants may find the group setting or environment inhibiting. How one determines the membership or composition of the group and how one decides on sampling frames is tied very directly to the nature of the research question. (See Thomas et al. 1992 for a more detailed discussion.)

Reference groups are really another form of focus group being used for the specific political purpose of eliciting information from stakeholders or representatives of stakeholders in the social context of the research project. It is often hoped that by setting up a reference group and inviting stakeholders to be members of such a group, the researcher/s will be able to sympathetically take into account and/or 'head off' any interests which might negatively influence the research process.

The benefits are clear. In-depth interviewing of key informants in a group can alert the researcher/s with regard to what is considered significant and/or contentious within that arena—be it a specific focus, the style of questioning or the personality of the researcher. On the other hand, there are two obvious problems inherent in setting up and relying on a reference group. Firstly, working out *who* the key stakeholders are in the research context may not be so simple (see chapter 3). A great deal of exploratory research (a project in and of itself) may need to be done before you could correctly or usefully identify such stakeholders. Even if you correctly identify them, they or their representative, for whatever reason, may not wish to participate in the reference group. Secondly, the researcher may become so reliant on the views solicited from the reference group that they might not be as open to other data and information which might be just as significant.

All members of the reference group will have their own interests to represent and these may conflict with the researcher's sense of integrity in responding to the concerns and interests of the different members. The researcher may be pressured to side with one member of the reference group, irrespective of the parameters and role of the group being 'laid out' at the beginning of the project. The researcher may also feel morally obliged to follow the interests of some reference group members and not others. It could be argued that all such pressures can be avoided by clearly and carefully structuring the role and purpose of the reference group to all participants, but we believe that this does not always prevent such pressures from occurring.

Memory work is another form of group interview developed by Frigga Haug (1987) in order to examine 'how we become ourselves and the part we play in that construction' (Kippax 1990, p. 93). The 'we' here refers to women, and this group interview method was developed specifically as a feminist methodology. The method is one which is aimed at illuminating the meanings individuals attach to their memories as they are understood by the participants at the time and as they are currently viewed. Haug set out a programme of steps for the carrying out of memory work which is detailed (and we can not elaborate on it here). The research question determines the composition of the group but there are debates as to whether a heterogeneous or homogeneous group is more useful to the process. The size of the group is usually between 8–10 people. Memories are shared, recorded and analysed collectively with each member of the research project actively participating in the research process. It is similar to participatory action research in that it operates with the ideal that all participants are equal co-researchers and that the participants as a group give form and meaning to the data.

In-depth interviewing

Unstructured and semi-structured (or focused interviewing) are two ways of doing in-depth interviewing. In-depth interviews, according to Taylor and Bogdan's useful definition, are *'repeated face-to-face encounters between the researcher and informants directed toward understanding informants' perspectives on their lives, experiences or situations as expressed in their own words'* (1984, p. 77).

There are several significant assumptions inherent in this conception. Firstly, that these encounters are *repeated*, which implies that a greater length of time is spent with the informant. This is regarded as beneficial for rapport enhancement and for the greater understanding that may follow the increased social interaction. Secondly, that the encounter is *between* researcher and informant. This implies an egalitarian concept of roles within the interview which contrasts with the imbalance of power between the roles in survey methods. Thirdly, rather than focusing on the researcher's perspective as the valid view, it is the informant's account which is being sought and is highly valued. Finally, that we try to retrieve the informant's world by understanding their perspective in language that is natural to them. This reduces the possible distorting effect of symbols and language which are not part of their everyday usage. Hence, there is a significant move from the interrogative process used in a structured interview toward that of a more conversational process.

The fundamental legitimation for the use of in-depth interviewing is based on acknowledging that:

> The world of nature as explored by the natural scientist does not mean anything to molecules, atoms and electrons. But the observational field of the social scientist—social reality—has a specific meaning and relevance structure for the beings living, acting and thinking within it. By a series of commonsense constructs they have pre-selected and pre-interpreted this world which they experience as the reality of their daily lives. It is these thought objects of theirs which determine their behaviour by motivating it. The thought objects constructed by the social scientist in order to grasp ... social reality, have to be founded upon the thought objects constructed by the commonsense thinking of men living their daily life within their social world (Schütz 1962, p. 49).

This quotation encapsulates the essential elements of the assumptions underlying interpretive research. In-depth interviewing is a method used in such research. The subject matter of the social scientist 'answers back', unlike the inanimate objects studied by the natural sciences. This is a fundamental difference between the natural and social sciences. Consequently, the use of natural science methodologies is regarded as inappropriate for the social sciences or at least some researchers think so. The underlying assumption of Schütz's statement is that we need to know what people think in order to understand why they behave in the ways that they do. This, in turn, is predicated on the belief that people act in the ways that they do because of the way in which they define the situation as they see it or believe it to be. That is, they interpret the facts as they see them.

Tied to this idea is the belief that when we are engaged in in-depth interviewing, what we are actually interested in is people's experience of social reality through their routinely constructed interpretations of it. If the researcher develops theories which are not grounded in the informant's experience of social reality, then he or she runs the risk of constructing and imposing on that informant a fictional view of their reality.

For example, let us say that a woman has just given birth to a baby. She feels depressed and lethargic, and this continues for months after the delivery. A doctor conducting a traditional clinical interview for the purpose of diagnosis and treatment may come to the conclusion that the woman is suffering from postpartum depression and needs treatment. Alternatively, if the doctor is aware of in-depth interviewing as a means of understanding the woman's interpretation of reality, then he or she might spend an hour engaged in such an interview and discover that there are alternative interpretations of the problem being discussed. The woman may tell the doctor how her body and self-image have altered in a negative manner due to physical changes during and after pregnancy; that she doesn't enjoy being overweight; that she is no longer independent because she has another human being totally dependent on her; and that her husband is not supportive. Her husband is reported to assume that all women 'get the blues' after giving birth and that she should 'pull herself together and not be neurotic'. She states that this lack of understanding and support is making her depressed. The woman's definition of the situation is that she is legitimately unhappy with the social situation in which she now finds herself. She argues that being depressed is a reasonable response under the circumstances. In this situation, the interviewer (doctor) can construct an interpretation based on the woman's own conception of her social reality. If the doctor accepts the meanings that the woman attaches to her actions he or she may be in a more advantageous position to 'diagnose' the problem than is the woman's husband. He has imposed his definition of the situation without taking his wife's understandings into account.

This example emphasises the interviewer's ability to reconstruct the reality of the informant through the process of listening to that informant. In other words, in-depth interviewing focuses on, and relies on, verbal accounts of social realities. This is somewhat different from participant observation which relies on participation in, and observation of, behaviour or action in the context in which it occurs. It is often argued (Taylor & Bogdan 1984) that the participant observer is in a better position than the interviewer to gain access to the everyday life of the informant or group of informants because the participant observer directly experiences the social world which the informant inhabits, rather than simply relating second-hand accounts. At one level this is certainly true. However, each method has its advantages and disadvantages, depending on the research question that is being asked, and on the manner in which the researcher is seeking to answer it. Often the researcher is interested in the second-hand account. In that case, in-depth interviewing is regarded as one of the more effective means of gaining access to that account. This debate relates directly to the types of in-depth interviewing available to researchers and clinicians and the situations in which they choose to use them.

Types of in-depth interviewing: when are they used?

There are at least five distinct research situations in which one can use in-depth interviewing:

1 The in-depth interview is used to gain access to, and an understanding of, activities and events which cannot be observed directly by the researcher. Accounts of action and patterns of living are provided by those who have directly participated in or observed them, such as in Minichiello's (1987) study of decision-making processes related to the entry of the older people into nursing homes. He interviewed the older people living in nursing homes and members of their families in order to find out about events which he could not directly observe or participate in because they had occurred in the past. Eastop's (1985) study of the rural community's reaction to the Ash Wednesday fires is another example of this kind of interviewing.

2 In-depth interviewing is used in the life (or oral)-history approach which is actually a more specialised form of the above-mentioned situation. Using this method, the interviewer attempts to elicit and understand the significant experiences in the informant's entire life by means of in-depth interviewing, sometimes combined with exam-ination of letters, photographs and personal effects. This method has also been called a *case study* approach because it is the individual informant's subjective experience that is desired. The sociological *autobiography* differs from biography and traditional autobiography, in that the life history of the informant is produced as a result of interaction and collaboration with the researcher. A more detailed account of this type of in-depth interviewing can be found in chapter 6.

3 In-depth interviewing is also linked to the purpose of the research project. It is intended to enable the researcher to gain access to groups of people in order to provide a broad view of situations, people or settings. For instance, Aroni's (1985) longitudinal study of the impact of schooling on Jewish identity was based primarily on in-depth interviews with nearly 300 Jewish matriculation students attending Jewish and non-Jewish schools. This particular use of in-depth interviewing enables the researcher to study a larger number of people over a shorter time than if they had chosen to use participant observation. If Aroni had decided on the latter method she would have had to have attended at least twenty schools and also participated in the home life and peer group interactions of 300 students. It would have taken a great deal longer to complete such a study.

4 The type of in-depth interviewing examined here is the clinical interview. It has been developed from three other kinds of interview: the sociological semi-focused interview, the medical model of interviewing the patient to obtain a *case history* and the counselling interview. It has been adapted for use in the clinical setting. A more detailed examination of this type of qualitative interviewing can be found in chapter 7.

5 In-depth interviewing can be conducted with a group of informants. The group interview is where the interviewer gathers together a group of informants and provides them with the opportunity to engage in discussion. This can include analysis of any argument or debate that may arise if group members' subjective perceptions of the issues, context or subject do not concur. Alternatively, if there is an agreement then this is analysed. This type of in-depth interviewing enables the researcher to examine the dynamics of the group, and to interpret the views of the members of the group irrespective of whether their views are consensual or in conflict. One reservation about this method is that informants in a group interview will tend to provide views that can be publicly stated. If they had been interviewed separately, perhaps there would be greater chance of hearing more private interpretations of their reality. Nevertheless, this method allows both meaningful use of the in-depth interview and different interpretations of the same experiences. All forms of in-depth interviewing from semi-structured or focused interviewing to unstructured applications rely on similar interviewing techniques.

Advantages and disadvantages of in-depth interviewing

There are advantages and disadvantages in trying to retrieve the world of the informant through in-depth interviewing. This is because, as many texts (Benney & Hughes 1970; Burgess 1982a; Denzin 1989; Deutscher 1973; Foddy 1988; Taylor & Bogdan 1984) point out, the researcher's definition of the situation is open to the vagaries of the informant's interpretation and presentation of reality. The researcher is not usually in the situation of being able to directly observe the informant in his or her everyday life. Thus they are deprived of the *ethnographic context* which would give a richer understanding of the informant's perspective.

If we return to our earlier example of the woman suffering from post-partum depression, we can illustrate the problems inherent in all forms of research relying on verbal accounts. One might ask how does the researcher (in this case the clinician) know that the informant (the patient) is telling the truth, and whether the informant's definition of the situation is accurate? The interviewer cannot know for sure simply from engaging in the interview. The strategy of cross-checking through subsequent interviews can be used however to assess the accuracy of information. In the matter of 'truth telling' it is important to ask who has the power to define what counts as truth in the informant's social world. She, or her husband, or the medical practitioner? Secondly, whose definition of the situation can be regarded as accurate? How do we determine this and does it matter? The researcher who uses in-depth interviewing would argue that the informant's definition is paramount, because that is the focus of the research process. How we, the researchers, subsequently interpret and analyse that information depends on our aims in carrying out the research. This, of course, is directly related to the motive for doing the research. It may be to provide clinical understanding and advice, or to delve into the unresearched area of the postnatally depressed mother's perception of self and how it relates (or does not relate) to the social and political context in which all women and men live. These concerns are discussed in chapters 8 and 9.

This raises a serious question for the interpretive researcher. If you cannot determine such matters by using in-depth interviewing, why not use participant observation where the researcher is more directly involved in the informant's world? We argue that, even when researchers use participant observation, they are still seeking the 'definition of the situation' of the group or individual under study. This may be enhanced by their ability to interpret and reinterpret actions on the spot rather than relying on verbal accounts. However, if we are still trying not to impose our own assumptions of the informant's world, then the problem remains the same, irrespective of whether we are researching as participant observers or as in-depth interviewers. It is interpretation as such that is the issue and not the technique. This issue is discussed in more detail in chapter 11.

Some researchers (Klockars 1977; Oakley 1988) suggest that these problems can be overcome by the in-depth interviewer using intrusive yet ethically sound methods. That is, the researcher should adopt a highly interactive role in the interview process in order to allow a collaborative approach to be taken by the informant (see chapter 9).

Alternatively, Schwartz and Jacobs (1979) suggest that Cicourel's approach is useful in coming to terms with this issue. Their suggestion is that in an interview situation, the informant operates within an ethnographic context, that is, the informant has an everyday commonsense working knowledge of his or her own life history, the cultural milieu of which he or she is a part, and a sense of self identity. It is from within this ethnographic context that the informant makes decisions about what to say to the interviewer. The informant knows the exact meaning and significance of what he or she is saying (as it would be perceived by an insider of that ethnographic context, such as a family member or close friend). Schwartz and Jacobs point out that interviewers should try to make provision for the ethnographic context in which the informant is operating. Otherwise he or she risks the problems that we discussed earlier—that is, of trying to interpret what the informant means as opposed to what he or she says. The interviewer should confirm the interview using the actual version of the information sought.

In-depth interviewing as the method of choice: why and when?

Why?

The decision to use in-depth interviewing as one's research strategy or data-collecting method is linked to theoretical and practical concerns. There are two major rationales given in the literature on choice of method. The first relates to the researcher's view of what social reality is and how it ought to be studied. As Bilton et al. (1981) argue, different ontological and epistemological positions generate different methodologies. That is, different models of reality lead to different propositions about what reality is, and therefore demand different ways of establishing what can be accepted as real; different ways of validating or justifying the data relevant to reality; and different strategies for collecting such data. The way we go about getting at knowledge and the techniques we use to collect evidence are directly related to our image of social reality; the way in which we think we can know it and the way in which we think it ought to be studied. Therefore, if we believe (as most researchers using qualitative methods do) that social reality exists as meaningful interaction between individuals then it can only be known through understanding others' points of view, interpretations and meanings. If meaningful human interaction depends on language, then the words people use and the interpretations they make are of central interest to the researcher. In-depth interviewing is an appropriate method to gain access to the individual's words and interpretations.

The second rationale for deciding to use in-depth interviewing is based on the view that practical issues determine the choice of research method. Quantitative and qualitative research are simply names for different ways of conducting social investigations. They can be thought of as being appropriate for different types of research question. Bryman points out that when this view is taken, quantitative and qualitative research strategies are regarded as 'different approaches to data collection, so that preferences for one or the other or some hybrid approach are based on technical issues' (1988, p. 5).

When?

When you choose to use in-depth interviewing is also related to the why of your choice. If you opt for the first rationale and you hold a *symbolic interactionist perspective*, then you would use in-depth interviewing alone or in conjunction with participant observation.

If you opt for the second rationale then you would recognise that the types of in-depth interview described in this chapter are each appropriate for particular circumstances. For instance, when the researcher wishes to highlight subjective human experience, then the case-study or life-history approach is an appropriate form of in-depth interviewing. This methodological strategy enables the researcher to understand and interpret social reality through the meanings that the informant attaches to their life experiences. Thus, depth of understanding is achieved by focusing intensely on one person or one setting. Taylor and Bogdan (1984, p. 81) point out that life histories enable the researcher to evaluate theories of social life by using them as 'a touchstone'; they refer to their own research with the mentally retarded 'whose life histories challenge myths and misconceptions of mental retardation'.

Another instance in which it is appropriate to choose in-depth interviewing is when the type of research depends on understanding a broad range of people or settings in a short time. That is, when there are research questions which lend themselves to in-depth interviewing rather than other qualitative methods because the researcher either has time constraints or has reasonably clear and well-defined research interests. Connell (1985) and Aroni (1985) both aimed at understanding a broad range of school students. Connell wanted a better understanding of children's constructions of politics. Aroni was interested in examining students' perceptions of their education in relation to ethnic identity. Both studies necessitated understanding the interpretations of a broad range of people. Participant observation would not have presented a useful alternative in these circumstances as it would have been too time consuming, and/or some of the activities (for example, playground discussion) were inaccessible to the researchers.

In-depth interviewing and theory building

It is significant that all forms of in-depth interviewing are not predominantly used as *hypothesis*-testing modes of research but as theory-building ones. It is more usual to see this method being employed as part of an exploratory study where the researcher is attempting to gain understanding of the field of study, and to develop theories rather than test them. Leggatt's (1981) research on schizophrenia used in-depth interviewing to understand the relationship between schizophrenia sufferers and their families. She was not testing a hypothesis. Rather she went into the field with some hunches based on her reading of the sociological literature on mental illness.

She had a hunch that symbolic interactionist theory somehow was not dealing adequately with the nature of reality that these people experienced. She wanted to find a method which would enable her to understand and explain their 'definition of the situation'. During the research process she engaged in a process of theory building, based on the data she was gathering and her experiences of the actual interaction in the in-depth interviewing. Leggatt utilised the Glaser and Strauss' (1967) model of *grounded theory*, that is, theory drawn or teased out of the data gathered. She developed a sophisticated interpretive approach and suggested that madness existed and in a fashion which was different from the symbolic interactionist portrayal. She concluded that government policies dealing with schizophrenia should be based on the informed view of the family members in whose everyday lives it plays a great part. The important point here is that Leggatt's conclusion rested on the views, attitudes and definitions of her informants. She had no formal hypothesis, and kept her hunches at the back of her mind while she listened and tried to comprehend the everyday reality of her informants. Further 'suspicions' were developed throughout the research, and when she had nearly completed the project these contributed to hypotheses or theories for further testing. More will be said on the topic of grounded theory in chapter 11.

Chapter 5

Interview processes

Interviewing techniques

There are no set rules for how to go about doing in-depth interviews nor for how to be a good informant. Yet we all have some idea of how we might behave in this situation. The following comments and suggestions are just that—comments and suggestions. Some authors (Benney & Hughes 1970; Goode & Hatt 1952), *do* provide rules, however we feel this is not possible because each in-depth interview will take place in a different socio-political and cultural context which may influence the social interaction that occurs. For example, if we were interested in the views held by occupational therapy students of their own profession and its status in comparison with that of other health professions, we might decide to present our research problem in a very direct fashion. However, if we knew that there was conflict between these students and physio-therapy students then we might decide to present the research issue, and one of us as the researcher, in a less direct and obvious manner in order to create a non-threatening atmosphere. Alternatively, we might decide to heighten the focus of the research issue to the prospective informants in the hope that this would capture some of their current definitions of the situation more accurately. Thus, even the initial approach can differ depending on the social context as it is perceived both by the researcher and the informant.

So instead of providing rules, we will discuss what was or was not help-ful to us as researchers based on our experience and the experiences of other researchers who have used in-depth interviewing. Before you start your research, it might be a good idea to read chapters 3, 4, 5 (this chap-ter), 8 and 9 in conjunction with one another. This will help you to avoid some of the problems that others have encountered. In practice, the issues raised in chapters 8 and 9 are inextricably tied to the processes discussed here. For ease of understanding, we have discussed these issues separately. However, when we reflect on the actual *process* of in-depth interviewing as most of us have experienced it, then integrating the material would have given a more accurate representation of those experiences.

Why bother discussing this at all? Specific issues of publication influence all who publish their research or write about the research process. Writing and publishing have an influence on, and are part of, the social context and structure of the interview and inevitably influence the process. It is important to recognise how such factors play a part in in-depth interviewing. It is also important for the reader to understand that interview processes are very closely tied to the political and ethical world view of the researcher (see chapter 9). If one is engaged in participatory action research or particular forms of feminist or ethnic research then the interview processes will alter accordingly. What we discuss below follows a generalised framework in order to make the notion of interview processes and pragmatics of interviewing more accessible to the novice. Due to this need, and for the sake of brevity, we feel that even though our description of interview participants (researcher and researched) seems to be a little positivist in style, it is inevitable for the expository purposes of our text. We encourage you to examine texts, such as Wadsworth (1991) and Harding (1991) for presentations of models of in-depth interviewing in participatory action research.

Strategies for starting an interview

Designing a piece of research, deciding on who should be interviewed, sampling strategies, and gaining access to your informant/s are all practical, ethical and political issues which are part of the research process. Let us assume that you have decided on a research strategy and informants have been selected on the basis of the sampling procedures you have employed.

How many interviews are you going to organise with your informants? With in-depth interviewing, the researcher does not know, prior to speaking with the informant, how many interviews would be useful. They can range from one or two long sessions (anywhere between one hour to four hours) to more than twenty sessions in the case of life histories. This will depend on the relationship that builds between researcher and informant and on the informant's volubility.

How do you approach the informant? The more complex answer to this question is another question, 'What impression do you want to give the informant about the research project and their involvement in it?'. We have found that most researchers wish themselves and others to see their research as bona fide and significant. Most people when approached to participate in a research project are willing if not flattered (Taylor & Bogdan 1984), and they will agree to be an informant if they 'can fit you into their schedules'. The opening gambit that Taylor and Bogdan use is very similar to those used by many researchers in the field:

When approaching potential informants, we tell them that it seems like they have had something important to say and that we would like to sit down with them and talk about it some time, if they seem receptive to the idea, we schedule the first meeting (1984, p. 86).

Sometimes the researcher uses this approach. The notion of an unstructured interview with minimal direction from the interviewer even prior to the actual interview is appealing. It is one which provides the informant with little information about the research, aiming to avoid biasing the informant's understanding of the issue toward the researcher's interests. The intending interviewer is often counselled to behave as though he or she is unsure about which questions to ask and that they should be willing to learn from the informant (Taylor & Bogdan 1984).

Alternatively, the researcher may decide that this sort of approach is ethically and politically inadequate for what should be collaborative research, and will introduce him or herself and the research issue in a more precise manner. This will be done by telling the informant a little about the general nature of the research issue and how the researcher intends to conduct the entire project. This approach is usually taken when the researcher wishes to involve the informant in a collaborative undertaking (see chapter 8). The topics usually covered are confidentiality and *anonymity*, the motives and intentions of the interviewer, and who gets the final say on the manuscript. It may also be appropriate to discuss whether the informant should expect any remuneration, monetary or otherwise. Other pragmatic issues discussed are the interview schedule, place of interview, and what method is to be used to record the interview/s.

Many researchers talk about what will happen in the interview prior to its occurrence, thus structuring the mutual contact in so-called unstructured interviewing strategies. These discussions centre on setting the tone, producing a *productive interpersonal climate* or establishing rapport. Usually such issues are discussed in the framework of the practical details of doing in-depth interviewing. This issue is related to the social experience of the interview for both parties and to the structuring of the questioning process.

In-depth interviewing: control and structure

In-depth interviewing, contrary to the image presented in figure 4.1 (see chapter 4), should not be seen as unstructured interviewing in the psychoanalytic model of free association. The reality of the social experience is that the conversation process, while not formally structured, is controlled to a certain degree. This inevitably produces an inequality in the relationship between the participants. However, in idealised accounts of in-depth interviewing, this is 'painted out' (Bell & Encel 1978; Oakley 1988). What is talked about is *establishing rapport* or establishing a *productive interpersonal climate*. These broad terms describe how interviewer and informant feel about their relationship. No researcher has suggested a specific method to create or guarantee rapport with the informant. However, it is regarded as important because it is assumed that if the informant and the researcher 'hit it off', then the informant will be more communicative. They will talk more freely because they 'get on' with the researcher.

How to establish rapport

Research methodology authors enthusiastically recommend that the interviewer establish rapport with the informant but none give the novice interviewer a specific technology for achieving this ideal. It is assumed to emerge somehow from a combination of the goal statement, and the individual's life experience. The question that remains in the mind of the novice is 'How do I actually do what is recommended?'. The how to of the interviewing process is addressed in another body of literature which we have not seen linked to research despite the obvious advantages of doing so.

Bandler and Grinder (1979), mathematician and linguist respectively, have developed a technology of communication from an original interest in how some therapists (such as Virginia Satir, Milton Erickson and Jay Haley) achieved their successes. From comparative studies, they have distilled a description of how to understand another person's model of the world which in turn permits the establishment of rapport and the pacing of interaction for the desired outcome. This model (*neurolinguistic programming*) explains how some interactions are easy while others are very difficult for the interviewer and how the easy and the difficult interviews differ from interviewer to interviewer.

Bandler and Grinder show that people vary in the reliance and emphasis they place upon different aspects of the perceptual information which they receive from the world. The particular emphasis chosen will determine what they conclude about that world. Information about the world is received through seeing, hearing, feeling or smelling. Our culture tends to discourage using olfactory data so we will discuss the first three channels of information only. If you listen to what people say you will hear understanding indicated by: I hear ..., I see ..., or I feel ... then elaborated by using language which is systematically linked to the perceptual channel originally referred to. There are those who 'hear' their understanding, or who speak in auditory terms of sounds and sound qualities; for example, volume, pitch, frequency; while the visual processors will 'see' brightness, colour, clarity; and the kinaesthetic 'feelers' will express their meanings with emotional metaphors and refer to such aspects as textures and temperature.

Different perceptual patterns link with different and characteristic eye movements, postures and breathing patterns. These can be used to guide the interviewer to understand the informant rapidly and accurately.

Rapport with another person is basically a matter of understanding their model of the world and communicating your understanding symmetrically. This can be done effectively by matching the perceptual language, the images of the world, the speech patterns, pitch, tone, speed, the overall posture and the breathing patterns of the informant.

Having matched and harmonised with the informant on these elements, the interviewer can lead the other person into areas of discussion which are significant in relation to the research problem, while maintaining understanding. (We recommend that you follow up these brief comments by reading King, Novik & Citrenbaum 1983.)

Bandler and Grinder also propose a metamodel for effective gathering of information (Cameron-Bandler 1985). This will not be discussed here because many of the recommendations concur with the sociological literature which is cited in this text. Suffice to say, we find the model a valuable way of synthesising recommendations and emphasising the claims that richer responses are elicited from informants by the use of open-ended how, when, or what questions rather than by asking the unanswerable why.

Taylor and Bogdan (1984) talk of setting the tone of the relationship with the informant. This involves conversation with the informant prior to the interview. They caution the researcher not to ask directive questions when initiating the interview because this may predispose (bias) the informant's perception of what the researcher regards as important to talk about. Rather, the researcher should, in the first few interviews, appear as someone who is not quite sure what questions to ask and is willing to learn from the informants.

Interview structure: the recursive model and asking questions

A number of writers (Schwartz & Jacobs 1979; Stewart & Cash 1988) refer to the patterned organisation or structure of conversations and, specifically, interviews. They speak of three parts to the structure— openings or beginnings, topical sections or middles, and closings or endings. Each part of the structure is said to incorporate its own organisation. They also raise another model of interviewing structure and organisation called the recursive model which was introduced in chapter 4.

The *recursive model of interviewing* refers to a form of questioning which is consistently associated with most forms of in-depth interviewing. It enables the researcher to do two things—to follow a more conversational model and, by doing this, to treat people and situations as unique. The interaction in each interview directs the research process.

Recursive questioning relies on the process of conversational interaction itself, that is, the relationship between a current remark and the next one. The researcher chooses how to use this method to best effect. This choice occurs at two levels. First, the interviewer needs to decide to what extent prior interaction in an interview session should be allowed to determine what is asked next. Secondly, the interviewer needs to decide on the extent to which the experiences and information of previous interview sessions with an informant or group of informants 'be allowed to determine the structure and content of current interviews' (Seaman 1987, p. 45). This means, irrespective of the type of question you are using, whether open or closed ended, whether decided on in advance or asked spontaneously, that you choose how recursive you want the interview process to be.

The researcher who chooses the recursive model as the strategy for conducting in-depth interviewing has chosen the most unstructured version of in-depth interviewing. This model relies on the natural flow of the conversation to direct it. The criticism levelled at the recursive model is that if the responses to the initial questions continue in the recursive manner, then it is possible for the interview to go off on a tangent. Interviewers have developed tactics to try to solve such problems. They use *transitions* to refocus the informant's attention on the topic or issue. Transitions are 'accomplished by connecting something the informant has said with the topic of interest, even if it is somewhat far fetched' (Abrahamson 1983, p. 339). The advantage of the recursive model of questioning is that it enables the interviewer to 'treat people and situations as unique and to alter the research technique in the light of information fed back during the research process itself' (Schwartz & Jacobs 1979, p. 45). This is close to the ideal form of research for those researchers who follow the *interpretive approach*.

As our discussion has indicated, there are a number of choices researchers need to make in relation to the degree of structure and control before and throughout the interview process. This includes the issue of how focused on a particular topic or problem the questions will be? It also raises the question of interview schedules or guides—to have or not to have?

The interview guide

When researchers are involved in large-scale survey research which utilise standardised (structured) interviewing techniques, they use a structured interview *protocol* or schedule. This usually includes the full list of questions in their appropriate order with instructions on how to ask certain questions, when to probe, how to cross-check and so on. This is obviously inappropriate in the context of in-depth interviewing, as it does not allow for recursively defined questioning, but rather a fully structured, controlled, survey-style interview. The quantitative model of interviewing ascribes various functions to the interview schedule which do not fit the *methodology* inherent in qualitative research. With the standardised or structured interview it is the interview schedule itself which acts as the standardising instrument by providing the question and response formats. Most research methods texts (Babbie 1989; Bailey 1982; Kidder 1981; Polgar & Thomas 1991) provide detailed discussions of the requirements for designing a good interview schedule for standardised interviews. They are usually less forthcoming about the different processes and needs of in-depth interviewing, and the nature and purpose of interview schedules in that context.

The in-depth interviewer needs to remind him or herself of certain areas which need to be discussed in the interview session/s. The researcher does not suddenly overnight become Superman or Wonderwoman by virtue of the fact of choosing to engage in in-depth interviewing. The researcher does not suddenly gain a flawless memory which can retain all the necessary information to be remembered in the interview setting. Rather, it is recognised that in such a predicament, the researcher utilises the means at hand to do a good interview.

So what does an *interview guide or schedule*, or, as Burgess (1982) refers to it, an *aide memoire*, look like? Usually, it consists of a list of general issues that the researcher wants to cover. It is used to jog the memory of the interviewer about certain issues or concerns. Unlike the interview schedule used in survey interviewing, this interview guide is revised as informants provide information which has not previously been thought of by the researcher.

Knowing what to include in the initial interview guide involves researchers in some preparation work before they enter the field. For instance, Aroni (1985) knew something about the Jewish community in Melbourne because she was a member of it. However, until she did some preparation work, she was not aware of all the studies that had investigated Jewish identification and identity among adolescents or the methodology of such studies. After doing a literature search and review, she gathered copies of questionnaires and interview schedules that had been used in those previous studies and examined them in order to analyse the content of the material. She isolated several themes which kept recurring in all the different studies and topics which she felt had not been dealt with in these studies. At that point, she compiled a brief list of themes which she felt might be useful to her for in-depth interviews. These themes were revised substantially after the first five interviews because the informants had alerted her to a number of issues which neither she nor previous researchers had thought were significant. Those first five interviews followed the structure and approach of the recursive model. She gained a great deal of information from the informants in terms of their interpretations of the impact of schooling on their ethnic identity and identification.

The *aide memoire* or the interview schedule does not necessarily determine the order of the conversation in an in-depth interview. As

Burgess (1984) points out, when he was interviewing primary school students, he had originally prepared to start each interview by explaining that he had an agenda. This included topics on themes that he wanted to cover in the discussion. His agenda or list of topics was structured around the chronology of the students' school lives. In keeping with this, he intended to start discussions with the obvious sequence of a chronology. However, even though he covered many of the topics and themes he had listed, he found that 'the order in which they occurred was different in each interview as these pupils had considerable freedom to develop strategies for answering my questions' (1984, p. 108). Rather than considering the issues chronologically, some informants started talking about the issues 'at the end, first'. In other words, they put the topic he had planned to ask about last 'at the top of the agenda'. He had to work his way back to the question he wanted to ask first about their early school experiences. This example highlights that one of the most significant aspects of the use of interview schedules in in-depth interviewing is that there is no set of preconceived, structured questions. The asking of questions is in no pre-set or fixed order. The interview process negotiated in the conversation in the interview participants is what orders questions and answers. The questions revolve around topics of conversations because the interview schedule merely suggests the kinds of themes, topics and questions that might be covered rather than any actual questions that might be used (Burgess 1984). The point here is that 'no individuals (other than perhaps other sociologists) think about themselves and their lives in the terms which sociologists use' (Burgess 1984, p. 1). Even the manner and language in which we phrase questions may be meaningless to the informant. Rather, we need to listen as well as speak, in order to continue the conversation we call an in-depth interview. A more detailed account of such background issues can be found in chapter 3.

Once a researcher has worked out some form of interview guide, made the introductions and set the scene or established rapport with the informant then he or she needs to start asking questions. But which questions? Do you start directly on the topic you are concerned with? Do you launch into asking about one of the themes on your interview guide and then quickly follow on with another theme question? Or do you opt for the recursive model? This reflexively defined structuring of the interview process enables the researchers to start with some questions on a theme, and then he or she allows the conversation to meander according to the informant's responses and the subsequent verbal interaction between him or herself and the informant. Perhaps you opt for some form of descriptive questioning or follow the *funnelling* method or the *story-telling* method?

The choice of strategy is dependent on the perspective the researcher holds on theory and methodology, on the research question being asked, and on the social interaction between the participants of the in-depth interview. There is no best way to phrase, order or commence questioning. The following strategies have been useful to many researchers engaged in trying to answer different research questions.

Funnelling

Funnelling refers to a process of questioning in which the interviewer controls the flow and type of information being asked by starting the interview with questions of a general and broad nature. These initial questions are designed simply to start the informant thinking about the issue in general terms. Then, as the participants engage in conversation, the interviewer guides the informant's view towards more specific issues by using questions which narrow the area. Finally, the interviewer begins to ask specific questions directly about the issue being examined. By using this strategy, the interview process can be a more relaxed and non-threatening conversation. The informant can reflect at ease on general questions. It is only later in the conversation that he or she is required to be more specific in response.

For example, let us assume that you wanted to know something about adolescents' views of their body image and whether those views had any connection with eating disorders. Using this strategy, the researcher might start by asking some general questions about the media and body images of men and women. What are these images? How realistic are they? The researcher could ask the informant what he or she regards as healthy eating habits and unhealthy eating habits. Then the researcher could continue by asking if the informant knows of any forms of eating disorders. From this point, the questions could narrow down by asking what the informant regarded as the ideal female and male body and what they personally regarded as an attractive body. Then the researcher could ask the informant what actions, including eating habits, could be taken to achieve their ideal body. The next step would be to ask questions dealing directly with the informant's own body and self-image, and eating habits.

The assumption made in using this strategy is that informants and interviewers would find it uncomfortable to start talking directly about an issue which may be personally threatening or uncomfortable to think about. It is often assumed that it is more difficult to commit oneself to personal, revealing commentary than to a general level of debate. Tied to this is the researcher's fear that the informant may decide not to continue the interview because it is too personal or invasive of privacy. General questions at the beginning of the interview allow the informant to consider issues at a non-personal level. Only as rapport develops are they asked to interpret their own personal circumstances. Abrahamson (1983) describes this process as being non-directive and yet it is in many ways extremely directive though not in the same manner or to the same degree as standardised or structured interviews.

Story telling

An alternative strategy to funnelling is one suggested by Askham (1982). She proposes using the device of asking questions in such a fashion that the informant would respond with a story. The rationale for encouraging stories is that they can be used as part of the process of analysis specifically for purposes of clarification. *Story telling* is a feature of many non-interview, ordinary conversations. In in-depth interviewing, it is used to parallel the social interaction of an ordinary conversation. She argues that there are basically two types of interview questions. The first one is similar to the notion of descriptive questioning described by Taylor and Bogdan (1984) where the interviewer asks for a record or description of an action, attribute or feeling, such as, 'When did you last see your ex-wife?', 'How many brothers and sisters do you have?', 'Did you get bored waiting for the speech therapist?'. The second type of question she refers to is when the interviewer asks the informant to perform more sophisticated analysis upon the raw data of their experiences before answering. These are questions which ask interviewees to generalise, classify, summarise, quantify or explain, such as, 'How often do you see your ex-wife?', 'What do you think the average family size is for people like yourselves?', 'Why did you get bored when you were waiting to see the speech therapist?' (Askham 1982).

Interviewers rarely ask directly for a story. However, in the case of a life history, this is very often what is called for. The strategy that Askham used in her research on marriage was to imply that she wished the informant to talk in more detail about how an event occurred. She would phrase the question to refer to a specific time period, such as a month before the wedding or the time after the marriage, and then ask the informant to fill in the events occurring during the specified time, or, as she puts it, 'artificially forcing a story by setting its beginning and end, and requesting the recounting of more than one event within these limits' (1982, p. 561).

Another example of the first kind of question could be the one used by Aroni in her interviews with Jewish high-school students and their views on their schooling (1985). All students were asked, 'Tell me *something about* how you *came to be attending this school*?'. The phrasing is significant because 'something about' and 'came to be attending this school' imply that attendance at that particular school was part of a process which needs to be answered in story form. The second type of story-telling question was one in which informants were asked if they could remember their last Jewish studies class, or to inform the researcher about the schools they attended before the current one.

Not all these questions will result in stories. Often informants will just string a few sentences together. However, Askham (1982) and Aroni (1985) both found that one of the strategies which seemed to lead to story telling was to ask informants for examples of the generalisations which they made during the conversation. Stories also emerge from the informant's train of thought or speech when he or she is actually reflecting on something which is only indirectly connected to the preceding question or has nothing to do with it. The kind of question you ask does influence whether the informant responds with a story giving his or her interpretation and analysis but there are other influencing factors also. One of the ways in which the interviewer's behaviour can encourage this story-telling process is to cue the informants that one is receptive to listening to their stories. This can be achieved by 'showing a lack of any hurry, by engaging in preliminary chatter oneself, and by appearing to enjoy any detailed accounts from the start of the interview' (Askham 1982, p. 570).

Problems with stories as data. In-depth interviews are constantly referred to as providing rich and detailed descriptive information which is valued precisely for its closeness or fit with 'reality'. However, stories are usually structured and take on a form which may be excellent for listening impact. An informant may create a good story by distorting the discussion of his or her perceived reality, in order to enhance the interviewer's image of them. Conversely, stories can be used by informants to avoid providing analysis of a situation. The major advantage of the story-telling process for both interviewer and informant is that it allows the informant greater latitude in answering questions 'rather than having to mould his answers into a format which the question requires' (Askham 1982, p. 572).

Three other strategies need to be mentioned briefly. Taylor and Bogdan (1984) refer to these as *solicited narratives, log interviews* and *personal document use.* All three strategies are used predominantly by researchers attempting to engage informants in in-depth interviews of a particular kind—life histories. These strategies have also been used with in-depth interviewing of other kinds such as clinical interviewing (see chapter 7).

Solicited narratives

This strategy is best described by its name. Solicited narratives refer to the interviewer soliciting a written narrative from the informant. This is a story-like account written by the informant which is then used either as a discussion point for subsequent in-depth interview sessions or is added to the background knowledge that the researcher amasses in order to classify and analyse the received information. It combines the strategies of asking descriptive questions and eliciting stories from the informant. One can be more or less directive in asking the informant to provide a written narrative. Often researchers ask for the informant to produce a chronology of their lives prior to being interviewed or simply to write their own story. This latter approach is very similar to that mentioned by

Askham. Others, such as Taylor and Bogdan (1984), have used the solicited narrative approach to ask their informant to provide a detailed chronology prior to being interviewed. They then use the narrative as the basis for their in-depth interviewing of the same informant.

For instance, Shaw (1966), in his study of delinquents, used a more directive approach in producing the life history of his informants. The sequence was a little different from those mentioned above. The youth 'Stanley' (a fictitious name) was first interviewed in order to ask him to prepare a detailed chronology of his delinquent acts and experiences. Shaw then gave the first solicited narrative back to 'Stanley' and asked him to use it to guide him in writing a second narrative—his life story. Stanley was directed to provide 'a detailed description of each event, the situation in which it occurred, and his personal reactions to the experience' (Shaw 1966, p. 23).

The advantages of such an approach are obvious. The informant is providing a written account of his or her life for the researcher who can then use it in a number of ways to inform the research process. It can provide the *ethnographic context* of the informant for the interviewer, or it can provide material for analysis and probing in the interview context. Solicited narratives are also used by researchers in conducting life-history interviews. The advantage is that the account is written in the informant's words. Consequently, during in-depth interviewing, it is argued that the interviewer plays a less intrusive role in the informant's original account and interpretation of his or her own life. There are also disadvantages. Not all informants are able or willing to engage in research if it requires them to write about their views or experiences, or they may feel obliged to provide either an embellished account or a more socially acceptable one because it is in 'black and white'. It is a captured account.

The *life-grid approach* is one form of solicited narrative. The informant is asked to complete a diagrammatic chronology of their life for the researcher. This method is often combined with personal in-depth interviewing and/or with the *log-interview* or *diary-interview method*. This method is a specific version of the solicited narrative. Rather than providing the researcher with a chronological account of his or her life and experiences up to date, the informant is asked to 'keep a running recording of their activities for a specified time period which is used to provide a basis for in-depth interview' (Taylor & Bogdan 1984, p. 91). Personal documents, such as informants' diaries, photos, letters, calendars, formal records and other memorabilia, are also used to jog the memory of informants regarding their life and experience.

These three strategies do not by their nature impose structure on the informants' interpretations of their own lives apart from asking for a chronologically ordered account. In most cases, they are used in conjunction with in-depth interviews to provide the researcher with some means of legitimately asking probing questions and addressing the informants' views in their own language as found in the written form. They provide a framework for the interviewing, that is, an interview schedule which is written by the informant.

Types of questions

So far, we have discussed the asking of questions by examining the way in which they can be ordered to structure and control the interaction between the participants of the in-depth interview. Questions can also be related to the type of information which they are supposed to elicit. For instance, we could ask informants to provide descriptions of events, people, places and/or experiences. This is known as *descriptive questioning* (Spradley 1979; Taylor & Bogdan 1984), which is often used to start interviews because it enables informants to discuss their experiences, placing their own interpretation on these in the process of describing them. In addition, it is regarded as a non-threatening strategy because the interviewer is not probing for specific answers to specific questions but is allowing the informant to take control of the flow of information.

Several researchers (Burgess 1984; Spradley 1979) mention two other types of questioning which are used in in-depth interviewing, often in tandem with descriptive questioning. First, *structural questioning*, by which we mean questions aimed at finding out how informants organise their knowledge. For instance, if the researcher asks a nursing student about how clinical training occurs at a particular hospital then he or she is asking a descriptive question. When the interviewer asks which areas of clinical studies the student has been involved with (other than the current one), then he or she is asking a structural question. The researcher is trying to determine the study categories which the informant perceives he or she has been engaged in, and the way in which the informant stratifies these studies.

Another form that questioning can take is *contrast questioning*. This enables the informants to make comparisons of situations or events within their world and to discuss the meanings of these situations. For example, the interviewer may then ask the nursing student during the same interview if he or she perceived any difference between the clinical training received by a tertiary-trained nurse and a hospital-trained nurse.

Patton (1989) mentions another question form apart from descriptive questioning. He mentions *opinion/value questions* which are aimed at gaining access to or understanding the cognitive and interpretive processes of people. That is, finding out what people think about a particular person, issue, event or experience. The interviewer might ask, 'What is your opinion of that?', or 'What do you think about it?'. In contrast to this, Patton discusses '*feeling questions* which are geared to understanding people's emotional responses. For example the interviewer might ask "How do you feel about that? Do you feel happy, sad, confident, intimidated, anxious ...?"' (1989, p. 207).

A researcher might also want to ask the informant what Patton calls *knowledge questions* which are used to 'find out what factual information' the informant has. According to Patton (1989), the underlying assumption of questions is that the informant 'knows things'. The point is to find out what the informant considers to be factual, to elicit the informant's view on 'the empirical nature of the world that is being elicited' (p. 208).

Sensory questions, as the name suggests, are those questions asking the informant about what has been seen, heard, touched, tasted and smelled. They are used in an attempt to induce informants to describe 'the stimuli to which they are subject'. For example, the researcher might ask the informant, 'What did you see when you walked into the classroom?'. They are a form of descriptive questioning, as *background demographic questions* also are. These questions are used to provide the researcher with some characteristics which can be used to identify the person being interviewed in relation to other people in society. Therefore, it is usual to ask the informant to specify their age, sex, education, occupation, place of residence, and so on. As Patton so poignantly states, 'Background and demographic questions are basically boring; they epitomise what people don't like about interviews' (1989, p. 211). Some people argue that it is preferable to ask such questions at the end of the interview or tie them to the same phase as descriptive questioning at the beginning; nevertheless, they provide valuable data for analysis.

Probing

Probing questions are used to elicit information more fully than the original questions which introduced a topic. In essence, it is the fact that probing is sanctioned as part of the research process that differentiates in-depth interviewing from normal everyday conversations. It is an indicator that the researcher is aware that he or she cannot take for granted the common sense understanding that people share because these may be differently interpreted by informant and interviewer. The example that Deutscher (1973) gives is appropriate. He points out that words which seem to be objective such as temperature descriptions hot and cold can actually have different meanings when used by different groups of people even though they are all speaking the same language. Translating his American example to the Australian context, we could say that an Australian truck driver may stop at the pub. The truck driver is complaining to the bartender that his drink is warm and the soup is cold. As Deutscher puts it:

> the 'warm' liquid may have a temperature of fifty degrees fahrenheit while the 'cold' one is seventy five degrees fahrenheit ... The standard for the same objects

may well vary from culture to culture, from nation to nation, from region to region and, for that matter, within any given social unit—between classes, age groups, sexes; what is 'cold' soup for an adult may be too 'hot' to give a child (1973, p. 191).

The use of probing questions is a method of clarifying, and gaining more detail, especially when you are trying to understand the meanings that informants attach to original or primary questions (Stewart & Cash 1988). *Original or primary questions* are used to begin the interview or introduce new topics. They can stand alone out of context and still make sense. *Probing or secondary questions* are used as follow-up questions. They are introduced to elicit information of greater detail than that which was drawn from the primary question or previous probing. These probes are used when the informant's statements seem incomplete, and vague, or when the informant gives no answers.

Schatzman and Strauss (1973) suggest several question-asking strategies which act as probes. However, these suggestions are tied to that stage of interviewing where the interviewer feels that they have established rapport or, as Schatzman and Strauss phrase it, that they have developed inter-personal familiarity and comfort. These strategies are more directive and aggressive. Their first suggestion is eliciting new information from the informant by asking the *devil's advocate question*. This form of leading question is often used for clarification. The question format 'deliberately confronts the informant with the arguments of opponents as abstractions within or outside the universe now being studied' (Schatzman & Strauss 1973, p. 81). The basic intent of this questioning tactic is to provoke the informant into elaborating on previous comments, either to provide the interviewer with more detailed information or to test the validity of the interviewer's interpretation of the informant's position on a particular issue or matter. It may provoke a specific retaliatory response or a more careful and detailed outline of a previous statement made by the informant.

Another means of leading the informant is to propose a *hypothetical question*. This is done by the interviewer suggesting a number of possible or plausible scenarios, options or occurrences and asking the informant to guess at his or her own attitude and/or behaviour response to such options.

A third means of leading the informant to further revelation is what Schatzman and Strauss (1973) call *posing the ideal*. This form of questioning can be used to ask the informant to describe and perhaps analyse the most ideal situation that they could conceive in relation to their current life situation. Another form of posing the ideal does not allow the informant to take the lead. Rather, it is the researcher who poses an ideal according to their perception of the situation. Whichever variation is used, the data elicited make the study available to the reader by allowing a comparison between the perceived ideal and 'reality'. These techniques enable the researcher to gain greater insight into the interpretations and views of the informant.

The most-often used form of probing is the *nudging probe* which is used when the informant has either given what the interviewer regards as incomplete information, or is hesitant to continue. Usually an interviewer will try to 'nudge' the informant into speaking or continuing to speak by using body language. This can include silence on the part of the researcher perhaps combined with eye contact, quizzical facial expressions or nodding of the head. If this first strategy is not effective then the researcher might attempt to use verbal nudging. For instance:

> Tell me more ...
> Oh, really?
> Go on.
> And then ...
> I see.
> Is that so?
> Please continue.
> Yes?
> Hmm ...
> What happened then?

Alternatively, if an informant has discussed an issue in a vague or superficial manner by using jargon or including generalisations, then you might use certain phrases to obtain clearer and deeper answers, such as:

> Tell me a little more about ...
> Why did you?
> What did you have in mind when you said ...?
> Just how small was ...?
> What happened after ...?
> I'm not sure I understand your point ...

On the other hand, the conversation between you and the informant may have taken a different turn. You may feel that some statement the informant has given suggests a particular feeling or attitude on their part. If this is the case, the researcher might decide to ask:

> How did you react?
> What did you think and feel about that?
> Is it the way you think and feel now?
> Why do you think and feel that way?

Sometimes in the exchange of conversation a comment made by the informant may seem irrelevant. For example, if the interviewer asks the informant to answer a question about new regulations being administered in a public hospital, such as, 'What are your attitudes to the new regulations?', and the informant answered, 'A lot of my colleagues are grizzly and grumpy because of the implementation of the new regulations ... ', then the informant has avoided answering about his or her own attitudes. Rather, he or she has concentrated on analysing and reporting the definitions of others. The researcher might try redirecting the informant by repeating the question, 'What are *your* attitudes toward the new regulations?', stressing or emphasising 'your' in order to elicit a more relevant response.

If the researcher is not sure that he or she has correctly understood what the informant has said or implied in answer to a question, he or she might try using the *reflective probe* strategy. This entails reflecting the answer back to the informant in order to clarify or verify the information. This double-checks the researcher's interpretation of an answer.

> You meant your daughter, didn't you?
> You mean the 1990s, don't you?
> She said that to you?
> Once every fortnight?
> Am I correct in assuming that you still hate his attitude?

The reflective probing strategy is similar to the *mirror* or *summary question*. When using this latter form of probing, the researcher is trying to ensure that they have gained an accurate understanding; the interpretation of the discussion summarises the conversation.

> Let me see if I have this straight? You actually ... and then ... and after that ...
> So to summarise your situation, you began by telling me that ...
> It is my understanding that in the past six years you have ...

Researchers need to be very careful when using these two forms of reflective probe. In some cases, the use of such forms of probing can appear to be questioning the informant's integrity, knowledge or intelligence by communicating disbelief, undue pressure or even entrapment. This may result in the informant not answering or even discontinuing the interview. However, if either or both the reflective probe or the mirror probe are used effectively, they can help the interviewer avoid making the mistake of assuming that they have accurately understood the informant's statements or implied meanings. Foddy (1988) discusses this issue in relation to the utility of closed-ended and open-ended questions in eliciting information which is accurately communicated between the participants.

Non-answering

An informant may at some point in the interview decide not to answer a question. If the researcher assesses that the asking of such questions is not overstepping the bounds of privacy then he or she tries to change this by using a number of strategies. Of course, the informant may disagree with the researcher's assessment and decide not to provide any answer to questions that he or she regards as overly intrusive. This is the informant's right. The researcher may decide to restate the question, rephrase it, or if that fails, tactfully ask the informant why they did not answer. Sometimes an informant may decide that he or she is either unable or unwilling to answer a particular question or to allow the conversation to be directed to a particular area. He or she may or may not give a reason for this action. If you receive a reason listen carefully before deciding on which, if any, question you will ask next. Be prepared to either explain or expand on the answer or information required, why you have requested it and its potential use. If these forms of probing are unsuccessful be prepared to abandon questioning.

There are many reasons why informants may not adequately answer questions. Some are related to the social interaction of the interview process. First, the informant may be unsure of the type of comment or detail in which the researcher is interested. Does the researcher want a simple yes or no, or is he or she interested in a detailed explanation? Second, the informant may not understand the question. This may be because the researcher has relied on language use or phrasing which is unfamiliar to the informant.

Third, the informant may not have adequately discussed a particular topic or issue because he or she does not have the knowledge or information required. Whether this is because he or she had not previously had access to the information or that it has been forgotten due to memory lapse is irrelevant. The point is that the informant in such an instance is unable to answer. Fourth, the informant may be unable to express inner feelings and thus cannot adequately provide an answer for the researcher.

Several additional reasons may explain an inadequate answer or a non-response. The informant may feel that the researcher could not comprehend the answer because the topic or issue is outside the researcher's experience, or because it is too technical. And the informant, as mentioned above, may think that a question is too personal and constitutes an infringement of privacy.

Cross-checks

It has been emphasised in this book that the in-depth interview is aimed at gaining access to the perspective of the informant. Thus, the researcher using the in-depth interview tries to elicit an honest account of how the informants see themselves and their experiences. How does an interviewer do this when people may be 'exaggerating their successes and denying or down-playing their failures' (Taylor & Bogdan 1984, p. 98); hiding important facts about themselves and their experiences (Douglas

1976); or that they 'lie a bit, cheat a bit' (Deutscher 1973, p. 191) when giving their definition of the situation? It is obviously difficult for in-depth interviewers to know the difference between exaggeration and distortion purposefully employed, and authentic perspectives which are inevitably biased and subjective. The answer is that the in-depth interviewer cannot be 100 per cent sure about the difference. However, the qualitative researcher is not primarily geared to finding out the truth *per se* but rather the truth as the informant sees it to be. As Shaw puts it in his introduction to *The Jack-Roller*:

> ... the validity and value of the personal document are not dependent upon its objectivity or veracity. It is not expected that the delinquent will necessarily describe his life-situations objectively. On the contrary, it is desired that his story will reflect his own personal attitudes and interpretations. Thus, rationalizations, fabrications, prejudices, exaggerations are quite as valuable as objective descriptions, provided of course, that these reactions be properly identified and classified (1966, pp. 2–3).

In essence, the interviewer is responsible for obtaining the informant's account and asking cross-check questions in order to make this genuine from the informant's perspective and to identify and classify distortions. This can be attempted in a number of ways. One can check the informant's stories and statements for consistency. This is done by seeing if the informant's description, interpretation or analysis of an event, experience or issue is consistent with his or her account of it in another interview or in some other part of the same interview. The interviewer can compare the versions given at the different times.

An alternative method of cross-checking that has been suggested as useful in dealing with seeming contradictions is to directly confront the informant with evidence of the problem, but in a gentle manner. For example, one could say, 'I'm a little confused. Perhaps you can clear this up for me. In one of our interview sessions you told me ... but this week you said ... which doesn't seem to fit in with what you told me before. I don't understand this'. As Taylor and Bogdan point out:

> If you know a person well enough, you can usually tell when he or she is evading a subject or 'putting you on' and the interviewer can then gauge the degree to which he or she should press the point (1984, p. 99).

However, an important factor that needs to be kept in mind is that people can hold logically contradictory views simultaneously and that these form a valid part of the account. Cross-checking will not provide the researcher with a more genuine account if these contradictions are discarded.

Closing the interview

Let us assume that several in-depth interviews have taken place. You, the interviewer, have made your intentions clear as to the nature of your research and what you require from your informant. You gained access and began your interviews in a congenial atmosphere after establishing and maintaining rapport and the informant's interest in participating. You have related your questions to the overall intent of the research design and you have made them as clear to the informant as possible. In addition, you have listened attentively and sensitively to the comments, statements and queries made by the informant and progressively analysed this information in the process of the conversations. You have used probing questions to clarify and extend your understanding of the meanings they intended with their use of words. Now you wish to end the interview. How do you go about this?

Several factors must be taken into account. Firstly, you may wish to re-interview the informant at some later date. Thus, you need to maintain rapport even though you are closing off the immediate relationship. Secondly, you should realise that the social process of in-depth interviewing creates a relationship between the participants and that such relationships create expectations. This may commit the researcher to fulfil prior promised actions such as contacting the informant when the research is published. The point is that taking a deep breath, heaving your shoulders and physically or verbally showing that you are glad it is all over may be gratifying to you as a tired researcher, but may be detrimental and hurtful to your informant and can be damaging to your research. It is important to show that you respect informants, their stories and their generosity in sharing them with you. There are both verbal and non-verbal cues that the interviewer can use to signal that the in-depth interview is coming to an end either for that session or for the total series of interviews with the informant.

Verbal techniques

The most commonly used strategies are similar to those of normal everyday conversation. These can be listed as follows:

Explaining the reason for closing. This is a forthright method in which you, the researcher, tell the informant directly that you must close the interview and why it must finish at this point. This can take three distinct forms. First, you can announce that the task or purpose of the interviews has been completed to the best of your mutual abilities. For example, you might use any of the following or similar forms of phrasing:

> 'Well, all that we've discussed should give me plenty of food for thought.'
> 'Well, I have no more questions, just now.'
> 'Well, with this interview, the series is complete.'

Alternatively, if you have previously agreed on a time limit for the interview then signalling that time is up is another form of explaining the reason for closing. However, the researcher should be careful not to be in an unseemly hurry to quit the scene, nor should he or she be perceived as responding to the informant as one of many in a production line rather than as a unique individual. For instance one could say:

> 'Well, that's all the time we have for today.'
> 'Goodness, it's 10.30 p.m. already; our time just raced away today. Our time is up.'
> 'I'm sorry, we'll have to leave our discussion there today as I have an appointment waiting.'
> 'I must leave in five minutes because I have a class at 4.00 p.m.'

Clearing-house questions. Use clearing-house questions as an indication to the informant that you are closing the interview. Clearing-house questions enable the researcher to focus on areas which may not have been adequately covered up to that point. This can be done by asking the informant if you have answered all his or her questions or covered all the topics. For instance, one could ask,

> 'Is there anything else we should discuss before I leave? I think that we have covered everything that is necessary. Can you think of anything that I have missed?'

Alternatively, you can offer to answer questions such as the following:

> 'If you have any questions I would be happy to try to answer them.'
> 'Now it's time to ask if you have any questions.'

This signals your completion of the task and your desire to include them as a full participant.

Summarising the interview. This is another conversational strategy which cues the informant that the interview is at the closing stage. It is a common form of closing which enables the researcher and the informant to formally recognise the areas of discussion that have been covered in the conversation:

> 'So do we agree that today we talked about ... and that we should continue next week by thinking about ...?'

Making personal enquiries and comments. Making personal enquiries and comments is another more involving manner of closing the interview. This strategy makes evident one's genuine interest in the informant. For example this can be done by asking about their family, job or situation:

> 'How is your son going with his final exams?'
> 'Do you think this is the right time of year to take a holiday in Hong Kong? Isn't it the monsoon season?'

This type of question indicates two things to the informant. First, that the interview issues are no longer the centre of discussion, and second, that even though you are a stranger, you have taken an interest in his or her life and the things that he or she has mentioned to you. It indicates that you are really listening.

An alternative to this questioning is exhibiting concern. This does not mean that you should pretend to care. If you do not care or you have not developed a relationship of that type and level, then it is not only inappropriate but also unethical to claim otherwise by making such comments. However, if the relationship has developed to that extent then, comments such as these are appropriate.

> 'Please look after yourself and I will see you soon.'
> 'I hope you pass all your exams with flying colours.'
> 'I know we didn't discuss this, but if you run into any problems like that just call me.'

Express thanks and satisfaction. Finally, one of the most obvious forms of closing a conversation is to express thanks, appreciation and satisfaction because you as the researcher have received information, from the informant, through the gift of his or her time and concentration. Thus, it is appropriate to close by saying something like this:

> 'Thank you for the time and effort you put in.'
> 'I've really enjoyed our discussions and I appreciate the fact that you agreed to participate in the study.'
> 'Well, now that we've covered the areas which are important, I want to let you know that we've done extremely well to get to this point in relation to ... Thank you for your time.'

Non-verbal closing strategies

There are many non-verbal actions which can indicate to the informant that the interview is about to close. These range from looking at your watch or a clock in the room, to straightening up in your chair as if ready to move out of it, putting the cap on your pen and closing your notebook, unplugging the tape-recorder or offering to shake hands. Any one of these movements will cue the informant that you consider it is time to finish the conversation. There are obviously many more that could be mentioned. Most researchers find that the relationship with the informant will help determine what the best method is of closing the interview, and whether closing will be initiated by the informant or interviewer. Researchers use verbal and non-verbal cues together.

One of the most significant factors in closing an interview is knowing when to stop. You do not need to drag it out until the allotted time if you have actually finished discussing the matters of interest. Nor do you have to probe everything in depth.

Your access to knowledge and information will be influenced by the relationship and the interaction you have developed with the informant.

The previous sections dealing with structuring the interview process, and the forms that questions can take, are obviously not exhaustive. There are as many strategies and tactics as there are researchers. The afore-mentioned options have been discussed in order to give the reader some idea of these processes and situations as they have been experienced by others.

Recording the interview

Interviewing as a method relies on the assumption that people are able (and willing) to give verbal accounts of their attitudes, beliefs and actions. This assumption is in turn dependent on the idea that human beings are reflective about their own actions, or can be put into a situation to become so. Keeping this in mind, most interviewers need to make a decision about how to record the interview.

Tape-recording and note-taking are two of the most commonly used methods and they are sometimes used in combination. There are advantages and disadvantages inherent in either technique. You can take notes during the interview, or if you think this is disruptive, rely on your memory to reconstruct the conversation soon after the interview. Or you can tape-record the conversation and transcribe it after the interview. The questions that must be asked regarding note-taking and tape-recording as methods of recording interview material are as follows:

- How effective is this technique in generating accurate data?
- How fair is the use of this method to the interviewer and the in-formant?
- How valid is the material gathered by this method?
- How helpful is this method in analysing the material?

Note-taking and tape recording should not be seen as simply altern-ative techniques or strategies for achieving similar ends but as different ways of doing research.

Tape-recording

Tape recording is one means of obtaining a full and accurate record of the interview. It can enhance greater rapport by allowing a more natural conversational style. The interviewer is free to be an attentive and thoughtful listener. The raw data remains on the record. Therefore, all the material is available for analysis when the researcher has the time to concentrate fully. Schwartz and Jacobs (1979) point out that there is greater analytic depth because the anecdotal information and the ambiguity of response is still available to the researcher. A more accurate picture remains because both questions and answers are recorded. Validity is enhanced by this preservation of authentic data.

If you are going to buy a tape-recorder, we suggest that you purchase a small unobtrusive one which looks less intimidating than a large machine. Also, a researcher who constantly checks the tape-recorder is distracting to the informant. Check that the equipment and batteries are in good working order prior to conducting the interview. It is frustrating to discover that the conversation was not recorded because the batteries were dead!

Tapes should be clearly labelled with the informant's identification, the topic and date of interview. Long-playing tapes should be used so that the conversation is not regularly interrupted because you have to change the tape. Low-quality tapes should not be purchased. They can be easily damaged by the machine due to frequent use.

However, there are problems with tape-recording which are worth mentioning. Both interviewer and informant may find that the tape-recorder inhibits interaction. Some people feel vulnerable, fearing that someone may recognise their voice if the interview becomes public. The informant may feel he or she has to be interesting or dramatic and this can alter the account the informant gives. One of the most significant problems is that you cannot record the non-verbal data unless you use a video camera. Video recording is now becoming more popular with researchers, particularly with group interview situations (see chapter 4). There is now a greater awareness, acceptance and understanding of body language and silences, as an important part of social interaction—and filming is a good way of recording such data for analysis. Video recording is also useful in maintaining a faithful account of verbal data as it can capture the interplay between verbal and non-verbal communication and the effects on the process of interaction. Of course, all the same issues and concerns that are raised by audio taping are also raised by video taping.

A common concern voiced by informants is that there is the feeling that once something is on tape (audio or video) it is indelible. There may be concern that the recorded account may be misinterpreted at a later date when the informant is not present to interject, correct or change an interpretation. The ethics of using a tape-recorder will be discussed in chapter 10. This gives the interviewer more control and power in relation to the informant and may upset the balance of interaction in the conversation. Electronic recording can lead to a recessive style of research where the interpretive process occurs during the editing and selection of extracts from the transcripts rather than during the interaction process. Recorders can also lull the interviewer into a loss of concentration.

One of the most tedious and time-consuming aspects associated with electronic recording is transcribing the data. Taylor and Bogdan (1984) estimate that a one-hour interview will result in up to forty typewritten pages of data. The work associated with transcribing can be reduced if you use a transcriber. A transcriber is especially designed to play back tapes at slow speeds. A clear tape can also save many hours of trying to transcribe inaudible words and sentences. The tape-recorder should be strategically placed so that it can pick up the conversation effectively without being obtrusive. Video recorders should be used in a similar manner.

If you plan to have someone else transcribe the tapes then it is important that you work closely with that person. The transcript must accurately reflect what was said. It should not only include sounds but also the non-verbal messages (for example, pauses) expressed by the researcher and informant. This contextual information can influence how you listen to and interpret the text. It should be pointed out that the major advantage of typing your own transcript is that you become more familiar with the data. As you are taking down the text, you become engaged in data analysis. Data analysis of video film is more complex initially, but in essence it is still the analysis of text, albeit a more detailed one. Interpretation of such text is still the concern as it is with all in-depth interview data (see chapter 11).

Note-taking

Note-taking pulls the researcher into analysis and interpretation earlier in the research than tape-recording. As you make notes, you tend to use your own version of shorthand which also incorporates interpretation. In researchers' interview notes, it is quite common to find commentaries about the discussion offered by the informant. This is a useful practice to adopt. Note-taking also enables the researcher to record body language in relation to speech patterns, although a tape-recorder is a better way of recording the modalities of speech.

Note-taking allows partial analysis to occur. However, this can also lead to a prematurely fixed conception of data where little or no re-selection of raw data occurs. This is because the notes are in a form that makes deletion and addition unattractive. Non-verbal contact may be restricted and discourse constrained because the researcher will be taking notes rather than interacting naturally. Rapport with the informant is obviously at risk. Nevertheless, note-taking tends to make the researcher listen more carefully to what the informant is saying.

If you decide to rely on your memory to reconstruct the interview, then we recommend that you follow some simple rules about note-taking. First, you should concentrate your attention on key words and ideas, and follow these as they develop in a conversation. The emphasis is not to recall and reproduce all that was said in exactly the same words, but to recall the meanings of remarks. Recalling conversation is a skill. It involves learning how to be attentive and reflective. Researchers who have mastered these skills can conduct up to two hours of interview without the use of a tape-recorder (Bogdan & Biklen 1992). Second, we repeat, it is important that you write your *fieldnotes* soon after you have finished the interview. We suggest that you should not spend more than one hour 'in the field' and that the 'fieldnotes' should be written on the same day. The day after may be one day too late for your memory to be accurate. Diagrams of the setting or sitting charts can help you to trace the conversation and recall its details.

Many researchers use tape-recorders in conjunction with taking notes. This is usually done in the hope that one can gain the advantages of both and cancel out their disadvantages.

Listening analytically

The role of the interviewer is not simply to record and process responses but to participate in a conversation with the informant. Participation means more than listening, nodding and note-taking. It means answering, commenting and attending to conversation sensitively. It also means thinking about each verbal interaction and its theoretical, political and ethical direction; when to probe for clarification or elaboration, and when to sit quietly and acknowledge the silence of the informant. Thus, the researcher needs to fully participate in the initiation, maintenance and closing of the in-depth interview but at the same time to sustain a critical inner dialogue. As Adelman points out:

> One problem with using talk lies in its familiarity. To penetrate beyond the 'ordinariness' of talk, to attribute social categories, value judgements and other cultural features requires the researcher to separate out his own knowledge as a member of the culture from the talk being used by a fellow member of the culture. This separating out allows the researcher to sustain a critical inner dialogue ... Such reflexibility comes through attention to what people say ... (1981, p. 24).

The process of listening is a crucial part of the interview process. It acknowledges the value of the informant's participation in the interview. For the researcher, it is the means of engaging in the conversation as part of normal social interaction while at the same time being distanced enough to sustain that critical inner dialogue which enables analysis of the data. This analytical ability enables the researcher to analyse what is happening at the same time as participating in the interaction and the discussion.

Some researchers regard listening as 'art' (Douglas, Roberts & Thompson 1988) whereas others regard it as a strategy (Schatzman & Strauss 1973) for maintaining the flow of communication. Both interpretations are applicable. We regard it as a matter of ethics (see chapter 9). The most significant point to remember is that the in-depth interview is social interaction and listening can act as a stimulation for further interaction or as a response to such interaction. The fundamental principle of in-depth interviewing is to provide a framework within which informants can express their understandings in their own terms. That framework is negotiated through talking, listening and reflecting.

Listening as support and recognition

In-depth interviews should operate as two-way communication and not feel like interrogation to the informant. This involves letting the informant know that you support his or her continuing comments and discussion of issues by listening carefully and indicating this attention both verbally and non-verbally. This can include 'smiling' with your eyes, nodding and making 'listening noises'. Empathic listening allows the researcher to reduce emotional tension by providing a supportive response and endorses the informant's feeling of value.

Sympathetic and patient listening allows the informant to refine his or her ideas and interpretations while articulating them. This assumes that the researcher is non-judgmental. Frowns on the interviewer's face should indicate lack of understanding, not disapproval! The tendency to evaluate, judge, approve or disapprove of a statement made by another person occurs in everyday conversation. However, in-depth interviewing requires the researcher to give a non-judgmental or tolerant appearance to the informant because the continuation of the social interaction may rely on such perceived tolerance. When we use the term non-judgmental, we are not advocating the same sort of distancing as is used in survey-style research. Rather, we are suggesting that the researcher should not come across as being overly critical. Nevertheless, listening involves response. A glassy-eyed passive interviewer, hanging on every word, leaves the informant feeling unrecognised, uncared for and often intimidated and unsure of how to interact with that interviewer. Useful and effective listening involves giving feedback to the informant in a normal conversational form.

Modes of listening

It is obvious that listening occurs at more than one level. Listening is not just hearing words spoken. We have all sat in a lecture theatre and forgotten what was said. This is hearing—listening at a superficial level. Yet, when the lecturer introduces material that is directly examinable, we 'tune in' to understand and record. During an in-depth interview, you can focus on information on at least two levels. One level is the explicit content or verbalised information given by the informant. The second is the implied or unstated information, or what is not said. Listening at both levels helps you to decide what you want to listen to, that is, when you want to probe. This gives you, the researcher, a certain degree of power and control over the structure of the conversation.

Listening skills

Researchers often need to develop their listening skills. One way in which we can improve our listening skills is to work out what some of the 'subskills' of listening are. Some of the ones we have noted during our own interviewing are as follows:

- adjust to the informant;
- identify the informant's attitudes;
- perceive and recognise differences between similarly worded statements;
- resist being overly influenced by emotion-laden words and/or arguments;
- distil the meaning intended by the informant by making valid inferences;
- use 'contextual clues' to determine the meanings of words and phrases used by the informant;
- take note of the sequence of ideas, comments and details;
- try to avoid the effects of projecting one's own perceptions on informants' statements;
- try to reflect on and analyse one's own listening;
- capture the main ideas being put forward by the informant;
- recognise supporting ideas put forward by the informant;
- learn to listen in undesirable or bad conditions;
- learn to check the accuracy of new information;
- learn to retain all relevant information;
- maintain sensitivity to persuasive techniques used by the informant;
- be alert to contradictory statements made by the informant.

Obviously, there are many other subskills involved in listening. The question is not how many subskills there are, but how can one develop these skills. Some people have developed such skills as part of their natural repertoire in their everyday interaction and they simply need to practice and refine them. (It is for this reason that interviewing is often referred to as an art, rather than a science.) However, most people have not adequately developed these skills. One means of developing such skill is to adopt Adelman's (1981) notion of *critical inner dialogue*.

What the researcher might think would be as follows: 'What is this informant saying that I can use? Is this interesting in relation to my research problem? What are the central ideas this person is putting forward in this account? Have I fully understood what this person is saying? Maybe, maybe not. I had better use a probe. Oh, yes I did understand. Now I can go on with a follow-up question'.

We think a great deal faster than we speak and this enables us to develop and use to advantage critical inner dialogues during the interview process.

Another means of improving our listening skills is to concentrate on the preparation aspect of listening. If you are as fully prepared and informed as you can make yourself on a topic, issue or person then you may be more capable of hearing and appreciating the implications of the comments and statements made by the informants. This preparation can be carried out by reading, immersing yourself in the social setting or taking studies examining the area. You must also involve yourself in the social interaction of the interview situation. This is essential as involvement prevents a lack of interest which might encourage concentration lapses. Concentration is a matter of both involvement and self-discipline. If you focus on what the informant is saying, how he or she is saying it, the body language that accompanies the verbal message, and the relevance the comments have to what has gone on before in this or previous interviews, then you won't have time to allow for mental wanderings!

A strategy for doing this is to link information by making mental links between the original questions, the answers and the logically following questions. This is called recursive structuring of the interview or following the *recursive model of interviewing*. Recursive questioning is an excellent means of maintaining concentration. When researchers use this strategy, they tend to integrate the informant's statements and comments into organised patterns or trends which help arrange the pieces into a total picture. They then reinterpret and analyse the information as it is given. The use of the critical inner dialogue is part of this overall process. Obviously, we have not given a total account of the strategies and processes involved in doing in-depth interviewing; as such, a task that is impossible by its very nature. What we have provided in this chapter, as discussed at the beginning, are some features which we have noted in our own research practices.

Chapter 6
Life history

A *life history* is precisely what it says it is—the history of an individual's life given by the person living it and solicited by the researcher. It is a sociological *autobiography* drawn from in-depth interviewing and/or solicited narratives (see chapter 4). It is an attempt to gain an account of a person's life told in their own words. This chapter discusses oral or life history as a means of extending and developing our understanding of in-depth interviewing. The concept of an oral or life history is defined and a rationale for its use is provided.

The usual form in which life histories can be found is in full-length accounts of the person's life, stated in their own words. Sometimes, these accounts appear with the introduction and conclusion written by the researcher in order to frame the informant's account in a sociological context; or an informant's story may be interspersed with a great deal of the researcher's interpretive material. The life history can be regarded as distinct from traditional autobiographies because it is recognised that in the more conventional autobiography what we read is what the author wishes us to know. In the sociological version, what we read is mediated by the researcher's interaction with the person during the telling of the story, the coding, analysis and interpretation of it.

The life history has also been called *oral history*, life story, document of life, case history or personal history. These terms, which are often used interchangeably, all refer to specific forms of research. For instance, the case history is drawn from clinical models in which the informant is asked questions so that the clinician can determine a more fitting diagnosis of the informant's 'state of health' in the light of past experiences. The aim in oral history is to gain information about the past whereas the central concern of the *biographical life history* is to elicit information detailing the individual's development. The sociological life history aims to understand the ways in which a particular individual creates, makes sense of and interprets his or her life.

Life histories are not simply the domain of sociologists. They will inevitably be different in form and content, even when the substantive research area is the same, because different people will have done the history for different purposes. These can range from sociological research to psychoanalytic investigation; from work histories to clinical profiles.

According to Denzin (1989), if we clarify the various terms used to describe this method, it is easier to understand the forms it can take. So, for our purposes, a life is the unfinished process of the lived experiences of a person and is given meaning by that person and his or her significant others. History is an account of an event or events including an attempt to explain why it occurred. A story is a recounting of events which is subjective and may be fictional. A life history is the experience of a person, group or organisation and is somewhat different to a case history which is a 'full story of some temporal span or interlude in social life' and focuses on a process not a person (Denzin 1989, p. 185). Oral history should not be confused with personal history which reconstructs a life based on interviews and conversations. However, it is quite obvious that in practice most researchers merge the two.

If we examine figure 6.1, we can see that elements of these terms or methods can be utilised depending on the purpose and aim of the research project. The wavering between the terms life-history and oral history, in fact, reflects the disciplinary antecedents, history and sociology. Whenever you read the terms (used interchangeably), it is because the author is utilising aspects of both traditions. (The less charitable view, of course, is that he or she is simply unsure of the exact meaning and is having a bet 'each way'.) Many social scientists prefer the term life story to designate the retrospective information itself without the corroborative document evidence often implied by life or oral history.

Researchers using this method assume that informants can make sense of their past and that public records are not always meaningful or the

Term/Method	Key Features	Forms/Variations
History	What happened? How?	Oral, life, personal.
Fiction	An account of something made up, fashioned.	Story (life, self).
Biography	History of a life.	Autobiography.
Story	A fiction, a narrative.	Life, personal experience.
Discourse	Telling a story.	First, third person.
Narrative	A story, having a plot and existence independent of the teller.	Fiction, epic, folklore.
Narrator	Teller of the story.	First, third person.
Life history	Account of life based on interviews and conversations.	Personal history, edited, complete, topical.
Case	An instance of a phenomenon.	Event, process.
Case history	History of an event or social process, not a person.	Single, multiple, medical, legal.
Case study	Analysis and record of a single case.	Single, multiple.
Life story	A person's story of his or her life, or a part thereof.	Edited, complete, topical, fictional.
Self story	Story of self in relation to an event.	Personal experience, story, fictional, true.
Personal experience	Stories about personal experience.	Single, multiple episode. Private or communal, folklore.
Oral history	Recollections of events, their causes and effects.	Work, musical, family.
Personal history	Reconstruction of life based on interviews and conversations.	Life history, life story.

Figure 6.1 Forms and varieties of the biographical method
Source: Drawn from Denzin, N. 1989, *The Research Act: A Theoretical Introduction to Sociological Methods*, 3rd edn, Prentice-Hall, Englewood Cliffs, NJ., p. 188.

most valid source of information. For example, if gerontologists wanted to understand the impact of ageing on Australian lives, they could examine and analyse statistical evidence derived from the Australian Bureau of Statistics or tabulate responses from surveys dealing with independence of older people. However, it is only from such *life history interviews* as provided by Blythe (1979) in *The View in Winter: Reflections on Old Age* that we vicariously experience the meanings of ageing in our society. We gain access by reading from the personal and subjective accounts given by older people about their lives and their perception of the progression from youth to old age.

A history of life histories

Life histories, as they are currently used in sociological research, follow the examples given in other disciplines particularly history, anthropology and clinical work (case histories). Each discipline focuses on the individual case for different reasons, in order to achieve different aims.

Oral history

The telling of one's life story is not unique to the social sciences. Most societies have some oral tradition of passing on information from one generation to the next. Autobiographies can be attested to even in ancient tomb inscriptions (Misch 1951). The use of oral evidence in historical research is not new. Much knowledge and information (evidence and data) in literate societies has been passed on by word of mouth. Throughout Western history, from the Middle Ages until the beginning of the Enlightenment, there were very few examples of introspection about the nature and concept of one's inner self. Most personal accounts were documents either of 'memorable events (memoirs) of great deeds done (resgestae) or philosophers' lives' (Plummer 1983, p. 9). From the Renaissance and Enlightenment periods came the diaries of Samuel Pepys, and the autobiographies of Rousseau and Goethe. These latter documents were seemingly motivated by a search for an understanding of one's inner self. Later in the Victorian era, biographies became popular.

In Australia, the oral tradition was significant in Aboriginal life whereas written documentation was not. According to Douglas, Roberts and Thompson (1988), Australia's first white settlers wrote a group of foundation narratives predominantly based on oral evidence. In the eighteenth and nineteenth centuries, historians also relied a great deal on oral evidence to write their accounts of history. Yet by the nineteenth century, when the writing of history became a professional occupation, the critical analysis of written documents became the preferred mode of 'doing history'. Oral sources of knowledge were spurned as limited, inadequate and biased compared with the reliability of documents.

In the last forty years this method has regained popularity for both theoretical and political reasons. In the 1960s, oral history in Australia developed as part of the increased interest in social history. There was a movement away from simply examining chronologies and biographies of great men and great events to a 'people's history'—an understanding of history through the eyes of ordinary folk by talking and listening to them. Their views were regarded as politically worthy. The examination of written documents coming from kings, queens and various social institutions was replaced by the methodology of oral history. (For a more detailed account of the development of oral history in Australia see Douglas, Roberts & Thompson 1988, particularly chapter 1, from which this discussion has been drawn.)

Here, it is sufficient to point out that oral history is currently flourishing. At least three significant oral-history projects were publicly funded in Australia in the 1980s. The Migrant Oral Histories project invited members of various ethnic groups to do their own recording under the direction of an experienced oral historian. This project was initially funded in 1984 by the New South Wales Ethnic Affairs Commission. At the same time, the La Trobe Library funded an oral history project eliciting responses from the Chinese in Victoria (Douglas, Roberts & Thompson 1988). One of the largest and most recent oral-history projects was established in 1985 at the federal level by the Community Employment program in conjunction with the National Library of Australia—*The Cultural Context of Unemployment: An Oral Record*. Over sixty people were employed to capture and document the personal experiences, traditions and contemporary culture of groups of the unemployed. These projects indicated, both in the political arena and the academic domain, a shift in what was and is regarded as legitimate historical evidence.

These developments in the discipline of history intersected with developments in the theory and practice of Australian sociology. The life histories which were produced by sociologists had a profound influence on the acceptance and encouragement of oral history within academic and non-academic history circles.

There has also been a modest spillover in the last fifteen to twenty years in the clinical research fields (for example, from nursing, occupational therapy and physiotherapy journals) as is shown by the increase in discussion of qualitative methods in general. As will be seen in the next chapter, clinical interviews have drawn on a combination of this model and the medical traditions.

Life history

The history model has been discussed above. The anthropological antecedent was ethnography in which researchers were also trying to illustrate a true-to-life picture of what people say and do in their own words. Psychology's use of the case history was also known to sociologists, particularly the works of Freud such as his accounts of 'Dora' and 'Little Hans' (Freud 1977).

Life history and symbolic interactionism

Over the last thirty years in Australian academic sociology, the symbolic interactionist perspective and the qualitative methods which came with it became very popular (Bryson & Thompson 1972; Connell 1985; Davies 1966; Wild 1974). In sociology, the use of personal document and life history has been related to symbolic interactionist theory and to the perception that case histories, oral histories and life histories were useful in providing the salient experiences of a person's life and that person's definitions of those experiences (Taylor & Bogdan 1984). In fact, it has been argued (Plummer 1983; Schwartz & Jacobs 1979) that there is a fundamental affinity between the central-tenets of symbolic inter-actionism and life-history research, especially in the legacy of the Chicago School of sociological thought and practice of the 1920s and 1930s. The following discussion is drawn from Plummer (1983) in which he discusses three theoretical assumptions which are common to life-history research and *symbolic interactionism*:

1 life is viewed as concrete experience;
2 life is regarded as an ever-emerging relativistic perspective; and
3 life is viewed as inherently marginal and ambiguous.

Life as a concrete experience

This was central to the view of 'doing sociology' held by the Chicago sociologists. Their view held that there was no point in studying abstractions of individuals or of social life. Rather it was more pertinent to recognise that 'a separate individual is an abstraction unknown to experience, and so likewise is society when regarded as something apart from individuals. The real thing is human life' (Cooley 1956, p. 67). The central consequence of being concerned with life as concrete experience is that 'in every case of study, we must acknowledge that experiencing individuals can never be isolated from their functioning bodies and their constraining social worlds' (Plummer 1983, p. 54). The Chicago sociol-ogists focused on the necessity of considering the combination of a social and an individual phenomenon. Life-history research is in accord with this view because it is aimed at examining life as concrete experience.

Life as an emergent perspective

This is central to symbolic interactionist thought. The social world is seen as constantly changing and in a state of flux. W. I. Thomas' dictum 'If men define situations as real, they are real in their consequences' is applicable here. Human beings experience reality through their def-initions of it. These definitions of the situation in turn alter in relation to their experience of it. 'The reality shifts with a person's life and people act towards things on the basis of their understandings, irrespective of the "objective" nature of those things' (Plummer 1983, p. 56). If we accept this view then it must be acknowledged that we can gain access to the objective world only through our precariously negotiated subjective views of it. These subjective views and conceptions of reality are inherent to the people who experience them. Thus, if one accepts these theoretical assumptions then the most central and fundamental source of knowledge is the personal document, the life history which elicits 'the sense of reality' that human beings hold about their own worlds.

Life as ambiguous and marginal

This is tied to the previously mentioned views. If we have taken one person's subjective reality seriously in a life history, and then consider it in relation to another person's, then there is always the possibility that ambiguity and incongruity will become evident in their definitions of the same situations. This is also related to the informants who have traditionally been chosen for such research particularly by members of the Chicago School. In sociological research this is what has been called 'studying down', where the researcher is interested in groups which are lower down the social scale than they are themselves. The informants are often from marginal groups—those with less credibility than other groups in social hierarchies; members of so-called deviant groups—thieves, transsexuals, the mentally retarded, the immigrant, and so on. As Plummer (1983) points out, the researcher using the life-history approach operates with these three assumptions, the first two leading them to study marginal groups 'whose voices may not be so readily heard'. This issue is discussed in more detail in chapter 9.

The message to the researcher was to move away from studying abstractions and get at the particular, the detailed and the experiential, that is, 'concrete human experience'. It was said that this allowed the researcher to grasp the ambiguities and inevitability of different perspectives, particularly those of marginal individuals and groups.

An example of a life history

The best-known and most discussed life history in sociology, is also claimed to be the first major one in the twentieth century, was Thomas and Znaniecki's *The Polish Peasant in Europe and America* (1958).

The significance of this piece of research lay not in its size (originally five volumes) but in the use of the life-history method as a means of examining a social issue and its concern with developing social theory. Approximately one-quarter of all immigrants to the USA between 1899 and 1910 were Polish. The impact of immigration, settlement, marginality, and community were questions of public concern. The method used by Thomas and Znaniecki was regarded as distinctive. The study included an abridged but major life-history statement made by a Polish peasant named Wladek, and then several other life histories; over 700 letters which were arranged into fifty series; third-person reports drawn from court records and social work agencies; documents collected through social agencies dealing with people who wished to emigrate from Poland and those arriving to settle in the USA; and a set of newspaper documentation taken from the archives of a Polish peasant newspaper (see Plummer 1983 for a more detailed account).

The use of the life-history method and the letters made this study famous. The same period gave rise to a number of life-history studies being done by American sociologists (Anderson 1961; Burgess 1925;

Cavan 1929; Park 1930; Shaw 1966; Sutherland 1937). There has been a revival of interest in the life-history method in sociology since the 1960s and 1970s at approximately the same time that symbolic interactionism was also coming into vogue. This is evidenced in the appearance of research methods texts such as Taylor and Bogdan's *Introduction to Qualitative Research Methods* (1984); N. K. Denzin's *The Research Act* (1970) and H. Schwartz and J. Jacobs' *Qualitative Sociology* (1979). All these volumes dealt with qualitative methods which included life-history methods. Later, we have the appearance of Thompson's *The Voice of the Past* (1978) which examines the resurgence of interest in oral history and D. Bertaux's (1981) focus on the renewed interest in the life story.

The use of the labels life history, oral history and ethnography in Australia also indicates that the tradition of doing such research crosses disciplinary boundaries. The labels depend on whether the researcher is employed as historian, anthropologist, or sociologist. The use of this particular form of in-depth interviewing is evident in works such as A. F. Davies' *Private Politics* (1966) which was an examination of five Australians and their political socialisation; B. Wilson & J. Wynn's *Shaping Futures: Youth Action for Livelihood* (Wilson & Wynn 1987) which used four case studies to highlight attendant research on youth, education, work and inequality; Claire Williams' *Open Cut and The Working Class in an Australian Mining Town* (1981) and R. W. Connell's *Teachers' Work* (1985) which provides five personal accounts of teachers' perceptions of their lives in relation to their work.

Types of life history

There are two basic approaches which underpin the type of life history the researcher might choose to carry out—the nomothetic approach or the *idiographic approach.*

The nomothetic approach is based on the idea that theoretical generalisations are drawn from systematic experimentation which usually employs statistical validation and on the idea that such generalisations should be applicable to many individuals. Researchers adopting a nomothetic approach believe that the life history or case study is only useful as a means of learning theoretical constructs in the social sciences or perhaps generating new discoveries. However, that is where their utility ends because they argue that one cannot generalise from single cases (Schwartz & Jacobs 1979).

On the other hand, the idiographic approach advocates that it is scientifically valid and methodologically correct to examine the behaviour and/or perceptions of one individual as an independent totality. Generalisations may be developed from the individual's story. This approach stresses that the goal of the social sciences is understanding human behaviour and social realities not quantifying them. Schwartz and

Jacobs point out that these two approaches can be seen as complementary so that 'in the course of acquiring and analysing the contents of a series of life histories, and searching for patterns within each one, the researcher may purposefully or serendipitously uncover patterns between them' (1979, p. 69). Whichever approach is adopted, it will inform the type of life history the researcher will engage in.

Several researchers (Allport 1965; Denzin 1989; Tagg 1985) assume that the variations can be encompassed in three essential forms of actual practice:

1 The complete or comprehensive life history which aims to incorporate the full range of the individual's life experiences. It is usually a long and complex account and is a rarity in research practice, for example R. W. White's *Lives in Progress: A Study of Natural Growth of Personality* (1975) in which he focuses on the overall flow of life of three people.

2 The topical life history which focuses on only one phase, aspect, or issue of the individual's life. This can take either the comprehensive or limited mode. The comprehensive topical life history mode does not try to focus on the full life history but rather examines a particular issue. Good examples of this form of practice are Shaw's study of 'Stanley', examining his delinquency (1966); Sutherland's depiction of *The Professional Thief* using Chic Conwell's information (1937); Hughes' study of Janet Clark and her drug use (1961); and Bogdan's research of Jane Fry's trans-sexuality (1974). The limited topical life history is actually the same as the above form except that less material is covered. Usually these life histories will include more than one person per volume. For example, the Davies study of five people (1966).

3 The edited life history may use either the topical or the complete life history. Comments and analysis by the researcher are then either interspersed with the narrative or in a combination which includes introductory passages and analytical commentary after the narrative, or incorporated in a combined form. Examples of this include Wilson and Wynn's *Shaping Futures* (1987) and Connell's *Teachers' Work* (1985).

These three types of life history are differentiated in terms of the aims of the research process and what the researcher is looking for or trying to illustrate; and the degree of intrusion made by the researcher in the production of the final document.

Aims of doing life-history research

The aims of the research process will inevitably influence the choice of research area and the type of research you choose to do. Glaser and Strauss (1967) have examined this issue in relation to doing life-history research. They point out that researchers need to decide whether they are producing a case history or a case study.

The case history has as its central goal the eliciting of the fullest possible story for its own sake, such as that of the mining community (Williams 1981) or the bushfire disaster (Eastop 1985). The case history is inductively evolved. The case study on the other hand tries to utilise personal documents, oral or written, for a theoretical purpose. You start with a theory or analytic abstraction and use the life history to illustrate or to verify some theoretical abstraction. An example of this is Douglas' use of suicide stories to lend validity to his version of suicide definitions (1967).

Researcher intrusion in the life-history document

The degree of researcher intrusion in the final document is the other distinguishing feature between types of life-history research. Such intrusion usually occurs in the process of interpreting the story and/or editing it.

Interpretation of a life-history document can occur at several stages and is predominantly done by the informant and the researcher. It can occur during the in-depth interview stage when the researcher listens to the informant and decides on what to ask next. Interpretation can also occur when the researcher decides on whether to use alternative sources of personal accounts such as letters, diaries, photos, etc. to accentuate or verify the story as told in the in-depth interview. Which of these elements he or she regards as significant is also a matter of interpretation. Obviously the informant is engaged in interpretation throughout the process by deciding what to mention or what to highlight. Finally, interpretation occurs in the written presentation of the life history.

Editing is the form that interpretation takes in the written presentation of life histories. It can range from minimal interpretation by the researcher where the raw data is presented in entirety without any interpretive commentary, through to 'verification by anecdote' (Plummer 1983, p. 115) in which the researcher's theoretical understandings of a particular sociological problem are predominant. The informant's interviews or quotations drawn from them are used as examples to illustrate and highlight the theoretical position being argued.

The most crucial methodological issue confronting the researcher using the life-history method is the problem of interpretation and selection of data at all stages of the research process but particularly in the final publication. As has been pointed out by Allport (1965, p. 21), it is 'This process of interaction between theory and inductive material ... [which] is the essence of the methodological problem with personal documents'.

Editing occurs in the presentation of all forms of life history. We have not yet found a publication of life history which did not use some form of editing. This can range from simply cutting out the verbal repetitions and the *ums* and *ahs*, to extensive cutting of the account and arrangement in chronological sequence, to the use of selected quotes to accentuate theoretical arguments. Plummer notes in his discussion of this issue that:

> The Polish Peasant story was twice as long in its original form, the *Letters from Jenny* were abridged to approximately one third of their original length ... Don, the Sun Chief's 8,000 page diary was reduced (for publication purposes) to one fifth of its original length (1983, p. 108).

In many cases, editing is carried out with the purpose of easing the work of the reader. The researcher attempts to make the life-history interview a more communicable experience on the page by reformatting the text which is then used as the major empirical component of the research (Bertaux & Bertaux-Wiame 1981; Chalasinski 1981). In other cases, the researcher does a great deal more in editing the material. Connell (1985, p. 3), in his examination of school teachers, makes comments about the necessity to maintain confidentiality, and says, that to do this, he and his colleagues felt constrained not to 'print actual biographies, even with names, dates and places changed'. We feel it is worthwhile reading his rationale as an example:

> Given the rule of confidentiality under which this research was done, we did not feel entitled to print actual biographies, even with names, dates and places changed. Yet as we worked through the evidence it seemed more and more important, for readers' understanding of the social processes we were studying, to convey in the published report the sense of biography, the way things hang together and take shape (and sometimes fall out of shape) in teachers' lives. As a slightly uneasy compromise, I have settled for constructing composite biographies, which are presented in Part One. Every detail in them comes from the interviews, but they come in each chapter from more than one. 'Terry Petersen', 'Rosa Marshall' and the others are therefore not real people. But I think reading chapters 1–5 as if they were, will give more insight into the lives of the actual teachers from whom the evidence comes than would a topic-by-topic, cross-sectional presentation of the same evidence (Connell 1985, p. 3).

Doing life-history research

The actual research processes used in life-history research involve the same issues as outlined in chapter 4 as well as issues relating to the researcher's choice of informant and the inclusion of alternative sources of data (other than the in-depth interview).

As can be seen in figure 6.2, there are innumerable variations to choose from when one engages in doing life-history research.

Choosing an informant

On what basis is someone chosen as an informant in life-history research? What is the appropriate sampling strategy? The answers to these questions can be found in the research design and the research context.

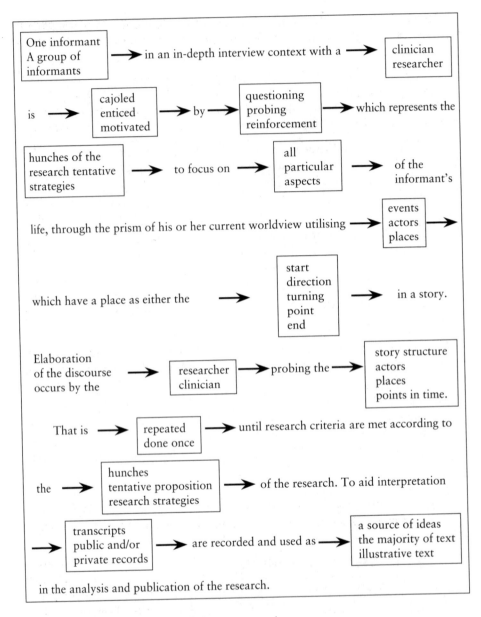

Figure 6.2 Variations of doing life-history research

Source: Based on Tagg, S.K. 1985, 'Life story interviews and their interpretation', in *The Research Interview: Uses and Approaches*, eds M. Brenner et al., Academic Press, London.

Life histories are usually based on data elicited from one or a very small number of people (at the most five or six individuals). The researcher can base his or her choice on theoretical or methodological criteria such as trying to find a particular type of individual who has had certain experiences, for example a professional thief (Sutherland 1937), or a trans-sexual (Bogdan 1974). Alternatively, researchers may use pragmatic or logistic criteria in choosing an informant, such as, whether the person has the ability, desire and time to give a detailed account of their lives and experiences.

How does one find an informant? Sometimes the researcher is engaged in a research programme involving other methods and stumbles across an individual who stands out as having a story to tell, or as highlighting significant issues related to the original project. In other cases, the informant is found directly in relation to the research problem being examined.

The other area of choice is explicitly ideological. That is, does the researcher choose the great or famous individual, the marginal person or the ordinary person? The literature indicates that the marginal individual has been the choice for much life-history research. Researchers assumed that marginality was being 'condemned to live in two antagonistic structures' (Stonequist 1961). The assumption was that a marginal individual living and experiencing life on the boundaries between the cultures would be more aware of conflicting expectations. The researcher hoped that this awareness could be tapped to give a more revealing picture of social reality.

The famous or great individual is much harder to recognise and is chosen more by historians and psychologists (doing what is known as psychohistory) than by sociologists. The rationale for choosing such an informant is that they can illuminate the issues, values and crises of a particular time due to their significance in that era. Erikson's case histories of Luther and Gandhi are well-known examples of this approach (1958, 1970). A more recent example is psychologist Graham Little's (1989) publication of his television interviews with currently famous individuals in Australian society.

Choosing an ordinary person as an informant is not as simple a task as one might think. After all, how do you define someone as ordinary? The actual basis for choosing someone as a life-history informant, using the idiographic approach, is that there is something unique about them (Plummer 1983; Schwartz & Jacobs 1979). However, sociologists have sought out those informants who are not particularly famous or marginal (as Connell chose teachers, and Wilson and Wynn chose teenagers). The oral historian often tries to choose an ordinary person for ideological reasons. Part of the popularity and resurgence of oral history as a research method at present is tied to the political and ethical concern with expanding knowledge of the interpretations of ordinary people in contrast to an earlier emphasis on the wealthy or famous.

The most significant factor about choosing an informant, maintaining a relationship with that informant and publishing his or her life history is that the person be someone who is aware of, informed about and involved in his or her own cultural world and able to articulate his or her own views. This is what the researcher can define as a good informant.

Data gathering

There are three major modes of data gathering when doing life histories:

1 soliciting narratives;
2 in-depth interviewing of many sessions;
3 use of multiple research strategies which may or may not include 1 and 2.

Soliciting narratives

In chapter 4, we said that soliciting a narrative account from an informant is often used to gain access to the person's story either through the log-interview method or the life-grid approach. Diaries of a more extended nature than log interviews have also been used to good effect but they have been used more often by psychologists and anthropologists than sociologists. Anthropologists and sociologists found it difficult to legitimate such usage as scientific, whereas psychologists argued that such methods directly revealed the subject matter in which they dealt. The assumption by researchers incorporating this data is that it provides a daily record of events which are regarded as significant by the informant. These are two of the three ways in which diaries are used. The third is an analysis of a single day in the life of the informant.

In-depth interviewing as life history

The nature of in-depth interviewing when it is used to elicit life-history information is not different from anything described in chapter 4. However, the researcher usually needs many more interview sessions. Establishing and maintaining good relations with the informant is vital to success. The life-history in-depth interview is also more dependent on tape-recording so that a full account is available and the relationship between researcher and informant is not overly hampered by detailed note-taking. The conversation between researcher and informant in the life-history interview is often dominated by the voice of the informant. This is sometimes difficult for the informant to get used to because his or her perception of an interview is one in which the researcher asks lots of questions and the informant simply answers them. The researcher needs to facilitate story telling as in Askham's model delineated in chapter 5. To do this, he or she must create a situation in which the informant not only feels at ease but wants to discuss details in full.

One strategy for extracting further detail is the *informal post-interview*. The researcher ties up loose ends by thanking the informant, going over some or all of their discussions in an informal manner, and checking on the informant's feelings about the sessions and the extent to which they made clear what they were trying to say. In effect, the informal post-interview chat is an attempt to make some checks on the validity of the account according to the informant's perception.

A number of ethical considerations are raised by life-history research such as, 'Who owns the account or holds copyright?', 'What does the informant get out of participating in the research process?'. In addition, there are the other usual issues of confidentiality, anonymity and control. These issues are discussed in detail in chapter 9.

Use of multiple research strategies

There are a number of sources the researcher can use to elicit personal accounts which do not rely on in-depth interviewing. Denzin points out that life histories can use any record or document, including the case histories of social agencies, if they throw light on the subjective behaviour of individuals or groups (1989). This same point is made somewhat more expansively by Plummer (1983) who lists nine sources of personal accounts which include life histories and oral histories. He aptly calls them 'documents of life'. We agree with his assertion that life history 'at its best' incorporates in-depth interviewing with intensive observation of the informant's life, interviews with the informant's friends and/or family, and access to and analysis of pertinent 'documents of life' such as diaries, personal letters and photographs.

Life-history researchers may employ more than one form of personal document. We have already mentioned in-depth interviewing, solicited narratives, diaries and letters. These accounts may be used individually or together to provide a cohesive or more informative description of the life experiences of the informant. Alternative sources of data are also available to the researcher. The researcher may decide to use questionnaire data in the same way as the diary- or log-interview method, that is, to help initiate the interviews. Photographs, films, self-observations and possessions can also be used to provide data for cross-checking against interview material. Systematic self-observation can also be used, although it is often regarded as not being adequately scientific (see chapter 2). According to Plummer 'We can never really know another's world, we might just know our own' (1983, p. 34). The example he cites is Anderson's publication of *The Hobo* (1961). Anderson used his own life experience as a member of a hobo family to inform his research even though he did not admit or discuss this until much after the publication.

The informant's possessions may be used as talking points to trigger discussion with the informant. They can be examined as a means of identifying the significance that individual informants attach to them and to the events or people which they symbolise. Films and photos can be utilised in the same manner. Another factor which should be taken into account is that informants may emphasise or de-emphasise their own role in difficult periods of their lives depending on how they wish to present themselves and so on. As stated earlier, the researcher will recognise this possibility and, in some instances, may wish to cross-check information to define a true account according to the informant's subjective reconstruction.

The utility of life histories

The significance and utility of the life history in sociology is based on the central tenet that it provides 'an account of individual experience which reveals the individual's actions as a human agent and as a participant in social life' (Blumer 1939, p. 29).

Yet, there is more to it than that. In many ways, the life history is a means of focusing on the relationship between biography, structure and history. It is unique as a form of social research because it can actually encompass those features of social life by dealing with concrete human experiences such as talk, feelings and action as they occur within the constraints of the social structure. The social structure is unique to the historical period in which the informant lives. The constant criticism of life histories has been that they are too individualistic, neglect history and are therefore not theoretically useful. This criticism has been made without taking into account that the life history enables us to view the totality of the biographical experience.

This totality enables us to see an individual in relation to the history of their time, and how he or she is influenced by the religious, social, psychological, political and economic ideas available to them in their world. It enables us to perceive the intersection of the life history of human beings with the history of their society, thus enabling us to comprehend and develop theories about the choices, contingencies and options open to the individual as they move through history and structure (Plummer 1983).

In addition, it must be pointed out that life histories constitute a significant strategy in incorporating history within the theoretical framework of symbolic interactionism. Plummer argues that this is achieved by the dual focus that occupies life-history research—'The changing biographical history of the person and the social history of his or her lifespan' (1983, p. 70). This is evident in the three modes of life histories: the oral history in which the historical problem rather than the biography becomes the key issue; the 'career' approach which is derived from symbolic interactionism and focuses on the changing meaning of an individual's life course as he or she moves through personal crises side by side with a given age cohort in an evolving historical culture; and the psychohistory approach which consists of two streams. The first stream, following Erikson and Lifton's work, examines the 'great men' of the period in order to illustrate that the concerns of the historical period are mirrored in the concerns of these 'great men' (see Plummer 1983). The second stream focuses on shared psychohistorical themes such as those things which are regarded as collective symbols of an historical period. Lifton's examination of the collective trauma of the survivors of Hiroshima—*Death in Life* (1968)—is a good example.

Social processes and social change

Life histories enable the researcher to examine the ambiguities and inconsistencies which are a part of everyday experience. Most social scientists speak of social change, social process and the constant state of flux in which human beings interact. Many researchers using attitude scales or questionnaires end up providing accounts of social reality which are far more ordered, rational and unambiguous than the way in which we experience it. It is with life history that the researcher can capture some of the ambiguity that is evident in our lives. As Becker so succinctly points out, 'sociologists like to speak of on-going processes and the like but their methods usually prevent them from seeing the processes they talk about so glibly' (1963, p. xiii).

Chapter 7

In-depth interviewing and clinical practice

Health professionals offer a service which relates to an aspect of the health or well-being of someone else. The terms 'health professional' or 'practitioner', as used here, could indicate a dentist, a medical practitioner or any specialist. They could also refer to a nurse, physiotherapist, occupational therapist, orthoptist, podiatrist, physiotherapist, speech therapist, to a counsellor, psychologist, social worker, or any other health worker, regardless of whether the endeavour truly meets the complex sociological definition of a profession (Maykovich 1980). Holding detailed and more or less in-depth conversations, referred to as the *clinical interview*, is an integral part of health care practice used by many professionals in their day to day work to elicit information, to support diagnosis, to provide or support treatment.

Clinical interviews are interviews which take place in the clinic. Clinic refers to some professional setting in an institution, agency, or surgery offering health care. The interview is an encounter in which both parties understand that one of them is there as a representative of some such institution. The clinical interview is accepted as a mode of discovering information, part of the professional practice of one of the participants.

In that sense, the clinical interview is an interview conducted by a recognised clinician (or therapist) and could even take place outside a designated clinical building.

The clinical interview is a part of applied social science—that is, it is an application, in the world of practice, of procedures based on theory. In particular, it is an applied in-depth interview, hence its inclusion here. This book is devoted to the in-depth interview, theory and practice, and argues throughout that the in-depth interview is one of the best ways to investigate people's minds, lives and life meanings. In the practice of applying the general theoretical principles relative to the in-depth interview (the psychology of both participants, the socio-cultural context and politics) to clinical work, various adjustments have to be made. Previous chapters have described how to go about doing an in-depth interview. This chapter will discuss how one might adapt the techniques described to the applied clinical setting and how this version of in-depth interview can be used for research in the clinic. We will look at the ways in which the clinical interview differs from the research interview, and the ways in which it is similar. In order to commence this process we note that clinical interviews are divided into expert interviews given in the clinic and counselling interviews given in the clinic (see figure 7.1). These differences and their relationship to research will also be explained.

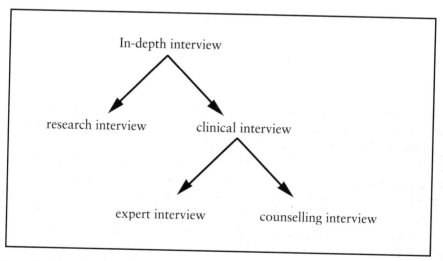

Figure 7.1 The relationship between different forms of the interview

The chapter is not meant to supply a comprehensive theory of clinical practice. Even less is it a handbook of clinical technique. However, much clinical practice can be improved by the clinician becoming self-conscious about the interviewing approaches advocated in this book (the skills of asking and listening) and conversely well trained clinicians already possess many of the skills needed for undertaking in-depth interviewing research. A well-conducted clinical interview may form the basis of research if the clinician is aware of the possibility and integrates the research needs into clinical work by exploring ways of interviewing people for overlapping purposes. The study on therapeutic counselling and living with HIV/AIDS described in the Appendix was developed in relation to the provision of clinical services and based upon audio-taped records of clinical interviews.

The skills and tasks of the clinical form of in-depth interviewing link with the central clinical issues of rapport building, maintaining a therapeutic relationship, and treatment itself. These are actions upon which all clinical engagement should be based. They constitute the nub of clinical inquiry (more or less supported by appropriate investigations and measurements). Depending upon the field of practice, they may form either the background to intervention, as, for instance, in surgical nursing, dentistry, or physiotherapy, the foreground to intervention as in psychosocial occupational therapy, or the matter of intervention as in counselling, clinical psychology and aspects of social work practice. Professional actions have a range of expression, from those where the major emphasis is on expert technical skill, like brain surgery, to those that require high levels of interpersonal skill, like counselling psychology, through those that require a balance of interpersonal and expert technical skill, like obstetrical nursing.

Training

Interviewing skill develops out of personal proclivity and educational processes. Some people, as a consequence of personality or experience, are naturally aware and sensitive to both their own inner processes and those of others with whom they interact. For most, however, education is vital to the development and refining of skills. Some professional training programmes, where the interpersonal is highly valued as the central focus of action, commit a great deal of training time to refining these skills, while others, where the practice focus is less personal and more technical, spend less, little or no time on training interview skills. There is, however, growing awareness that every professional action directed to helping another human, whatever its expert technical/interpersonal balance, will be more effectively achieved if its practitioner is sensitive and trained in interpersonal interviewing.

There has been a great deal of criticism of some professions and groups within professions because of insensitivity to the interpersonal domain of practice. Much of this has pointed to the perceptual distortion in interviews of unacknowledged gender bias or social discrimination and the effect on diagnosis and treatment. Baker Miller (1984) noted the 'permanent inequality' based on race, sex, nationality, or other characteristics which produces profound psychological responses of dominance and subordination in relationships. Carmen, Russo & Baker Miller

(1984) examined how an unequal perception of women, devalued and discredited in mental health care, biased the services provided (generally by men). They took equality to mean equal right to participate in society and to pursue unique psychological potential. Other socially marginalised groups have racial, sexual (in contrast to gender) or poverty characteristics which provide the basis for the prejudice of others. We will explore these interview-distorting influences in a later section.

Scientific scepticism is a good basic attitude for the well-trained practitioner to hold. The practice truths of a particular era are based upon the current state of knowledge and present practices are not always later shown to have been best or even scientifically based practice. We no longer put babies to sleep on their stomachs because that position has been shown to be implicated in sudden infant death, whereas many past generations of babies slept on their stomachs for fear that they would choke if they slept on their backs. Theoretical developments in counselling and clinical psychology have changed the main treatment emphasis from analytic uncovering of deep seated intrapsychic conflicts to cognitive-behavioural educational emphases. In all health care areas theory continually challenges practice. We must take care to heed client communication even when it opposes practice orthodoxy. If the medical dermatologist in the early 1940s had heard the concerns of the mother of a six-month-old baby and not proceeded with isotope implantation into the child's neck to treat a spider nevis the child-as-adult would have been spared years of surgical and psychiatric suffering.

Communication between medical practitioner and patient has been cited as the source of considerable patient dissatisfaction, at all socio-economic levels (Steven & Douglas 1988). Feeling rushed and being discouraged from asking questions were fairly common concerns. A recent court case awarded damages of over $400 000 to a young woman with cervical cancer whose doctor did not listen to her description of unusual continued bleeding and whose pathology result, although equivocal, was not further investigated (O'Shea *v*. Sullivan). She has since died.

A practitioner must listen carefully to what is said by the client and integrate what is heard into treatment for the best clinical outcome. The expert clinician and the counsellor, like the research interviewer, must always be vigilant for leads to follow to reveal a fuller or more accurate story.

The educational function of practice is often inadequately addressed by practitioners. The busy surgeon may wish to blame the radiologist who in turn may implicate the oncologist when the stoical patient finally complains of excessive pain because none of these highly trained specialists thought to warn him that swelling in his leg (lymphoedema) after surgery, radiology and chemotherapy, should be reduced by surgical stocking and massage and should not be tolerated till his leg had become twice its normal size.

Although much of this criticism has been directed to medical practitioners, the need for active listening in clinical practice is not restricted to one group of practitioners alone. All clinicians offering health services need to recognise that their enterprise involves another human being, no matter what the state of that person, and include the principles of human communication in their actions.

The rise in societal levels of general education and changing expectations of health care, from paternalism to participation, requires that the patient be given appropriate education by the practitioner to observe, understand and manage his or her own situation. This principle will, of necessity, be applied differently in the expert clinical interview and in the counselling interview because of the different goals of each (see the future sections on the expert and counselling interviews).

There is an increasing awareness in society of the rights of the individual which has emerged with consumer education, expectation, and political sensitisation. As well, there is a growing understanding of the integral connection between mind and body and the healing influence of practitioner actions that promote feelings of well-being and enhance treatment acceptance and compliance (Rossi 1986). Both influences serve to force practitioner vigilance. The first through fear of legal challenge, the second through responsibility for providing the best assistance possible to his or her client.

Research and health professionals

A profession is responsible for the regulation of its policies, statutes and membership. Beyond self-regulation, it provides service, education of its members and the public, and undertakes research into the theory and application of its service area. Allied health clinicians have a good record of achievement in education and service, however, much could be done to improve the quantity and relevance of research in some health professions. For example, concern about the absence and apparent lack of interest in research by clinicians in psychology and occupational therapy has been expressed (Barlow 1981; Polatajko et al. 1989).

Although a great deal of medical research exists, it is almost all quantitative and biomedical in its approach and undertaken mainly by medical research institutions. This means that while causal connections are being explored there is less medical research interest in issues of personal values, meanings and perceptions that can be investigated using a qualitative research approach. Investigation of the research methodology used by various health professions in researching clinical questions was undertaken by searching publications listed in the *Cumulative Index to Nursing and Allied Health Literature* (CINAHL) for the years 1983–93. This index samples English-language publications world wide (see chapter 3). While one cannot assume total coverage of all work done from one index, it shows that the publication of journal articles using a qualitative research approach, and in-depth interviewing research specifically, is numerically much greater in nursing than in other health professions, including medicine, occupational therapy, physiotherapy, and social work. However, despite the much larger number of in-depth interviewing studies shown in CINAHL as published by nurses than by other professionals (387), the total of 407 in-depth interviewing studies published world wide, in English, over ten years, suggests that clinicians undertook little research during that time. In understanding these brief indications we need to realise that the world wide total number of nursing professionals is probably numerically much greater than the total number of other allied health professionals. In addition, we should note that it is not known how many of the given number of articles written about research into professional issues have emerged from research undertaken in the clinical environment by clinicians working in those environments and how much was undertaking by researchers who gained entry to the clinical setting specifically for the purpose of the investigation. The following titles from this search indicate some of the issues investigated, and, more particularly, illustrate topics amenable to in-depth interviewing research in clinical settings. Many questions with characteristics suitable for in-depth interviewing investi-gation emerge from the practice setting. These include questions relating to all aspects of the service and its staff, their manner of working, the meanings they attribute to their work, the clients of the service and their response to the service, their medical or psychological condition, and the meanings they attribute to the illness, their need, or help offered. You will probably be able to think of many questions across the range of issues occurring in or related to the clinic and these will be discussed further in the final section of this chapter. These are a few examples of the titles of papers included in the index search described above:

> 'Visually impaired patients' perception of their needs in hospital'
> 'What psychiatric nurses say about constant care'
> 'Adults with an intellectual disability: a practice perspective'
> 'The emotional effects of sport injuries: implications for physiotherapists'
> 'The caregiver career'
> 'The meaning of activity: day care for patients with Alzheimer's disease'

It is interesting to recognise that lack of interest in research seems to be endemic to practitioners whose choice of career focuses on the interpersonal domain. One could conjecture that attraction to aspects of a profession, which draws initial selection for training by students, is located in personality and personal preference, more than in marks or prediction of future recompense. It has been shown (Barlow, Hayes & Nelson 1984) that practitioners gain expertise and information from clinical practice and their clinical peers rather than from research articles. Clinicians spend most of their time practicing professional skills even while paying lipservice to the practitioner–scientist model of practice (Barlow, Hayes & Nelson 1984; Raimy 1985).

It is not the intention here to impose the over valuing of research activities, commonly perceived in universities, upon clinical practice. Rather, the message of this book is that there are many questions in clinical practice which could benefit from sustained investigation. If the practitioner is able to prepare for research by being research-knowledgeable and if work conditions permit it, then in-depth interviewing is a useful and appropriate research approach to answering many clinical questions. The great advantage of this method is that the interviewing in clinical practice can support research as long as one understands the issues and plans in advance.

The activities, skills and gratifications of interpersonal 'helping' are very different from those which characterise the traditional research endeavour. Interpersonal activities require interest in relationship participation, empathy, and social concern. Positivist research demands an individualistic, cognitive and measurement emphasis as well as numerical skills. Even when faced with clinical problems that require investigation in the workplace, clinicians rarely undertake research. This may also be explained by lack of inclusion of research activities in clinical job-role descriptions, and in the inadequacy of therapists' understanding of the variety of research methodologies available for analysis of different research questions in which clinicians may be interested. Particularly lacking may be an understanding of in-depth interviewing research, a methodology which has considerable affinity with the interpersonal awareness and skills of any well-trained clinical practitioner.

It is our contention that in-depth interviewing research is harmonious with the practitioner world view and that it is appropriate for investigating many clinical questions where little previous research information exists. The skills required for in-depth interviewing are familiar to the well-trained clinician, and only require the understanding of how to frame them into research mode, for the clinician to function as a researcher as well as a clinical practitioner.

Clinical interviewing skills and in-depth interviewing research skills

The relationship between professional practice skills and the skills required to undertake in-depth interviewing research can be discussed in relationship to three questions. First, what interview skills and tasks are required for research, second, what interview skills and tasks are required for clinical practice, and third, to what extent are these skills related?

In-depth interviewing research, with participant observation studies, and increasingly the study of diaries and personal effects, are major strategies in the qualitative research arena. In-depth interviewing is also a major data collection mode in heuristic research (Moustakas 1990) and phenomenological research (Giorgi 1985) These qualitative (or post-positivist) approaches allow for a recursive uncovering and discovery of meaning and the essence of human experience.

Research strategies in these approaches connect with different aspects of clinical work such as the practitioner skills of relating, talking and listening to clients, gathering clinical data by observation, and the study of writings and personal lifestyle in order to better understand a person. The basis of the relationship between clinical practice and research rests (ideally) upon a shared interest and respect in both clinical practice and qualitative research for the meanings invested in life and action by human beings, and in the narratives which they construct to develop and support individual life meaning. The skills and tasks of in-depth interviewing especially, link with the central clinical issues and methods of establishing a therapeutic relationship, rapport building, diagnosis, and effective treatment. These are found particularly in the counselling interview although they also support and facilitate the expert interview even though the main emphasis there is on the application of a technical action.

Research skills

The goal of in-depth interviewing research is to have the informant reconstruct his or her experience of the topic under study so that the concrete living of people in that content area and the meaning that their experience has for them becomes known. The intellectual and emotional connections within the informant's world make the topic meaningful through the stories which he or she constructs.

According to Strauss and Corbin (1990) a qualitative researcher requires theoretical and social sensitivity, the ability to maintain analytical distance while at the same time drawing upon past experience and theoretical knowledge to interpret what is seen, astute powers of observation, and good interactional skills to adequately manage the research tasks. It is important that the interviewer has a genuine interest in others and respect for the stories told. These are part of the meaning-making process. The interviewer questions, responds, and clarifies experiences, working with the material and selecting from it, interpreting, describing and analysing it. While operating within constraints set for the research (time, area of questioning), theory must be allowed to develop from the informant's words without distortion or bias. This requires self awareness as well as awareness of the other, both verbal and non-verbal. Non-verbal awareness calls for finely developed skills of observation:

Becoming a skilled observer is essential for qualitative evaluation work even if the evaluation concentrates primarily on interviewing because every face-to-face interview also involves and requires observation. The skilled interviewer is also a skilled observer, able to read non-verbal messages, sensitive to how the interview setting can affect what is said, and carefully attuned to the nuances of the interviewer-interviewee interaction and relationship (Patton 1990, p. 32).

Questioning is carefully constructed to balance the research interest with informant freedom and ease of response. It is open-ended and recursive. These requirements exactly describe what makes good clinical action if we simply change the word research to read clinical.

Clinical skills

Practitioner education and practice train observational and interpretive skills so that therapists understand verbal and non-verbal communication, and the person–person, and person–environment interaction. The theory base for these skills is integrated into practice from psychological and counselling theories. Psychological understanding either forms the background to all interventions or sometimes becomes the specific matter of the therapy, depending upon the area of practice involved. In either case, the therapeutic relationship relies on the clinician facilitating the intervention process through interpersonal skills, encouragement and understanding.

Professional practice skills have been described as tacit and not easily subject to verbalisation (Dreyfus & Dreyfus 1986; Polanyi 1967; Schön 1983, 1987). The greater the clinical expertise the more embodied and automatic becomes the knowledge base which informs practice. This knowledge base comprises factual information from various disciplines (anatomy, biology, pathology, psychology), applied scientific understandings such as how to treat a particular condition, as well as tacit clinical knowledge derived from an amalgam of practical experience. Complex information about the client is used to hypothesise the nature of each client's unique problems. This is a dynamic rather than static process with all new information being assimilated to gain a greater understanding of the person.

Mattingly (1991a, p. 983), discussing phenomenological clinical reasoning, proposes that it is 'primarily directed not to a biological world of disease but to the human world of motives, and values and beliefs—a world of human meaning'. In treating the illness experience of the patient/client, clinical reasoning becomes applied phenomenology recognising and engaging with the meaning of the illness for the individual. Using Bruner's (1986) proposition that humans think both paradigmatically and narratively, and Schön's (1983, 1987) work on clinical thinking and reasoning, Mattingly (1991b) adapted the notion of narrative thinking to explain one aspect of clinical thinking. Narrative thinking occurs when the therapist attempts to understand a particular case and is primarily a way of 'making sense of human experience' through investigation of motives. 'The therapist must try to imagine how it feels to the patient and to various family members to have this disease, how they are experiencing it, and how it enters and changes the life story of a patient and his or her family' (Mattingly 1991b, p. 1000). The therapist also uses narrative in structuring the therapeutic sequence for the patient, providing a short story embedded in the longer life story, using an understanding of human motives in each story for the most effective clinical outcome that can be achieved.

Comparison between in-depth interviewing research and clinical skills

Schein (1987), writing about the clinical perspective in research, said that all researchers who deal with human systems must have some degree of clinical training with specific emphasis on responsibility to clients and the consequences of data gathering interventions. He believes that all research on humans must be informed to some degree by a clinical point of view.

Probably the major factor discriminating between clinical and research interviewing is the initial request and the overt primary beneficiary of the action. Therapy is sought or prescribed for the apparent benefit of the patient/client, though its provision also benefits the practitioner (by fee or salary; through personality need or professional endorsement). In-depth interviewing is initiated by the researcher for his or her own purposes (advancement, scholarship, professional activity). Despite careful management to protect and support the informant, and the personal gain which can accrue to the informant as a result of telling his or her story to a sympathetic listener, the major goal of research activity is the researcher's interest in learning about a phenomenon. An extreme view was put in Marxist terms by Patton (1990) who described the interviewer as both capitalist and labourer, capable of treating the words of participants as commodities to be exploited.

Similarities between the research and the clinical interview

Many of the skills demanded by the methodology and approach of in-depth interviewing research can be said to be analogous to the skills and the philosophical assumptions of clinical practice. As a clinician uses clinical skills to facilitate the intervention process, the qualitative researcher also requires clinical skills to facilitate the research interview. Qualitative research methodologies depend upon the researcher having good interpersonal skills which become the primary research tool and create the matter of the research. Such skills are vital to the research process where, as in clinical practice, dilemmas and issues become clearer as the work evolves. This, in fact, differentiates the method from other research approaches.

We have called the clinical interview an applied piece of social research using the in-depth interview as its technique of discovery. That implies, given what was said in earlier chapters of this book, that it will take an open, loose-textured form to facilitate the holistic interpretation which is the aim of such an interview. It may have a protocol, but any such protocol will be determined largely by the course of the interview itself, rather than by the prior expectations or interpretations made either by interviewer or client. The questions will not close off the possible range of responses, and their form will often be determined by previous responses. The aims of the interview will be subject to change at any time during its course. So will the meaning ascribed to the statements of the client (and of the clinician for that matter) as the interview proceeds. The clinical interview will acknowledge throughout that its process is one of inter-subjective interaction and interpretation, just like any other well-conducted in-depth interview. For the health practitioner, clinical skills not only make for more effective research but skill and practice at research can assist the clinician to become a more effective practitioner because of the involvement of similar skills in each set of actions.

Differences between the research and the clinical interview

The process of inter-subjective interaction is likely to be more complex in the clinical interview than in the in-depth interview directed at research. The aims of the participants in the research interview are likely to be relatively simple, symmetrical and mutually congruent: the researcher wants to understand what is going on, and—more or less—the informant wants to tell him or her.

For instance, the researcher wants to know what it feels like to have a diagnosis of breast cancer and the woman with the diagnosis tries to tell him or her. Of course, both of them may have other, extra or hidden agendas for the interview, and these may make it hard for the two of them to find and hold onto one another's wavelengths, but usually both have a reasonable understanding what each is about. In the clinical interview, however, there are apt to be systematic differences of perception between the two in terms of both the aims and meaning of the interview. For instance, the client or patient may be sure that she has heart trouble (her mother had it at the same age) and that the solution to her problem is to be put on Workcare. The clinician, on the other hand, sees her as having terminal breast cancer, thus a success for diagnosis, a problem for medical research, and inappropriate for chemotherapy. In the clinician's eyes, she has the personal and social problem of coming to terms with her imminent death. They are both therefore likely to misunderstand what the other is saying, and why they are saying it. (The dialogues quoted from Taylor (1988) in chapter 1, are painful instances of such mutual struggles towards comprehension.) In this way they resemble domestic disagreements over sex or annual holidays. Instances like the one above in which the patient has made her own diagnosis and determination of treatment are only extreme forms of the chronic problems of translation and *negotiation* which occur in all social interactions.

In the research interview, there is a general presumption that the informant has the required information which the researcher lacks. The researcher may add a few details, but essentially his or her aim is to interpret the experiences of the informant by placing that informant in a social and theoretical context which may be of little or no interest to them. In the traditional textbook version the informant provides the data and the researcher provides the explanation, so allowing a neat division of expertise between them. The client, at least, is the expert on him- or herself.

In the clinical interview, as in other types of in-depth interviewing, this neat division between data-expert and interpretation-expert breaks down. The clinician may see something straight away about the client—'Have you noticed that your eyes are bright yellow'—which supplements the facts supplied by the client, alters their interpretation, and sharpens the aims of the client from a general desire to feel less awful to specifically wishing to have his or her illness treated. All this depends on clinician and client negotiating a shared perception of the facts as they go along. The client, for instance, agrees that she has been feeling very weak and feverish since dining at the restaurant last Saturday, acknowledges that she has a temperature, volunteers that she has not had hepatitis before, and accepts knowledge from the clinician that she has the *signs* and *symptoms* of hepatitis. This example shows some of the ways in which we interpret and negotiate meaning. 'I've got a pain in my heart' is sometimes made true and intelligible by being interpreted tentatively as 'I've got a pain in my upper intestine'. The beliefs systems of client and clinician are made to overlap sufficiently for negotiation and action to take place.

The expertise of the clinician has a different import to the expertise of the research interviewer. The clinician's opinion makes a big difference to how the client sees his or her world, and to how he or she achieves goals within it. Their interaction is not simply a meeting of minds; it depends on a shared understanding that the beliefs and aims of both will change and develop. Indeed the expectation of learning has always to be counted as part of the aims of both parties in a way which is not always true of the research interview. In some clinical interviews this growth towards change and development in the participants' belief structures is directed not towards understanding but towards action.

Expert and counselling interviews

Clinical interviews can be further divided into expert or counselling interviews, as shown in figure 7.1. In cases in which the client has come to the clinician for his or her *expertise and technical skill* we shall call this the *expert interview*. In cases in which the clinician's expertise applies to the process of the interview itself and to understanding the client's behaviour as the primary treatment mode we shall speak of the *counselling interview*. The distinction is not watertight; in practice a continuum exits with many shared characteristics. Each form of interview is a clinical interview, but their theory and structure are sufficiently different to make it worthwhile to discuss both. In doing so we will also draw some connections with the research interview and research possibilities in the clinic.

In terms of the degree of control over information exercised by the clinician, the counselling model is at the opposite end of the clinical interview continuum to the expert interview. In an expert interview client and clinician will disclose information to one another about how the world works, including how bodies work, and how institutions such as hospitals work. In this way clinical work involves teaching, and educational methods will become appropriate. For instance, the clinician may check whether the client correctly understands medical or legal terms; whereas in a counselling setting the question of factual correctness frequently does not arise. Even more strikingly, one of the goals of the expert interview is likely to be action taken by the professional on behalf of the patient, because the patient has neither the skill, nor the knowledge to carry the action out. The action might be anything from cutting out a brain tumour to issuing a writ against his mother for making nuisance phone calls to his wife; from putting a patient on the right kind of antidepressants, to writing a certificate authorising work absence for his employer. This invokes the classic meaning of the word patient, which implies that he or she is the passive recipient of someone else's (the agent's) action.

The aim of counselling is the growth and development of normal human beings coping with normal human problems. It must be 'distinguished from psychotherapy, which is a more intense process, focusing on deep-seated personality or behavioural difficulties' (Ivey 1988, p. 10). However, most of the principles of the counselling interview can be applied to the psychotherapy interview and even to the psychiatric interview which falls closer to the expert interview end of our model. Often, in reality, the boundaries between situations are not as clear as theorising attempts suggest.

In some ways the counselling model is at the opposite pole to the medical interview. Especially (but not only) with Freudian approaches to psychotherapy, enormous emphasis is placed on allowing the client time to unfold his or her own story in his or her own way. Obviously, this fits in very nicely with the holistic approach we are taking here. We have two reservations about it, however. These are, first, that counselling usually allows a very small place for providing or feeding back information or attitudes to the client; second, that most counselling theory plays down the goal of understanding in favour of talking about such personal attributes of the therapist as warmth and liveliness.

In most counselling, at least as conventionally described, information provided in the interview flows one way, from client to therapist. Many therapists refuse to provide information about themselves or about their social circumstances on the grounds that these are outside their professional role, or would constitute an irrelevant change of topic within the interview. According to them, the client is likely to find out, on his or her own accord, most of the relevant information about himself or herself if the therapist acts as no more than a 'mirror' to the client. These clinicians may indeed see the interview as inter-subjective, but most of the 'perception' allowed to occur is of the client only. Clinicians coming from this background will accordingly often be shocked by the directness of client demands for information in other clinical settings. For instance:

> AIDS patient: 'How long have I got to live?'

or perhaps

> AIDS patient's mother: 'How did he get it?'

These are everyday demands in some clinical settings, which it would be grossly inappropriate to meet by replying, 'That's a matter of how you see it, don't you think?'. Most clinical interviews are more fully inter-subjective in the sense that both parties to the exchange are likely to alter their views and attitudes, and are in some sense committed to doing so.

Much of the literature on counselling places great emphasis on the personal attributes of the therapist. The therapist in particular should be 'psychologically minded', a 'skilled helper', a 'good listener' with an 'empathic' attitude who knows how to prevent his or her own feelings and attitudes from interfering with the 'therapeutic process'.

In summary, clinical interviews range from expert medical case history-taking, on the one hand, to counselling on the other. Clinical interviews must take a holistic view of the client's belief system (not just a case history), but they must also include a mutual inter-subjective exchange of information, including specialist education of the client (in the case of the expert interview), and can lead to the therapist using this information to become an effective agent on behalf of the client (like a doctor but not a psychotherapist). The stages of the clinical interview of both kinds will be discussed after consideration of other issues that influence the process.

Process models versus goal models

A distinction has often been made between the goals of the clinical interview, on the one hand, and the process of the interview on the other. The goal of the in-depth interview is the understanding of the world of the informant by the clinician. The goal of the clinical version of the in-depth interview is the development of a *shared* understanding of the world of the client, whether the main purpose is expert skill application or counselling, leading to concerted action by both clinician and client to alter that world for the better. The process of the in-depth interview is one of testing and negotiating theories about the meaning of the informant's world. We have already said that the process of the clinical interview is a dialectic in which the interviewer contributes 'facts' as well as interprets them. This process will be one of accumulating facts and increasingly sharpening and redefining therapeutic (expert or counselling) aims.

The clinical interview proceeds by mutual exchange, each step depending on the previous ones. In this sense, it has an intrinsically *dialectical process*. The argument of this book is that all meaningful conversations proceed in this way; but the clinical interview has a step-wise dialectic of a very forceful kind. The clinician may have a general aim to exercise his or her expertise and the client a general aim to experience it. For such expertise and experience to occur, the client needs to disclose the facts as he or she experiences them (the symptoms), the clinician needs to collect information possibly unsuspected by the client (signs like having yellow eyes), make a preliminary interpretation, elicit further signs and symptoms, share further possible interpretation with the client, and discuss possible courses of action with him or her. In all of this dialectical process, the meaning of each step depends on the preceding ones. The only fixed assumptions are that full information is needed to act correctly, and the clinician is state-licensed to act correctly. A prior assumption which is open to question is that the clinician will interpret 'correctly'. This issue is raised in more detail in chapter 9.

The clinician's expertise is legitimated by the state, (for expert and usually for counselling purposes) and carries with it a license to treat, that is, to act on the client's body or property or social circumstances. The in-depth interview itself provides part of the *legitimation* of clinical work, part of the general role played by state-endorsed science in supporting professional membership and practice. The clinician is licensed to collect the information, and certified by his or her education as being capable of doing it well. The client may resent the fact of doing things the clinician's way; but this does not alter the asymmetry of social legitimacy: the clinician is the authority in a way that the client is not.

The principles of good interviewing apply in each situation, even when the primary emphasis varies from the fact seeking and information giving of the medical interview to the feeling exploration of counselling or the deep conflict resolution of psychotherapy. Psychological knowledge informs each applied action either as the basis of treatment in counselling or as the best way to ensure patient compliance in an expert interview.

Applying psychological theory

Clinicians make use of insights from a wide range of basic study areas in psychology such as human development (child and adult), information processing, perception, brain-behaviour relationships as well as therapeutic systems, from cognitive behavioural therapy to family therapy. This may be either as the basis of primary intervention in psychotherapy and counselling or to support and inform other forms of health care provision. A child's truanting from school is more effectively resolved if the link between his behaviour and his mother's cancer, which the whole family is denying, is recognised and dealt with in family interviews. This requires skilled handling from a specifically trained clinician. Conversely, the tonsillectomy hospitalisation of three-year-old Sarah is likely to be medically and surgically smoother and shorter and healing quicker, if she is informed and prepared in advance of the event and accompanied by her parents throughout her time in hospital. In the first example, the clinician employs the insights of psychology as the treatment mode, while in the second, understanding of aspects of behaviour led him or her to instruct Sarah and her parents about the best way they could act to support her tonsillectomy.

Different counselling and therapeutic endeavours make use of different aspects of psychological theory, depending upon the chosen emphasis (Corsini 1989; Patterson 1986). A different focus will lead to different therapeutic tasks and actions being undertaken. Thus a behavioural approach endeavours to change external, observed behaviour and employs to do so some direct methods with specific outcome goals. At the other end of the prescriptive scale of therapeutic endeavour is family therapy intervention. Here, and in those individual therapies most closely allied to recent thought in this area, lies the greatest similarity with in-depth interviewing research interviewing.

Anderson and Goolishian (1988) describe this approach as a language-generated, meaning-generated system, where meaning and understanding are socially and inter-subjectively constructed. This is a linguistic system which is problem organising and problem dissolving, leading to change by the evolution of new meaning through dialogue. These writers argue for a therapist role which combines the actions of participant observer and participant manager of conversation. The first position includes the therapist as member of a 'problem system', in a collaborative, respectful and mutual relationship, as a learner 'in there', co-operating, 'attempting to understand, and work within the clients' meaning system. Clients' ideas, stories and narrative are the only available tools we have to keep ourselves and our clients open to the development of new meaning and understanding (Anderson & Goolishian 1988). No one's meaning or integrity is challenged.

The task of therapy involves therapist and client creating together the therapeutic realities, collaboratively exploring new themes and descriptions for self-organisation and organisation. As participant manager of conversation, the therapist creates and maintains dialogue with certain characteristics, that allow new forms of social organisation to develop. The participant manager of conversation is part of a circular interactive system. He or she does not influence conversation toward a particular direction of change or content alteration. Therapists must be prepared and able to abandon old meanings in order to find new ones, just as is expected of clients.

White and Epston (1989) offer a rich diversity of therapeutic initiatives by involving in clinical endeavours many of the materials that qualitative researchers use for reconstructing and uncovering meanings. Letters, declarations, predictive statements are written, exchanged, and pondered over by protagonists on both sides of the therapeutic relationship. White and Epston invoke the notion of narrative to explain their use of literate means, and 'propose the analogy of therapy as a process of "storying" and/or "re-storying" the lives and experiences of persons who present with problems' (Tomm 1989, p. 7). They propose that documenting events and meanings contributes to the creation of new, liberating narratives. Most people have a multiplicity of stories about themselves and their relationships with others which reflect personal constraints or empowerment. The dominant story generally gives the major meaning to life and action. Additionally, it is acknowledged that therapists are never void of values or the views that develop from them through having their own life stories and experiences. Awareness of this inevitability and consciousness of one's own values are important. Clinical neutrality includes the possibility of having a position, being clear what it is, being flexible enough to allow it to change and where necessary making it explicit.

Many studies (Atkinson et al. 1987 give a summary) have shown that there are severe limits on the capacity of human beings to retain and process information. Even under ideal conditions, few people can juggle more than eight or so items of information in their heads and subsequently retain the items in memory. It follows that clinicians should not expect their clients to remember to tell them all the details which the client thinks to be relevant if the details are numerous and varied. Often these details will only be offered with prompting in the course of the interview. Nor should the clinician expect himself or herself to be any better without taking careful notes. The moral should be clear.

Moreover, clients in the clinic are very likely to be tired, confused, in pain, disoriented, depressed or anxious. All these factors have been shown severely to limit whatever capacity for processing information the client may possess, and the clinician should take it for granted that severe limits are being placed on getting and giving information by the clinical set-up. There seem also to be only a few realistic ways around this: whenever possible, we should place our clients at ease and give them time to get used to us and the clinical room. Taking notes for them as well as for ourselves is often useful. And having a friend or relation of the client present is often a good way of checking, extending and corroborating stories—theirs and ours.

Checklists and routines

Previous chapters, particularly chapter 2, have discussed the desire for sure-fire techniques and set procedures as guarantees of scientific legitimacy. It is not surprising that in the clinical literature this desire often appears as a taste for checklists and step-by-step procedures. Our response to such desires is threefold. Firstly, these are very good ways of checking out causal hypotheses about clients. In many clinical interviews there will be an important place for checking such propositions. For instance, in an interview with a plastic surgeon about having a nose reconstruction, there will much routine factual material collected:

> 'Are you allergic to any anaesthetics?'
> 'I'd like to have a look at the bone structure inside your nose.'
> 'Is there any history of high blood pressure in your family?'

All these and many other enquiries are part of routine factual checks which should be carried out before any plastic surgery procedure. Other questions relate to factors which are likely to affect any investigation, no matter what the problem such as the question of age.

Once the practical problems with which the clinical interview is concerned are sufficiently defined, such questions follow routinely. Therefore it will be appropriate to have a routine checklist of questions to ask and items to look for in the expert interview. Typically, as in the examples given above, there will be a mixture of verbal queries and physical or other investigations:

> 'What is your medicare number?'

Notice, however, that such a checklist is determined by how the problem is defined. But just what the problem is may be unclear or confused or contended through much of the clinical interview. So just what checklist to use may be undecidable for much of the time.

Then there are those factors which, considered purely in terms of their far-reaching effect on nearly all the problems of the clients, should be on all checklists, but which in practice may be so explosive or subversive of the course of the interview that they should be asked circumspectly or not at all:

'What is your sexual orientation?'
'Is there any alcoholism in your family?'
'What is your ethnic background?'

Secondly, checklists and fixed routines provide a poor way to reach interpretive understanding of anyone, and are likely to lead the interviewer into a false sense of security, believing that understanding has been achieved because the standard procedures have been followed. The best they could safely provide would be a heuristic reminder that we should not jump to conclusions too soon about what the client is speaking about; we should move from areas of neutral and unalarming detail towards more important matters only after we have established rapport with our client; we should observe a general movement from sharing facts to sharing decisions; and we should be conscious at every stage of the need to negotiate the client's understanding of, and consent to, our clinical decisions. These recommendations may seem harmless enough, and possibly bland and useless, too. On the other hand, we are very conscious that most of the nostrums for conduct of the clinical interview which occur in the published literature have about them a spurious air of professionalism, and, in fact, work to close off our receptivity to what the client is actually saying and doing.

Thirdly, clients are likely to be very conscious that the clinician is following a set routine. This can be reassuring to the client, as for the clinician; it can also give the client a sense of regimentation, of having to surrender passively to a process beyond his or her control. This, in turn, can lead to resentment of, or indifference to, the conclusions and suggestions of the clinician. This spell can be broken by asking the client:

'What do you think is causing the problem?'

Symptom checklists make sense from the point of view of causal explanation. There are only so many probable illnesses, and each is defined in terms of a handful of discrete symptoms, so by collecting lists of symptoms it should be possible to decide, within limits, what is the illness of the patient. Bleaching the interpretations of the client is, of course, a necessary preliminary step to making this clinical decision. The background to this procedure is the one we have seen before in previous chapters: causal explanation allows us, to a large extent, to fragment the evidence and to deal with experience in separate parcels. None of this will apply to the attitude of the patient to his or her illness, nor to large parts of psychiatry.

Clinical objectivity

The training of health practitioners stresses the value of detached, objective observation, leading to test results records, open to public inspection, which satisfy the goals of valid and reliable measures. But this kind of public objectivity is just what we cannot hope for in holistic explanation. To aim for it would be to apply the right standard to the wrong material.

Medical writers often distinguish between signs and symptoms in discussing the information gathered in a clinical interview. Signs are the pieces of information collected by the clinician, regardless of whether they have been noticed by the patient. Symptoms are the pieces of information noticed by the patient; in that sense, they define the problem, at least at first. They have their meaning within the personal world of the client: the signs have a meaning within the world-view of the clinician. This distinction between signs and symptoms is a useful one for dividing the origins of the pieces of information used in the interview. It is not useful as a way of indicating how they might be used. Both signs and symptoms have to be evaluated and used within the belief-systems of both client and clinician. Ultimately, those belief-systems must come to coincide for effective diagnosis and treatment to occur, and in that process signs and symptoms will become assimilated to one another.

Stages of the clinical interview

We will now consider the stages of the clinical interview and in doing so will further distinguish the difference between the expert and the counselling variants. Figure 7.2 presents the action sequence in each case, following several initially similar steps.

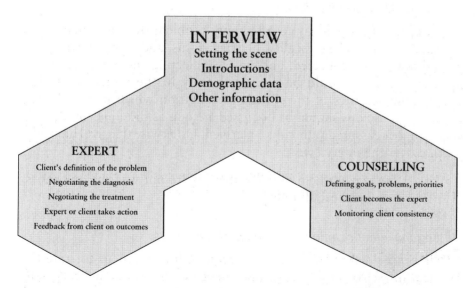

Figure 7.2 Comparing the stages of the clinical interview: expert and counselling

Stages of the expert interview

The stages listed below are given somewhat optimistically. It is hard to imagine any effective interview which completely dispensed with them; but there are many good interviews which double-back from earlier to later stages in order to correct errors of interpretation or understanding. The stages are described largely from the point of view of the clinician, just as the interviews outlined elsewhere in the book are described from the point of view of the researcher.

Setting the scene

It's important to have a setting in which the client can feel comfortable and safe to make confidences. Sound-proofing and freedom from interruptions (including phone calls) are important. So are comfortable and similar (same status) chairs, not too far apart (cold) or close together (frightening), with a view of both persons' bodies unimpeded by any desk or table—the movement of people's bodies provides us with information we may need.

Introductions

Names, explaining the role, including sometimes the financial and legal responsibilities, of both interviewer and interviewee. Sometimes it emerges straight away that the client has actually come on someone else's behalf; or that the clinician does not have the right qualifications to handle the client's problem. Perhaps the client thought you were someone else; or that they were at another clinic ... Make all this clear at once.

Collecting demographic data

Some information is likely to affect any problem the client may have. Basics of age, sex, class, locality, married status, and employment status should always be collected, and unless collecting them is likely to be distressing, they should be discussed early in the interview. Other conspicuous features of the client's presentation which may make the client self-conscious should be discussed as soon as the clinician feels the client can be reassured rather than alarmed. Otherwise they will hang like a cloud over the interview:

> 'Jay, I can't help noticing that you're not wearing any shoes. Are your feet all right?'

Getting the client's definition of the problem

'What can I do for you?' This is a request for the client to state the problem (or set of problems) in the client's own terms. Medically, this would cover finding their symptoms. This will encompass the relevant experiences of the client, along with the client's possible explanations of how these problems came about. It does not help to force on the client a premature separation of symptoms from aetiology. Nor is it helpful to propel the client into a rigorous exposition which does not match how confused the client may actually feel. On the contrary, this is the best time to let the client's narrative stumble across paddocks of distress and reminiscence. 'My Mum died of cancer at the age I am now' hints at a theory which fear of ridicule may prevent the client from voicing directly. The more time the clinician spends simply listening the more the client understands that, for the moment, anything may be spoken of.

Perhaps it can be said that, in many psychotherapy interviews, this stage is as far as the process goes. Indeed, therapy over many months may consist of no more than allowing the client to define and re-define the problem causing so much distress. In the counselling interview, then, the remaining apparatus of negotiated diagnosis and treatment will be irrelevant. In other counselling settings our emphasis on expertise and problems may be inappropriate: the client need only become clear as to what he or she wants—to define his or her goals—for the interview to do its work. This kind of interview is discussed below.

Collection of information

History taking is directed to developing an understanding of what is the matter with the client; how they got to be like this; how their social or physical setting is likely to respond to your interventions; whether they have seen other professionals before and with what result. Of course, some of this material will already have been elicited by getting the client's definition of the problem. But now is the time for systematically pursuing hypotheses and collecting evidence. Symptom or other checklists, phone calls, referral for X-rays—all may be in order now. Naturally, some of these procedures may require the interview itself to be suspended until another time.

Though it may not seem directly relevant to the client's view of the problem, this is also the time to assess the client's psychological state: are they angry, outraged, despairing, indifferent? Often the client's psychological state is an important part of the problem itself. At other times, the client's psychological state will be a good index of how seriously he or she is appraising the problem, and how well able to take in new information about it.

Diagnosis

This is your initial definition of the problem. You might have alternatives between which you can't decide, at least to begin with. You might want to check your reading, consult with colleagues, reflect on what you have seen and heard. But, however tentatively, you have a set of initial hypotheses. It would be very foolish at this stage to be precipitated into a hasty conclusion (unless of course the client is in physical or social danger). In some cases, the client may need to wait for some days, or even for some sessions, before the clinician feels able to speak helpfully on the matter.

Feedback to the client on the diagnosis

This includes instructing, informing, and teaching the client about how the world—their body, the law—works. This, of course, has special implications for what you and the client are going to do about it—for your 'treatment'.

Feedback from the client on the diagnosis

The validity of your assessment has to be negotiated with the client. For one thing, you may be wrong and they may know better. The client may respond to your diagnosis by revealing a mass of new facts which did not previously seem relevant. Or the client may agree with your diagnosis, but then show that there is another, more important, problem concealed behind the one you have isolated.

For another thing, you need the client's collaboration in your diagnosis before you can get the client to co-operate with your 'treatment', that is, your carrying out some suitable action, for instance, removing the client's toe-nail or appearing for him or her in court.

Proposing a course of action

Between you, outline and explore the various possible courses of action available. If the problem is a medical one, this will constitute your options for 'treatment.' These courses of action will often include some that only you, as a professional, are qualified to take.

Feedback from the client on the proposed course of action

Just as diagnosis has to be negotiated with the client, so does treatment. Are you going to refer them to someone else? Are they coming back for weekly visits? What are they going to do while they are at home? Have they the time and money to sustain the course of action you have jointly chosen? It is often at this stage that the most sophisticated proposals founder and client and clinician must return to an earlier stage.

Action!

The lawyer takes out a court injunction; the social worker rings the Ministry of Housing to say that the client will have the rent by Friday; the optician sends to have lenses ground to the correct specification; the doctor orders an X-ray of the broken leg ... This is the point at which the expert interview differs from the counselling interview. Here the expert takes action.

Feedback on the success of the course of action

Almost any clinician will understand the value of a follow-up meeting to see what happened and how the client feels about it. But not all clinicians are willing to hear that their diagnosis or treatment has been inadequate. Don't oblige the client to say what a great success you are. This is the time to remind yourself that clinical work is unending.

Recording the expert interview

In some circumstances it will be appropriate for you to record the interview on a cassette tape. As we've discussed earlier, this must never be done without the client's *informed consent*. At other times it is preferable to take detailed notes of the interview as you go along. Almost any employing institution will demand that the clinician keep some case notes as part of the job. Where suitable, the interviewer should also take notes of the setting of the interview, the client's body language and the side-comments made by the client.

Write up your case notes—in full sentences, not in point form—so that they are clearly legible and written in language which your client and colleagues can read if they ever need to do so. In most clinical settings your client is legally entitled to see what you have written, and you should write your notes with this in mind. There are only very rare cases in which you should want to conceal your opinion from your client. More likely, your notes will be read by a colleague taking over your job. He or she should be able to understand exactly what your overall impression of the client was, and what were the relevant details which determined it. Therefore, as a good clinician, your notes will be long, detailed and discursive.

Unless you have some reason for wanting to present them in an unusual form, you might write up your case notes in an order which roughly follows that of the interview's stages:

- client's name;
- demographic data;
- client's psychological state where relevant;
- client's definition of the problem if it differs from yours;
- client's history;
- your diagnosis;
- treatment;
- follow-up and success of the treatment.

Stages of the counselling interview

Ivey (1988), among others (for example, Bernstein & Bernstein 1985 and Egan 1982), has outlined possible stages which should be followed in a successful counselling interview. We have adapted his work to our purposes, and have given the stages names which bring out the parallels between the counselling and the expert interview. Even more so than for the expert interview, our attitude to giving stages to counselling interviews is less than realistic. Good counselling sessions range all over the place. Also, it is even more important in discussing the counselling interview than with the expert interview to emphasise that we are setting counselling in the context of the research interview, not presenting a training course in counselling.

Setting the scene

This stage will be much the same as setting the scene for an expert interview. With luck, the counsellor will be able to contrive a more informal setting than most professionals can manage.

Introductions

As in the expert interview, clarify the names of both people present, explaining the role, including, if appropriate, the financial and legal responsibilities of both interviewer and interviewee. All this is as for the expert interview. But the fact that the interviewer is not here to give advice may be one of the main points the interviewer must make clear. Another is just how much structure the interview is going to have. Taking a stance of complete and open receptivity, as advocated by many psychotherapists, is admirable provided it doesn't induce in the interviewee a crisis of paranoid embarrassment. The aim should be to provide a framework within which the client can feel secure enough to say and feel what is really happening. Make clear (if it is true) that you are going to leave most of the structure of the interview to the client; that you have fifty minutes to spend with them; that if they would like to they can come back at the same time next week. The more the counselling interview shades from the expert interview towards psychotherapy, the more it will tend to be structured not by the client's problem, but by time itself. This is also a good moment to clarify another important matter—if you or your employer charges fees, these must be negotiated and finalised before the main work of the interview begins.

Collecting demographic data

As in an expert interview, some information is likely to affect any problem the client may have, and basics of age, gender, class, locality, married status, and employment status should always be collected. Besides, in a counselling interview, this is likely to lead directly to the client's problem, and to be charged with strong feeling:

> 'Where do you live, Jo?'
> 'Well, that's the problem. My partner has asked me to move out and I'm living at my mother's place now.'

Collecting information

In an expert interview, this would be the place to record the client's history. But the history of what? In a counselling setting, the client's interests are likely to be multiple, disguised, interlocking. Labelling one area as the problem might lead to a premature exclusion of more important matters. Labelling one outcome as the solution can conceal the ways in which human beings have a range of inexplicit and incompatible goals which need to be evaluated before good choices can be made. On the whole, we prefer to emphasise an overall process of funnelling, as we call it in chapter 5, where the definition of both purposes and roles moves from the broad to the narrow and from the vague to the precise as the interview proceeds. At the vague end, the client's discourse will often float on a sea of anxiety or anger. This allows both client and clinician quickly to reconnoitre the client's universe, its passions included. Both the structure of that universe and the client's feelings about it may surprise both interviewer and interviewee:

> 'You seem to be more angry that your son has married some-
> one from Zimbabwe than that he hasn't repaid your loan.'
> 'Yes I am. I'm not a racist. I really like her. I just think he's
> married her for the notoriety.' [Makes another angry face.]

Defining goals, problems and priorities

This stage consists of the therapist and client making explicit and reconciling the facts, problems, solutions, goals and urgencies which have emerged from the client's discourse. Client and counsellor are both likely to focus too early on what seem to be open-shut solutions. But if the client's goals are confused or complex, a proposed solution to an explicit problem is likely to undermine possible solutions to inexplicit ones. This can be a particular problem when the client prefers to focus on problems which are psychologically or morally more comfortable, to the exclusion of more distressing matters. For instance, a client may prefer to focus on her husband's drinking and the solutions to his problem rather than discussing why she has stayed married to him, thus evading a set of complex fears, desires, pains and satisfactions to be had from marriage to an alcoholic. In an expert interview, the interviewer tends to accept the goals for treatment of the client as unproblematic; in the counselling interview, the counsellor is more likely to mount a critique of the client's values from within the client's own belief system, exploring alternatives and confronting client ambiguity (Ivey 1988). (The question of which problems to work on first is controversial among counsellors. Some counsellors choose to take the obvious and immediate problems first, and deal with others if and when they arise. Other counsellors have theoretical reasons for sometimes going for the best hidden problems much earlier. These disputes are not our concern here.)

It may strike you that these definitions of goals are just as important in the expert interview as in a counselling one. Often this is true. A patient in counselling assessment for a sex-change operation cannot be assumed to have his or her life goals all tidily worked through, and just to provide what seemingly is being asked for would be a failure of clinical responsibility. At other times there is such a close agreement between the values of clinician, client and society—for instance, on the value of removing toothaches—that no explicit evaluation of gaols is thought necessary.

The client becomes the expert

In an expert interview there occurs an essential though incomplete transfer of responsibility and power from the client to the clinician. The client cannot be expected to master all the required facts or carry out all the required actions. But counselling interviews cover just those cases when the client can perfectly well become his or her own expert. Once he or she knows what he values and feels and is conscious of the range of options available, what need is there for the clinician to take control of the client's life? Consequently, steps in the interview which correspond to the later steps of the expert interview cease to be stages within the interview and come to occur outside the clinic. The client has no need to reconcile his or her values with those of the clinician. Nor, usually, is there any need for the counsellor to become an educator or the client's agent. To do so would be to 'disempower' the client. What remains is for the client to monitor how consistently the feelings, goals and choices made explicit in the interview are carried into action beyond it. For that reason nearly all counselling interviews wind up with a final stage: monitoring, in a return visit, how the client coped.

The socio-political setting of the clinical interview

All variants of the clinical interview take place in a social setting. Aspects of this social setting include how each participant in the interview sees and understands the other's purpose and how each fits into the broader social structure. These will exert important influences upon all interviews which the interviewer (at either end of the spectrum) must recognise and manage for an effective outcome.

Client information control

Goffman (1959) has given a useful account of the general manoeuvres we use to form the information about ourselves into an acceptable social impression. In presenting ourselves to others, we are not usually concerned to let others see us as we 'really' are, but as we want them to perceive us. We are involved, in all our transactions with other people, with controlling the flow of information about ourselves, including deleting, embellishing and sometimes inventing information, so as to manage the impression others form of us. We present to others a *front* of contrived appearances.

We have already said that the clinical interview is concerned with the two-way flow of information between therapist and client. Now we can see that if either or both of these people is engaging in large-scale impression management, then the ideal we have set ourselves of achieving a shared holistic understanding in the clinical setting is likely to be threatened, or achieved only in a fake or spurious form.

According to Goffman's *The Presentation of Self in Everyday Life* (1959), clients (and therapists) are apt to show a front to the therapist rather than passively or unreflectively letting the facts about ourselves unfold themselves. Few of us trust the conclusions others might draw about us so completely to chance and charity. *Front* is the actively presented body of information we show to others. Often this performance requires us to make visible—give dramatic realisation to—information which might otherwise be sceptically regarded. It is always useful to have the high temperature or the coughing fit right in front of the doctor, rather than limply explaining that you had one at home just before coming to the surgery.

We notice others' limited capacity for accommodating complex information, and so present an idealised simplification of the facts: our leg has been hurting non-stop since Thursday, we have never missed a day at work, and we love our spouse without qualification and without ceasing. And we only maintain such unbelievable things ... in order to be believed.

We preserve the pretence that most if not all the things that happen to us and to our bodies are intended by us. We meant (so we pretend) to get angry when you pointed out that we had wept, or we meant to start coughing just when we did start. Throughout, we kept to the maintenance of expressive control, as Goffman (1959) calls it. Obviously the problem of the maintenance of expressive control is going to be particularly pressing when we are working with physically damaged clients, especially in hospitals. Finally, when necessary to preserve the desired impression, we are prepared to lie, concoct false identities and false histories, or to leave large and deceptive areas of mystification about potentially embarrassing areas of our lives. 'The doctor doesn't need to know that I drink two bottles of wine a day, or that my wife earns twice as much as I do. If the doctor wants to know those things, let him or her ask.'

Social aspects of the clinical population

One of the most striking facts about clinical populations is the oppressed and marginalised nature of many of the people coming (or being brought) for institutional help. Such people are far more prone to illness of most kinds, and far more prone to seek assistance from hospitals and other 'helping' agencies. So are people who are habitually heavy users of drugs, including alcohol and tobacco. So are those people who are intellectually retarded or educationally disadvantaged. To these we can add those people who are criminally or sexually or psychically or interpersonally *deviant* (for instance, those of us who are inarticulately angry about the state of the world much of the time; or those of us who were sexually exploited as children). Working-class clients are not necessarily deviant by virtue of their class membership, but they are just as likely as any social deviant to feel defensive and lacking in legitimacy; so if the following discussion identifies the working-class client with deviant groups, this is done with good reason.

Worse, if someone is a member of one of these groups, then he or she is very likely to be a member of one or more of the other groups, too: deviant and disadvantaged groups have a high tendency to overlap. So, for instance, the level of alcohol and drug abuse is statistically very high among gay men: the level of heart disease is high among people with criminal records.

Worst, those members of society who are found among these overlapping deviant groups are the heaviest users of our helping institutions. You may not be surprised to read that 70 per cent of males in Australian prisons are there for drug-related offences; but not everyone knows how much time and money in welfare agencies, schools and hospitals is consumed by these multiply-deviant groups. To the clinician, it often seems that these people are taking away all the clinic's time from its 'proper' clients. But the researcher sees that often these multiply-deviant clients are the clinic's proper clients. Therefore the clinician can expect similar themes to recur in the stories and world-view of these clients. These recurrences allow him or her many shortcuts in dealing with them. They also can lead to many traps of *stereotyping* clients as supposedly 'typical' drug-users or prostitutes.

These deviant clients know all too well that they come from deviant groups. They know all too well that they are not highly regarded by the custodians of society's values, and rightly or wrongly they usually see clinicians as just such custodians. This is to say that these clients are *stigmatised* and will behave so as to manage the 'spoiled social identity' (Goffman 1963) that being stigmatised entails. Because stigma leads clients actively to alter or suppress information, it can decisively affect the success of a clinical interview: people in stigmatised groups deploy exaggerated forms of the self-presentations employed by all of us.

Stigma-management

Goffman (1963) has paid special attention to the impression-management of those people who have a social stigma—something to be ashamed of. (Notice that shame here has to do with what others think is wrong with us, regardless of our own opinion of ourselves. What we find wrong with ourselves is perhaps a matter of guilt. In these terms, shame and guilt have little to do with one another.) Regardless of whether we are personally responsible for our failure to measure up to society's norms—by wearing a colostomy bag, beating up old people in parks or growing to one metre in height—we are charged by 'normal' people with the responsibility for endorsing those norms by appearing as normal as possible. Obviously, the different ways which stigmatised people use to preserve social appearances will vitally affect their behaviour in the clinical interview.

By far the most common way of managing stigma is suppressing information or putting out counter-propaganda designed to lead people to believe that you are not stigmatised. Because the point of this exercise is to pass yourself off as 'normal' or 'straight', this form of stigma management is known as *passing*. Alternatively, you might try *migration* away from sources of social exposure—for instance, the country town you grew to feel ashamed in, or withdrawal, having as little contact with others as possible (withdrawal from social contact is a major source of depression among people from stigmatised groups).

Brazening it out is another possible solution. You dare the 'straights' to put you down; to refuse to accept your shame. You adopt what Goffman (1963) calls a *militant* stance as a self-proclaimed member of your stigmatised group. Or you might attempt to form an improvised ghetto of the excluded. The term *splitting* usually refers to divisions within the individual mind; here we use it to describe a process of coping with stigma. The ruse here is to divide your stigmatised group into two: the socially acceptable and the socially unacceptable—good Jews and bad Jews, for example. Clients choosing this ruse will launch fierce verbal attacks on 'poofs' or 'dole bludgers' who, to all external appearances, are little different from themselves. The clinician should be alert to the personal defensiveness implied by these attacks, and fail to join in. Both good Jews and bad Jews are still Jews: poofters, however defined, are just one subgroup of gay men and women; and encouraging our clients to split their group is only to feed their sense of social insecurity. By now, you will be getting a sense of how underlying all these ruses, and many others we haven't space for, is one fundamental stratagem: angle for *acceptance* in the way most likely to succeed with your interlocutor.

Accordingly, an experienced clinician will forestall all such ruses by showing from the very beginning that he or she is what Goffman calls *wise* or, to put it another way, showing that you understand what it feels like to be a member of the stigmatised group. This is the familiar quality, holistic understanding. Though not necessarily a member of the stigmatised group, he or she nevertheless understands what it *feels* like to be a member of the group. (Often one finds inexperienced therapists pretending to group-membership in an attempt to seek respect: acceptance is what is required, not fellowship.)

Social theory often disputes whether there is any such thing as a real self beneath or beyond the social roles we have internalised. What is not in dispute is that there will be aspects of the client which might be excluded by playing the narrow range of roles seemingly allotted by the hospital or clinic. When we allow the client to step outside these, he or she has the sense of unconstrained personal expression. It feels to both of us as though he or she has been permitted to show a 'real' self. And when that free-floating expressive self is acknowledged, most clients find the experience deeply satisfying. The clinician seems to meet a need for intimacy, to be acknowledged as a person beyond playing a mere social part. To share that intimacy can be for the clinician a motive more powerful than any other.

Institutional limitations on the clinical interview

So far we have outlined the limits on clinical understanding imposed by the client's *front*. But there are many other limits which are likely to be imposed from outside the clinical room. Foremost among these is the limitation of time. The in-depth interview is necessarily time consuming, and the ideal length of the interview is to some extent unpredictable because of the holistic nature of the material. Yet almost all institutions and clinics in our society are overcrowded with clients waiting to see too few therapists. Even in private clinics or in private practice, the pressure to earn enough money to cover costs means that time is scarce. Therefore, the institutional interview is apt to remain rather shallow, and its validity and reliability rather doubtful.

The clinician as an agent of the state

High among threats to the validity of the clinical interview must rank the suspicion that the institution of whom, like it or not, the clinician is a representative, is seen by the client as potentially hostile to his or her interests. Only naive clinical workers believe that their hospital is purely interested in the welfare of its patients: hospitals are primarily clients of governments, and must constantly refer to government priorities on health, employment and welfare spending. These priorities insinuate themselves into the clinical interview whenever the clinician finds himself or herself saying that you can go on the methadone program, or that you can't get free access to a hospital bed no matter how distressed you might feel. Moreover, when the client realises that you are indeed an agent of the state (like it or not), then he or she is likely to tell you the versions of the truth best calculated to produce the action from you which he or she desires. In other words, the client is likely to become manipulative rather than frank. And when you think about it, your own attitude as agent of the state is likely to be a manipulative one too, though you will perhaps try to conceal this fact from yourself. Obviously, when both parties to the social interaction are trying to manipulate the other, largely through the control of information, then the kind of shared holistic understanding which we set as the goal of the clinical interview is likely to be compromised.

The client as an agent of others

If the clinician is apt to be a stand-in for wider institutions of the state, so too is the client likely to be present on behalf of other groups—pursuing the agendas of, for example, members of his or her family, work or church. The client may only have come to the clinic in the first place at their behest. Even when the client has come for treatment independent of others, his or her intentions are likely to be modified or censored by an awareness of what, for instance, would be acceptable to, say, the children, when it comes to admission to a retirement home. So both clinician and client are sitting in the room secretly wired for messages back to unseen headquarters. Then there is likely to be a definite idea in the head of both client and clinician of how a clinician is expected to behave, in other words, what it is to be professional. We have discussed earlier what it means to society as a whole for someone to be professional, but for clients it usually means that the clinician will be punctual, well-dressed in appearance, confidential, not impertinent, not advance his or her sexual or status interests through the interaction, and generally preserve an air of middle-class decorum. But having expected, and sometimes insisted, that the clinician will gaze at him or her from an alabaster pedestal, the client is also likely to be intimidated by his or her perceived social distance from the clinician; just as the clinician is likely to feel cut off from the client, while at the same time hiding his or her own anxiety behind a cool, professional front.

Subverting pre-ordained clinical roles

But there are good ways around these problems, so long as we are aware that they are indeed problems. The clinician should make it clear at the appropriate time that he or she is unwilling to be manipulated without a corresponding exchange of true information by the client; and he or she will usually find in any case that the client sets the clinician a test of his or her integrity—not as state agent, but as fellow human being who knows what it's like to struggle with and through bureaucratic systems.

Most useful here is a habit on the part of the clinician of self-disclosure. Telling the client relevant facts about yourself can throw light on the client's problem. But even better, it can show the client that you are quite capable of hopping off your pedestal when required and perhaps sharing his or her attitude and, if the situation forces it on you, able to subvert the system in order to see that justice is done. But the clinician has to be prepared to make a commitment to this line of action, risking the institutional consequences: fake radicalism doesn't fool the humblest and slowest client when his or her welfare is at stake.

In-depth interviewing research in clinical practice

It is clear from the previous descriptions of clinical interviewing (expert and counselling) and from the sociological context of these activities, that many questions will arise that could be investigated using in-depth interviewing research. These will be wide-ranging questions dealing with issues of basic or applied science concerning the lived experiences of patient and clinician in relation to the condition, the service, each other and significant others. Hopefully it is also clear that clinicians, well trained in the art and issues of the clinical interview, can develop in-depth interviewing research because of the connection between the research process and their clinical-work actions and skills. Working clinicians are in the enviable position of being able to easily make contact with research samples and also to make research endeavours overlap their normal work activities because of the affinity between these actions which was described earlier. Questions may be investigated in a clinical setting where the data pre-exists as a consequence of the normal clinical recording practices. Alternatively, questions may be specifically developed for a research project which then becomes located in the clinic involving present clients, and collecting research data at the same time.

Clinical reports and clinical interview recordings provide an easily accessible base for research. Clinical reports can be written so that they may serve two purposes. The questions must preferably be identified first and the limitation on recursive interaction with the client be recognised. Pre-existing notes do not allow you to ask for clarification and interviews in the present are constrained by the clinical purpose. Diaries and client writing could be used to support and extend the data available for the research purpose.

Viney (1986) found content analysis of clinical records to be a useful way of estimating change in psychological state. She suggests that this taps into people's experience without interfering with it. It is important, however, to remember that as in any interviewing research, case notes will not answer questions that require analytic probing, just as computers will not perceive the underlying meaning in an analysis. The clinician must pick below the surface in a way neither notes nor computers can do for the underlying nuances and theoretical connections of comments to emerge. Knowing what to look for is largely theory directed and must be done by the researcher prior to the research, and during the research and the analysis.

Taped clinical interviews, especially where a number of clients in the same category of clinical concern are seen in a clinical setting, such as people with HIV, families of individuals with acquired brain damage, sexual assault victims, and people with schizophrenia, can offer valuable research opportunities. Clinical interview tape-recordings, used for research purposes, have similar implications to those discussed earlier in relation to written clinical records. The pragmatic issues discussed in chapter 9 regarding handling of the tape-recorder, coding of material, and data storage are relevant here. The intention to research using any aspect of the clinical process must always first be cleared with the institutional *ethics committee*, and client consent must be obtained after a full explanation has been given (see chapter 9). This applies whether the researcher plans to use material which is to be collected in the future or to use material which exits in the files of the clinic as a consequence of past clinical work.

While the counselling interview has greatest affinity with the in-depth research interview, as we have seen, all clinical interviewing could support research purposes using the methodology described in this book. We see it as important for clinicians to be aware of these research approaches and to realise that in-depth interviewing research is a flexible tool which can be adapted to suit many different clinical research needs and possibilities. Armed with this knowledge, practitioners can decide if they can or will undertake research and whether the questions in which they are interested could be investigated using in-depth interviewing methods. We suggest that once you have absorbed the research ideas here and increased your research awareness, you will find many ways of introducing those ideas into your work because of the flexibility of this research approach.

Chapter 8

The pragmatics of in-depth interviewing

The pragmatics of conducting research using in-depth interviewing as the primary method are inextricably interwoven with the methodological stance we take; the moral and ethical issues that are raised throughout the research process and the political context in which the research takes place. More will be said on this subject in chapter 9. Here we examine the pragmatic issues raised in the *doing* of research.

By pragmatic issues we mean the practical concerns of the researcher in accomplishing his or her task. These practical concerns include how one designs and does research, decides on sampling procedures, gains access to informants, establishes rapport, and leaves the field. They also involve assessing bias and objectivity throughout the research process, gauging the validity and reliability of the research process and the data, and deciding whether to employ multiple methods.

Research methods texts usually present the reader with a linear model of research; a sanitised, idealised account of how research ought to be done, progressing tidily from research design to data collection and then from data analysis to publication of results. Or, they tell us how complex and untidy research is, and that one must recognise that 'social research is not just a question of neat procedures but a social process whereby interaction between researcher and researched will directly influence the course which a research programme takes' (Burgess 1984, p. 31).

We argue that the research process is complex and untidy. Rarely does it follow the path laid down in the traditional texts. However, using a linear profile of the process of in-depth interviewing is helpful for heuristic reasons. It is the simplest way of incorporating into the discussion some of the issues, problems and untidiness that may arise in the research process. It is obvious, however, that each piece of research will raise its own dilemmas for the researcher and the researched.

Research design

Linear models of research describe specific stages of a project. These usually include generating or testing hypotheses, gathering data, analysing data, and then writing a research report. However, several researchers (Bell & Encel 1978; Bell & Newby 1977; Burgess 1984; Roberts 1988; Shipman 1972) have acknowledged that the reality is far more complex than it is usually portrayed. The social interaction between informant and interviewer can influence not only the direction of the discussion but the research project itself. Throughout in-depth interviewing research, the methodology and the research design are negotiated and renegotiated by both researcher and informant. However, prior to entering the field, the researcher needs to make an initial choice of a research problem or question.

You might decide to examine a particular question or issue because it is an important social issue of the day, an assignment problem set by your lecturer, or an issue related to your experience and understanding of the world which you wish to further explore. Whatever the motivation, research begins with asking a question and is carried out in an attempt to answer it. It is a means of understanding and explaining the world. Research begins before you put together a research design.

An example

Initial motivations are numerous. Often researchers are interested in a particular issue and decide to read more about it. They discuss it with friends and/or colleagues. Personal experiences may induce an interest in an area. A research problem may be developed or generated by the interplay between the researcher's theoretical and methodological training and personal experiences within a social setting (Burgess 1984). For instance, Aroni (1985) selected her research topic after many dinner-table conversations. These discussions included speculation about the relationship between Jewish schooling, and the production and maintenance of Jewish identity. Her sociological training enabled her to perceive it as a topic for research. It was only after some preparation work (see chapter 3), which included reading research literature in the field and talking to other researchers, that she designed a research project. Even then, the sociological problem was revised several times after preliminary discussions with some informants, members of the Jewish community and colleagues. She then formulated a research problem and turned it into a working title. After this, she wrote a research proposal outlining a design for the research project.

James (1984) provides detailed discussion of the practical issues facing a researcher prior to defining the research problem and subsequent reclarification of the research topic. Her account of doing research as a nurse in a cancer ward outlines how the entire process began, how she narrowed the question and then how she began with a research proposal or design which altered in response to suggestions made by prospective informants. Her account provides commentary on her position as a postgraduate student, the manner in which this influenced the framing of the topic, the people she discussed the project with and the help and encouragement she received in actually selecting a suitable topic.

The process

You begin the process of defining the research problem by working out why you are asking the questions. This is an important issue because it will influence:

1 the sort of research you would like to do;
2 that you, in fact, are able to do;
3 who it is for; and
4 how you go about doing it.

The questions you might ask at this point are:

• What prompted me into thinking about this problem?
• What is the real problem that underlies this?
• What are my values and interests in relation to asking this as a research question?

Most researchers begin with general topics and then clarify or narrow these to a few questions. A good way of doing this is to write down everything you can think of in relation to your topic. Then choose those ideas on which you want to focus and write a clearer statement of your research question. Once you have selected the issue of particular interest, reformulate it and revise it in the field. We have found that it is useful to broaden the research problem or topic again at the end of the research process as it helps to balance your overall understandings of the theoretical issues.

Substantive and theoretical questions

There are two categories of questions which researchers use—substantive and theoretical. Substantive questions focus on particular problems or issues in a specific setting such as nursing homes, schools, hospitals, and so on. Theoretical questions are those which relate specifically to conceptual categories such as deviance, social control, identity formation, group identification. A good research design is one which asks both questions. Also, as mentioned in chapter 1, the research problem or question in qualitative studies is usually flexible and open to change throughout the research process.

A manageable research question

A manageable research question is one that is clear, concise and answerable within the practical constraints imposed on the study. These include limited time and money and the ability of the researcher to maintain sanity throughout! But how do you make a research project manageable? There are no hard-and-fast rules. One useful way is to 'unpack' it and examine the assumptions underlying the asking of the question in the first place. For example, take the question, 'Does body image have an influence on eating habits?' You might ask yourself, why would we be interested in examining the relationship between body image and eating habits? The following statements are hypothetical answers:

- I have experienced bulimia and want to understand myself better.
- I am a psychologist working with anorexia nervosa sufferers and I want to know whether there is any real relationship between body image and eating habits.
- I am a feminist with theories about societal influences on women's health; and since it is predominantly women who suffer from eating disorders, I want to find out if body image influences behaviour. If this is the case, I want to find out where people get their ideas about bodies from.
- I am a nurse who wants to explore this commonly held assumption because I have worked with people who have a negative body image but do not suffer from eating disorders.

The implication one can draw from the given statements is that who you are will influence what assumptions you bring to the asking of the question and how you go about narrowing it down to a specific research project.

The research design should outline the initial aims and objectives of the project and give an indication of the methodology to be employed. The researcher should provide a preliminary indication of the theoretical concepts to be used. This includes their relationship to the research problem, and the methods employed to collect and analyse data. The research design should not be rigid but should be used as 'a base against which modifications can be made as the research continued' (Burgess 1984). After all, you may find, even with preparation work behind you (reviewing the literature, talking to informants socially), that your original research question is inappropriate and does not fit with the data 'on the ground'.

Sampling

The purpose of sampling, be it in qualitative or quantitative research, is to produce either a *sample* which is representative of a chosen *population* or which may 'illuminate a situation, get insight, or collect information about a particular event' (Wadsworth 1984, p. 14). Below are a set of terms used to define different forms of sampling.

Population sampling. The population refers to the entire set of people you intend to study. A sample is a subset of that population which is considered to be representative of it in some fashion. Population sampling strategies can be divided into two basic types, probability sampling and non-probability sampling. The difference between these two types of sampling can be explained as follows:

> In probability sampling every unit in the universe under study has the same calculable and non-zero possibility of being selected. Meanwhile with Non-Probability Sampling there is no means of estimating the probability of units being included in the sample. Indeed there is no guarantee that every element has a chance of being studied (Burgess 1984, p. 54).

Probability sampling. There are several forms that probability sampling can take. Some examples which are well known are random sampling and stratified random sampling. (For a detailed discussion see Bailey 1989 and Polgar & Thomas 1991.)

Random sampling is regarded as providing the most representative form of sampling, because the sample is chosen so that every member of the population being examined has the same probability of being included. You list all members of the population. Then, using some method such as dice or random number tables, you select your sample from the list of the population. The advantage of random sampling is that it provides a group that is representative of the population. The major disadvantage is that you need to be able to list every member of the population. In many clinical settings this is just not possible. Also, in many instances, the cost is prohibitive, being much more expensive than using readily available groups.

Stratified random sampling is a variation of random sampling in which quotas are filled rather than a random sample being taken right across the population. The advantages of stratified random sampling are that all the significant groups are proportionately represented and the exact representativeness of the sample is known. The disadvantages are again a prohibitive cost for a very small gain in accuracy and the need for a remarkably detailed amount of information about your population.

Non-probability sampling. There are a number of forms which non-probability sampling can take. These include: incidental sampling, quota sampling, snowball sampling and theoretical sampling. These are briefly discussed below.

Incidental sampling (also referred to as judgment, convenience or opportunistic sampling) involves the selection of people, actions or events at random. When a TV interviewer stops passers-by in the street and interviews them, that is incidental sampling. Replication is impossible.

Consecutive or quota sampling is an improvement to incidental sampling in that, if you were the TV interviewer standing on a street corner, you might keep on interviewing until you had interviewed forty-nine men and fifty-one women because those are the proportions of each sex in the population. The problem is that the fifty-one women you met would not necessarily be representative of all women in the community.

Snowball sampling relies on the researcher's knowledge of a social situation. This approach involves using a group of informants with whom the researcher has made initial contact and asking them to put the researcher in touch with people in their networks, then asking those people to be informants and in turn asking them to put the researcher in touch with people in their networks and so on as long as they fit the criteria for the research project.

Theoretical sampling is a process of data collection which is generated by, and is used to generate, theory. The researcher concurrently collects, codes and analyses his or her data. He or she then makes decisions about what further data should be collected in order to develop the emerging theory. This is explained in more detail in the following section.

Sampling in qualitative research

Qualitative research tends to rely mostly on the use of non-probability sampling, particularly snowball sampling and theoretical sampling. Burgess (1984) argues that in theoretical sampling, case data collection is essentially controlled by the developing and emerging theory. As it will be discussed further in detail, the researcher has to decide for what theoretical purpose the groups and sub-groups are used, and which groups or sub-groups are used in data collection. As he puts it, 'Theoretical sampling ... involves researchers in observing groups with a view to extending, modifying, developing and verifying theory' (Burgess 1984, p. 56). The term *saturation* when used in conjunction with theoretical sampling refers to a process where no additional data can be found that would add to the categories being developed and examined. That is, you have reached saturation level. It is this process that makes qualitative research systematic.

Let us provide an example. Aroni (1985) drew informants from both Jewish and non-Jewish day schools in the Melbourne metropolitan area in order to provide a comparison of the patterns of identification in their responses. The choice of metropolitan schools was made not simply for pragmatic reasons but in direct relation to demographic data. This showed that the majority of Victoria's Jewish population are urban dwellers congregating in enclaves within various suburbs of Melbourne. Only students from schools located within or close to these enclaves were approached. A major problem in the sampling procedure arose in deciding who was to be included as an informant (in the absence of agreement regarding objective criteria for determining who is Jewish in the modern context). Aroni decided that for the purposes of her research the only objective criterion designated was that of having a Jewish parent (not necessarily the mother as designated by Orthodox Jewish Law as this would exclude a number of individuals who subjectively perceive themselves to be Jewish).

In addition, identification of Jewish students in non-Jewish schools was a legal problem in two ways. Firstly, schools are prohibited from differentiating their students on grounds of religious criteria. Secondly, they are bound not to release certain information about students such as their home address and telephone number. To do so is regarded as infringement of privacy. The snowball technique of sampling was used to overcome this problem. Students at Jewish day schools were asked to introduce the researcher to their Jewish friends attending non-Jewish schools, where she did not already have initial contacts. It was also an attempt at gaining access to informants who did not publicly identify with being Jewish.

Applying the principles of theoretical sampling

As discussed in the previous section, the fundamental process of theoretical sampling requires selecting informants on the basis of relevant issues, categories and themes which emerge in the course of conducting the study. For this reason, sampling cannot be predetermined before entering the field. The process for selecting cases must allow for some degree of flexibility to enable the investigator to make the most of data which arise from the fieldwork. This suggests that sampling is cumulative and dependent upon categories which have been justified as relevant. Such categories are recognised by the researcher because 'they are repeatedly present or notably absent when comparing incident after incident' (Strauss & Corbin 1990, p. 177). For example, in the *analytical file* presented in chapter 10, the researcher's initial theoretical sampling model included a number of sampling categories which represented situations identified from the literature review as possibly influencing the practice of safe sex in young men who have sex with men (MSM). However, consistent with grounded theory (see chapter 11), the researcher revised the sampling model during the course of the data collection, and discusses the rationale for incorporating these changes in the analytical file. For instance, the researcher used the category 'connection to gay community' to recruit men who had different levels of involvement with the gay subculture, ranging from purely sexual through social and even political/cultural. Upon entering the field, the researcher found that sampling according to this category proved to be inadequate because the data suggested that it was not the level of involvement in the gay community that was influential for sexual safety. Instead, he replaced this category with 'sexual pathways' which included the various kinds of male-to-male sex culture that men become involved in (for example, the commercial gay scene and informal male-to-male-network), and how this culture was situated in relation to their social life (for example, central, peripheral or irrelevant). Theoretical sampling then covered the diversity of these pathways.

In theoretical sampling the objective is to identify the full range of possibilities which have proved to be theoretically relevant to the evolving data. This is why sampling in qualitative research is referred to as 'theoretical' sampling. Researchers can derive their samples by combining the following two case-selection procedures. Persons, places and situations can be purposefully selected (Category I types) because these have been identified as relevant categories in the literature. In addition, the researcher can fortuitously discover and recognise (Category II types) the analytical importance of an event, incident, place or situation emerging from the ongoing data, and add categories which represent these in the sample framework. Categories included in the sample can vary according to the characteristics of people, their beliefs, knowledge and attitudes, the social situations they find themselves in or their organisational contexts.

The process of selecting cases is guided by the search for contrasts, which are needed to clarify the analysis and identify emergent concepts or themes (Strauss 1987). Negative case analysis makes sampling in qualitative research rigorous and systematic. Locating negative cases allows the researcher to compare and test the propositions being put forward as the data evolves. Strauss and Corbin note that negative cases:

> denote not necessarily an error in our thinking but a possible variation. When a negative instance of action/interactions appears, it becomes very important to trace the line of conditions leading to it, in order to determine if this is failure or change in action/interaction (1990, p. 187).

A brief example of how theoretical sampling can be applied in qualitative research is now provided. Let us say that we are researching how older people construct their sexuality. The broad aims of the study are to:

1 explore the meaning of sexuality from a life-span perspective in order to better understand how older people construct and negotiate sexual expressions;
2 identify a typology of sexuality in later life that is grounded within personal and social contexts which includes, for example emotions, relationships, life experiences, interpretations of the self, and gender roles; and
3 understand the importance of physical and romantic sexual expression in later life.

A qualitative research design is chosen because we want to collect grounded contextual data on how older people give meaning to sexual intimacy and how such meanings unfold within the context of interpretations of the self. Qualitative methods are based on the premise that social reality exists as meaningful interaction created by individuals and is known through understanding the meanings people give to their human experiences. As discussed in chapter 1, this method is usually employed when the researcher is attempting to understand the phenomena under study in order to develop conceptual insights rather than test hypotheses.

The aim of the study is to account for differences in the meaning older people give to sexual expressions. This requires searching for a diverse sample of older people who hold particular characteristics and/or find themselves in social situations which may have some influence on the construction of the sexual self in later life. We have reviewed the literature on the specific topic of sexuality and older people, and the broader literature on sexual health and gerontology. The analysis of this literature has helped us to identify sampling categories which are conceptually relevant to the research questions asked in the study. For example, the sampling categories we will include in our model are gender, age, relationship status and reported level of sexual activity. The following rationale is provided:

Gender. Past research has shown that among older people, men and women attach different meanings to sex in their relationships (Traupmann, Eckels & Hatfield 1982). Research has also shown that men and women construct their sexuality and negotiate sexual expressions with their partners along different lines (Moore & Rosenthal 1992).

Age. Gerontological research has clearly demonstrated that within the category of 'old people' there are significant cohort differences, for example, in terms of health, availability of partner, attitudes and lifestyles (for a review see Minichiello, Browning & Aroni 1992). Not surprisingly, studies have reported some relationship between sexual activity and age. It would be important to contrast the views and perceptions of those who are 'young old', 'middle old' and 'old old'.

Relationship status. Previous research has shown that sexual activity in later life is partly dependent upon on the availability of a partner (Turner & Adams 1988) and contrasting the views of those currently in a sexual relationship with those who are not may reveal important insights into the social processes by which intimacy is given meaning.

Reported level of sexual activity. A number of patterns of sexual functioning in old age have been reported, ranging from decreasing to increasing sexual functioning (Turner & Adams 1988). This category has been chosen to provide a contrast between older people who have never had a sexual relationship with those who have, and a further contrast between those who have reported changes in their sexual functioning with those have maintained a stable pattern.

The particular dimensions for each category are specified. For the sampling category 'gender' the obvious dimensions are 'male' and 'female'. For 'relationship status' it might be 'currently in a sexual relationship' or 'currently not in a sexual relationship'.

These four categories represent purposefully selected cases. The informants reflect the characteristics described in each cell as shown in figure 8.1, for example, a 'young old' man (aged between 65 to 74) who is currently in a sexual relationship and reports an increase in sexual activity in later life. Using these categories the sample may provide a basis for comparing how older people are making sense of and interpreting their sexuality in later life. For example, the specific dimensions of reported level of sexual activity maximises opportunities for discovering how previous levels of sexual activity in life (and its associated reference point and expectations) may be influencing how older people interpret the importance and significance of sex now that they are older.

Several important points are worth noting here. First, the above theoretical sampling framework is not fixed. Rigidity in sampling would hinder theory generation. Consistent with the analytical induction method (see chapter 11), figure 8.1 is only a proposed sampling model. The model would be in the 'early days' of the project, and 'edited' as the researchers collect data which inform them about the validity of the sampling categories.

Several kinds of changes are likely to occur. The researchers may discover the analytical importance of Category II sampling categories (fortuitously identified in the data), which are currently not included in the model. For example, the data may reveal the significance of sexual identity in influencing sexual expression. We may want to interview people who identify themselves as heterosexual or homosexual. In

Theoretical sampling categories			
GENDER	AGE	RELATION-SHIP STATUS	REPORTED LEVEL OF SEXUAL ACTIVITY
Female	Old Old	Currently Not in a Sexual Relationship	Same
			Decrease
			Increase
		Currently in a Sexual Relationship	Same
			Decrease
			Increase
	Middle Old	Currently Not in a Sexual Relationship	Same
			Decrease
			Increase
		Currently in a Sexual Relationship	Same
			Decrease
			Increase
	Young Old	Currently Not in a Sexual Relationship	Same
			Decrease
			Increase
		Currently in a Sexual Relationship	Same
			Decrease
			Increase
Male	Old Old	Currently Not in a Sexual Relationship	Same
			Decrease
			Increase
		Currently in a Sexual Relationship	Same
			Decrease
			Increase
	Middle Old	Currently Not in a Sexual Relationship	Same
			Decrease
			Increase
		Currently in a Sexual Relationship	Same
			Decrease
			Increase
	Young Old	Currently Not in a Sexual Relationship	Same
			Decrease
			Increase
		Currently in a Sexual Relationship	Same
			Decrease
			Increase

Dimension of categories

Figure 8.1 Proposed sampling framework for the 'Older people and sexuality' study

addition, further into the fieldwork, analysis of the subsequently published literature may provide the researchers with the opportunity to further refine or modify Category I sampling categories (purposefully identified from the literature) and its dimensions (for example, to include 'never had a sexual relationship' to the category 'reported level of sexual activity').

Second, the informants represented in the sampling model exist in theoretical terms but they may not be found in the real world. For example, there may not be any older person who holds all of the following characteristics: an 'old old' (80 years and over) women who is currently in a sexual relationship and, prior to this relationship, did not have any sexual experiences. If such a person can not be located, the researcher may, of course, speculate as to why such persons do not exist or, if they do exist, consider and discuss the methodological issues associated with locating such informants. These discussions can inform the conceptualisation process of the study as they force the researcher to identify the boundaries of the research.

It should be obvious by now that in locating informants theoretical sampling requires detective work. A range of information sources will have to be identified and called upon, including existing data sets which provide information on the sampling categories; lists held by various agencies about people; or asking informants to nominate someone they believe 'fits' the designated characteristics the researcher has described to them. For example, sampling according to requirements of the theoretical sampling model described in figure 8.1 would be easier if an earlier survey had been conducted and provided information on older people's gender, age, reported level of sexuality activity, and current sexual relationship status.

The complexity of locating informants will depend, in part, on the kinds of sampling categories included in the model. For example, it is much easier to access sources which provide the researcher with information on the gender of informants than their particular beliefs and attitudes. Rarely do such lists exist, unless they have been collected in a previous survey or held by organisations, who may be cautious about releasing such confidential information. The snowballing method may offer a practical solution to identifying people who hold particular beliefs and attitudes. A word of caution is required here, however. Someone may refer to you a person that they think is 'conservative'. But definitions of conservative vary between people. People's definitions can not be taken for granted. The researcher needs to validate whether the informant does indeed represent the sampling category (that is, conservative).

Third, no theoretical sampling model will ever be exhaustive or complete. The researchers will have to place 'brackets' around what is possible. For example, it would be interesting to include in the sample Australian-born and non-Australian-born older people and investigate the influence of culture on sexuality. This additional sampling category would, however, increase our sample size. This may not be feasible given our resources, research aims and the time requirements to complete the study. The researcher could of course acknowledge the importance of culture on sexual expression in the conclusion section of the report. Decisions about sampling will be influenced by a combination of conceptual, methodological and practical considerations, and these have been described in general terms elsewhere in the book

Fourth, the sample size will be determined by the number of sampling categories and the dimensions of these categories. For example, the model presented in figure 8.1 will generate a total of thirty-six cases. The researcher may also wish to replicate cells in order to achieve, as discussed earlier, theoretical saturation of the category. By 'saturation', Strauss and Corbin (1990) mean until:

1 no new or relevant data seem to emerge regarding a category;
2 the category development is dense, in so far as all of the paradigm elements are accounted for, along with variation and process; and
3 the relationships between categories are well established and validated.

And finally, samples generated by theoretical sampling will never be representative of a particular population in a statistical sense. But statistical representativeness is not an objective of this sampling technique. Rather, theoretical sampling is purposely designed to allow the researcher to include variations identified as relevant to the study in terms of both preliminary assumptions and provisional findings. Informants are, however, representative in a colloquial sense. They illuminate important aspects of people's ideas and experiences which have general applicability to understanding the social phenomena under investigation. Strauss and Corbin summarise the purpose of theoretical sampling as a tool which assists the researcher to address the following questions:

> Is there evidence of this category's relevance? If so, what form or meaning does it take here? Is it the same or different from previous situations? What are its properties here? What conditions led up to it? What is the specific context? What intervening conditions have come into play to give this variations? (1990, p. 185).

Issues in sampling

Sample size is an issue which is often raised by researchers and students. In most qualitative research, the sample size tends to be small for a number of reasons. First, in-depth interviewing is time-intensive research. Unless there is a research team engaged in the project, it is very difficult for a single researcher to be involved in more than 100 long and complex social interactions. Second, there is a tendency for qualitative researchers to utilise theoretical sampling. This does not encourage large samples by its very nature (especially when linked with the concept of saturation).

Time and space sampling

The time/space dimension is one of the least discussed aspects of doing qualitative research. Where it has been discussed, it has been in relation to how much time the interviewer has available to complete a research project, how long it actually takes to complete it, and how that relates to a budget (Wadsworth 1984). The would-be in-depth interviewer is charged with several pragmatic concerns including arranging times with informants, not overtaxing their own or their informants' concentration span, and making a choice between doing longitudinal or *cross-sectional* (static comparison) *studies*.

It seems to be stating the obvious when one points out that social activity occurs in time and space but that 'neither have been incorporated into the centre of social theory; rather they are ordinarily treated more as environments' (Giddens 1979, p. 202). Nevertheless, the geo-political context may have some bearing on your choice of topic, access to informants, and the willingness of informants to trust you. For instance, in the case of Aroni's research, had she decided to do her research a year earlier perhaps she might have gained access to one of the schools using 'frontdoor methods'. Perhaps if she had conducted the interviews during the 1973 Middle East War the informants' perceptions of their Jewish-ness might have been different. Perhaps if she had decided to interview Year 11 students instead of Year 12, the students would not have been as willing to talk because they didn't need to create displacement activity to the same extent as those studying for final year high-school exams.

It is important to remember that informants are not 'cultural dopes' or 'clean slates' but rather individuals involved in everyday living. This includes a consciousness of relations to family and peer groups, exposure to media discussions and active participation in the historical context. In addition, it is important to remember that informants will have different activities occurring in relation to their own social rhythms. Thus, if you are interviewing people who are health professionals working in hos-pitals, they will be involved in the routines that are associated with such institutions and may be influenced by such, in their ability and desire to converse with you. For instance, if a person has just finished a long night shift, he or she may not be interested in, or capable of, engaging in an in-depth interview. In addition, if a hospital staff or nurses' strike has just been announced, the political climate may not be conducive for con-ducting interviews or for gaining access to informants.

The time and space dimensions of social reality lead one to consider the twin issues of selection of research location and selection of time. The space dimension is closely tied to the time dimension in that it forms part of the structures that individuals create and yet are restrained by. Growing up in Melbourne, or any other city for that matter, may play some part in the formation and reproduction of both informants' and researchers' world views.

The selection of research location is not always a matter of choice but is tied to the exigencies of the research project. It may be tied to access. *Gatekeepers* may have specified certain locations as available or unavailable to the researcher. The researcher may also be concerned about the physical comfort which can be attained in certain locations in order to put the informant at ease. For example, Aroni found that students did not wish to be interviewed at the school they attended as they regarded the school precincts as 'enemy' territory.

Longitudinal research

The selection of time varies according to the nature of the research project itself. There are some projects where the passage of time is significant to understanding the phenomena being researched. It provides 'the possibility of comparing changes in identifiable individuals over time and the possibility of meeting the criticism ... that ... (other studies) cannot identify who actually changes in some respect' (Bulmer 1979, p. 11).

Bulmer's description of longitudinal research design is a traditional explanation of its advantages over other forms of research labelled as static group comparison, single case study or the comparison of different populations at two points in time. However, if we examine Aroni's research, the advantage of using a longitudinal design was not only tied to the identification of who actually changes, but also to the understanding that 'the study of social activity involves the elapse of time just as that activity itself does' (Giddens 1979, p. 199). In addition, it must be pointed out that conducting a longitudinal study does not necessarily involve an expectation of social change (as implied by Bulmer's statement). Rather, it may be examining the continuity over time of the meanings and values informants attach to events, behaviours and attitudes. Thus, a longitudinal design allows the recognition and examination of patterns.

In this context, the longitudinal design also enables the investigation of time-space relations by following informants through cycles of social activity which are demarcated through 'time-geography (which) deals with the time-space choreography of individuals' existence over given time periods: the day, week, year or whole lifetime' (Giddens 1979, p. 205). Thus, in Aroni's research, the subjective meaning structures of the students typifying their Jewishness were examined in their relationship to the locale of the school. The term *locale* here refers to regionalisation on a time-space basis by which the 'aspects of ... settings ... are normatively implicated in systems of interaction, such that in some way they are "set apart", for certain individuals, or types of individuals' (Giddens 1982, p. 40). The informants are then followed through from the end of that episode in their lives through to alternate locales, regions and episodes (university, work, college or unemployment). Thus, the researcher is able to analyse the continuity or otherwise of the informants' meaning structures from one episode in their everyday living to another, by means of a longitudinal research design.

Gaining access ('getting in')

Once a sample has been decided upon, how does the researcher get people to agree to being interviewed? How do you gain permission and from whom? Which strategies are useful in seeking co-operation? How do you present yourself? How much detail or information about the research project do you disclose to the informant? Is your study an overt or covert one? Do you need to 'strike a research bargain'? Do you need to promise your informants anything in the research process or after it? To what extent does the manner in which you present yourself influence your ability to gain access to the informant and/or the setting? There are a number of discussions about the difficulties of gaining access to informants (Cohen & Taylor 1977; Pettigrew 1988; Spender 1988) but they do not provide adequate information regarding negotiation techniques for overcoming the problems nor who one negotiates with.

Gatekeepers

Gaining access is fundamentally an issue of getting permission to do in-depth interviewing. The question is, from whom do you need permission? If you are engaged in research with a small sample, such as in a life-story project, then it would be the informants who need to give permission. However, you may wish to interview patients in a hospital, school children, factory workers, or prisoners. These people as we have just identified are members of a bureaucratic hierarchy. In order to gain access to them you may confront what are known in the jargon as *gatekeepers*. Gatekeepers are 'those individuals in an organisation that have the power to withhold access to people or situations for the purposes of research' (Burgess 1984, p. 39).

The problems raised by asking permission from gatekeepers are related to how the researcher comes to be seen in the eyes of the informant. Burgess (1984) raises this issue in the context of researcher/informant relationships. Let us assume that you are interested in exploring factory hands' perceptions of their working lives. What credentials do you, the researcher, come with if you have to contact both the head of the firm and the shop floor steward in order to gain access to your informants? What sort of rapport and trust can you build if the initial contact with the factory worker is predicated on contact with those who have control over him or her? The inevitable question will be whose side are you on? Will the worker suffer or feel pressure to participate because they are fearful of the job consequences if they do not participate? In these circumstances, the researcher needs to clarify his or her position in order to establish a good relationship with the informant. Is the owner or manager of the factory acting as a sponsor of the research project? How much access will he or she have to any cassettes or notes of conversations? Answers to such questions have to be given before they are asked. Assurances need to be made.

Examples

One example where access was denied by gatekeepers was found in Aroni's (1985) research. In order to actually speak to informants, she used what are known as back-door or illegitimate measures to find her sample. She was denied access at the 'front door' by the gatekeepers, so the strategies she used involved going to other individuals in the organisational hierarchies and changing her sampling strategy to the snowball technique whenever she was confronted with poor or no access. Some prospective informants did not agree to participate because she did not have the appropriate credentials. That is, she did not have the school's 'blessing' and people wondered why she had been denied it. Others who did agree to participate did so on the understanding that if she did not have the school's blessing 'she must be okay' because she must have done something to 'buck the system'.

In Aroni's case, access was denied to the class lists of the school that was sponsoring another research project. The board members refused access. This presented a serious threat to the viability of her research as the school was, in enrolment terms, the largest Jewish school in the state. Most of the other schools (both Jewish and non-Jewish) agreed to allow access to student lists although some sent letters home to parents to request permission for names and addresses to be released. In other cases, the principals of the schools allowed senior staff to make the decision to grant access. Other principals refused to provide any class lists with Jewish students' names listed on the basis that this might be prejudicial or at least seen that way by parents, peer group or teaching fraternity. Other schools, particularly the Jewish ones, allowed Aroni access as she had 'insider status'. As a member of the Jewish community, she was regarded as 'friendly' toward the community and as not harbouring any sinister or ulterior motives. More will be said on this later in the chapter.

Another example is given by Burgess (1984) who interviewed school students while also being their part-time teacher. He comments on how his access to students increased because they negotiated interviewing times to coincide with unpopular classes in order to avoid those classes. He highlights that gaining access is not just access to informants, but also to print documents which might provide a broader understanding of the research environment and the informants.

Access needs to be clearly negotiated with all parties involved. Obviously, the research activities that occur during this part of the research process 'will influence the ways in which those who are to be researched define the research and the activities of the researcher' (Burgess 1984, p. 85). Once permission has been given by an informant, an agreement or a research bargain should be established between the researcher and the informant regarding the type of interviewing to be engaged in or the use of other research strategies, and how and when they will be employed (see chapter 10 for greater detail).

Leaving the field

Most qualitative methods texts refer, at least briefly, to 'leaving the field' when discussing various forms of ethnographic research, particularly participant observation. The problems of leaving the field for the researchers engaged in in-depth interviewing are much the same. It has been recognised that disengaging from the research context is a process rather than a single event. This process can have a significant impact on the informant/s, the researcher and possibly future researchers depending on how the process was orchestrated and carried out. The political and ethical aspects are obviously tied to the practical concerns of successfully leaving the field.

The researcher should realise that leave taking is inherently influenced by the manner in which he or she entered the field, the bargains they made throughout, and the nature of the social relationships that they had formed during the interviewing. In recognising these influences, the in-depth interviewer—whether engaged in eliciting a life history, a clinical interview or in any other form of in-depth interviewing—would have to face the knowledge that there is more to this process than their physical removal from the research setting. Emotional disengagement for both researcher and informant occurs. Much of the literature focuses on the hurt that might be experienced by the informant and provides details of how to extract oneself so as to cause the least amount of distress to the informant or the research community.

If we accept that in-depth interviewing necessitates establishing and maintaining a good rapport with informants then it should also be recognised that such a process is never devoid of some form of emotional commitment from both sides of the fence. If emotional commitment is a two-way process then emotional disengagement must also be such a process. Yet, very few researchers prepare themselves for exit, and even fewer report on the process when providing details of their project. It is usually in the reporting of life-history research (Liebow 1967; Whyte 1955) that there is discussion of the intimate relationships that exist between the researcher's academic and personal involvement with the informant/s (Altheide 1980). In these discussions, it is acknowledged that the pragmatic concern of finishing one's involvement with informants is a psychological and social problem as well as a tactical one.

There are at least three ways of leaving the field that have been suggested to researchers: withdraw gradually, withdraw by cutting relations quickly and completely, or do not ever withdraw entirely. For instance, that Aroni was a member of the community she studied meant, in many respects, she could never leave the field (Aroni 1985). The three options are tied to one's view of the research process. There are no natural or routine means by which one can end the researcher-informant relationship. The strategies employed vary with the setting or research context.

This aspect of research is not always as easy as it sounds. In the process of disengaging from the informants and the context, there are certain moral obligations which must be fulfilled, the most obvious being that the researcher should thank all participants in the process appropriately. Questions that the researcher should ask himself or herself are: Have all agreements been adhered to? Who benefits from the process and the publication of the research? The research process can be regarded as successful when the researcher can answer these questions with a sense of having sustained a position of personal and professional integrity in relation to the informants.

Pragmatic concerns

The pragmatic concern is with what is the most advantageous way of leaving the field. That is, to decide which process is going to enable the researcher to complete the research project successfully. Our interpretation of successfully includes maintaining access to informants during the analysis and writing-up stages so that the interviewer is not prohibited from obtaining any other critical data. After completing the task according to one's research design, totally distancing yourself from informants may disadvantage you if during a later stage you need to clarify some points. Successfully also means not disappointing, offending or distressing informants throughout the research. This includes the process of leave-taking so that if you, or some other researcher, wishes to engage in further research, you have not 'queered the pitch'.

To achieve these goals, the researcher can at the beginning of the process set a time frame so that both parties are prepared for a leave-taking to occur. If one has made promises, one should keep them.

Another strategy is to gradually break the routine that has been established. For instance, if you have completed the supposedly last interview, tell the informant that this is the formal end of the research but that you will maintain contact. Then gradually ease down the number and type of contacts so that hopefully the emotional and intellectual impact of the breaking down of the routine of the research process is not so great. Contact can then be maintained, or not, at a level which is negotiated between researcher and informant.

Alternatively, you may feel that setting up social distance and cutting relations totally and quickly is the most appropriate form of leave taking. You regard it as a clean break and as the mode of leaving the field which would provide the least possible future complications. Researchers using this approach have negotiated set time frames with informants at the beginning of the research process and have renegotiated them throughout so that when the last interview has taken place both parties expect a leave taking to occur. Obviously, if you wish to do follow-up research, or you are involved in a longitudinal study, then this would not be an appropriate approach to take. There are no rules. The pragmatics of leaving the field are directly tied to the foregoing research process, and the political and ethical stance the researcher has adopted in that process.

Objectivity

> Be a good craftsman. Avoid any rigid set of procedures. Above all seek to develop and use the sociological imagination. Avoid the fetishism of method and technique. Urge the rehabilitation of the unpretentious intellectual craftsman yourself. Let every man be his own theorist; let theory and method again become part of the practice of a craft (Mills 1959, p. 224).

Nearly every student entering introductory sociology courses would have heard the above quotation in Australian lecture theatres for at least the last twenty years. The underlying premise is a sound one. Mills is arguing for flexibility and creativity of thought. Nevertheless, the validity and reliability of qualitative research is often examined closely precisely because researchers try to carry out Mills' exhortation.

It has been argued that objectivity can be divided into two components: reliability and validity. Reliability is the extent to which a measurement procedure yields the same answer. Validity is the extent to which it gives the correct answer, or a finding is interpreted in correct ways (Kirk & Miller 1986). How are these concepts applied in qualitative research? As we pointed out in chapter 2, people often confuse the terms and cannot perceive how they are distinct and yet related notions.

Objectivity is a difficult concept to define because the term is used to refer to different ideas and is often used ambiguously. Usually it is used to describe the goal or aim of scientific investigation, that is, objective knowledge. The assumption underlying this usage is that objective knowledge is free of bias or prejudice. Abercrombie, Hill and Turner (1988) suggest that there are divisions of opinion as to whether objectivity or objective knowledge can be achieved. They also debate whether it is possible to be objective in social science research, and in particular qualitative research, using such strategies as in-depth interviewing. They present five arguments which have been advanced to say that social science research is not and cannot be objective:

1   Social science judgments are subjective, being coloured by the actors' own experiences.
2   All propositions are limited in their meaning to particular language contexts.
3   All social science theories are produced by, and limited to, particular social groups. Such a doctrine is often taken to be an outcome of the sociology of knowledge which treats all knowledge as a function of social location.
4   All observations are necessarily theory-laden.
5   In that all members of society have different values, social scientists will unconsciously, but necessarily, have their arguments influenced by their values (p. 170).

The significance of this approach to objectivity is that the arguments used to state that social science research is not objective can be applied to all forms of science (Kuhn 1970). Objectivity is an aim or goal which is not really an achievable one. In fact, many theorists (Fay 1980; Wadsworth 1984) argue that it is not necessarily desirable. The researcher should be critical and espouse particular values in an explicit fashion.

The second usage of the term (which is related to the first) is one which is generally acknowledged (Douglas 1971; Kirk & Miller 1986). The aim of objectivity in research is to be able to share knowledge. As Douglas points out, shareability is defined by members of the academic community who are interested in such knowledge. Truth (or what provisionally passes for truth at a particular time) is bounded by the tolerance of empirical reality and by the consensus of the scholarly community (Kirk & Miller 1986). If one takes this consensus into account then the objectivity of a piece of qualitative research can be examined and evaluated in terms of its validity and reliability.

Validity

In in-depth interviewing, the researcher tries to stay close to the empirical world in order to ensure a close fit between the data and what people actually say and do. According to Taylor and Bogdan (1984), this is attempted and achieved by calling things by the right names or being concerned with the validity or correctness of one's understanding of the informant's perceptions, view, attitudes and behaviours (see chapter 2).

Our ability to identify a perverse use of terms as perverse depends on the assumption that there is such a thing as calling things by their right names, and this in turn depends on the assumption that there is a common world and that language's relation to it is not wholly arbitrary (Graff 1979, p. 90).

The in-depth interviewer is constantly engaged in checking perception and understanding against a host of possible sources of error to draw tentative conclusions from his or her current understanding of the situation (Kirk & Miller 1986). Probing, cross-checking and recursive interviewing are forms of validity checking. When using these techniques, the interviewer will sooner or later discover the discrepancies in the informant's story.

Why are such discrepancies a matter of interest for the researcher? Interview statements should not be treated as accurate or distorted versions of reality. We would argue, along with Silverman (1985, p. 176), that interview data 'display cultural realities which are neither biased nor accurate but real'. The researcher's focus should be aimed at analysing the moral and cultural forms that are displayed as they can provide a rich source of data of how people 'account for both their troubles and good fortune' (p. 176). Therefore, bias and accuracy are still relevant issues. However, they should rather be seen as problems arising 'only in the analysis of data, not in the form or content of data (except in so far as participants are troubled by bias or accuracy)' (p. 176).

In-depth interviewing as a validity check

There are three types of error which are said to make research invalid. A *type one* error is believing a principle to be true when it is not. A *type two* error is rejecting a principle when in fact it is true. A *type three* error is asking the wrong question. The latter is the source of most validity errors in qualitative research (Kirk & Miller 1986). A wrong question is one which is not understood by the informant or is regarded by the informant as evidence of misunderstanding on the part of the researcher. Employing strategies to avoid asking the wrong question are vital to the in-depth interviewer. The use of multiple research methods is a commonly used strategy. If understanding derived from the asking of a question or series of questions in a conversation can survive 'the confrontation of a series of complementary methods of testing, it contains a degree of validity unattainable by one tested within the more constricted framework of a single method' (Kirk & Miller 1986, p. 30).

Research has external validity when it shows something that is 'true' beyond the narrow limits of the study. If the findings are appropriate and 'true' not just for the particular time, place and people in the study but are generally so, the research is regarded as externally valid. The only way that one can 'objectively' assess external validity is to see if the results can be repeated in another time and place with different people and procedures. The more variations in places, people and procedures a piece of research can withstand and still yield the same findings, the more externally valid the conclusions. External validity is similar to reliability.

The researcher can never be ultimately sure that he or she has understood all the meanings and cultural implications elicited in the in-depth interviews. However, as Kirk and Miller suggest, 'the sensitive, intelligent fieldworker armed with a good theoretical orientation and good rapport over a long period of time is the best check we can make' (1986, p. 32). Enhanced validity is one of the legitimations for the enhancing of rapport and building a good relationship with your informants in the face to face interaction of the in-depth interview.

Reliability

For a technique of data collection to be reliable, we must show that the research can be repeated or replicated. However, it is not often that researchers are rewarded for simply repeating research, either their own or someone else's. Replications are often regarded as less creative and interesting than new discoveries, and are more difficult to publish.

Research that repeats the ideas or concepts rather than the procedural details of previous studies serves two purposes. Firstly, it may provide some new discoveries about another set of events; and secondly, it can provide a conceptual replication of previous ideas. Exact replications of procedures and results demonstrate that the results are reliable. Conceptual replications of ideas and conclusions demonstrate that the research is externally valid.

Reliability in in-depth interviewing involves checking the strength of the data. The concern is whether or not, and under what conditions, the interviewer would expect to obtain the same finding if he or she tried to do the research again in the same way. The question to be asked, then, is how one assesses the reliability of research projects using in-depth interviewing as their primary method.

It is often pointed out that 'the claim to fame' of qualitative research is its ability to provide valid understandings of the meanings informants attach to behaviour, events, attitudes. It is also claimed that its major flaw is in providing and assessing reliability because of the difficulty of replicating such research. In order to reasonably assess reliability when using any research method, including in-depth interviewing, it is necessary for the researcher to document his or her procedure. This should be done in such a manner that any reader or prospective researcher can find details of how and why the researcher made certain decisions in the research process; their perceived impact on researcher and informant/s; how the data were collected (interviews only or personal documents in addition to in-depth interviews or multi-method use); and how they were analysed. Thus, the researcher provides a fully documented account of ethnographic decision making (Kirk & Miller 1986).

One way of improving the researcher's ability to provide an account which enables replication is to adopt a language for coding the scientific behaviour of the researcher. Kirk and Miller propose that in writing an account of the research process, interviewers (or rather, qualitative researchers or ethnographers as they refer to them) might wish to use their four-phase model of science to outline their procedures and processes. They argue that qualitative research is the same as all other forms of science. There is an invention phase in which the research question is decided and a research design developed; a discovery phase in which data are collected; an interpretation phase during which analysis and theory building occurs; and an explanation phase in which the entire research process is packaged for communication.

This approach is useful in aiding the interviewer to write a detailed and literate account of the research process to allow for an assessment of reliability. However, there is a limitation in using this model when a research project is based on in-depth interviewing. This is because attendant analytical processes occur throughout the project. It is not so easy to determine when a researcher is engaged in which phase. They might, when engaged in probing, be involved in both the discovery phase and the interpretation phase. It is essential that, as researchers, we acknowledge the non-linear nature of research. Analysis in research using in-depth interviewing does not occur in a neat ordered fashion immediately after the data gathering but in fact simultaneously with it.

Objectivity in selection of research problem

Let us assume that we have a certain piece of research in mind and, for ease of argument, let us assume, in this instance, that we are speaking of just one researcher. How did I come to choose this topic? What were the motivations? Is it chosen because I am studying research methods and I have been given a limited choice? Perhaps I have chosen to examine physiotherapists' attitudes to body image—their own and that of patients—because I have been treated by a physiotherapist, noticed some disparaging responses from her during treatment and wondered if it affected her ability to treat me. Or perhaps I've decided to interview nurses about their vision of the role of nursing because I have been politically active on behalf of my own union for twenty years. I want to know what might motivate nurses to be more or less involved in industrial action. On the other hand, I may be a sociologist, psychologist, or clinician who has been working in a particular field, and I wish to expand my knowledge of that field by conducting research. Even at this stage of the research process, that is, the choice of research area or topic, the decision is very rarely a detached, neutral, objective, value-free choice. As was discussed in chapter 5, the rationale, and/or motivation will inevitably be predicated on my world view, my life experiences, my age, ethnic background, gender, class and occupation. These factors are usually discussed as possible influences on researchers regarding their ability to ask questions appropriately. They are only fleetingly glossed over as factors focusing choice of research area.

'You can divorce your wife or abandon your child, but what can you do with yourself?'
'You can't banish the world if it's in you. Is that it, Joseph?'
'How can you? You have gone to its schools and seen its movies, listened to its radios, read its magazines. What if you declare you are alienated. You say you reject the Hollywood dream, the soap operas, the cheap thriller? The very denial implicates you' (Bellow 1973, p. 113).

This quotation makes it abundantly clear that human beings cannot escape the social world which they have not only socially constructed, but also internalised. The question that should be asked is should they feel that they need to, in order to be scientific? This is a methodological issue for the researcher. As previously stated in chapter 2, the concept of an objective, neutral, value-free stance has been arbitrarily agreed upon by some members of the community as a useful criterion by which to judge research as being within the domain of science.

Methodologies and methods are not constructed or chosen in isolation from ontological and epistemological positions. Rather, the manner in which we gain access to knowledge and our choice of the techniques for collecting evidence are directly related to our image of reality and the way we think we can know it. Obviously, our choice of research topic or question will be influenced by our world views or meaning systems.

The issue of objectivity within interpretive approaches to social science is a contentious one. There are those theorists who argue that when one has attempted to understand and interpret the actor's view of reality then one is in a position to give an objectively valid explanation of the nature of this socially constructed reality. On the other hand, there are theorists who argue that objectivity is not really possible. The researcher is simply another social actor interpreting and attributing meaning to the world through his or her interaction with others.

The researcher's account, even though it allows for a critical and professional understanding, does not necessarily provide a more objectively true account of society than the competing versions of others, whether they are social scientists or not. Therefore, the researcher's explanations and understandings, even of the topic, are subjective. The view put by some theorists such as Giddens is that the construction of social science explanations (in choice of topic, area, analysis and so on) is predicated on analysing a pre-interpreted world in which knowledgeable social actors create and reproduce frames of meaning in conditions not of their choosing (Giddens 1979, 1982). To be able to analyse social life, the researcher has to penetrate these frames of meaning using skills similar to those whose conduct or action he or she is attempting to understand. According to Giddens (1979, p. 145), the purpose of mediating these frames of meaning is 'to generate descriptions of them that are potentially available to those who have not directly participated in them'. The researcher is then able to reinterpret or transform these frames of meaning into 'the technical terminologies invented by social scientists' (Giddens 1982, p. 13). Subjectivity is almost a requirement for interpretive research such as in-depth interviewing. The notion of bias however is still there. After all, if one is a pro-nuclear activist, an anti-nuclear activist or a journalist, and wishes to interview members of a local community about their attitudes and understandings of nuclear energy, then whichever stance taken, one could still be accused of bias, irrespective of personal and professional integrity. The assumption is that all our understandings of the world are theory laden, and that this is something which must be accounted for in the research process. There are a number of ways of doing this. One can either take an explicitly political stance and state one's own position throughout the various stages of the research project, or one can state prior assumptions and understandings of the research area at only the writing-up stage and let the reader be the judge. The bias is inherent, it does not go away. It is simply counted in to the research process. Taylor and Bogdan (1984) suggest the option of critical self reflection, that is, examining one's own perspectives, logic and assumptions.

This methodological issue is raised before the researcher has made contact with the informant/s and is also tied to a number of other factors. These are: for what purpose is the research being undertaken, or, as Wadsworth (1984) puts it, for whom is the research? This is a question that is not dealt with in most introductory research methods text. There is usually a sharp division drawn between 'knowledge and the uses of knowledge, between questions in the philosophy of social science and those in political philosophy, between scientific activity and political activity, and between theory and practice' (Fay 1980, p. 12). What Fay is ultimately drawing our attention to is the 'role which values have as part of the conceptual framework which defines what it is to have real, that is, scientific knowledge about some phenomenon' (1980, p. 15).

If we accept a critical and interpretive framework and assume that there is an interrelationship between the actor's and the researcher's typifications and frames of meaning; and that social agents (human beings—both researchers and researched) are both knowledgeable and capable, then we are not simply engaged in an analysis of action, but are also implicitly taking a political stance. This is because we recognise that the findings of the social sciences can be understood and taken up by those to whose behaviour they refer and that this is integral to their very nature.

As Giddens notes:

> It is the hinge connecting two possible modes in which the social sciences connect
> to their involvement in society itself: as contributing to forms of exploitative
> domination, or as promoting emancipation (1982, p. 14).

Researcher bias?

This last point raises two methodological issues: firstly, the insider/out-
sider status of the researcher; and secondly, the time and space continuum
in which research takes place (examined earlier in this chapter).

Although there is now a growing literature on the effects of gender in
qualitative research (Oakley 1988; Roberts 1988)—and it is recognised
that a fieldworker's gender, age, prestige, expertise or ethnic identity may
limit or determine what he or she can accomplish—very little has been
written on the effects of ethnic identity in the field, especially in terms of
research strategies employed. We wish to elaborate on this particular
aspect of the interviewer's identity and image because it provides a good
example of the possible impact that the researcher's attributes may have
on the informant and his or her relationship with that researcher.

Even though much attention has been focused on the ethical problems
of minority or ethnic research, very little has been directed at the
methodological problems raised, and the techniques used have not been
modified to any degree. Also there is little written regarding the conditions
faced by ethnic scholars conducting research in ethnic communities.

An example: the insider–outsider controversy

The most commonly discussed methodological issue in research examining ethnic groups has focused on the 'insider–outsider' controversy (that
is, who should carry out such research?). It is argued on one side of the
debate that insiders have a special knowledge of their own group, that
they are 'endowed with special insight into matters necessarily obscure
to others, thus possessed of a penetrating discernment' (Merton 1972,
p. 11). On the other side, it is argued that 'unprejudiced knowledge about
groups is accessible only to non-members of those groups' (Zinn 1979,
p. 210). This controversy is also applicable to other social groups, such
as professions. Thus one could ask whether only nurses should research
nurses, or occupational therapists research occupational therapists, and
so on.

Merton's position paper on the sociology of knowledge was written as
a response to the view held by many black American scholars that white
researchers ought to be excluded from research in black communities (a
view which he considered elitist and exclusory). In this paper, he
concludes that the debate can be overcome if researchers take heed of his
plea for 'insiders and outsiders in the domain of knowledge [to] unite.
You have nothing to lose but your claims. You have a world of understanding to win' (Merton 1972, p. 44).

Obviously, Merton did not consider several important methodological and empirical issues which are directly related to the politics of the setting. One of these is the perception that members of the ethnic group (with minority status) might have of the research enterprise itself. Past studies, particularly in the USA, have revealed a hostility toward and distrust of researchers by the communities being investigated (Blauner & Wellman 1973; Moore 1973). In the case of Jews in Melbourne, a community suspicion of non-Jewish researchers exists (Aroni 1985). Merton's call for unity ignores the larger context of ethnic relations in which the research process is carried out. For instance, in the case of Aroni's study, the advantage of being an insider was that her 'credentials' were evaluated as acceptable because of past associations with members of various groups in the Jewish community. She was identified as politically non-threatening in the context of Jewish and non-Jewish relations in the public arena. It was assumed that she 'understood' the community and would not 'misinterpret' various practices and the meanings attached to them. However, within the Jewish community any investigations of Jewish day schools not sponsored by communal organisations was regarded as potentially threatening to their image. Even though she was an 'insider' in terms of the Jewish community, she was not an 'insider' as far as the administrators of one of the schools was concerned.

In considering the insider–outsider controversy in terms of entrance to the field, insider status can have advantages in gaining access to the field. Of course, by the same token, that status also has its limitations if one is not readily identified as being politically sympathetic toward the institutions under examination. Ethnic researchers conducting studies within their own communities may experience problems common to all researchers, as well as the dilemmas posed by their own ethnic identity.

The methodological issue inherent in the insider–outsider controversy focuses on who can provide more satisfying or better sociological knowledge. In discussing this issue, Zinn (1979) contends that it is the lens through which minority scholars see that enables them to ask questions and gather information others could not. A number of researchers believe that insider researchers pose different questions due to their insight into various nuances of behaviour which an outsider may interpret as merely typical of the entire sample under investigation (Blauner & Wellman 1973; Ellis & Orleans 1971; Valentine & Valentine 1970; Zinn 1979). Ellis and Orleans, in their discussion of 'race research' in America, argue:

> Undoubtedly, white social scientists are as capable of engaging in race research as their non-white colleagues even though their everyday experiences differ. However, because they come to the task with different backgrounds they are likely to see different problems and pose different questions. The intellectual and practical concerns may overlap, yet their analyses and recommendations will

almost necessarily differ insofar as these are tempered by differences in the individual sense of urgency and conception of the possible (1971, p. 18).

The view attached to this position is that traditional theoretical frameworks do not fit minority experiences. Insider researchers are more likely to challenge such frameworks due to their supposedly more attuned interpretation.

The most obvious objection voiced against this view is that the subjectivity of insider researchers 'will lead to bias in data gathering and interpretation' (Zinn 1979, p. 213). However, those who voice this objection assume that somehow the observations and interpretations of outsiders are value-free. This in turn implies that social science and/or natural science is based on a perspective which sees the logic of knowledge construction as being neutral. As has already been stated, if one accepts the view that all observation is theory-laden (following Feyerabend), it seems logically, and politically, impossible to accept such a view.

Making knowledge able to be shared is the goal and aim of objectivity and is defined by members of the academic community who are interested in the collection and use of such knowledge (Douglas 1971). The researcher needs to provide systematic evidence of the actual research methods used to collect and analyse data so that there is some possibility of replication. This is one means of acknowledging one's stance as a researcher who retains political and personal integrity by maintaining scientific reliability and credibility.

However, even though the ethnic researcher (insider) may be more attuned to the informant's meanings, this in itself could present a problem. The ethnic researcher (insider) must guard against assuming a taken-for-granted stance toward the informants' meanings, languages and concepts. The danger is that the researcher might not probe for details which may or may not indicate different interpretative schemes being used and/or relied upon by the informants. The assumption that an insider researcher is privileged in terms of 'in-group understanding' presupposes that the ethnic community is monolithic in nature and that there is little differentiation between various individuals' views on certain subjects. To retain the integrity of the phenomena, the ethnic researcher must attempt to straddle his or her insider's perspective with his or her outsider's stance.

An additional methodological problem is raised by doing research in one's own community. Once the existence of a research project becomes public knowledge in that community, it may or may not be considered that the degree of perceived political significance may impinge on the researcher's consciousness in a number of ways. Actual research strategies and methods need to be evaluated in terms of being appropriate within the political environment (which is also part of the process of the research project). For clarification and elaboration of this point, one can consider the impact of the political context of the Jewish community for Aroni as a researcher.

Apart from the work of Bullivant (1975), who was not regarded as an insider, most research conducted in Melbourne by Jewish social scientists examining issues of identification and/or education had relied on data elicited by the administration of a questionnaire. Bullivant's ethnography of the Yeshivah Boys' College was informed by a phenomenological and social anthropological methodology. It provided subsequent researchers (Aroni included) with sociologically useful and relevant material. However, the study raised much controversy within the Jewish community when it was published. The discussions centred on the claim that Bullivant's interpretations were derived not from proper scientific techniques but from his personal, subjective participation in school life as a teacher who was not an insider (and therefore whose ability to understand was curtailed by his status as ethnic outsider). The ethnographic mode of research was tarnished in the eyes of various members of the Jewish community because the results were evaluated as being ethnically based misinterpretations. Tied to this are the understandings, meanings and values various influential members of the Melbourne Jewish community have and hold regarding what constitutes valid knowledge upon which to base policy decisions. Their interpretations of validity (which will be discussed later) were influenced by their knowledge and experience of prior researchers in the area, most of whom opted for methods usually associated with positivistic methodologies. Apart from being professionally socialised in the positivist paradigm (most of them being 'trained' at the time when that paradigm in sociology was predominant), they were aware that facts and figures were what was required of them by communal policy-makers in order for their data and conclusions to be acceptable and used. In the case of Aroni's research project, the political implications due to the history of sociological inquiry in the Melbourne Jewish community influenced her choice of research strategy to include the administration of a questionnaire, even though in-depth interviewing remained the central strategy.

Obviously other factors were also involved in this choice, such as enabling comparability with previous research—thus partially satisfying the requirements of the academic sociological community as a *critical reference group*. If one accepts Merton's references to the 'corrupting influence of group loyalties upon the human understanding', the 'native' or 'insider' must somehow acquire distance in order to gain some objective perspective (Merton 1972). Heilman (1980) argues that the researcher's status becomes that of 'stranger', as Simmel (1894) defines it, and not that of outsider.

The conceptualisation of objectivity inherent in the stranger's role is tied to a distinct structure of opposites where there is an alteration between remoteness and nearness, indifference and involvement. Obviously, the issue is related to the negotiation of position of the researcher in constructing sociological explanations as both participant and researcher. What has to be taken into account is that such categories as insider, outsider, native and stranger, should not be conceived of as absolute, but rather as terms of type and of degree. By conducting in-depth interviewing, the researcher (particularly the 'native-as-stranger') is in a good position to access social cues and intended meanings which would not be accessible to more structured methods.

Bias: interviewer and informant relationships

To this point, we have discussed one example of how the interviewer's non-professional identities (that is, other than that of researcher) might infringe on the informant's perception of the researcher and the interview process altogether. There are a number of other perceptions that may influence or bias the informant's communication during the interview.

The background of the informant is something that he or she will inevitably bring in to the interview. When we are interviewed by someone, we do not suddenly discard the fact that we belong to a family, an ethnic and/or religious group and are members of a class or gender. We also see ourselves as being members of a particular age group, working in a particular occupation, and having a particular physiological status. We have all grown up in a particular time and place, in a particular group with a particular set of circumstances which we have experienced. This background comes with us into the in-depth interview. Obviously, not every role or group membership has 'potency or relevance' (Kadushin 1988) for developing or determining the informant's interaction/s in the interview situation. Rather, those roles, attitudes and beliefs which the informant has decided are most relevant and relate to the perceived purpose of the interview will be drawn upon. The perceived purpose of the interview can be what the interviewee interprets as being the reason that the researcher has engaged in the research process but it can also refer to the reason for the informant's participation in that process. This can range from simple curiosity through to a desire to portray oneself in a favourable light even if only in the eyes of a social researcher. Even though it is understood that interviewers can influence an informant's discussion, the reverse is also the case.

Informants can manipulate the researcher's interpretation and definition of the situation—just as the researcher can—by half answering questions, not answering them, or making misleading statements. This may be done for a variety of reasons ranging from trying to impress the researcher, to simply trying to control any social interaction in which he or she might engage. For instance, the informant may have perceived the researcher to be someone who holds a very strong feminist stance, and may then gear his or her communication with the researcher to take this into account. They may wish to portray themselves as sympathetic to such a stance and frame their language to fit in with it; or they may wish to antagonise the researcher by using overtly sexist language to illustrate their own non-adherence to or defiance of such a perspective.

How does the researcher deal with these intended and unintended consequences of the in-depth interview situation and their relationship with the informant? There have been a number of suggestions made in chapter 6 as to how to carry out the interviewing process in a manner which enables the researcher to gain as accurate an understanding of the informant's interpretations as possible. However, as we discuss in chapters 2 and 11, the process of analysis involves a great many decisions about the unit which you are examining and how you can examine it— are you analysing the words, the phrases, the stories or the beliefs and meanings the informant attaches to these when you are interpreting their communications with you? This issue is discussed in greater detail in chapter 11.

One way of dealing with these issues is to try and use different methods to cross-check information so that even though you are focusing on the subjective view of the informant, you take into account and examine what you regard as possible sources of bias in his or her account and your own analysis and interpretation.

Use of multiple research methods

In-depth interviewers are often confronted with problems of validity when they are asked what effect the interviewer's presence has on the informant's generation of data (that is, internal validity) and whether the data that are obtained in studying one situation can be generalised to another situation (external validity) (Burgess 1984). Many researchers advocate the use of *triangulation* which is also known as multiple strategies of field research or *mixed strategies* as a means of overcoming problems of validity and bias (Burgess 1984; Campbell & Fiske 1959; Phillips 1985; Webb et al. 1966). Triangulation refers to the combination of different techniques of collecting data in the study of the same phenomenon, and its most well known proponent is Denzin.

There are two reasons for the use of triangulation. Firstly, that the 'deficiencies of any one method can be overcome by combining methods and thus capitalising on their individual strengths' (Blaikie 1988, p. 1). Secondly, that it can be used to overcome the problems that stem from studies relying on 'a single theory, single method, single set of data and single investigation' (Burgess 1984, p. 144). All the advocates of this strategy only provide us with more variations on the same theme. It is regarded as a means of enhancing validity and decreasing possible bias.

Blaikie argues that triangulation is a metaphor that was originally drawn from surveying and that it is an inappropriate one for social science researchers. This is because in attempting to overcome problems of bias and validity 'the ontological and epistemological incompatibility of some methods is ignored' (1988, p. 7). In fact, Blaikie points to the fallacy of Denzin's arguments by asserting that 'he has abdicated the interpretivist concern for the primacy of meaning in favour of a positivist concern about validity and bias' (1988, p. 11). Blaikie is not the only critic of Denzin's lapse. Silverman also provides a very telling critique of the misuse of triangulation:

> to overcome partial views and present something like a complete picture. Underlying this suggestion is, ironically ... elements of a positivist frame of reference which assumes a single (undefined) reality and treats accounts as multiple mappings of this reality. Interestingly, Denzin talks about 'measuring the same unit' and quotes from a text which supports multiple methods within a logic of hypothesis testing. Conversely, from an interactionist position, one would not expect a defence of hypothesis-testing nor, more importantly, of social 'units' which exist in a single form despite their multiple definitions.
>
> For an interactionist ... without bias there would be no phenomenon. Consequently ... actions and accounts are 'situated'. The sociologist's role is not to adjudicate between participants competing versions but to understand the situated work that they do.
>
> Of course, this does not imply that the sociologist should avoid generating data in multiple ways ...The 'mistake' only arises in using data to adjudicate between accounts (1985, pp. 105–6).

The relevant point for qualitative researchers is the final one made by Silverman. There is nothing wrong with generating data in multiple ways. However, if one wishes to remain ontologically and epistemologically consistent, then one might conceivably use 'different methods in a time sequence stage in the research process' (Blaikie 1988, p. 15). Aroni does this by using a questionnaire to initiate data collection in her research on Jewish identity and schooling. The material drawn from the questionnaire was used as a 'bouncing off' point for her in-depth interviews. The questionnaire was the method used in the brief initiating phase of the research and the process of administering it personally was used as a means of establishing rapport prior to the interview. Informants were also offered access to their questionnaires and to the research results.

Chapter 9

Ethics and politics

There are a number of factors which must be clarified and reiterated in a chapter on ethics. The politics and ethics of social research should not be divorced from any part of the research process. Each decision that we, as researchers, make involves not only a practical or methodological component but also an ethical and political one, even if this is not immediately apparent. The interrelationship between these various elements of research is inevitable in the practice of research. The reasons we have separated these factors into distinct chapters are twofold. First, if we tried to capture the complex interrelationships on paper, then we would have no chapters or headings. This is because in the process of writing a book on in-depth interviewing, we would simply try to follow the intertwined complex relationships between theory, method, pragmatic issues and political and ethical concerns as they have occurred in the research process. This would be useful as an appendix or an accompanying volume providing a phenomenological account of in-depth interviewing, but in and of itself may not clarify the issues that are raised if one is planning to engage in in-depth interviewing for the first time. Second, we think it is important to highlight these issues as central to any research enterprise. As previously stated, the political and ethical factors inevitably influence the theoretical, methodological and practical choices that are made.

We are not providing a list of *do's* and *don'ts* because each researcher will have to decide those for him– or herself in relation to the context of the research. Rather, we hope that you can use and draw on our discussions to help make the decision-making process a little easier and more overt. The rest of the chapter will delineate the dimensions of politics and ethics as part of the researcher's explicit recognition of the impact of power on social relations—including the special social relations encountered in doing in-depth interviewing.

Each research process will engender its own ethical and political dilemmas. Research projects which are essentially based on in-depth interviewing may strike all the same possible ethical quandaries as other forms of research. The political context of the research can influence the nature of the ethical considerations brought to bear during the process. When we use the term political here, we include the politics of interpersonal relations, the politics of inter-group relations, the cultures and resources of research organisations—including universities, hospitals and other clinical settings, government and private research units and the power of the state. The politics of these contexts influence not only the outcomes of research projects, their design and implementation, but also what the researcher will perceive as presenting moral dilemmas. Obviously, what is implied in this discussion is that power relations are inherent in all social interaction including the social interactions that take place in research. The political domain is the usual arena in which power relations are played out either implicitly or explicitly. However, since the popularisation of the feminist dictum that 'the personal is political', it has become acceptable (at least in some circles) to recognise the power structures of interpersonal relationships ranging from the sexual to the clinical to the research relationship.

Let us raise another issue of significance at this point. Using in-depth interviewing and being faithful to the informants' perceptions is not a guarantee for producing a moral piece of research. Techniques can be used to provide data for immoral purposes, just as well as moral ones. The debate that has occurred in the literature on ethics has centred on the reasons for doing research, and whether these reasons 'fit' with an ethical world view. What constitutes an ethical world view is, in turn, tied to the ideology you espouse in the first place—which underpins your reasons for doing the research. Who decides what counts as an ethical world view? What is ethical about gaining knowledge for knowledge's sake? If you do openly partisan research, who is to decide whether you have chosen to be partisan to the group that has the moral high ground? Is it possible that competing groups can both have the moral high ground, and that it is not a matter of deciding who is right but of deciding between 'two rights'? Should we engage in participatory action research or opt for a more traditional research approach? Which is more ethical? Put more clearly:

> The liberal sciences accept the Baconian edict that those who best obey nature will in the end command it, or in other words, that an interest in practice is best served by a refusal to allow that interest to shape or influence the content or form of theory. According to the edict in the long run, the most effective strategy for improving or bettering anyone's condition is by not allowing one's interest in improvement to influence one's understanding of the nature of the condition. Participatory research rejects Bacon's edict and aims at a social theory based on a social practice (Root 1993, p. 143).

Recently, researcher's using different world views, such as feminist research and critical ethnic research, have opted for participatory action research models because they believe that such models by their re-distribution of power and control to the research 'subjects' produce more socially just and equitable research processes and outcomes. The assumptions such researchers make is that if the social sciences (and for that matter natural sciences) are not neutral, then the ethical and political question to be asked is *for whom* and not *whether* they should be partisan. Particular forms of feminist research (see Stanley & Wise 1983) operate on the principle that research focused on women is only relevant (read— ethically and politically viable) to women when they as subjects of research become equal co-researchers by 'having the say' over which questions are asked, how the research process is conducted, and that they benefit by participating in the process and utilising the results. The degree and range of participation varies from project to project but the under-lying assumptions remain the same.

Research conducted on, in and with ethnic groups usually raise ethical and political concerns related to two specific issues. The first, and most common, is tied to a critique of knowledge production, that is, 'an examination and perhaps revision of formal epistemologies, theories, methods, data interpretation styles, and patterns of knowledge dis-semination' (Stanfield 1994, p. 182). An example of such work is Anderson's (1994) commentary on ethics, health research and Aboriginal communities (discussed later in the chapter). The second critique is that little has been done to develop indigenous 'ethnic' models of qualitative research. Rather, we have produced an increase in the literature on how researchers who are members of dominant ethnic groups can be more sensitive in doing research in minority ethnic settings. This, of course, is seen politically and methodologically as a half measure and not having complete ethical and political integrity. (See Stanfield 1994 for a full discussion of these issues.)

Definitions

Ethics is the study of standards of conduct and moral judgment. In this context, the term is used to denote the system or code of morals we apply to the research process, be it as individuals and/or as members of a profession. Social research ethics involves the consideration of the moral implications of social science inquiry. There are three elements which are usually considered when examining research in terms of ethics and politics:

1 The morality of the practices used, and the personal and professional morality of the researcher who used them.
2 The integrity, both personal and professional, of the researcher.
3 Social justice in relation to the informant/s, the community, the profession and/or the society at large.

The central ethical and political questions that must be asked of any research programme are, 'Who is it for?' and 'What is it for?' (Wadsworth 1984) and how can the research be done so that the above-mentioned three elements are sustained?

There is a question which underscores all these elements and highlights their contentious nature. Who decides what counts as personal and professional morality, integrity and social justice in any circumstance, including research? The answer we give is that those individuals, groups or institutions who hold power are the ones who usually decide what counts. One might ask, 'but what of the moral viewpoint of the dis-empowered?'. We would contend that it is no less valid but is often less likely to be given due consideration. Power and control in social research are also specifically and inevitably raised in the social interaction between the interviewer and the informant. Figure 9.1 gives a brief suggestion of some of the ethical and political issues raised in research using in-depth interviewing. This is not an exhaustive list (see Punch 1986).

As mentioned in the previous chapter, choice of research topic and research design is influenced by who you are, what group you belong to and the allegiances you recognise, the socialisation processes that you have been involved in (both personally and professionally) and the social and political climate of the era.

Thus, if you grew up in Australia in the 1960s and 1970s, and studied social sciences in the 1980s during your nursing studies, then your choice of research topic and method would be influenced not only by your

Research processes	Ethical & political issues
Design of research project	• Is the researcher competent and capable of conducting research? That is, were they credited with professional integrity?
Sponsorship	• Does the researcher pay for the research, or is it some other group or institution? • Who benefits from the study? • Who has access to data and results? • How do you maintain confidentiality of informants if you are not the only 'owner' of the raw data (tapes/notes/transcripts, personal documents)?
Access	• Who controls the research process? • How ethical are the methods that the researcher is prepared to use to gain access to informants?
In-depth interviewing	• Who has control of the interactions? • Whose interpretation of the situation is accorded validity? • How is confidentiality maintained and trust developed? • What effects does the research have on the informant? • To what degree can the participants strike and keep a bargain? • If the researcher controls the recording process, is the informant's view of what should be recorded given equal weighting?
Analysis	• Who has control of storing of data and the maintaining of confidentiality? • Is the researcher's analysis 'keeping faith' with the informant's account?
Presentation of data	• What effect does the informant as audience have? • Who owns the research report—sponsor/s, researcher/s or informant/s? • What is the purpose of publication? • Who has control of publication and/or censorship of the report?

Figure 9.1 Idealised account of some ethical and political issues raised during research

personal background but also by the theoretical perspective you learned; your views as an individual and as a member of the nursing profession; and the exigencies of trying to complete a piece of research within a limited time period for a specific reading audience. This sentiment was stated much earlier by Max Weber (1958) in his essay 'Science as a Vocation', where he discusses the relationship between facts and values and their implications. Weber argued that all research is tainted to some degree by the values of the researcher. There is no such research as value free research. More recent formulations suggest that research cannot proceed unless it is driven by values which make problematic some situations (and not others) and thus lead to particular questions and drive fieldwork and analysis. In most Australian tertiary institutions and in most clinical settings, the research project would also have to be approved by the institutional ethics committee (more on this shortly).

Costs and benefits: a difference in values

The ethical and political questions raised in the choice of topic and the design of research revolve around weighing the potential benefits of asking the research question against the anticipated costs. This is of necessity a subjective assessment of two sets of values. One value or right is that of the social scientist to inquire, to gain knowledge and to advance scientific theory. The social scientist hopes to advance knowledge which will be of practical value to society and the research participants (Kidder 1981). The other value, or right, is that of the informant to maintain privacy, dignity, and self-determination (Kidder 1981). As Kidder points out:

> A discussion not to conduct a planned research project limits the first of these rights. A decision to conduct the research despite its questionable practices with research participants limits the second (p. 308).

Ethical absolutist or situational relativist?

The researcher can be an *ethical absolutist* or a *situational relativist* in dealing with ethical and moral dilemmas in the research process. The ethical absolutist position is one in which researchers want to establish specific principles to guide all social research. Such principles are often developed and devised into a professional code of ethics which is to be adhered to by all members of the profession.

The situational relativist holds that there can be no absolute principles of ethical research behaviour or absolute guidelines. They argue that the social science researcher is faced with the same ethical and moral issues that he or she confronts in everyday life and has to handle them both in the same way. That is, they have to come to an ethical decision according to their individual interpretation of the situation at hand. Ethics are up to the individual's conscience.

There are advantages and disadvantages in taking either stance. If social science researchers hold to the absolutist position, then there is some form of collective responsibility which helps to prevent individual researchers besmirching the integrity of all researchers. On the other hand, the use of a formalised code of ethics may produce social research which is unadventurous and sterile. Researchers may be too confined to ask useful and creative questions which overstep guidelines.

The option that seems to take into account the informant, the researcher, and future potential researchers is the one where the professional body representing the discipline devises a set of guidelines or a code of ethics which still empowers the researcher to make appropriate personal ethical choices in the context of the research process itself.

Let us now examine how discipline-devised codes of ethics are constructed and operate within the wider community. Academics and other professional researchers are still members of the wider society in which they exist and work. They are subject to all the social pressures, ideologies and influences that the rest of us are. It is inevitable that the discipline-based codes of ethics will incorporate some comprehension and accommodation of ideologies, social pressures and influences that are external to (but often concomitant with) professional understandings and requirements for 'integrity-based' research.

The way this occurs in practice in Australia is that researchers become aware of ethical and political dilemmas in doing their own research and then come together with colleagues in national and international fora, discuss issues and then construct regulatory statements. Such regulatory statements are designed to protect the research practitioners, the research participants and the research process itself. Often, such statements need to 'fit in' with prior models of ethics codes, such as those developed in the health sphere. Most Western post-World War II codes of ethics are written with the Nuremberg Code and the Declaration of Helsinki as their historical backdrop. These statements were written as a response to the Nazi experiments on humans which were conducted with no respect for human life or dignity.

In Australia, the National Health and Medical Research Council (NH&MRC) has operated as the provider of a benchmark statement on research ethics. The NH&MRC 'Statement on Human Experimentation and Supplementary Notes', in conjunction with the NH&MRC subcommittee, the Australian Health Ethics Committee, have outlined and influenced (both in interpretative and structural terms) the ethical and operational principles guiding institutional ethics committees (IECs). The principles outlined in the statement are used to assess whether proposed research projects are 'ethically acceptable'. Whether a research project is ethically acceptable and conforms to the standards outlined and implied in the Statement is monitored by IECs. Current debates in this arena have focused on whether such guidelines sufficiently recognise and deal with 'the risks of breaches of confidentiality' and the potential for research projects to cause 'social harm' due to their origins in the field of medicine and health (see Foddy 1994 for an outline of this debate in an Australian research setting). Another area of contention has been the way in which research projects are assessed in terms of methodology, ideology and 'fit' with international, national, local and/or institutional research policies.

Institutional ethics committees (IECs)

Discussions of research ethics have usually focused on the impact of the practices of the research process on the informants and the integrity of the individual researcher in 'maintaining faith' with the informants There has been little written on the impact of, discipline-located (for example, sociology or philosophy), institutional (for example, hospital or university), local (for example, Melbourne), national (Australian) and/or international research policy as a direct influence on research ethics. Research policy, whatever its origin, is important because it provides the social, political and ethical framework within which research is carried out. Sometimes these groups are in conflict, either with one another's perceptions of what constitutes a good research policy; or with individual's desires to engage in research which does not fall within the parameters set by the research policy. Little is known of the impacts of these differing viewpoints on the ethical and practical choices made by individual researchers. Most of the data we have on this is anecdotal. Nevertheless, the ethical and political questions must be asked. Is the research policy or its direction unethical? How do research policies influence the individual researcher in choice of research topic, or for that matter in choosing to do research at all. For example, in the health sphere, the process of undertaking research 'could in itself constitute a moral obligation' as in the case of clinicians in order that they fulfil a moral obligation to patients to 'improve the scientific quality of their clinical decisions, improve communication, rapport with patients and empathic understanding of illness' (McDonald 1994, p. 112).

On the other hand, a government directive to fund research which is politically or economically prioritised may mean that researchers have to choose whether to apply for funding in these approved areas (which may or may not be consistent with their personal and professional ethics in terms of the choice of subject matter, the conceptual focus and framework to be adopted); or to choose professional obscurity by not applying for the funds. This issue is particularly relevant in terms of the research culture that has developed in Australia since 'Dawkinism'. There is a tendency to assume that if the research that you are doing is unfunded and/or not for a degree, then it cannot be 'real' or 'important' research. After all, if it was not funded then was it a question of an unethical proposal, an inadequate research design, not a priority area, or the use of an inappropriate sampling frame? The construction of research policy in these terms has led to a reconfiguration of the intellectual, and subsequently, ethical landscape. In fact, the moral legitimacy and technical adequacy of proposed research projects are assessed and judged by the ethos of state-defined economic rationalism. This brings us to the nature and role of institutional ethics committees.

The problems of double standards in relation to acceptance or otherwise of research projects with methodologies differing from those favoured or understood by IECs members, the lack of uniformity in ethical decision-making across IECs, the relationship between ethical and scientific merit and ethics in general and IECs in particular, now form the backdrop against which this dispute is being played. Research and the issue of research ethics in the health sphere have made these concerns clear. The nature, composition and role of international, national and local educational, tertiary and hospital or clinical IECs are influenced by the history of their evolution and, in turn, influence the ethical issues which are raised in these contexts regarding research.

Almost all research must receive the approval of an institutional ethics committee before participants can be approached. However, approval from one of these committees does not guarantee that research will be conducted in an ethical manner for two reasons. The first is that even though there may be a committee whose responsibility it is to monitor research practice, the members of such a committee may not agree on ethical values and research models. Secondly, the applicant for approval may disagree with the committee's concept of ethical research. Some IECs chairpersons may have strong ideological commitments to particular forms of research, for example, collaborative, and may be less approving of other approaches. The workings of IECs raise a whole host of ethical and political concerns which cannot be properly examined in this book except to say that in their role as official gatekeepers they will increasingly influence the type of research that will take place.

Power and control: who and what is it for?

A significant part of your choice of topic is working out what it is you actually want to find out. This is, to begin with, a practical problem but it is tied to two questions: 'What are my values and interests in choosing this topic?'; 'Who and what is the choice of this research project for?'. The identification of who and what the research is for is crucial for any research undertaking.

These questions, 'What is the research for?' and 'Who is it for?', are interdependent and have an impact on the research design. Who is the 'critical reference group?' (Wadsworth 1991). What are its interests according to its members? Is the research area, topic or group being chosen to provide the researcher with increased status in the academic community by being able to complete a PhD? Does the researcher wish to provide the group being researched with some information which may empower them in the political arena? Is the researcher trying to achieve both aims? Or is the researcher employed by other interested parties or groups such as universities, foundations, charitable institutions, government bodies, unions, etc. where the critical reference group is the employing body?

Wadsworth (1984) clarifies this issue in her discussion of reference groups. She points out that, in answering these questions, the researcher needs to understand that the 'who' and 'what' research is for, will be tied to the research design, practice, ethical stance and what the researcher does with the results once the research is completed. She identifies four conceptual possible answers to the question of 'who': 'the researcher or researchers, those the research is for (to help meet their interests, solve their problems); the researched and those who may need to be convinced by the research (such as funders or managers)' (1984, p. 8). She argues for the privileging of those who the research is ultimately meant to benefit and calls them the critical reference group. She also notes that it 'is important where you as the researcher/s are located in terms of these four groups' (p. 8).

There is a form of research known as 'action research' which is said to be done to aid those being researched. Action research is 'the way groups of people can organise the conditions under which they can learn from their own experience' (McTaggart 1989, p. 170). This brings us back to the audience for the research and the issue of access and sponsorship. This audience may include a range of reference groups such PhD examiners and other sociologists, psychologists and/or clinicians, the people who were the informants, the people who you wish to influence by doing the research and/or the general public. In Wadsworth's terms, the critical reference group would be the ultimate beneficiaries of the PhD findings. For example, if you were researching caregiving for people with Alzheimer's disease, then those suffering the disease who are meant to benefit from the care might be the critical reference group. Others believe that all the reference groups mentioned in the list above constitute critical reference groups, because their theoretical and methodological perspectives differ in terms of the research rationale and they are all 'critical' reference groups for the researcher.

An example: history of a process

Let us examine the initial stages of Aroni's (1985) study as an example of our discussion to date. She had decided on a research question after hearing an issue discussed at many dinner-table conversations among her peer group. In the Jewish community of Melbourne (of which she was a member), there were many assumptions made regarding the impact of schooling—just as in the general community there is a belief that schooling makes a difference. However, the precise nature of the effects of schooling was a debated issue. Jewish communal leaders, teachers and parents commented on the rise in the assimilation and intermarriage rates of Jews into the surrounding non-Jewish society. They assumed that if their children attended Jewish day schools then this might prevent or at least slow down the rate—by inculcating Jewish children with Jewish values the schools would instil Jewish identity. They felt that this was the task of the school, just as they felt it was the task of the school to provide the students with an education that would enable them to succeed in the majority culture while retaining their own ethnicity and religious identity.

Aroni noted that the majority of the comments were made by concerned Jewish adults—either parents, teachers, communal leaders and/or Jewish social researchers—and not by those who were directly affected by the results of decisions regarding Jewish schooling in Melbourne, namely, the students. The purpose of Aroni's research was to examine if, in the view of the Jewish students, attending or not attending a Jewish day school had any impact on their sense of Jewishness in terms of identification and/or personal identity. If so, in what manner and to what degree; and if not, what other factors did they evaluate as significant?

From the perspective of the researcher, the study had four critical reference groups: members of the Jewish community who participated as informants; those Melbourne Jews who are involved in forming the Jewish schools' educational policy; the academic community of sociologists; and the researcher herself. All these groups influenced the researcher, not only from the point of view of ethical commitments, but also in terms of methodological stance and choice of research techniques and strategy. She herself shared the values and interests of some members of the Jewish community. These values and interests included the perpetuation of a strong, viable and committed Jewish community in Melbourne. However, she also shared the values and interests of the academic community of sociologists. This meant that she had to display personal and professional integrity not only to the group which was being researched but to the group which would critically examine the research from an alternative perspective. The questions of bias and objectivity are again raised here as issues of personal and professional morality and integrity, not simply as concerns of methodology. We raise them as issues of critical awareness, honesty of examination and evaluation versus dishonesty and fraud (and not in terms of the subjectivity of value commitment). After all, what else but emotional commitment and engagement enables you to sustain the effort required to complete a research project? What stimulates that commitment we leave open to your imagination.

When reading reports of research, the reader is heavily reliant on the integrity of the researcher in terms of detailing the nature and number of interviews, the data analysis process and the criteria for the selections included in the research report. Usually the personal logs and diaries of the researcher are not available, the interviews are not always quoted at length and the reasons for selecting and specifying particular quotes and incidents are not articulated (Punch 1986; van Maanen 1988). The reader then depends on the academic integrity of the researcher:

> in coming clean not only on the nature of his data, how and where it was collected, how reliable and valid he thinks it is, and what successive inter- pretations he had placed on it—but also on the nature of his relationship with the field setting and with the 'subjects' of the inquiry (Punch 1986, p. 15).

The researcher needs to maintain his or her personal and professional integrity by establishing competence in choice of research topic, research design, and conduct of the research project and what to do with the results. This involves establishing credibility in the eyes of the critical reference group/s. In the case of the academic community and the Jewish community, Aroni's research design needed to state her personal com- mitments so that they could be taken into account by anyone assessing the research project.

Race, ethnicity and research ethics in the 1990s

Another issue of ethical concern in terms of choice of research area, design and who the research is for, is the politically and ethically fraught arena of race relations. The most obvious example in the Australian context is that of the relationship between the Aboriginal and white communities. An issue which needs to be addressed is: does the asking of the research question itself cause harm to a particular group? So again we ask who is the research for? For example, it has been argued that much of the recent interest in doing research focusing on the health of Aboriginal people is in fact part of a shift 'from a predominantly assimilationist form of colonialism into welfare colonialism' (Anderson 1994, p. 91). Anderson contends that since the creation of an Aboriginal primary health system, there has been an increased and increasing tendency for academics to define Aboriginal health problems rather than actively taking into account local Aboriginal communities' under- standings of what their health needs are. As a researcher, your sensitivity to the concerns of the particular group you choose to focus your research on may not be an ethically adequate or appropriate position to take. This is especially the case when the historical circumstances indicate that the inequities between the racial and/or ethnic groups are of such significance (as in the case of the Aboriginal and white communities in Australia) that the research enterprise is itself morally flawed. This is due to its potential and/or actual exploitation of a community by the researcher. The evidence suggests that the published research on Aboriginal health does not fit or match with the perceived health needs of the different Ab- original communities in Australia (Lake 1992). Utility and ethics are obviously intertwined in this context.

The National Aboriginal and Islander Health Organisation (NAIHO), in conjunction with the National Health and Medical Research Council (NH&MRC), developed a set of guidelines on ethical issues for research in indigenous Australian communities (NH&MRC 1991). This was in response to a formal clarification and outlining of what constituted 'priority issues' in health research for Aboriginal communities (see the National Aboriginal Health Strategy (Commonwealth of Australia 1989) for details of these priorities). Ethical implications were also raised as part of this statement. Aboriginal and Torres Strait Islander controlled organisations have also set up their own ethics committees and some states have developed their own research guidelines (Maddocks 1992).

If you examine the NAIHO/NH&MRC guidelines, it is clear that they constitute a framework designed specifically to protect Aboriginal people from exploitation by researchers. According to Anderson (1994), the guidelines include principles which are intended to govern processes of ongoing consultation and negotiation with Aboriginal communities in terms of having opportunities to make informed assessments of research proposals, participate in the research process, be paid for resources and make decisions regarding the ownership and publication of data. In this case, it has been seen as important, first by Aboriginal communities, and subsequently by the academic community, to formalise the research relationship because of the wider social and political context. Anderson's lucid discussion of the ethical concerns of health research with Aboriginal communities applies equally to any other substantive area of research. The significant issue raised in his discussion of what he terms 'the ethics of utility' (assessment of the project's benefit) and 'the ethics of exploitation' (the power differential inherent in the relations between the researcher and community, intended or not) is whether the research projects and the strategies they wish to employ ultimately benefit or harm the communities.

Another ethical, and concomitantly technical concern that needs to be considered is your moral position when you are a member of the group that you are researching (see chapter 8 for a more detailed discussion). If you are a member of the group that you are researching, then determining the values and interests of the group beforehand may be easier. However, it is important to remember when interviewing members of your own group that such entities are not homogeneous. All members do not necessarily have the same views or values. As the researcher, initially you may need to examine how interests, views, ideas, etc. come to be shared (or not); to identify who shares the interests and who the research is intended to serve.

The clinical interview: who and what is it for?

The ethical considerations that are pertinent to in-depth interviewing in non-clinical settings are equally significant in the clinical setting. It is quite clear that in the case of the clinical interview, the nature of the clinical contract with the patient, that is, one of a duty of care, takes moral and ethical precedence over any other concern. However, in the clinical setting the in-depth interview in the form of a diagnostic taking of history or a therapy session is inevitably made up of 'a continuous series of ethical events each of infinitesimal dimension and often inconspicuous to the participants'. This is what Komesaroff (1994, p. 26) calls the 'microethical structure' of the clinical relationship. He argues, and we agree, that in the typical flow of conversation (the interview) the clinician is constantly dealing with the ethical decision 'What should I do?'. What he then describes is very much like the reflexive processes engaged in recursive interviewing (see chapters 4 and 5). The following questions are provided as examples of the typical self-talk engaged in by clinicians in the course of a clinical interview. 'How ... should I ask this difficult or potentially intrusive question? ... How should I express the diagnosis of lung cancer to this elderly woman?' (Komesaroff 1994, p. 26). The significance of this process in the clinical interview is that these self-talk questions occur constantly, require immediate, continuous ethical decision-making and have a direct bearing on clinical outcomes. This is because it is through such inter-subjective processes that moral actions actually take place. In terms of the everyday language of clinical life these ethical quandaries are resolved in the in-depth interview process of conversational response and counter response.

Each verbal or physical response occurs as an ethical decision. Komesaroff contends that the clinician's responses can take the form of either 'a particular choice of words or manner of delivering those words, or it may be embodied in the pitch of the voice, the length of the pause or the softness of touch' (Komesaroff 1994, p. 26). Whichever form this ethical decision-making process takes, the patient or client inevitably responds and the clinician in turn continues to respond to that response. The microethical decision-making process is part and parcel of the model of diagnostic interviewing that the consumer lauds as 'good care'. It is experienced as good care precisely because the ethical decisions were incorporated in the reciprocity (give and take) of the social interaction that constitutes the interview. In addition, this microethical decision-making is tied to the wider context of the social, political and cultural structures within which clinical interactions are set. For example, a paediatrician may discuss the options of treatment and care of a severely physically handicapped and brain-damaged newborn with the parents of that infant. In the interview process it becomes clear to this clinician that neither parent is able to cope with the situation. He or she engages in that self-talk of 'Should I introduce the idea of euthanasia and how should I do it? It is illegal, but in this instance would it be the morally appropriate decision to make for all parties concerned? What are the consequences for all of us if I make this suggestion (however I frame it)?'.

In the ethical arena of the wider social and political context the practice of active euthanasia in Australia is illegal and the clinician is fully aware of the legal consequences of making the ethical decision to speak on this subject and act on the responses of the parents. The microethical domain is intertwined with the wider social and political context—called the 'global ethical level' by Komesaroff (1994, p. 26)—in an overt manner in this example . However, in many instances the connections are not quite as transparent. It is in those cases that the clinician engaged in microethical decision-making may encounter ethical dilemmas which cannot easily be solved in the conversational interchange of the clinical interview.

There are two other major ethical issues of concern in the clinical setting. First, should one interview those who are physically or mentally ill, or who are engaged in therapy at all? Second, should one use data drawn from clinical interviews, when the participants are long gone from the scene and your research interest is not directly tied to an exploration of their perspective? The issues are tied to the question of whether one is potentially causing harm, versus obtaining knowledge which would be beneficial to future patients or clients in these settings or the participants themselves. The timing of interviews in such settings is also an issue of ethical concern. The other concern is also an issue of consent. We argue that in all research each case needs to be weighed individually with regard to the impact of agreement on the proposed participant. Impact can go well beyond the formal completion of the research project.

Sponsorship

Who initiated the research project? Was it the researcher? The group being interviewed? Or another interested party such as a government research body or private industry? How can this affect the research project?

Discussions of this issue usually refer to the impact of sponsorship on researchers' conduct, loyalties and understandings of why they do research. As Roberts (1988, p. 201) so succinctly put it, 'To whom does our primary duty as researchers lie and how can we maximise the effectiveness of the work we do?'. Does our loyalty go to those being interviewed or those who commissioned and funded the research project (assuming that they are not the same)?

If we return to our earlier example of Aroni's research, we can see some of the problems raised by sponsorship of research. One of the members of the governing body of one of the Jewish day schools had sponsored another researcher to investigate almost exactly the same research question. Aroni discovered this and discussed two issues with her supervisor. First, did it matter if there was more than one research project examining similar issues and dealing with the same informants, and, secondly, would it be appropriate to join the research team that was being employed by a member of the school board?

These questions were discussed in terms of whether another researcher would 'spoil the field', that is, make it difficult for future researchers such as Aroni to interact with informants (who were already jaded by participating in a research project, particularly one dealing with similar issues). By joining a research team paid for by a member of the school board, what sort of control would each team member have in deciding the research strategies to be employed and the mode of analysis to be used?

To what use would the research be put, and how would the time and manner of the publication of results be influenced? Would there be problems with the sponsor if some or all the analysis was unfavourable to his or her school and, if so, would there by any attempts to suppress data? Aroni, in conjunction with her supervisor, decided that the independence of her research might be threatened—independence was a critical factor in the assessment of doctoral dissertations—and that the costs both ethically and methodologically were too great. She decided to make contact with the informants without the backing of the other parties in the field. After informing them of her decisions to go it alone she discovered what the term gatekeepers meant! This brings us to the political and ethical concerns of gaining access to the population which you wish to study.

Gaining access and informed consent

What sort of methods are you prepared to use to gain access to your informants? Will you be overt or covert in your approach? How ethical are these methods particularly when your research is jeopardised by intransigent gatekeepers? Are you prepared to use back-door methods? How do you decide if the end justifies the means? What if the gatekeepers are in 'the right' and safeguarding some people from harm?

Access and acceptance are critical to in-depth interviewing (as they are to any form of research). For instance, the reputation of one's institutional affiliation can influence access in either a positive or negative fashion. If you are a researcher who has presented documentation and credentials establishing your project as being carried out under the auspices of a prestigious university, you are more likely to gain access to informants than someone who simply knocks on the front door and introduces himself or herself as a student who wants to ask about attitudes to euthanasia. However, in some settings, certain credentials, including academic ones, may be irrelevant or harmful. You may be investigating attitudes to euthanasia with predominantly devout Catholic informants. They may know that the head of department who has authorised your research and signed your letter of introduction is well known for his or her humanist views. They might not be happy to participate in a study that was associated with this individual. In this case, the research would be influenced by being seen as an extension of the academic sponsor. The politics of the social context will have determined the prospective informant's perspective of the researcher's integrity and ethical stance.

The term informed consent is drawn from the medical sciences where there is a possibility that actual physical harm can be done to participants and patient's rights can be violated. It is important to acknowledge this background because the attempts that have been made to control biomedical research and protect patients is the model upon which social science has based its codes of ethics in relation to informant participation and protection. It has been pointed out that we attempt to protect the rights of vulnerable groups (children, the aged, prisoners, the institutionally confined mentally ill, etc.) because their rights have been violated in past research, particularly in biomedical research (Punch 1986). Professional and ethical codes have been drawn up to include principles which cover the 'dignity and privacy of individuals, the avoidance of harm and the confidentiality of research data' (Punch 1986, p. 35).

The question that has been raised is, how applicable is this model to social science research? The concept of informed consent presumes that the informants participating in research have the right to be informed that they are being researched and what the nature of the research is. How appropriate is this concept to in-depth interviewing? Informing someone that they are being interviewed is not usually problematic. However, how much do you wish to tell the informant about the nature of the research project, particularly if you feel that it will influence their discussion of the area which you are examining? In many cases, to provide full information would destroy the research project. In other cases, it may be the only way to secure access. It is also argued that such possible outcomes are precisely the reason that the researcher must negotiate fully informed participation. Alternatively, it has been argued that if you decide to not fully inform the participants prior to the research that you are ethically bound to fully debrief them at its conclusion, and preferably prior to publication of your report. In this instance, do we take the ethically absolutist position, or opt for the situationally relativist one?

Researcher–informant relationships

This brings us back to the political and ethical problems in research relations. The questions that each researcher must ask: What are the risks and benefits for those individuals who participate in research? What should participating individuals be told about the nature of the research project? How essential is informed consent and what is it comprised of? What form of protection might individuals who participate in social research need? How far does the researcher intrude before there is an invasion of privacy which is intolerable to the informant? What is the relationship between the researcher and informant? Are there any formal or informal controls on this process? If so, how valid and effective are such controls and how do they operate?

Overt or covert? Do the ends justify the means?

When establishing the researcher–informant relationship, it is also important to establish the moral ground in a concrete manner. We suggest that this is done by providing the informant with accurate information such as your aims and goals in doing the research, how the interview data will be stored, what you the researcher will do with the information and whether your plans for the final product will be of any benefit to the informant.

This is the ideal version. Yet, as has been debated by many researchers whether one should be involved in overt or covert research is a moot point (Bulmer 1979; Denzin 1968; Erikson 1968). Erikson has argued that the researcher is being unethical if he or she deliberately mis-represents (or fails to represent) his or her identity for the purpose of securing access to the 'private domain' of the informants. It is also unethical for the researcher to misrepresent the character and nature of the research in which he or she is involved. Denzin has responded to Erikson's comments by arguing that there can be no invasion of privacy if one does not accept the distinction between the public and private domain. All methods can pose a threat to participants. The essential debate boils down to whether one accepts that 'what is good for social science is inherently ethical', which is what Erikson accused Denzin of believing. The related question is whether certain pieces of research should be carried out at all, if they are so dangerous to individuals.

> Anyone who has been interviewed, even on trivial topics (such as which television programmes they watched last week) will know that the interview is a rare enough event for it to leave a mark on the interviewee. You find yourself rethinking what you said, aware of the gaps between what you wanted to say and what you were able to say. When interviewed on deeper topics, such as how you see your work or relationships within the family or your feelings about death, the effect is more marked. The interview both opens up areas of dialogue in taken-for-granted areas of your life and, at the same time, perhaps because of the conversational asymmetry in the relationship between the interviewer and the interviewee, fails to offer a sense of closure. As a result, the interviewee typically emerges from the interview with a feeling of being left stranded. It is the researcher who goes away with the data to rework it in his or her own fashion, to gain satisfaction from making it make sense, and who indeed has the context to do so (Walker 1989, p. 37).

This vision of the relationship between researcher and informant is unfortunate but seems reasonably accurate if one examines published accounts of the research process. The researcher very rarely addresses the social justice and validity issue of who the research is for, because it seems that it is for him or her. Establishing rapport for a period of time is regarded as a reasonable cost if it means publication of research! The nature of such a relationship is hardly ethical when it is primarily exploitative. This issue has been raised by Oakley (1988) in her discussion of 'feminist interviewing' where she examines the nature of the relationship between women who are informants and those who are researchers, using herself as the example. In her research she examines the problems of communication between female patients and male obstetricians. The argument she puts is that such communication problems occurred because the male obstetricians operated with a male discourse which does not utilise a notion of reciprocity in the same way as female conversation. She points out that inherent in the nature of normal human female relationships is reciprocity of conversation. While she is doing the interviewing, the least she can do for her informants is answer their queries and share their problems in the context of their social interaction. However, she points out that most textbooks would suggest that this is inappropriate behaviour for an interviewer. In post-positivist research, which utilises constructivist methodology (Guba & Lincoln 1989; McGuiness & Wadsworth 1992; Wadsworth 1991), the issue of reciprocity is taken to its logical conclusion. The role of the researcher becomes that of facilitator of dialogue between the relevant informants or participants of an inquiry. In this way, the concept of a 'community of scientists' extends to include all people who have an interest in learning from the research and who also may contribute views, experiences, data, analyses and findings of their own. In such research the boundaries between 'researcher', 'researched' and 'researched for' become less distinct as each 'informant' is recognised as having a greater or lesser claim to active participation in the inquiry.

Research which operates within such political, methodological and ethical frameworks goes some of the way in addressing the issue of unequal power relationships between researcher and researched. This way of doing research, however, does not guarantee that all ethical considerations will inevitably be met. The power structures that exist within organisations may make it unethical to encourage members of such organisations (any workplace such as hospitals, private industry, government departments etc.) to engage in in-depth interviews with one another as it may prejudice their security of position or employment within the organisation due to the lack of confidentiality and anonymity.

Confidentiality and anonymity

People often give consent to be interviewed when they know that they will not be individually identifiable because their anonymity has been guaranteed by the researcher. Hence, the researcher who promises to use conceal identities is more likely to gain access to a sample. Confidentiality does not refer simply to protecting names and keeping confidences but sometimes to protecting other information about the informant. This is often done by altering details in description of people, places and/or

events. The entire process takes the form of a bargain. It is based on the
notion that the individual will agree to take part in the research process
and become the informant if the researcher keeps his or her side of the
bargain by promising to create and maintain anonymity and confidentiality. The pragmatics of this process are not always as simple and
easy as the texts make them sound. Where does the researcher store his
or her own personal research diary (which probably includes the names,
addresses and telephone numbers of the informants particularly when
constant use is made of this to arrange interview times)? If one promises
to keep it under lock and key then is it to be kept locked in the home of
the researcher or in the workplace or elsewhere? The ideal situation
would be strict adherence to whatever is promised but this is rarely the
case. The issue is that it is important to make bargains and promises that
can be kept. Making initial contact with informants is not simply a matter
of gaining access and being courteous. The informant must be able to
trust the researcher and be confident in what he or she says. This is
essential to successful social interaction in most conver-sations.

As we have stated, much of the material written on the ethics and
morality of the research process utilise concepts from medical research
(such as informed consent). Many comments have been critical in relation
to the applicability of these concepts in non-medical research. On the
other hand, the basic underlying concepts are the same—the integrity of
the researcher in carrying out research, the morality and ethics of the
relationship between researcher and researched and what is discovered
in the research process, and the consideration of social justice issues in
determining who benefits from the research process and the publication
of results.

Data collection and dissemination: control and privacy

Let us again assume that you, as the researcher, have gained access to
informants; you have given them a brief introduction and explanation of
the research project as you see it and now you proceed to the asking of
questions and discussion of topics which might bear on your research
problem. How invasive should you allow your questions to be? At what
point is the informant's privacy infringed? Do you use trick questions to
elicit sensitive and private material from your informant? In some cases,
the informant will let you know in no uncertain terms that you have
infringed his or her privacy when you ask questions which overstep their
subjectively determined boundary. In other cases, you may decide that
unless you elicit information on certain areas and issues that an informant
regards as private and confidential, then you will not have a valid
understanding of those issues and your research project will not be worth
doing. The decision is based on your subjective consideration of the
ethical choice and whether your choice is morally allowable within your
own ethical frame work and boundaries, or, morally reprehensible and

not allowable within that same framework. The political pressures in such a situation are twofold. On one level, the pressure to produce many good research reports quickly may be very strong, particularly if future promotion and status are dependent on such publications. On the other level, there may be political pressure to present oneself as being a researcher of great integrity who maintains an ideologically and ethically sound stance in relation to participants (that is, in research projects which you initiate and carry out). Both pressures may be applied to the researcher and the choice is both a political and ethical one.

As stated in chapter 4, the interviewer usually has control of the interactions during the interview even though this may not be apparent to the informant. In many cases, it is an intended control. In others, even where the researcher has negotiated a more egalitarian relationship with the informant, it becomes an unintended consequence of the research process itself and of the social and political structures and settings in which it takes place. In this context, even though in-depth interviewing places the informant's interpretations and meanings at centre stage, it is often the interviewer's interpretation of the situation which is accorded greater validity. This can include decisions about which subject matter should be regarded as private and confidential and which should not. This becomes most obvious in negotiations about record-keeping and note-taking. In some instances, an informant will ask the researcher to turn off the tape recorder while he or she refers to something which he or she has defined as private or confidential. The researcher is often reluctant to do this because he or she anticipates that the forthcoming information might be significant to the research project. For the informant, the privacy issue is translated from the immediate context of the research process to the promises of confidentiality and anonymity which he or she had been given in terms of the storage of the data and its subsequent publication and future dissemination.

Issues of reliability, validity and practicality are definite concerns when one wishes to interpret narratives that are the data outcome of in-depth interviews. The production of these narratives is itself a matter of ethical concern for the reasons stated above, most especially in terms of keeping faith with informants' accounts and promises made to them in prior negotiations. Transcription of recordings and interpretation of the actual data for this purpose opens Pandora's box in terms of ethics issues. After all, if one wants to make the research more reliable by providing all or the greater part of the transcript material what methods can successfully maintain the anonymity of the informant/s without losing the specificity required for reliability.

The issue of unobtrusive measures being adopted as an inherent part of social interaction raises another issue of privacy. Let us explain. Kellehear (1993) argues that there has been a failure to use unobtrusive measures such as observation, audiovisual records or material culture (artefacts of the present day society). He views this omission as a significant flaw in the conduct of modern social science research. We agree that, if such measures are omitted, much valuable data are never brought to light. However, we would argue that good in-depth interviewers (technically competent) incorporate simple types of unobtrusive measures into the fabric of an in-depth interview. In the context of the interview, a good interviewer will observe, as discussed in chapters 5 and 10, and record the dress, manner and appearance of the informant and the nature of his or her physical surroundings, including, for instance, photographs, pictures and the wear and tear on the furniture. These observations can raise some ethical concerns. For example, in the course of an interview about the dilemmas of commencing IVF treatment, the interviewer happens to observe a letter from the clinic confirming the participant's acceptance into the program. In the interview the informant has not mentioned that acceptance has been received. Alternatively, a participant in a study of sexual and emotional development admits loving another person but does not reveal the full depth of emotion. Letters or photographs in the setting suggest an even greater depth of emotional involvement than the informant has consciously revealed. Is it ethical to allow this information to permeate the assessment or analysis of the data? Have we as researchers become overly invasive in the private domain of the informant simply by being competent in using the full range of our in-depth interviewing skills?

Most human beings hold inconsistent views across a range of topics. This makes interviewers often wonder whether their informants know that, strictly speaking, their views are inconsistent or whether they are lying to the interviewer. The classic example here is the observation that the same person can argue that it is wrong to destroy an unborn child and yet believe that every woman has the right to abortion on demand. Is this person lying about one or the other view? Have they compartmentalised their views so that they may co-exist? Is it ethical for the in-depth interviewer to inquire about this contradiction if it may cause harm to the informant by awakening in him or her an understanding of this compartmentalisation? There is a strong cultural commitment in Western societies to consistency of opinion so that pointing out inconsistencies may be taken as a moral and/or intellectual challenge. We believe that, in most cases, it would be unethical to query to the point where the participant feels threatened. Nevertheless, there are certain research topics where not to do so would be unethical, for example, exploring racist beliefs. If you are exploring how an intelligent and educated person can also be a racist, it may be mandatory for both intellectual and moral purposes to determine whether the racist point of view is part of an unconscious compartmentalisation process or whether the informant is expressing an acknowledged and fully thought out position. This is a clear indication of our values in this area!

It is often argued that there are no set rules apart from the subjective deliberations one makes in determining whether an action is ethically sound. However, in Australia currently the National Health and Medical Research Council (NH&MRC) has guidelines for the ethical conduct of research involving human beings. In these guidelines it stipulates that the informant must be free to withdraw at any time. Some researchers interpret this to mean to withdraw some or all material and to choose to discuss some issues but not others. Perhaps the most significant factor to remember is that researchers, like other professionals, are held accountable for their actions—be it by an ethics committee, their professional peer group, a research methods lecturer, the group or individual being researched, the general public and the researcher's own conscience.

Analysis and publication

The presentation and dissemination of data is also a stage of research which is fraught with political and ethical dilemmas. In relation to anonymity and confidentiality, the researcher should again try to keep faith with informants by disguising their identity and information so that the individual is not identifiable. This is usually achieved by the use of pseudonyms and slight changes of descriptive information. Is it desirable if you want to provide your readers with accurate information? The researcher is usually placed in the position of trying to balance the needs of the informant for privacy with the needs of the audience for accurate and detailed data which is accompanied by sufficient demographic information for them to judge the validity of your report. In many instances, this is not possible, especially when the group researched is part of a small community or the research was focused on well known or famous individuals. Then the initial promises should not have been made or at least stated in a qualified and realistic form.

It is often the case that when a researcher is engaged in coding and analysing data that he or she will discuss queries and problems with relevant associates and colleagues. When promising confidentiality and anonymity to informants, did the researcher explicitly extend his or her own access to and reading of the data to these colleagues? Were informants aware that someone else might read or listen to their statements in unreconstructed and undisguised form? We think that the most useful way to overcome such possible violations of promises is to try and identify ethical issues before they become problems (although foreseeing all such problems is not possible). For instance, the researcher should gain informed consent from the informant for the use of a tape recorder during interview sessions. This should be done with full explanations of the problems of maintaining confidentiality and anonymity in all research.

Fraud

The entire issue of fraud in research is a difficult area to deal with. It is often the unstated suspicion of people who read published research reporting on the interview process, that they do not have enough data available to them in the report itself to assess the validity of the conclusions being drawn by the author. Did the researcher just draw on extracts of interviews which support their conclusions? Did they censor the data and exclude non-confirmatory data? Did they collude with informants to produce a politically or ideologically helpful account? If it was a team of interviewers did they really do the interviews or did they fabricate the interview data? When you are running a large-scale interview project, it is usual to have a team of interviewers most of whom you hope will share your high standards of academic integrity and competence. However, it is important to build safeguards into the procedure to ensure that interviews are not concocted by the interviewers alone in the privacy of their own homes.

Fudging of data usually refers to alteration of statistics. However, in the case of interview material, whether the rationale be ideological, theoretical or methodological, the selection of quotes, the selective editing of quotes and the non-accessibility of data, that is, data which are not available in the published report or some form of appendix in suitably anonymous form, is considered unethical or at least open to ethical query. The conceptualisation of fraud is not debatable if one is referring to consciously chosen deceit. The situation is more difficult to deal with when researchers interpret discussions through the prism of their ideology and misinterpret the informants' meaning and do not recognise this. The outcome is fraudulent even if the intent to deceive was not there. It is in this and the area of reporting of data and its 'construction' that debates occur regarding the notion of fraud.

Who is the research for?

Another issue raised at this stage of the research echoes our initial question of who the research is for. Was the research sponsored? Were there any expectations on the part of the sponsor and/or the researcher which were not specified at the beginning of the project? Did any stated expectations change? The power relationship between *sponsors* and researchers exists whatever the topic of research and is often most felt when the researcher wishes to publish the results of his or her research and make the material public. It is when the research takes an unexpected turn, or the researcher comes up with embarrassing findings, or the analysis and explanation made by the researcher is not in keeping with the interests of the sponsors, as they see it, that the exercise of power is most likely to pose difficulties for researchers and expose their vulnerability in sponsored research. The ownership of the report is often at issue in such circumstances.

If the research was initiated by the researcher alone, there are still ethical and political concerns which must be faced. Data dissemination includes not only publication but also communication of the report orally and visually. Researchers, in the age of electronic media, are often invited to comment about their research on television and radio programmes particularly if their findings are regarded as controversial. Once data has been widely disseminated in the public arena, it means that anyone can utilise it for their own purposes. Researchers need to make political and ethical decisions in relation to how widely their reports should be disseminated and if they should have any legal brakes applied to them. In some cases, the researchers' interpretations of the meanings and events in informants' lives may differ from the informants' interpretation to such an extent that the informants might wish to prevent further publication or dissemination of the report. This can occur even though the researcher and informants agree that the report is truthful and accurate. It may nevertheless, or in fact because of this, be seen as harmful.

Some researchers, particularly those who have made the political decision to engage in action research, provide their informants with an opportunity to validate their studies. In some instances (Whyte 1955), this involves the informant reading the entire manuscript prior to publication or the researcher discussing drafts of the report with informants. In many ways, these approaches act not only as a means of maintaining an ethical stance in relation to informants but also as a final verification of the validity of the research. However, as Burgess (1984) points out, there are no solutions which are foolproof. It has been said that the 'only safe way to avoid violating principles of professional ethics is to refrain from doing social research altogether' (Bronfenbrenner 1952, p. 453).

The best one can do is to consider the ethical and political issues in asking a particular research question, determine the areas of concern prior to the research, take into account professional standards that have been established and then consider the ethics of the entire research process as an individual case with its own social and political ramifications.

We realise that many readers would wish us to conclude this chapter by providing guidelines and laying down the ethical law. We believe that this is neither possible nor appropriate. Ethical guidelines are difficult to propose in the abstract; a grand rule about, for instance, informed consent, is all very well in principle but the question of how to interpret what constitutes informed consent is a complex one. Many texts do set out lists of what constitutes morally good or morally odious acts in research settings. Rather, we would argue that the social and political context of research will exert its own demands on the ethics and integrity of the researcher. We can neither foresee nor forestall such demands.

Chapter 10

Assembling and organising the data

(With Damien Ridge)

The next two chapters provide a review of methods used for *coding* and analysing data. Few other publications examine the procedures for organising qualitative data. Learning how to store and manage the data is a crucial step in the research process because the quality of *data analysis* partly depends on the systematic recording of fieldnotes. (For a detailed discussion of the general issues presented here, see Bogdan & Biklen 1992, Lofland & Lofland 1984, Miles & Huberman 1994 and Strauss 1987.)

Although qualitative data are not usually susceptible to computerisation, they do need to be transcribed, coded and filed. This chapter discusses how to store the data into files (also called logs). These files assist the researcher to sort, focus and organise information in such a way that patterns and themes within the data become clearer. Specific attention will be paid to the following questions: What data do you record? How do you record it? What fieldnote system can be used for storing the data collected? Chapter 11 will discuss methods for discovering and testing concepts contained in the fieldnotes.

Data analysis includes both a mechanical and an interpretative phase. The work which surrounds the mechanical phase involves designing operations which retrieve, modify and transform data. Physically sorting out the data into files provides easier access to sections of it. Researchers often end up with over 3000 pages of fieldnotes. Trying to make sense of those pages without ordering and storing them may turn the interpretative work of data analysis into a nightmare. It is important for the reader to recognise that while the mechanical and interpretative aspects of data analysis are discussed in separate chapters, these two tasks are interrelated and occur simultaneously. The interpretative work presupposes that the data are organised according to a set of mechanical operations. Yet, at the same time, the interpretative work will dictate how the data will be sorted.

Fieldnotes: what do they contain?

Fieldnotes contain a record of conversations the researcher has had with people, observations about their actions in everyday life and procedures for collecting such information. While the data may be collected through a combination of asking, listening and looking, which of these activities is dominant in a study will vary with whether the researcher is using in-depth interviewing or participant observation. It should be stated, however, that whether we are conscious of it or not, all these skills are put into practice in our everyday lives. When we sit in a classroom, we listen to what is presented, ask questions to clarify issues, and observe the non-verbal gestures of the lecturer to assess the importance of what is being said. Unlike the ordinary person, however, researchers are more conscious of using these skills to study human life. As it was noted in chapter 5 when using in-depth interviewing, listening and asking are important skills to master. The interviewer, of course, is also observing as he or she talks to the informant. Much of what is written in the fieldnotes can be derived from observations made about the informant, the setting and the interview.

Fieldnotes contain more than a transcription of what the tape-recorder has registered. Experienced researchers include information in their notes that was invisible to the tape-recorder but perceived by the trained interviewer. The formal interview is only one component of the fieldwork experience. It may constitute about 60 per cent of the total time spent collecting data in the field. The rest of the time is spent contacting people on the telephone and talking to them before and after the formal interview. The researcher is also an observer. Information is collected about the facial and physical expressions of the informant, the details of the setting and perceptual impressions. This information places the interview in its larger context and provides additional information on the informant, the setting and the topic.

Fieldnotes include the researcher's reflection on what was said (or not said) and observed. The reflective account can include speculation about themes and connections between pieces of data; issues which arise while entering and leaving the field; reflections on methodological, sampling and ethical issues; and ideas on report writing. Researchers often prefer to keep the descriptive and reflective parts of the notes separate (Burgess 1982b). It is important to recognise that the reflective content of fieldnotes is a personal activity. The researcher is encouraged to adopt a writing style that will not inhibit note-taking.

The reflective comments should include information the researcher thinks is relevant at the time. An inexperienced fieldworker would complain that he or she did not write any notes because there was nothing important to report. Rosalie Wax (1971) warns fieldworkers to think twice about following the example of those would-be ethnographers who assert or boast that they take few or no fieldnotes. The fact is that most of the people who say that they are able to get along without taking notes tend not to write anything worth reading. While note-taking may appear to be tedious, and indeed even simply boring, it is crucial for the analysis.

Guidelines for writing fieldnotes

There are a number of basic principles for data recording that can facilitate the task of writing fieldnotes. (Burgess 1982b and Webb 1982 provide excellent illustrations and we recommend that the reader consult these sources.) The first basic rule is to write down any idea that enters your mind. These ideas can be lost if you do not write them down immediately. Many researchers carry with them a little notebook during the course of their study and enter comments at all hours of the day or night. Many good ideas are composed while you ride the tram, have a long hot bath, or pretend to be listening to a boring conversation.

A second rule is to set aside time for writing the fieldnotes. Your memory can play tricks. You must adopt the attitude that unless you write down everything you are thinking about, there is a danger that it will be lost. It is a serious error not to record or reflect on the data as soon as it has been collected. It is so easy to allow one's fieldnotes to pile up. As a general rule, the researcher should write the fieldnotes no later than the day after the interview. The objective is to minimise the period between data collection and data storing, and to reflect on the data before commencing the next interview. Most experienced fieldworkers note that the quality of their notes diminishes with the passage of time. Details are lost and episodes are forgotten or muddled (Hammersley & Atkinson 1983).

Note-taking should be viewed as compulsory. Like maintaining a personal diary, it involves discipline and hard work. Many of us at one time began writing a diary but gave it up because we did not invest enough time in the project. Fieldnotes, like diaries, must have periodic entries and include information that you might find of interest at some later stage.

Another important rule to follow is to make duplicate copies of your fieldnotes and to store these in separate places in the event of a fire or theft. There is nothing more frustrating than losing your data and realising that you do not have copies. Hours of hard work can be lost. As chapter 11 will illustrate, the duplicate copy can be used for cutting and pasting accounts of a single event or situation onto index cards.

Finally, the task of data coding and data analysis should not be separated. Both these tasks need to occur at the same time. As well as spending time to write and code the data into files, the researcher should be searching for emergent ideas in the data and sketching research strategies. Researchers can ask themselves how much knowledge they have gained, what they know and do not know, the degree of certainty of such knowledge and further lines of inquiry. Of course, what the researcher writes will depend on a continual reassessment of purposes and priorities. As Hammersley and Atkinson (1983) note, the standard practice of writing down everything you see and hear fails to take into account that with the accumulation of data, the researcher focuses his or her attention on what to write down, how to write it down and when to write it down. During the first days of a research project, the focus of the researcher will be general. As a result, fieldnotes will be much broader in scope. As the research progresses, and themes and concepts are identified, the notes will become more focused, 'dense' and selective.

Different types of fieldnote files

Although there are no general rules on what sort of information should be included in your fieldnotes, a number of researchers have suggested that the notes should address the who/what/when/where/how questions that surround the study (Bogdan & Biklen 1992; Burgess 1982b). *Who* involves reporting the identity of the participants and their relationships to others. *What* involves describing the activity or conversation seen or heard. *When* involves noting the reference to time, with special attention to recording the actual sequence of events. *Where* involves describing the location of the activity. *How* involves a description of whatever logistics were used to collect the data and an analysis of how ideas and patterns in the data have emerged.

The answers to the above questions, as illustrated in figures 10.1 and 10.2, are stored in the following separate files: a *transcript file* which contains the raw data of the interview; a *personal file* on the fieldwork experiences; and an analytical file which discusses ideas and conceptual issues. The rest of the chapter will discuss the form and content of these three files and present examples of each.

Transcript file	*Personal file*	*Analytical file*
Includes the transcription of the interview, observer's comments and a cover page. The text is centred in the middle of the page with margins containing observer's comments on both sides.	Includes a descriptive account of the actors and their settings, reflective notes on the fieldwork experience and methodological issues.	Includes a detailed examination of the research questions asked and ideas emerging as the study progresses.

Figure 10.1 Information contained in the file system

However, before we do this, we need to clarify an important point. Borrowing what Samuel Beckett said of memory, we might say of fieldnotes that they are as much an instrument of discovery as of reference. As such they need to be organised in such a way that their content can be easily found and accessed. Imagine if you simply dumped all of the contents of your fieldnotes into one continuous file, without headings or topic areas. You would be overwhelmed with the volume of your fieldnotes and the task of sorting and finding relevant material. As Sanjek (1990, p. 378) prudently comments, 'having notes is one thing, but using notes is quite another'. For this reason most experienced qualitative practitioners develop indexing procedures to organise their fieldnotes.

While the following discussion includes the separation of fieldnotes into distinct files, this is done in order to facilitate the 'unpacking' of fieldnotes. The creation of the transcript, personal and analytical files described in this chapter is a heuristic separation developed for writing and reading purposes rather than a reflection of how the fieldwork process and analysis unfolds. It is the researcher's attempt to impose the making of a 'neat record'. This 'neat' record is an artificial product of the fieldwork process as it does not reflect the full recreation of the inter-connection and interdependence between the notes stored in the different files. For example, issues dealing with establishing rapport, asking questions and modifying interviewing strategies to obtain data are events which occur at the same time and influence one another. Your rapport with the informants, for example, might give you access to important data. An analysis of why access to such data is only possible when a certain type or level of rapport is achieved might provide important analytical insights. So while you might describe the method used to achieve rapport with informants in your personal file, and the analysis of the data in the analytical file, some cross reference between the two is necessary to explain how you have gained this understanding. The files described below represent one of many ways in which you can organise your fieldnotes. (For alternative guidelines on how to organise your fieldnotes see Burgess 1982b, Strauss 1987 and Taylor & Bogdan 1984). Some researchers may wish to combine the personal and analytical files. Storing your personal and analytical files on a computer database file allows you to cross-reference material from both files and to compile all records on a particular informant or across informants.

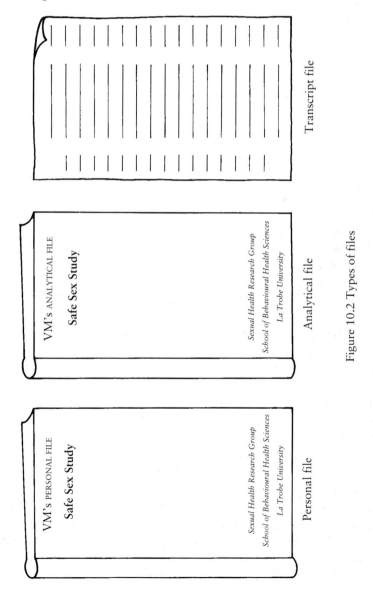

Figure 10.2 Types of files

The transcript file

As we discussed in chapter 5, there are a number of ways one can record the interview. We have stated that the use of a tape-recorder in conjunction with note-taking is the most useful means of capturing the full dimensions of the conversation. Regardless of whether or not you used a tape-recorder, the transcript file is a reproduction of the formal interview which took place between researcher and informant. The depth of information contained in the transcript file may be slightly different, depending on which of these two methods is used (Ives 1980). A conversation that was reproduced from a tape-recorder will contain an exact reproduction of the verbal conversation, while a memory recollection of a conversation will contain a combination of what was said and approximate remarks. Strauss (1987) suggests that researchers use quotation marks for exact recall, apostrophes to indicate less precision in wording and no marks to indicate proxy recall.

Typed notes are preferable to handwritten notes. For one thing, they are much more legible. It also makes it easier to code and cut up your notes to create index cards at a later stage (more will be said about this topic in chapter 11). Another way the transcript file can be prepared for analysis is to break up sentences into paragraphs which are organised around ideas or topics.

An example of a transcript file and accompanying diagram of the interview setting (below) is reproduced in figure 10.3. This conversation was transcribed from a recorded conversation between one of the authors and a clergyman. The focus of the study was to identify how ministers construct eulogies. This was the first of several interviews and only the first four pages are reproduced here. We include this transcript to illustrate guidelines for formatting the transcript file and provide an example of the rich data that can be collected through in-depth interviewing.

Subject:	Rev David Hodges, Interview No 1
Topic:	How do ministers construct eulogies?
Date:	8 January 1987
Place:	Rev. Hodges' home—lounge room, Melbourne.
Time:	Arrived at DH's home 1.10 pm; chatted for 20 minutes; formal interview began at 1.30 pm and finished at 3.00 pm; left DH's home at 3.45 pm.
Relevant Information:	United Church Minister for 30 years, recently retired, delivered many eulogies, trained in Scotland.
Special Circumstances:	Hot day (35 degrees C); permission to use tape-recorder was granted.

Transcript data

0000 **VM** David, I would like to begin by asking you what is a eulogy?

DH Well, a eulogy is an address (*cough*) to honour a person either living or dead I presume. But in my case (*smile*) it would be given for the dead.

VM So it is …

DH So it's a funeral address.

A case interrupting. I think this is a good question as it opens up the conversation.

VM What is the purpose of the address?

DH I think the purpose of it as far as a Christian service is concerned is to … it is part of a *ritual*. I think we need rituals at birth and birthdays and so we need a ritual for death because I think that just helps us to get through what can be a difficult time—so that is part of it. It's a part of a ritual which is a Christian ritual if you're a Christian. It's one of *those rite-of-passage* things in a way and that is common to everybody, not just Christians; when it is for a particular person in a particular situation then it becomes a recognition of their life. And I think usually a thanksgiving for their life. I think that is the main point.

Did not realise that a eulogy can be delivered for a person who is not dead. Need to understand if the construction of such eulogies are different from the funeral address.

Need to understand the concept of rituals, rite of passage can be applied to study eulogies.

Eulogy is a way of giving recognition to life. Would all ministers agree with this statement?

Picked up point of inconsistency.

VM You said 'I think'. Is there a difference between what you think and what the Uniting Church would think is the purpose of the eulogy?

Very informative response. David is doing most of the talking.

DH No, I think different Ministers would have different emphases. So there would be some ministers who would think that the most important thing at a funeral service is their reading of the Bible, the

0015 preaching of the word on this particular

Question—does the minister's views on the purpose of a eulogy influence how he constructs it?

0015 occasion with an emphasis on the Church's belief in eternal life, resurrection or whatever.

So some ministers would have that sort of, if you like, doctrinal emphasis in a service. They would emphasise that largely and they would minimise any recognition of the particular person. They would say that a service is about celebrating the gospel and the resur-rection rather than celebrating the life of a particular person. I would not deny that *(DH means he would not deny the importance of celebrating the gospel—the Christian aspect of the funeral address)* but there are other ministers, and I would be one of them, who would see a major focus of a funeral service and a eulogy in a service to be a thanksgiving for the particular person for whom the service is being conducted. So I would make that a very important part of what I am doing and, of course, it would be related to the Christian gospel.

One type of eulogy has a 'doctrinal emphasis'.

Another type— 'thanksgiving'. Are there other types?

But then I think that if you spoke to a minister who took a different approach, the opposite stance to the one I gave you, he would say that the important thing is 'here is a congregation' a lot of these people have got a very hazy idea of the gospel to those in faith is about and this is a real opportunity to preach the Gospel you see'. You say bam, bam, bam, which I think is ... frankly ...

I think that the occasion, the people have come because they knew, respected, loved this particular person. I think that they ought to be able to move through this critical point in their lives by being able to have expressed by me, what they want to say about him, what they want to think about him, what they want to feel about him. So my objective is to try to make the person who has died a sort of continuous living presence in that group. It's all about the person who has died for me.

Negative case— Uniting Church minister who uses the 'doctrinal emphasis.' What about ministers from other churches?

An aim of doctrinal emphasis is to preach the gospel to those in attendance.

DH sees himself as a voice which represents the audience. But who is the audience?

I should have asked a clearer question.

VM How do you do that? It must be a difficult thing because sometimes you come across people you knew, sometimes you come across people that you did not know very well and then you come across

I am following the conversation and 0086 the in-between people.

picking up on

David's ideas for follow-up discussion.	**0086**	**DH** Well it probably sounds ... it would be a strange thing to say I think that I find it easier if I do not know the person terribly well (*laughs*). Because the way I do it is to listen to the family and to friends and I would see them before the service. **VM** You would arrange to see them? **DH** Oh yes, always. And I would spend sufficient time with them. I would just simply talk to them about him and some of the things would be quite formal things, such as he was born in the country, or he was an accountant, or he had a partner who was so and so. The factual things about families. Those factual things do not worry me much. I do not believe the eulogy should be full of these sort of facts—Bill Smith was born in Mansfield in 1892 and lived here and moved there and qualified here and did this at this university, had so many children etc.—I think that is all adequate but everybody who is there knows most of those things anyhow. By talking to people, they will tell me the factual things of the person. But they will tell me about it in a particular sort of way, you know. They might say he always loved the country, and although his job brought him to the city he always had a great love for the country. And so I would just put that at the back of my head and you build up a sort of picture in your mind of the sort of person. You talk to his family, you talk to some of his friends. Even if you have not known him at all, why that is sometimes easier is because they distil the essence of him.	
I should have followed through and asked why DH thinks it is easier to do a eulogy for someone he does not know well. Instead, I introduced a different topic.		
		What are the factual things about the person? *An example of retrieving the 'essential thing' about a person and building a portrait.* *(This interview continues for another 27 pages.)*
	0116	

Figure 10.3 Diagram of interview setting and transcript file

Note: One of the author's analytical file on 'The Social Construction of the Eulogy' Project, ACSPRI Summer Program in Research Methods, January 1987. David—Informant number 1.

Transcript files should be organised to facilitate the process of coding data for analysis. The transcript file should have a cover page which is found at the beginning of each transcript. The type of information included in the cover page varies depending on what information is relevant to the study. Researchers often include the following inform-ation: the informant's name (or a code number if anonymity has been promised), the number of the interview, date and place of interview, length of interview, and background information about the informant (for example, gender, marital status). The cover page also includes a sketch of people, furniture, floor design and paintings on the wall. The diagram assists recall of the events of the interview and recaptures the events and feeling surrounding the interview.

Second, the text is centred in the middle of the page with wide margins on both the left and right hand of the page. The text should identify 'who said what' by designating the researcher and informant's initials. Corresponding numbers which locate the conversation on the tape can be included at the top and bottom of each page. The text includes the words spoken during the conversation, and dialogue descriptions such as gestures and tone of voice.

A transcript file should look as if it has been written, read and analysed. You should circle or underline key words in the text and write ideas in the margin. The observers' comments can be divided into two categories. One margin can be used to reflect on how the researcher's fieldwork experience. Good interviewing depends on paying attention, not interrupting, being reflective and probing (see chapter 5). The interviewer should critically examine whether he or she violated any of these rules. General ideas and coding categories, for example, can be entered in the other margin; these may be summary notes which are elaborated in the personal and analytical file.

The personal file

Burgess (1982b) argues that fieldnotes can be established on the basis of the substantive, methodological and analytical issues surrounding the research process. The *substantive notes* discuss the circumstances in which the fieldworker collected his or her data. A description of informants and settings, details of their actions and personal impressions of situations are included. The *methodological notes* contain a first-hand account of the processes involved in doing the research. The *analytical notes* record the researcher's initial questions and the ways in which these questions have been revised.

The personal file, described here, is an annotated chronological record or diary of the researcher's reflections of the substantive and method-ological issues which arise in the course of the study. The file is produced over a period of time. It is an impossible task to write the personal file at the end of the study. It becomes an instrument for discovering and organising ideas only if it is written while you are collecting data. There are a number of questions that need to be addressed concerning the format of the personal file. How do you record this information? Should you write down everything you are thinking about? Should you write in simple language? These are important questions. Before we proceed to discuss the specific contents of the personal file, a few words need to be said about the practice of writing it.

Writing a personal file

While each researcher is encouraged to devise a set of instructions which are congruent with his or her writing style and research interests, the following guidelines provide a framework for constructing notes. We suggest that you enter your thoughts in a journal. Put down on paper all of your thoughts and impressions. Do not omit events because they seem mundane. As discussed in chapter 1, you only partially know what particular events or situations will be relevant for the discovery of ideas when you are collecting data. What may seem irrelevant at the time can turn out to be a significant piece of information.

Your notes should be frank and unrestricted in length. Try to be detailed in your description. The notes must provide a full account of people, situations, decisions rather than summaries of these. For example, instead of

'Mr Rhodes looked distinguished'

you could write something like

'Mr Rhodes wore a three piece black suit with a matching vest and red tie. The suit was bespoke tailored and immaculate. He spoke with a soft gentle English accent. He was very articulate. I was not surprised when he later told me that, prior to his retirement, he was the vice-president of an insurance company. He projected the image of a business man. My first impression of him, based on visual cues, was of an independent elderly man who made up his own mind about things. The interview confirmed this assessment. He had made his own decision to move to a nursing home.'

Information can be entered under a principal heading to which the notes relate. The heading can be the name of the person or the title of the particular institution, depending on your *unit of analysis*. For example, if the investigation is centred around examining how the organisational structure of nursing homes influences staff behaviour, the essential item to record is the type of nursing home (for example, private nursing home, state nursing home, voluntary nursing home). On the other hand, if you are interested in studying how residents explain their admission to nursing homes, the major heading is the name of individuals. Sub-headings are used to further organise the material contained within the major heading. This carefully planned organisation of the material brings the facts under review in an arrangement that facilitates the discovery of ideas (Webb 1982).

People, settings and activities

Words taken out of context are difficult to interpret. Your fieldnotes
should read like a play script. A descriptive account of the actors involved
and the setting must be conveyed. This information places the interview
encounter in its larger context and is extremely valuable during the
analysis phase of the research. For example, one of the authors studied
older people living in geriatric wards. The paintings on the walls made a
strong impression on the initial visit. A number of the paintings were
about clowns and animals. These are the sort of paintings one would
expect to find in a child's room or kindergarten class. This observation
proved to be very important when the researcher analysed the interview
material. Patients spoke about staff members treating them like 'babies'.
The decor of the geriatric ward certainly gave credence to the residents'
views that staff perceived them in childlike terms.

In line with the theoretical underpinning of interpretative research (see
chapters 1 and 2), the fieldnotes must reproduce the perceptual states
experienced in the interview. The intent is to reconstruct the conversation
within the context in which it occurred. To simply rely only on the verbal
text ignores that the interaction evolved from assumptions people were
making about themselves, others and the setting. These assumptions
influence what people say.

People should be carefully described in the notes. First, a short biographical history that is relevant to the study should be given. This
biographical history could include information on a person's age, gender,
marital status, type of living arrangement, occupation and other information that would appear to be relevant to subsequent analysis. For
example, if you were studying older people living in a nursing home you
might include their medical history prior to entering the nursing home. A
study on sex workers may contain information about age of profession
entry, type of sex work and social class.

Second, a description of how people dress and present themselves is
included. You can learn important things about a person on the basis of
his or her general appearance and manner. People use 'impression
management' to influence how others think about them through their
looks and actions (Goffman 1967). The person's style of talking and
acting, as well as the mood of the interaction, can also be observed.
Researchers, like Goffman (see chapter 7), rely on their eyes to reach
interesting conclusions about human behaviour. For example, by
observing waiters working in a restaurant hotel, Goffman noted that
waiters presented themselves differently when they were in the dining
room than when in the kitchen. He developed the concept of 'front and
backstage behaviour' to distinguish between people's presentation of self
in formal and informal situations.

You, of course, are also an actor. The notes should include an account
of your own behaviour in the field. People's words and actions can only

be understood if they are examined in the context in which they are staged (Schwartz & Jacobs 1979; Taylor & Bogdan 1984). As an actor in the script, you are influencing how others act. An examination of your role in the field helps to access the influence your actions have had on the subject's remarks and behaviour. It also allows you to revise your field tactics or develop new ones.

Like people, settings need to be carefully examined and described. These can be sketched out in sufficient detail to enable imaginary recreation. An assessment of your impressions of the setting can provide useful insights and substantiate conclusions reached from other data sources (as illustrated in the above example of the geriatric ward study). An example of a personal file is presented in figure 10.4. You will notice that the personal file includes a detailed chronological description of the social experience of doing research and methodological issues which arise in the field. The personal file reproduced here was written by a student doing a fieldwork assignment. It is presented as it appeared in the student's diary. This has been done purposely because we did not want to mislead the reader into thinking that a personal file is written like a paper. A personal file should read as you speak, capturing your thoughts without being inhibited by the formalities of writing well as presented in a final manuscript. The student was studying how people define love. We include these notes to provide an example of the type of information that can be included in a personal file and to illustrate the discussion that follows. We suggest that you read through figure 10.4 below before you go on, and then refer to it as you read.

Getting in

I briefly considered who I could approach to be my first informant. I had decided that my sample had to include a *cross-section* of people from various social and cultural backgrounds, of varying age and a mixture of male and female participants. Age and gender would allow me to capture people who may be in different stages in the life cycle and experiencing different types of love. The person's social situation (for example, in a relationship) and cultural background may shape how they talk about and experience love.

Inspiration visited me one evening while I was watching television. The news mentioned the terrible battle that had taken place between two rival bike gangs a few years ago. I cannot remember the details of the news item. But the story immediately reminded me of one of my clients' husband that I had met last November. Peter and his wife had interested me a lot when I met them. I had never met a bikie before and was curious to know where all of Peter's scars came from. I had summoned up the courage to ask him about a particularly large scar at the top of his thigh (a large chunk of muscle tissue was missing, the scar was clearly visible as he was only wearing a pair of shorts). Peter's reply was 'someone's [sic] didn't like me and took a shot at me'.

Peter fitted the type of informant I wanted to interview. For my first interview I had a strong preference for someone of approximately my age, male and relatively unknown to me. I had met him before when I was present at their home birth, as their own midwife, Betty, was unavailable that night, attending another client. I had spoken to Sue on the telephone just once before she went into labour when I agreed to be 'backup midwife' and only once more after their son was born. Betty had continued on with the post-natal care, and I had visited them briefly once just before Christmas. I certainly did not consider them friends—simply very friendly people with whom I had shared a significant and moving experience; the birth of their son, Jesse. I suppose a certain degree of trust and rapport had already been built prior to the interview, and this made it easier for me to inquire into the private world of Peter's feelings about love.

On Sunday (23/4/89) I telephoned Sue and Peter's home and spoke to Sue. I asked Sue whether she thought Peter would mind being interviewed and explained to her the topic. I was anxious to ask Peter directly and wanted to hear Sue's opinion about the topic and whether she thought Peter would mind being interviewed on the topic. (Looking back I guess I was uncomfortable approaching a married man.) I figured that if Sue thought that Peter would not mind being interviewed then I could proceed and interview him without being too concerned about revealing the topic prior to the interview. I did not want Peter to know the topic beforehand as I wanted his responses to be spontaneous. Sue promised me that she would not reveal to Peter the topic.

When Peter came to the telephone he willingly agreed to be interviewed. There was no hesitation. After I put the telephone down I felt somewhat guilty at the conspiracy that I had engineered and wondered whether I should ring back and 'come clean'. I decided, however, that it was important to keep things as I had arranged. I felt good to talk to them again. They both expressed their delight at having the opportunity to see me again. Naturally when I spoke to them I inquired about their son's progress and was pleased to hear that he was healthy and had quite a fan club amongst their friends and family. I looked forward to seeing him again and seeing how much he had grown.

I telephoned Peter and Sue again on Friday (28/4/89) to confirm my visit the following day. Peter answered the call and in reply to my question, 'How are you, Peter', he said in a flat tone, 'Could be better', and handed the receiver over to Sue. Sue told me that Jesse had died suddenly on Wednesday. He had died of 'cot death'.

Sue gave me a vivid account of the events that took place on the evening that Jesse died and talked for a long time without stopping. I listened and at the same time wondered what, if anything, I could say. When Sue stopped talking I found myself saying how sad I was at the terrible news and was there anything I could do. (I also remembered our lecturer saying that when doing fieldwork one of the risks of establishing rapport with informants is that we can become involved with their world. In such moments we can share feelings such as embarrassment, sadness, excitement and so. I now knew what he was talking about.) Sue said that she was coping reasonably well. She asked me to attend the funeral to be held after the autopsy the following week. Sue did not cry on the telephone and said that she would let me know if there was anything I could do to help in the meantime.

When I put the telephone down and found myself alone in the house I poured myself a drink and sat in a daze for about an hour. I had never had the experience of losing one of 'my' babies before and did not know how to respond to Sue and Peter. I did not know how to handle my feeling of inadequacy. I did not know how to cope with my feeling of rage at this injustice. I still feel a physical pain in my throat and chest at the thought of Jesse's death. Indeed, in writing this account I find myself in the midst of these feelings again. I cannot see the keyboard because of my tears. I eventually rang a colleague of mine who is also a good friend. She had [had] a similar experience with one of her clients. She was lovely to talk to and after speaking to her I cried, off and on, for the next few hours.

On Saturday morning 1/5/89 I visited Sue and Peter. I ended up staying at their house for most of the weekend. The house was in semi-darkness because the curtains had not be [sic] drawn. Sue's mother was there. Sue and Peter talked constantly about many different topics, including Jesse. There were Jesse's toys and baby paraphernalia all over the house. Jesse's cot had been folded up and rested against the wall; his soiled nappies and clothes sat on top of an overfull laundry basket.

I stayed with Sue and Peter all day on Saturday and went home mid-evening. Both of them seemed to want me to stay and talk about Jesse. We looked at the photograph album which contained all of their son's pictures. Sue and Peter took great delight in talking about their son's birth. Sue's mother was very cheery and chatty for most of the time; but every now and then someone was crying.

The next day I rang Sue and Peter to see how they were. I was invited up to spend the day again. Sue's mother had gone home and we spent the day in much the same way as the day before. Sue and Peter talked about the funeral arrangements. I let them lead the conversation and I followed. As the hours went by I relaxed and so did Sue and Peter. Sue at one point commented that she had entirely forgotten about her loss more than once during the day.

I had naturally come to the conclusion that Peter would be in no mood to go ahead with the interview. I was wrong. Peter told me that he still wanted to do the interview. We arranged to do the interview on the following Tuesday; the day following the autopsy and the day before the funeral. I wondered whether I would end up with an interview on love or a discussion on grief. When I explained to Peter the topic and said that I would understand if he did not want to go ahead with the interview, he insisted on being interviewed.

Ethical considerations

Even though there had been a change in my relationship with Peter over the past few days, and the grief Peter was experiencing, it seemed to me wrong not to proceed with the interview because Peter wanted to do so. I wondered why he still wanted to go ahead. I often thought about the many times they had indicated how pleased they were that I was their consistent [sic] companion over that weekend. Was I taking advantage of their gratitude? Or was this their way of carrying on as though nothing has happened? I made it clear to them, and in particular Peter, that I would totally understand if the interview did not take place. They both made it clear to me that this was what they wanted to do.

I was deeply concerned that the actual interview situation may prove to be stressful for Peter. The topic of love—love for one's child—could surface in our conversation. I wondered about the use of the tape-recorder and wondered whether Peter would 'clam up'. Peter has expressed his feelings quite openly to me up until this point. I had valued his confidence in me. I wondered how much of an influence the tape-recorder would have on the conversation. I decided to go ahead and use the tape-recorder and explain to Peter why I wanted to use it.

The interview

On the day of the interview I thought about some of the important techniques about in-depth interviewing. I must remember how important it is to ask for permission to use the tape-recorder and to point out to Peter that the recorder can be turned off at any point. I wanted Peter to have control of the tape-recorder.

I wrote down some topic areas I wanted to cover during the interview as a guide I could refer to if I needed to do so. I decided that because I could remember the topics quite easily I would keep the notes in my bag unless I was at a loss for direction or words. I reminded myself to be reflective, not to interrupt or fill silent spaces with talk. I could remember quite clearly the words of our lecturer saying that we were after the interviewee's point of view, not ours. For reassurance I reminded myself that the interview was a form of conversation. In fact what I was about to do was no different to what I had been doing over the last few days: listen to Peter talk, that is, let Peter talk and I will follow 'his' conversation.

I arrived at Peter and Sue's home late morning. As usual their dog, Sheila, came trotting to the car in her usual friendly way, wagging her tail and waiting for a friendly pat. She escorted me to the front door and Sue was waiting to let me in. Their house is in the 'bushland' area of the north-eastern suburbs of Melbourne. Not an easy house to find without directions. Two houses share the same land. The tenants next door are friends.

Peter, Sue and I shared the usual hug that we had grown accustomed to over the last few days. Sue made a 'cuppa'. We sat and chatted in our usual relaxed fashion. Sue showed me some newspaper clippings about her son's funeral notice. I was reluctant to instigate any move toward starting the interview. After half an hour Peter suggested 'we get started'.

I explained to Peter that I was doing this interview as part of a learning exercise for my qualitative methods course. I explained to him, for the first time, why the class had chosen the topic of love. I explained why it was important for nurses to understand what love means to people and its implications for nursing and midwifery. I said how important it was for nurses to understand what lies behind people's emotional experiences; that this understanding assists us to provide care and support to individuals in times of stress. As I was explaining this to Peter I was aware that what I was saying was very pertinent to his recent experience [loss of child]. I was aware of my own discomfort but Peter showed no sign of being upset. I made a mental note that if I was too concerned about trying not to talk about sensitive topics that [sic] I was not going to get very far in my interview. At this stage I came to terms that I was talking about a very sensitive topic and that it was foolish for me to be too sensitive. I wanted to know what Peter thought about love—and this was going to mean talking about happy and sad times.

I reached into my bag and produced the tape-recorder. Peter did not object to the use of the tape-recorder. The tape-recorder, however, reminded Sue of the researcher who came to interview her the day after Jesse's birth. She told me how shocked she was at the time when the reporter produced a tape-recorder and she had been given no prior warning that one would be used. She had felt intimidated. The presence of the tape-recorder had greatly affected what Sue said during the interview as she imagined that the tape would be played to others without her consent. Her trust in the interviewer disappeared with the presence of the tape-recorder. Sue's comments gave me the opportunity once again to reassure both of them that the only person to hear the tape was me. I did, however, mention to Peter that the class would be reading the first few pages of the transcript. Peter was unconcerned. I could not help but think that the difference between myself and the researcher was that I had established rapport with Peter and Sue prior to the actual interview. Now I understand why establishing rapport is so very important. A trust is built and people are more likely to agree to participate in your study, and confide in you, than if you were simply a stranger who will have a brief encounter with them.

Peter and I were seated at right angles to each other. I was seated on the settee. Peter was sitting in an armchair. The large, heavily littered coffee table was directly in front of me. I placed the tape-recorder on it, on top of a pile of magazines and newspapers. I explained to Peter how the tape-recorder could be switched on and off, emphasising that he was welcome to stop the tape at any time he wished.

Sue asked if we minded her presence in the room. We both said we did not mind. It was difficult to ask her to leave the room as there was only the bedroom and bathroom available for her to retreat to; the kitchen was part of the living room. Sue was busy reading newspapers; searching for death notices addressed to Jesse. She was kneeling on the floor, on the other side of the coffee table with a pair of scissors in her hand.

As I was interviewing Peter I was aware, every now and again, of Sue cutting another notice out of the paper. Whenever she did this Peter would turn his gaze in her direction. I do not think I would interview another person in the presence of others. It was obvious that on more than one occasion Peter's train of thought was influenced by Sue's activity, and maybe even her presence in the room.

Peter looked very tired and was not as chatty as he had been recently. He told me later that he had been having trouble sleeping since Jesse's death. There were several references to Jesse's death during the course of the interview. Each time Peter referred to Jesse there was a long pause in the conversation. One such pause was particularly long and I just had to say something, anything to fill the silence.

He told me about his boyhood days. He had a succession of dogs as companions as a boy. But he lived close to a busy highway and the dogs kept getting killed on the road. He was talking about how he saw love as partially being a learned emotion. He quickly learned not to become so emotionally attached to his dogs as he knew that sooner or later they would be killed and he would feel sadness. It was almost like a self fulfilling prophesy as each dog in succession (as though) obligingly ran onto the road.

I asked him if loosing Jesse was seen by him to possibly have an influence on the love he will feel in the future for another child. He emphatically replied, 'No, no way. That is completely different!'. His reply was so forceful that I was immediately worried that I had hurt his feelings. Was I too presumptions to think I had the right to ask him such a personal question? Peter must have noticed my dismay and concern as he quickly followed his reply with a wide beaming and reassuring smile.

I was thrown off balance once again when during the course of our conversation Peter took a tray off the bookcase and proceeded to construct an immaculate, large cone shaped 'joint' cigarette. He casually lit the end took a few large puffs and handed it to me. I declined the offer but the smell of the joint brought me back to my younger days. I was hoping he would roll another joint before I left.

The joint in no way seemed to affect his behaviour. The conversation continued on as before. I asked him about his experience when he was falling in love with Sue. He said that he felt silly and related a delightful story of how each of them made it clear to the other that they were 'interested'.

The interview did not seem to come to a logical conclusion as I had expected. We both simply became tired and stopped. I suppose this is what Glaser and Strauss mean by 'saturation' or stopping when nothing else needs to be said. I think Peter was clearly restrained whilst the tape-recorder was on. He never really warmed to the subject as I had hoped would have happened. It may have been that the topic was something that he had never really given thought to or I was looking at it from the perspective of a women [sic]. (I suspect there may be some validity to the later explanation because Sue said that she was surprised at some of Peter's comments. Sue told me that she would have given me a completely different story and bezlieved that she would have offered more freely her thoughts.) His vocabulary seemed to let him down. He was floundering on many occasions for the right word, and several times simply resorted to saying variations of roughly synonymous words in quick succession. This made it difficult for me to follow what he really was trying to say. The interview ended when Peter looked at me with an expression which indicated he had enough. I switched off the tape-recorder and Peter said, 'Will that do you?'

When the recorder was switched off we both let out an audible sigh and we laughed. Peter mentioned that he felt that it was a very hard task to describe the topic of love into words. Sue felt that she would have had no trouble at all and argued that women thought about such things much more than men.

Peter rolled another joint and we all shared a smoke together (my wish has come true). Peter noted that if his mates had not brought him over a bag of 'home grown stuff', he would be on 'the Valium'. I must admit that I felt that this type of social self-medication (joint) appeared to be therapeutic. I was feeling very relaxed and content with the world at that moment! Peter took me for a walk down the garden to inspect the crop of plants that they were in the process of saving from the voracious local snails. On the way back up to the house he told me how happy he and Sue were that I had reappeared in their lives. We shared a big hug together and we both cried. At this stage I felt I had been immersed into their lives.

Maintaining relations

I telephoned Peter and Sue today (9/5/89) to see how they were. Peter was drunk. Sue told me that their dog, Sheila, had been destroyed by the rangers today because she was worrying the sheep. Peter is pretty cut up about it. It must be a terrible slap in the face for him.

I feel that I have developed a good and trusting relationship with Peter and Sue. I do not think I would have any difficulties in asking Peter to be re-interviewed. Given that this is my first interview, and my ideas will continue to develop as I listen to other people's stories about what love is, I may want to ask Peter further questions or get him to clarify some of his statements.

I visited Sue and Peter yesterday (28/5/89) in the evening and brought with me a copy of the transcript. Their friends, John and Ros, also dropped in to see them. John belongs to the bike club. Peter and John went out together for the night, leaving Sue, Ros and myself to chat. The conversation was a real education for me and provided further insights on the topic. (I suppose this is another advantage of qualitative methods; data collection does not have to be restricted to a point in time. It is continuous and in fact when it happens naturally, as with my conversation with Sue and Ros it provides real insights on the topic.) Ros and Sue were talking about their partners and the way the men's violent outlook on life affects their lives. Ros spoke to me about her concern over John's obsession with weapons, and particular guns and knives. She showed me her birthday present given to her by John. It was a ladies flick knife. It was a very heavy but it sat in Ros' hand very comfortably. The blade was razor sharp, 'good for cutting up steak' Ros informed me.

Getting out

I have no doubt that I will remain in contact with Peter and Sue. Sue and Peter were not at all interested in the transcript or what the group analysis revealed on love. I did not keep my original bargain of providing Peter with feedback on the research findings.

Figure 10.4 An example of a personal file

Note: A student's personal file on 'Perceptions of Love' Project, La Trobe University, April 1989. Peter—Informant Number 1

Reflections on the social experience of doing research

The social dimension of the fieldwork process involves four steps—getting in, learning the ropes, maintaining relations and leaving the field (see chapter 8; Shaffir & Stebbins 1991 and Shaffir, Stebbins & Turowetz 1980). An account of how the researcher has designed and executed each of these is important for two reasons. First, the researcher can learn new ways of behaving while in the field and possibly develop further fieldwork skills. Learning new skills is crucial for being successful in the field. Second, the final written product is the result of many decisions. These decisions influence the quality of data that is collected. A study cannot be properly evaluated unless it is placed within the larger context of how the data were collected.

Getting people to agree to be interviewed is a difficult task. Many anxious moments are spent thinking about ways to get people to say yes.

Yet the way you go about getting others to accept you and your study can either open or close doors. The personal file contains a detailed account of how you gained permission and the strategies used to seek co-operation. How did you present yourself? How much information about the study did you disclose? Were you doing covert or overt research? Did you strike a research bargain? What did you promise your informants? Did you present yourself differently to informants?

There are no simple formulae that guarantee successful entry. The tactics you use, and the issues you encounter, will depend on the research question and informants. For example, on first reflection, it would appear easy to interview people who are sitting in a park. After all, you do not need to negotiate with a gatekeeper (see chapter 8) to gain permission to go up to a stranger and talk to them. However, Karp notes that studying people in public places is not so easy:

> Strangers in public settings largely avoid each other. We try to maximise public privacy as we travel on buses, sit in waiting rooms, stand in lines, or simply walk along the street. The researcher is no different. Those who study conduct in public places will, like everyone else, be constrained by the rules that inhibit unnecessary verbal interaction (1980, p. 96).

Karp provides a useful description of the strategies he used to overcome the problem of access in public places.

Successful entry often depends on learning which suitable tactic is appropriate given particular situations or people. Hoffman, for example, provides a detailed account of the tactics she used to gain access to hospital boards:

> I began to choose my subjects on the basis of social ties, seeking interviews with all those board members who personally knew me or a member of my family. I usually wrote a letter first, outlining my interests in a formal, businesslike fashion consistent with the customary approach to executives. Most of these people must cope with large volumes of correspondence, much of which is non-business in nature, soliciting time, money, cooperation, information, or whatever. Unless something attracts their attention as they skim through the daily mail, executives are quick to refer correspondence to the waste basket or a subordinate. In order to catch attention or to compete with other requests, I included personal references in my letter (such as, 'I hope you might have the time between fishing trips ...' where I knew the board member often went fishing with a member of my family) and made certain my surname was written largely and legibly for them to recognise. In the letter, I usually stated that I would telephone to make an appointment (1980, p. 47).

The important point to remember is that the personal file captures the full details of the methods used to gain permission, as well as a reflection of whether such strategies failed or were successful.

The file also contains a detailed description and reflection on issues associated with 'learning the ropes' and 'maintaining relations' (Shaffir & Stebbins 1991; Shaffir, Stebbins & Turowetz 1980). 'Learning the ropes' involves attaining an intimate familiarity with the setting and its participants. Understanding people demands that the researcher learns to interact with informants on their own terms. 'Maintaining relations' is about establishing rapport and trust with informants.

You may think that learning about people, their setting and habits are of little scientific interest. This is far from true. Establishing a good rapport with subjects increases your chances of hearing the 'true' story. For example, Miller and Humphreys (1980) show how they were able to maintain ties with former informants involved in Humphreys' St Louis study of impersonal sexual encounters in public rest-rooms. The rapport he established with informants over the years allowed him to conduct further research on new questions that emerged in subsequent inter-pretations of the data and to gain an honest insight into the private sexual practices of men. Rapport is established slowly and with time. Much discussion and activities proceed it. In the example of the personal file (figure 10.4), four previous contacts were required before Allison felt comfortable to formally interview Peter. A record of the interaction and activities which have taken place during these contacts should be discussed. As the personal file shows, important information can be disclosed during these contacts.

The file also illustrates your reflection on the role you played within particular situations or settings. One of the authors quickly learned not to interview older residents living in a nursing home before morning or afternoon tea. He found that residents became agitated if they were interviewed before their tea time. These interviews were shorter. The researcher quickly understood that residents considered tea time to be one of their most important social activity.

Learning the ropes enhances the researcher's chances of becoming more familiar with the informant's views. Researchers who have studied deviant groups have reported in their notes how important it was for them to learn the informal language of these groups (Schwartz & Jacobs 1979). This special vocabulary provides clues about the group's basic assumptions about themselves and others. Familiarity with this know-ledge provides a solid basis for becoming attuned to the informant's life style. McCall (1980) discusses how the artists' terminology helped to explain the organisation of their social world. The categories she describes in her study—'professionals' and 'amateurs'—were derived from the expressions used by the artists themselves—'serious' and 'dedicated'.

Finally, the file includes details of how the researcher orchestrated his or her departure from the field. Was it a gradual or quick exit? Were the promises made at the beginning of the study kept? How did you negotiate the possibility of returning to reinterview participants? Will you maintain contact with the informant? An example of how this information can be presented in your notes is illustrated below. Altheide explains why he decided to make a quick exit from his study of newsrooms:

One reason I did not engage in a long and formal farewell was that I doubted it would be final. Also, however, I did not want to define a situation in which the news director could again demand that drafts of all written work be submitted to him for approval. He had insisted at one point in the study that he had veto rights over any report that came out of the research, even though we had never agreed to this unreasonable and unsatisfactory condition at the outset. So, in a manner of speaking, I had to slip out of the setting, noticed by several friends, but not in an eventful way that would have called forth the news director's wrath (1980, p. 308).

Methodological issues

Decisions made about the study's design are also presented in the personal file. Which informants were selected? Why were they selected? Who has been left out of the sampling frame? Your answers to these questions (as it was explained in chapter 9) can have important implications for data analysis and theory building. Cases are selected because they represent specific types of a given phenomenon. The researcher searches for contrasts that are required to clarify the analysis and obtain saturation of emergent categories through a process of constant comparison. This allows for the possibility of testing for falsification of propositions. The researcher should make explicit the rationale for selecting cases and its relevance to theory building.

The personal file is also the place where you include comments on methodological problems encountered in the study. Did informants object to the use of the tape-recorder? Were your questions too long? Did you interrupt? Were you being reflective? Did the interview follow the format of the recursive interview model? What ethical issues did you confront and what action did you take? Can you use an alternative method design? Your reflections on these issues will help you to think through the methodological problems you face and to make decisions about them. If you keep a systematic account of your research experience, these notes can be used to write the methodological section of the research report.

The analytical file

The analytical file includes reflective notes on the questions asked in the course of the research and ideas emerging from the data. These notes can be organised around several topic areas.

First, analytical notes can include an outline of topics discussed in each interview and changes to the interview guide during the course of the study. This will help you maintain a record of what issues were covered in the interviews, to identify issues which were not included and to follow up issues that the informant raised. Notes like this will assist in guiding future interviews.

Second, notes include a critical examination of what research questions are being asked, and how these changed as data were collected. Qualitative researchers enter the field with general questions. As the researcher collects and studies the data, he or she follows leads contained within it.

Slowly, the research question becomes more focused. The researcher learns what is feasible and what is of interest to the study. As the research question becomes narrower in scope, so does the information collected. The notes include a discussion about the preliminary questions asked, propositions developed and ideas that emerge gradually as the research winds down. You should put down on paper your reason for deciding what facts are relevant, what facts to collect, how you identified concepts, explanations for your decisions and the logic behind your attempts to give meaning to the data and the research process.

Analytical files should be organised in any way that makes sense to you. They can be written on paper (exercise and journal books), or alternatively, since files can often become quite lengthy, they can be stored in a database system for easy search and retrieval of topics (see chapter 3). The file is typed onto a series of cards on the screen which can be flicked through like a book. Each card should be designed with information about the date the file was entered, the informant's identification, a heading about the entry, and plenty of room for the entry. Despite the advantages of being able to quickly recall desired topics for comparison, it is difficult to record diagrams and it is not mobile like paper (unless you have access to a portable computer).

The analytical file is an aid in the analysis process. Just putting your thoughts into writing often forces you to think through ideas and speculation more systematically than just playing around with the ideas in your head. It is a good idea to keep a pen and notebook with you whenever it is practical. By jotting down your idea, you can write about it in more detail when you return to your analytical file. Additionally, if you are using a computer program to help analyse your data, such as *NUD.IST* version 3.0, you can graphically develop and modify codes (*nodes* on the hierarchical tree diagram), store index references to interviews at nodes, do sophisticated searches and build new nodes (and theory) all at the computer terminal. This interactive process is useful in clarifying and furthering your analysis, and can be recorded in your analytical file.

One of the shortcomings of keeping an analytical file is that you might immerse yourself in your file to such a degree that you feel like you are drowning in a sea of information. This makes it difficult to step back and take a fresh approach to your data. If you feel that you are not making progress in your analysis, or that your ideas have become stagnated or muddled, then it may be time to take a break or holiday from your file so that you can return to it refreshed. It is amazing how you can look at old issues with a new perspective after a break.

Writing an analytical file

The actual process of doing research follows a different course from that which researchers report in their published papers. Researchers often give the reader the impression that the study followed a predetermined linear plan of action. This hides the fact that doing research is a creative and imaginative process which occurs throughout the course of the research. Researchers often revise their research question and change their sampling or field strategies while doing the research. For example, MacIntyre notes that the published reports did not contain a full account of how the research design for her study changed while she was in the field:

> In the book describing the study I simply state that I used a mixture of prospective follow-up techniques and cross-sectional interview and observational techniques to obtain more information about certain points and key events. This implies, I suppose, that this was the original intention; from what I have said above I hope it is clear that this was not so, and in fact I initially approached the supplementary strategies with a distinct feeling of 'second-best-ism'. In retrospect, however, were I to do a similar study again, I would include such strategies as an integral part of the design from the beginning (1979, p. 766).

In qualitative research, data are collected in light of what you have found in previous observations. The journal should include a discussion of how past knowledge is influencing what you are thinking about and what data will be next collected. You should be asking questions such as, 'What is it that I know so far?', 'What do I not know?', 'What do I need to know?', and 'How do I collect this information?'.

An analytical file should be written with the view that this represents an opportunity for the researcher to reflect on issues raised in the data and to examine how these issues relate to larger theoretical issues. A number of strategies have been suggested to facilitate this process. Taylor and Bogdan (1984) recommend writing 'story lines' (see chapter 11) and using these to guide the analysis. The story line attempts to identify the main threads running through the data. It answers the question 'What conclusions can I reach from the information I have at hand?'. Strauss (1987) suggests scrutinising the data by asking the following questions to 'open up' the inquiry. These are, 'What study are these data pertinent to?', 'What is the main story here, and why?', 'What category or property of a category, or what part of the emerging theory, does this incident indicate?'. The purpose of asking these questions is to force the generation of categories which allow you to develop propositions. (Chapter 11 will discuss the importance of classifying data into categories.)

Of course, the analytical file becomes denser in information as the study progresses. The aim is to collect information that will generate insightful propositions relevant to the study, and to develop, refine and reformulate the questions asked. As tentative propositions are identified and modified, the researcher begins to focus on key issues and test the validity and reliability of the emerging propositions. Thus, the early days allow for the discovery of concepts and themes, while latter interviews focus on building, testing and establishing links between concepts. Not surprisingly, the entries at first will be general and descriptive. However, as propositions are developed, revised and expanded, the notes become more focused and centre around interpreting data and theorising.

A central feature of this work involves developing concepts. Concepts are abstract ideas generalised from empirical facts. Concepts are constructed to illuminate social processes and phenomena which are not readily apparent through descriptions of specific instances. You should maintain a record of concepts and themes emerging from the data. Every time a theme or concept is identified, include it in the notes. It is important that you remember that there are many styles of writing your analytical file. The notes included in figure 10.5 are offered as an example of one approach.

Speculation is an important aspect of any research. It plays a central role in developing ideas. Feel free to include in the notes any ideas that come to mind, and as long as they are plausible, write them down. You will have the opportunity to test the ideas as the data are collected. Too often researchers do not bother to write their ideas down because they have not collected all the data. The danger of being too cautious and over-concerned with having all the facts in front of you is that you may lose good ideas. As Bogdan and Biklen (1992) note, facts are important but they are not the end. They should be seen as a means to clear thinking and the generation of ideas. Facts can always be retrieved, ideas cannot!

Writing an analytical file: an example

The purpose of presenting the analytical file is to highlight a number of important features associated with qualitative data analysis. Firstly, framing the research question and developing themes and concepts involves a discursive dialogue between the researcher, the literature, other sources (for example, discussions with experts who have views on the topic), and the data being collected. Secondly, the initial research question is not fixed but is subject to constant revision. The refining of the analysis has some similarities to editing (see chapter 11). It involves making minor adjustments, re-doing substantial proportions of the conceptual work, further developing or clarifying themes, as well as removing 'clutter' in order to interpret and give more focused meaning to the data. Thirdly, as was noted earlier, it is only with continuing field experience and writing about that experience over a period of time that issues develop and become clearer. An analytical file can not be written over a few intense sessions. Emerging ideas need to be played with, investigated, set aside and re-examined in the light of new insights emerging from the data.

The following example of an analytical file (figure 10.5) has been taken from a research project (Ridge, Minichiello & Plummer 1994) which examines possible reasons and explanations behind continued HIV (Human Immunodeficiency Virus) infection among young gay men in Melbourne. The study was formulated within the context of understanding the meanings behind sexual interactions. Sex usually involves an interaction between more than one person, occurring in various settings, and within a broader sociopolitical context (Davies et al. 1993). It is important to note that the study described here is in its conceptualisation stage and the material presented includes a brief summary of the literature review, selected extracts from the analytical file covering the first three interviews with Martin, John and Nathan (names and places have been changed), and a commentary which provides a data analysis context for the extracts.

Discovering the meaning of masculinity

The researcher's conceptual understanding of just one category, namely 'masculinities', will be traced through his assumptions about the topic, a review of the literature and the first few interviews. The research period covered in the discussion of the analytical file covers the first five months of the project. A short summary of the researcher's thinking about the broad topic area is presented below with the purpose of describing how masculinity was conceptualised by the researcher.

The researcher had a hunch, based upon his own work experiences in HIV prevention at the AIDS Council, that masculinity, social class, sexual identity, and 'connection to the gay community' would be important in understanding the reasons and contexts for unsafe sex among gay men. After reviewing the literature and analysing the first few interviews, the researcher's understanding of these categories had changed. For example, the importance of becoming attached to the gay community for encouraging safe sex, as reported by Kippax, Connell, Dowsett and Crawford (1993), did not surface in the data after three interviews, despite the researcher's attempts to replicate this finding. This concept was gradually replaced with the idea of personal and collective sexual pathways for incorporating sexual activity into one's social life. Issues such as type of sexual partnerships (for example, relationships and episodic sex), the type of male-to-male sex culture that men became involved in (for example, commercial, community organisations, private networks) and the meaning of these pathways to the men were the notable issues that emerged from the data and were discussed in the analytical file.

The influence of the general literature

In everyday life, and in the biomedical literature, masculinity is often considered to be a natural biological trait in men (this is sometimes called essentialism). Others see masculinity as a sex role which is learnt and socially structured around stereotyped expectations between actors. The literature search generated hundreds of journal papers on sex-role theory. However, this literature did not help to clarify for the researcher how the concept of masculinity could inform the research question. Nor did it address the initial hunches about masculinity that the researcher had. Eventually, a book by Bob Connell titled *Gender and Power* (1987) struck a chord with the researcher's understanding about gender, pointing to its importance in sex. This text saved a great deal of time because it contained a critical review of a vast literature, and reflexively worked through issues and concepts that the author had spent many years developing. The researcher treated this text as just one part of the conversation between the general theory and the current project.

Connell (1987) highlights a number of conceptual problems in discussing masculinity as 'natural', 'biological', a 'sex role' or even an 'identity'. Following on from Connell and others, the researcher framed his initial understanding of gender within a comprehensive practice-based gender system, where gender relations are organised as an ongoing concern. Individuals do not simply have gender—it is a property of collectivities and historical processes. Since gender is soxcially constructed in practice, we can conceive multiple kinds of femininities and masculinities existing at any one time, and new ones emerging over time. Moreover, resources and power are connected with dominant forms of masculinity, accounting for the hierarchical and dynamic nature of masculinities. This suggests that there are dominant masculinities and subordinated masculinities. Connell has noted that gay men are mostly 'straight acting', and they are not necessarily excluded from valued (dominant) masculinities (Connell 1992). Yet, they often face 'structurally-induced conflicts' due to their sexual object choice being inconsistent with dominant masculinities.

In addition to Connell's work, recent HIV research has also made heterosexuality problematic in relation to sexual practices. This work shows how sex is situated in 'gendered power relationships' which often make it difficult for women to insist on safe sex. For example, women are often expected to be passive but responsible for fulfilling an uncontrollable male sexual desire (Holland et al. 1992). In another study, men generally only used condoms provided the women made the decision to use them, and did all the work to maintain their use (Browne & Minichiello 1994). These findings, along with theorising on gender relations, led the researcher to speculate that, in some way, a hierarchy of masculinities is operating among gay men, and that this may have implications for sexual safety.

Extracts from an analytical file

In analysing the interview material, the researcher was conceptualising masculinities in terms of gender relations, where multiple kinds of masculinities exist with different meanings attached to them. By the start of the first interview, he was still only guessing about what aspects of masculinity would be important for sexual safety in gay men. Three main categories of masculinity as outlined by Connell (1992)—hegemonic, complicit and subordinated—were used in the initial theoretical sampling.

The first interview was with a young gay man called 'Martin' who was later classified as representing the category of 'complicit masculinity'. The file reproduced below includes an analysis of Martin's first sexual encounter, the researcher's interpretation of the data, and the identification of further issues needing investigation.

19/8/93: First interview with Martin: issues related to masculinity ... *I think the first indicator of gender issues was when Martin 'panicked' about the encounter with the pizza deliverer (who he had invited into his home) because he didn't know if the deliverer was 'gay or straight'. He was worried that if he revealed that the videos in his drawer were gay pornography that 'he would be really upset, or ... bash me up or something like that'. Here, in Connell's terms, is a potential encounter with a dominant masculinity for Martin. Perhaps this fear of a more dominant masculinity is an important factor in Martin's acting as 'straight' most of the time in the wider world. This concern for possible conflict helped to maintain the uncertainty of this encounter, which turned out in the end to be Martin's first ever sexual encounter. Perhaps Martin's fear of violence or disapproval, by contributing to the maintenance of uncertainty about the sexual encounter, handed over control of the situation to the pizza deliverer. It was the pizza deliverer who had to end the uncertainty, by making obvious moves towards sex. Martin tried to interpret each move as non-sexual due to his fear, even when it would be clear to outside observers that the pizza deliverer was making sexual advances, for example the pizza deliverer went into Martin's bedroom, he told Martin that he had his first sexual experience with his brother. So, an encounter with a masculinity which appears threatening or more dominant can mean less control in sex, but probably not always since power in sexual relations has many sources. This fear of violence, force or even disapproval from a male is one that has been found in samples of heterosexual women to be important in influencing sexual safety. Here is evidence of its importance in sex between men who have sex with men. Hegemonic masculinity can be an important consideration in a man's first same-sex encounter when he is inexperienced, but is it still important in further encounters? Importantly, not being in control of this first encounter did not result in unsafe sex due to other conditions, for example the pizza deliverer did not desire unsafe sex, Martin was well informed and concerned about avoiding HIV. Future questions would need to ascertain under what conditions in an encounter with a perceived dominant masculinity would unsafe sex result. Notice how conflict was avoided by Martin in this situation (he hid his homosexuality right up until the actual sexual encounter) and how control can be taken up by one person with out any visible conflict emerging ...*

The extract shows how fear of other men can influence a sexual encounter. Mapping out ideas about the role of fear in sex, and strategies used by Martin to avoid conflict, allowed the researcher to follow and explore the significance of these issues. In subsequent interviews these ideas gained more analytical importance when they were mentioned and expanded upon by other informants (see example of 'John' later). The researcher was sensitised to ideas of fear and avoidance of conflict recorded in the analytical file, and could therefore explore them further in subsequent interviews.

Another extract later in the file contains the seeds of an emerging concept in the data about how male-to-male sex can lead to opportunities for men to experiment with, and reorganise their masculinity in situated activity.

It wasn't until Martin came to Australia (he was born in South-East Asia) and saw that gay men could be 'straight acting too' (he said that gay men were seen as 'effeminate' in his home country) that he began to see that he could identify with being gay ... Martin talks about not fitting into the macho image of Western society. This gives him some protection from his point of view. He feels he can get away with things that Australian men cannot for example, saying 'that's sweet' of an account summary sheet at work ... Martin says he tries to be straight acting most of the time. Identifying as gay has not meant that he has negated his masculinity (for example, he cultivates a muscular masculinity in the gay community). For Martin, what he actually says is important in the process of maintaining his masculinity. He will sometimes say something, but then realise that he shouldn't have said it, for example saying the word 'bitch' at work. He also controls what he wears. He will avoid wearing jewellery, for example. Yet, he still wears coded clothing that would in his mind signify that he is gay to other gay men. He also tries to be softly spoken—he is modifying how he says things. He finds this quite difficult. He considers the energy used to maintain this masculinity in a straight environment as 'wasted energy'. He is able to relax more in the gay world. He actually minimised the environment where he has to play straight—seems to be a way of saving 'wasted energy'— therefore all his friends are 'fag-hags' or gay, and he has distanced himself from his family ... Martin feels it is easier to be a guy in his workplace, because you 'can be more aggressive'. He believes that females are treated 'sort of patronisingly' in his workplace. He sees there being more work opportunities for males. He includes himself when he talks about all the males sitting around 'bitching' about a female worker who has been promoted, even though he has said men have more opportunities. Is Martin trying to fit into the masculinity of office, or does he really resent a female being promoted ahead of him? Martin would appear to have a complicit masculinity in Connell's conceptualisation.

The above extract attempts to explain how Martin was not negating his masculinity. Rather, he was cultivating a masculinity which was more appropriate under the various (gay or straight) circumstances. It is not until after more data collection and analysis that the researcher elaborates on this idea, and comes to label this phenomenon 'renegotiating masculinity'. This concept highlights how homosexuality provides opportunities to renegotiate a valued masculinity in various interactions and settings. Not all men will renegotiate in this way, since some may negate the importance of this strategy. The researcher is also trying to work out whether Martin has a hegemonic, complicit or negated masculinity (that is, Connell's masculine hierarchy) as in the initial theoretical sampling model. The lack of direct connection of these categories of masculinity to Martin's sex life alerts the researcher that he should also be exploring other aspects of masculinity.

The next interview with 'John' allowed for the comparison and contrasting of issues that emerged from the first interview; for example avoidance of conflict and fear of other men. For this sexually experienced gay man who identified as 'macho', fear of other men was an important part of his sex life in some settings.

30/8/93: Interview with John: issues related to masculinity ... *In a commercial sex-on-premises venue, John says he always thinks about whether or not the 'stranger(s)' he encounters will do 'something physically to my well-being'. So, he is not just thinking about safety from HIV, but also safety from more immediate physical danger ... He seems to fear other men and this is at a venue in which presumably he is dealing only with men who have sex with men (MSM), not homophobic heterosexuals ... it appears that a similar differentiation or hierarchy of masculinity (to the wider gender system) is also operating in this more unlikely environment. I wonder whether this is the same system that operates in the wider culture, or whether it is a micro-environment that reproduces the wider culture?*

It is interesting that dominant masculinity should be feared (especially by a self-confessed 'macho' male) at a commercial venue for men who have sex with men (MSM) where presumably hegemonic masculinity (defined as exclusively heterosexual in our society) is excluded. This suggests that fear of dominant masculinity is not just limited to fear of homophobic heterosexual males, first sexual encounters, nor to MSM who have more subordinated masculinities.

This insight supported the initial speculation about a hierarchy of masculinities operating among gay men. Yet, the analysis here is still unclear with regards to the conceptual significance of this finding. It fails to identify the possibility that male-to-male sex environments could do more than merely reproduce the wider gender system, but modify or even subvert it. After comparing the story-lines across the cases, the researcher became sensitive to the idea that the wider gender system is somewhat separated out from the immediate male-to-male sex environment. This separation means that the patterns of masculinities in the wider system and the male-to-male environment could be quite different.

It seems that in any environment, a system of dynamic masculinities can be set up and exist as a collective system for that environment separated from but not unrelated to the wider system of gender relations ... There will be competing masculinities in many environments, as well as zones of co-operation (for example, relationships). In a sex-on-premises venue, or any gay venue, there are usually obvious displays of masculinity which are important in sexual currency, for example in sexual attraction. Men may wear certain clothes or use their bodies in certain ways to indicate their masculinity. Some men may not be interested in winning a position of dominant masculinity in a setting or situated activity.

A 'conversation' with the general literature is then developed to further clarify concepts emerging from the data.

Layder's research map (Layder 1993) is important here. Although there is the macro social form (called context by Layder) of gender, there is also the immediate environment of social activity (the setting), the dynamics of face to face interaction (situated activity), and the biographical experiences and social involvements (the self) to be considered. Each element has its own history. So, even if a man doesn't have a dominant masculinity in the wider context (i.e. the wider gender system), he may be closer to the peak in a given setting and situated activity. He may or may not be interested in having a valued masculinity in a certain situation.

After analysing more data, issues associated with the concept of 'renegotiating for a valued masculinity' for men who move into a male-to-male sex setting are explained using Layder's (1993) research map. Towards the end of the analysis of the second interview, ideas about masculinity are summarised.

John's maleness is central to his identity ... He openly enjoys and acknowledges the benefits of being a male, but he indicates that this is part of an ongoing social process. To remain a male for example, he needs to be with men and cultivate correct body displays and attitudes. He also seems to fear male power to some degree, even in sex venues. It was important for him to maintain his maleness in his so-called 'coming out' process: 'looking as straight as possible'. Despite this, he is critical of some aspects of gay and straight male culture for example, exclusion of lesbians from gay venues. There is room here to rework masculinity.

It was important for John to remain 'straight' as he moved from a non-gay to a gay identity. This presented teething problems for John as he could not identify with the less than straight acting gay men. There is acknowledgment that a non-heterosexual identity was a flaw in his masculinity, and this may have contributed to his confusion during his recent transition to a gay identity.

'Beats' (secluded public places where men look for sexual partners) and sex venues appear to have presented John with an opportunity to renegotiate for a valued masculinity in a situation where compulsory heterosexual masculinity was largely excluded. However, unlike many gay men, John was also able to feel comfortable in heterosexual male environments. Beats and sex venues cultivate all male environments with overt displays of masculinity which can allow renegotiation of masculinity, and can act as sexual currency since masculinity is prized by many men. Evidence of dynamic masculine environments includes the fear John feels about physical harm even at sex venues where homophobic bashers would be almost entirely excluded. Renegotiating masculinity among gay men is ongoing.

John seems to retain a great deal of control over others, but backs down from confronting and challenging other men on various occasions. As with Martin, he avoids confrontation if possible, and this may be an important strategy in being able to maintain his masculinity. For example, he will steer a sexual encounter away from anal sex if there is no condom available rather than deal with a possible conflict in desires for anal sex if it was actually verbally negotiated. This is an example of a strategic skill which can enable safe sex to occur. For John, sharing in the 'benefits' of maleness (for example, access to sex as required) is enough usually to cover over any underlying conflict or power imbalances. On the occasions that conflict emerges, John uses strategies to cover over open conflict or aggression, for example, giving out a fake phone number to someone who insists on seeing him again.

Being in control is central to John, and this provides challenges in sexual encounters and relationships. Having this largely controlling or assertive masculinity, John's unsafe sexual experiences were actively sought in that he was in control. His construction of masculinity may have even given him a licence to go out and get sexual experience, including unsafe sex. For example, in one instance, his explanation of having unsafe sex was that he was 'really horny'. He had a sexual drive which would not be 'interrupted', allowing him to dismiss ideas of 'what am I doing?' for the time being ...

Masculine ideology is also used as sexual currency, and it can be used to interpret how other partners will act for example, 'passionate men' who are almost uncontrollable during sex ... Does this mean that men who have less control over other men are less able to negotiate safe sex when confronted by a man who is 'passionate' and barely under control? Even in a passionate session, John can indicate non-verbally what he wants done by his partner, and also, because men know what men like, many just seem to know anyway.

An 'in control' masculinity may be related to going out and actively finding sex (safe or unsafe, receptive or insertive) as a method of dealing with emotional troubles (for example, the confusion from being in a sexual identity transition) in that it is acting on the world. This instrumentality may have contributed to John's transient view of his place in the world as 'me against the world', and this was related to occasions of unsafe sex by symbolically 'fucking the world' ...

A 'storyline' on the category of masculinity is developed in an attempt to identify the main threads running through the informant's account. The first two interviews are also jointly analysed in order to bring these threads together for comparing and contrasting. Storylines and comparisons assist in answering the questions: What is it that I know now? What conclusions can I reach? What themes and concepts have I discovered? How can I build on these concepts, refine them, and establish links between them?

Both Martin and John feared male aggression, although John seemed to have a more assertive masculinity than Martin. Both attempted to avoid open conflict with their sexual partners, and this may have had implications for negotiating safe sex ... Being Asian, Martin felt he could get away with less than masculine behaviour, but John, who was of Southern European background, did not talk about being able to get away with feminine traits.

Martin acknowledges that his masculinity is self-conscious—he tries to be 'straight acting' in the wider context, and he finds it quite difficult and slips up at times. He is more relaxed in the gay world, and finds maintaining masculinity less of a chore here. Whereas John seems to actually identify as masculine and enjoy it, Martin seems to be using it as a cover ... (Unlike John) Martin appears to have failed to develop a physical 'macho' masculinity, but may have built a masculinity based on academic and rational achievement, which has delivered the goods in terms of good career prospects. John appears to have placed less emphasis in this area (possibly related to social class?) compared to physical displays. However, recently, Martin has taken up body building and John is trying to build a career.

The researcher goes on to speculate that perhaps an alternative categorisation of masculinity (to hegemonic/complicit/negated) is that of control/non-control. For example, Martin seems to have a less controlling kind of masculinity compared to John in terms of his ability to physically assert his will over other men. This speculation, however, is later refuted.

Perhaps it is better to assume that most men in this sample, (gay, straight or whatever) want to gain control over others, unless they have reflexively worked through issues about masculinity in a certain fashion and made conscious decisions to change for example, as have some men in the men's movement. Martin derives his masculine control over the environment more from rationality, whereas John derives his control more from a kind of physical display and assertion. This may be an important distinction in how control is exercised in relation to sex. Martin's rationality may have been important in his avoiding HIV. He had a good career based on rationality and he wanted to know the minutest details about HIV transmission in order that he could avoid ill health. John on the other hand also wanted to avoid HIV, but on occasions, he used his control to facilitate unsafe sex.

In analysing the third interview, the idea of men having an obligation to go out and secure sexual experience and learn sexual technique was proposed. This 'obligation' was not recognised as important initially, but was later discovered to be present in the stories of all three men. Just like straight men, gay men seem to have a need to acquire sexual technique by going out to get 'experience'. Nathan and the other informants often seemed to have sex when they were not even feeling 'horny', and couched it in terms of gaining experience. Indeed, for Nathan, sex with men became 'compulsive' and, at one stage, he felt he was totally unable to control his sexual encounters with men.

6/10/93: Interview with Nathan: issues related to masculinity. *Even during sex, he still liked the men to take the initiative, because he 'was sort of learning'. He felt 'inexperienced' early on. He even felt like he should be apologising for the 'fumbling'. He knew a lot about sex with women, but he 'didn't know anything about sex with men'. So, it may not just be a case of applying experience of sex with women to that of men. Why not? Certainly the activities are different, and it involves an understanding that sex is more than just penetration (certainly in Nathan's case where he wasn't having any penetrative anal sex with men). The wider society equates sex with vaginal penetration and so this new activity with men needs to be understood apart from this conceptualisation.*

So, in this training, I wonder where the transition from inactive learner to active participant occurs? The idea of fumbling that Nathan talks about seems to indicate a learning by trial and error. In these instructor/learner relationships, the instructor has the resources of knowledge and technique. I wonder why Nathan did not have unprotected anal sex in this situation? Perhaps it was not practical in the situation. Perhaps as part of his privileged-class background he was able to avoid this as a risk to his future and career? Perhaps he just wasn't in a situation that presented this option.

After the first few interviews, masculinity or 'modern male sexuality' emerged as important in explaining patterns of sexual safety. The simple hegemonic/complicit/negated masculinity and control/non-control masculinity concepts now appeared inadequate. It became obvious to the researcher that different conceptualisations for theoretical sampling were needed.

I could apply the concept of 'career' as described by Layder. He widens the concept of 'career' to take account of 'hidden' power differentials and the meshing of 'individual and collective forces'. So, I could look at masculinity as a kind of career. This would incorporate the idea that there are varying pathways through the gender system, and that male-to-male sex offers a particular opportunity to 'renegotiate' and even subvert aspects of masculinity. The state of a man's masculinity, and the way that it is reorganised or not reorganised through out a man's sexual career has possible implications for sexual safety as demonstrated in these first interviews ...

An alternative theoretical sampling plan was then developed in order to reflect the complexity of the data on masculinity, and select negative cases using the analytical induction method.

Over my holidays, I had the chance to read Anthony Giddens' new book called The Transformation of Intimacy *(1992). As I read through the book it occurred to me that he was tackling some of the issues about 'masculinity' or 'male sexuality' that I had found in my first interviews. He has tried to make sense of aspects of modern male sexuality including difficulties with intimacy, sexual 'compulsion', objectification, violence, dominance, control and conquest. Giddens' theorising may provide clues on how a masculine 'career' could be initially conceptualised. He makes an important point when he shows that some women now follow the masculine model in our society. I have had trouble thinking about how I could theoretically sample a concept of 'masculine career' and there may be a few clues here. I will need to identify different types of masculine career in order to select negative cases for comparison in the analytic induction method. Masculinity and male sexuality are far more complicated and slippery than I had imagined to begin with. After reading this book, I got the sense that 'masculinity', a gender relations concept, could be somewhat separated out from the idea of 'male sexuality', and this needs further thinking through.*

The researcher shifted his focus from being preoccupied with the kind of masculinity men had (for example, dominant, subordinate) to the constant 'renegotiation' of masculinities among gay men in situated activities (for example, attracting sexual partners) and various settings (for example, sex-on-premises venues, relationships). His understanding of masculinity and male sexuality was expanded to include themes such as control, body use, objectifying, issues of intimacy, competing and co-operation, autonomy, instrumentality, training for sexual skills, rationality, sex drives, and 'compulsive' sex. The analysis now focused on mapping pathways through the gender system and establishing links with other categories for example, sexual pathways and safety. Consulting the general literature again offered new insights on ways in which masculinity could be investigated.

The above discussion shows how over the span of the first few interviews the original conceptualisations and speculations about masculinity and sexual safety changed and became more conceptually complex. A host of issues about masculine sexuality, which were not anticipated by the researcher prior to entering the field (for example, sexual 'compulsion'), were located in the data.

Figure 10.5 An example of an analytical file

Note: One of the author's analytical file on 'Young Gay Men, Sexual Pathways and HIV Transmission' Project, conducted by the Sexual Health Research Group, School of Behavioural Health Sciences, La Trobe University.

Concluding remarks on note-taking

We have reviewed how notes are made, what format is used and what types of fieldnotes are produced. Fieldnotes can be organised into different types of files: transcript file, personal file and analytical file. These files assist the researcher to organise and reflect upon the information he or she is collecting and the strategies used.

Data recording is an essential component of the research process. It is a basic building block which permits the researcher to make sense of the information that is being assembled. Regardless of how interesting and rich the data are, they are of no use to anyone unless they are recorded accurately and systematically. For this reason, data recording needs to be carefully programmed into the research timetable. However, producing fieldnotes and transcriptions from interviews is but one part of the research process. We need to consider the interrelationship between producing fieldnotes and data analysis. This topic will be pursued in chapter 11.

Chapter 11

Analysing the data and writing it up

(With Rosemarie Stynes)

The purpose of this chapter is to teach students how to analyse, interpret and report qualitative data. We will describe basic approaches to making sense of data collected through in-depth interviewing. The key issues addressed are: how are links made between the data that are recorded and subsequent theoretical writings? And how are qualitative data presented in final reports? Before we address these questions, we would like to make a few general comments about issues relating to analysing qualitative data.

First, a definition of data analysis is required. The aim of data analysis is to find meaning in the information collected. Data analysis is the process of systematically arranging and presenting information in order to search for ideas. Data analysis can be broken down into a series of decisions. Taylor and Bogdan (1984) identify three distinct stages. The first stage involves coding the data, discovering themes and developing propositions. The second stage is refining one's themes and propositions. The third stage centres around reporting the findings.

Second, data analysis and data collection occur simultaneously in qualitative research. This point should not be overlooked. Unlike quantitative researchers who can employ a research assistant to collect and code the data, qualitative researchers lack a similar division of labour between data collection, coding and analysis. The ongoing analysis that takes place in qualitative research requires that the researcher develops an eye for detecting the conceptual issues while the data are collected. Without analysis occurring in the field, data has no direction.

Third, as shown in the previous chapter, the sheer size of data collected through in-depth interviewing can overload the researcher, and make qualitative data analysis an impossible task. Fortunately, there are techniques that you can use to overcome such problems. The data must be broken up into manageable units. This requires organisation so that you read and retrieve parts of the data that are relevant to the questions being addressed. It is important to remember that data analysis does not happen overnight. Many researchers read and re-read their notes and fieldnotes for several weeks or even months. This allows them to discover recurring themes or events which stand out. You should not commence intensive data analysis until you are completely familiar with your data.

The remainder of this chapter will discuss techniques for analysing and reporting data, and illustrate these with examples from our own research.

Analytic induction method

A central feature of data analysis is conceptualising data into theory. How do we transform strings of sentences (for example, raw data) into meaningful data which contribute to knowledge? This question cannot be answered without first understanding what data are. Data collected by using in-depth interviewing include the material the researcher has collected through talking to people. It should be obvious from our discussion in chapter 10 that people's accounts as presented in the transcript file are sentences about beliefs, feelings and state of affairs as they see them. These data are both the evidence and the clues from which knowledge and understanding can emerge. For data to become meaningful for analysis, the researcher has to identify common themes and/or propositions which link issues together, and ground the analysis in the informant's understandings and in scientific translations of it.

The main challenge facing qualitative researchers is how to collect and analyse data simultaneously. The analytic induction method uses induction not as described in chapter 2 to justify the theory but as a means of creating explanation in the data. It allows for ideas to emerge from the data as they are collected. Glaser and Strauss (1965) highlight the following steps:

1 developing a general statement about a topic;
2 collecting data to gain a better understanding of the topic;
3 modifying, revising and expanding the statement as data are collected;
4 searching for cases which provide the opportunity to revise the level of understanding reached by the researcher;
5 developing a satisfactory explanation.

The method described here is only one of many ways in which meaning into data can be constructed. There are two points worth mentioning. First, the classification of qualitative research as 'inductive' and quantitative research as 'deductive' presents too much of a black and white picture. Both methods include inductive and deductive reasoning in their analysis procedure. For example, quantitative researchers often rely on their computer (for example, step wise multiple regression analysis) to identify variables which are statistically significant. They then search for possible explanations for why such relationships exist. Likewise, qualitative researchers eventually reach a level in their analysis where propositions are being 'tested' in the field. Second, there are many different forms of qualitative analysis; each of these necessitating modifications in how the analysis is conducted. Tesch (1990) and Dey (1993) provide a useful description on the different types of qualitative analysis.

This chapter, however, focuses on applying the analytic induction method to collect and analyse qualitative data. Figure 11.1 illustrates how the principles of the *analytical induction method* are put into practice. Data are collected within a reflective model (Strauss 1987) where the researcher develops a general research question, conducts his or her first interview, thinks about and analyses this data, conducts another interview, then does more analysis and revision of the proposition, and so on.

The early days of the data-collection stage are often descriptive and exploratory. Let us move through the spiral displayed in figure 11.1 and illustrate this point with an example. You want to study why older people move into nursing homes. Not all of the factors involved in the decision-making process for entering nursing homes are known. (Of course, you have reviewed the literature and this has provided some leads.) You interview your first informant—Miss Jones. After analysing the transcript of Miss Jones' interview, you develop propositions about why older people move into nursing homes and refine the questions asked in subsequent interviews. On the basis of the material and analysis from the first interview, you decide that the research question should focus on understanding the processes by which older persons are included or excluded from the decision. You develop a general proposition: never-married people living alone make the decision to move into a nursing home because they anticipate dependency in their old age.

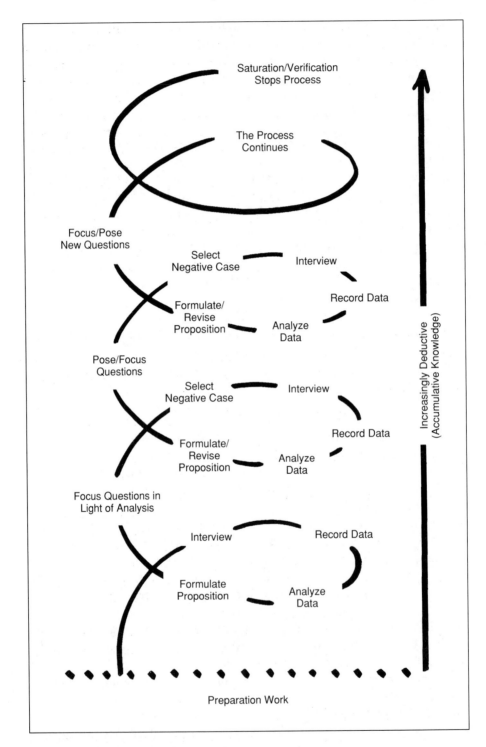

Figure 11.1 The qualitative research process

Source: Adapted from Eckett, J. 1988, 'Ethnographic research on ageing', in *Qualitative Gerontology*, eds S. Reinharz & G. Rowles, Springer, New York, p. 243.

The next step is to locate a negative case that will extend your understanding of the social processes by which older people enter nursing homes. Miss Jones represents a never-married person who made her own decision to move into a nursing home. What happens to our proposition if we locate a resident who has never married but had others make the decision for her? Will it still be true that making the decision to move into a nursing home is dependent on never being married? Are there never-married people who do not plan ahead? How does this information affect our understanding of the factors that determine an older person making their own decision to move to a nursing home? You continue this process until you have reached saturation, that is, until you feel that you have reached an adequate level of explanation. Thus, the early days of data collection and analysis involve the discovery of concepts and the development of propositions, while the interviews in the latter days focus on testing the links established between themes in order to assess the validity of propositions.

Philosophical issues associated with data analysis

All we assume here is the basic position taken in chapter 2; one cannot begin to undertake qualitative data analysis without understanding in detail the philosophical issues which underpin it. Before we proceed to present the mechanical aspects of data analysis, it is necessary to discuss conceptual questions associated with the issue of what to analyse. However, it is not the purpose of this chapter to provide a detailed exposition of how to make sense of human action be it physical or verbal. (For a detailed discussion see Boudon 1982, Geertz 1973 and Ricoeur 1974.) As we discussed in chapters 1 and 2, there are different ways of interpreting social phenomena. The distinction between positivist and interpretative approaches ultimately depends on the distinction between causes and reasons. That distinction depends upon another, that of persons and things. Is there an absolute difference between persons and things?

Understanding a person requires a constantly shifting global assessment of his or her beliefs, utterances, actions and cultural settings. It is assumptions made about individuals and their relationship to society that gives qualitative data a different form from that of quantitative data. These assumptions direct us to ask what is to be regarded as the unit of analysis.

What do you code?

The first issue is what gets coded? Or to put it differently, what is the unit of analysis? When you look at transcripts and notes from the interviews, are you looking for groups of words, phrases, sentences, themes or even the writing between the lines?

Some researchers suggest that the doing of content analysis can focus on several elements of the interview transcript or written document (for example, letters and diaries); and that these elements are counted in terms of their frequency of appearance (Berg 1989). We, on the other hand, suggest that these elements should not only be counted in numerical terms, but should also be examined for meaning. The elements or units of analysis we consider to be useful are as follows.

Words. Individual words are usually the smallest unit examined during a content analysis. Sometimes, the researcher does a frequency count—seeing how many times a word (which has been designated as significant) appears in the text. In other instances, the researcher also examines the way in which the word appears to be used for example, as a descriptor, as an expletive, incorrect semantic usage, in group and outgroup differentiation, and so on.

Concepts. Concepts are words grouped together in clusters to indicate particular ideas. Concepts are often used in the expression of themes, that is, a group of concepts such as delinquency and fraud may be linked in the informant's discussion with the interviewer, to indicate one specific theme in that discussion. The theme would be one focusing on deviance.

Sentences. Obviously, an interviewee will often explicitly say what the researcher is looking for. In addition, words, concepts and themes are all evaluated in terms of their various locations in sentences of discourse. Sentences in this way are the most fundamental and indispensable units of any analysis of qualitative data.

Themes. The researcher looks for themes as expressed in the transcript. The themes can be expressed in single words, phrases, sentences, paragraphs or even entire documents. When the researcher uses themes as the unit of analysis he or she is primarily looking for the expression of an idea irrespective of its grammatical location. It is often made up of concepts which are linked together either by the informant and/or the interviewer.

These units and elements are analysed in terms of the semantics indicated by the informant's usage of them. Obviously, it is a matter of how the researcher interprets that usage. For instance, the researcher could be interpreting what Berg (1989, p. 107) labels the manifest content of the manuscript, that is, 'those elements that are physically present and countable'; or the researcher might be examining what he calls the latent content or 'the symbolism underlying the physically presented data', that is, the message that is written between the lines. Whenever we interpret passages of transcript, we can choose to do either manifest or latent content analysis, or both. Where we read between the lines, we must ask ourselves whether our reading is consistent with the informant's perspective. This is not an easy matter to determine and it is the point at which any mode of analysis is open to criticism. Nevertheless, all social interpretation is dependent on this latent content analysis and it is inherent in the analytic enterprise itself. Any system of analysis must label some sentences as lies, jokes and sarcasm and apply some systems (for example, Freud and Marx). Many of our beliefs and purposes are hidden from ourselves and the researcher must hope to discover these hidden beliefs and purposes by complex analytic means.

Even when you have solved the question of what gets coded by selecting the appropriate unit of analysis, the following questions remain: How do you distinguish between key issues and peripheral issues? In fact, can we legitimately use such categorisations at all? Do we take statements at their face value? Do we look for hidden meanings which are not apparent in the text but are part of our understanding of the social interaction of the interview, the informant's views and our knowledge of the informant's situation?

This last issue highlights several possibilities. First, that the researcher, in conversation with the informant, can misunderstand the meanings that the informant intends (Brown 1983). While there is debate about ways in which researchers can deal with this methodological concern, a commonly used strategy is to listen to what the informant tells us, and to use ourselves to filter what he or she says without distorting the intended meaning—this can be done by checking back with the informant. Alternatively, it is sometimes the case that the informant unintentionally provides information and expressions of attitude which he or she has not consciously examined. It is only when the researcher recognises patterns of meaning in the conversation that the discussion becomes part of the analysis.

For the researcher to act as an interpretative filter in this way, however, requires that he or she needs to go beyond the mere reporting of what was said. The researcher needs to create a picture of what might be the meaning. This is done in the context of shared symbols, language, culture and historical moments. As Brown points out:

> [the researcher] can not rest content with a restatement of the facts, say, about a birth weight, age of mother, parity, complications and so on. He must go on to consider their likely meaning to those involved and for this the relevance of the wider social context must be considered. Concern with meaning ultimately reflects a commitment to explore the significance of a happening or situation in terms of the lives as a whole of those involved. Fortunately, since we all spend much of our time doing just this for ourselves, the human mind is a suitable instrument for the task, even if it is only that of the investigator (1983, p. 35).

Thus, as was explored in chapter 2, the focus of the hermeneutic tradition is to empathically grasp the minds of others, the subjective meaning of their behaviours, that is, using *verstehen* or empathic understanding.

Secondly, the researcher is operating both within the knowledge worlds of the informant and the researcher's own discipline. An important distinction made by Rose (1982) in relation to this is that between *participant concepts* and *theoretical concepts*. Participant concepts are created by informants and couched in their everyday language. Theoretical concepts are created by the researcher and not immediately recognised by the informants as part of their terminology. An example of a participant concept is the idea of 'not having a say' presented in the 1987 Minichiello study which examines the decision-making process behind moving to a nursing home. Bowers' concept of 'protective caregiving' (see chapter 1) is an example of a theoretical concept. Participants' concepts are learned by the researcher who then interprets these by giving them scientific order and meaning, and using a theoretical concept to do this translation.

But you may be asking how does the above discussion help us solve the question of what gets coded? Trivialising centuries of debate on this issue, our position can be simply summarised as follows—regardless of the choice of the unit of analysis, an important skill to master is learning to understand the logic of the informant's use of idiom, and how to translate it into a system of conceptual thought. This requires studying the whole text, not only in the context of what was said, but also in terms of what was not said, and within the boundaries of the paradigm which the researcher chooses to apply. This is an important point. The interpretation of the conversation is more than simply a quantitative content analysis of the words spoken. Williams (1981, p. 170) points out that the researcher makes 'claims not primarily about the dictionary meanings of words but rather about the context in which the informants' terms are'. The researcher's aim, when doing data analysis, is to extract the essence of the informants' meanings as they are verbalised either as intended and unintended accounts.

The second issue is related to recognising that there is a debate as to whether understanding is influenced by theory. According to Kuhn (1970), scientists operating in different scientific traditions with different paradigms, work in different worlds and therefore use different filters to interpret what people have said to them. In chapter 2, we quoted Quine (1960) as saying that nothing guarantees that there will be one definitive interpretation of someone's meaning. This may explain why researchers disagree with each other when interpreting the results of studies. For example, in reviewing Minichiello's (1987) study of the role families play in the decision to place an aged relative into a nursing home, Connidis states that she reached a different conclusion because:

> the view of the older person as victim, and family members as coconspirators with outsiders ... is also a function of Minichiello's fairly compelling application of Goffman's work in Asylums to the plight of older persons at the time of entering nursing homes (1989, pp. 189–90).

In other words, she argues that Minichiello bases his analysi. use of a particular theoretical framework drawn from sociology. R. than casting family members as part of a conspiracy, she notes that famn, members play an advocate role and act as information sources for older people by informing and assisting older people in dealing with the bureaucratic structure. She argues that the family and health-care organisations operate as a partnership with those institutions (for example, nursing homes) that control various services. Connidis reaches a different conclusion because she uses a different sociological approach.

Techniques for doing qualitative data analysis

A number of researchers have developed techniques for analysing qualitative data. These include interactive reading, developing coding categories, writing *case summaries*, *typologising*, and computer analysis. While these techniques are discussed separately below, researchers often employ a number of these techniques together to analyse their data.

Interactive reading

Data needs to be read in an 'interactive way' in order to analyse it, a process which Dey (1993) compares to loosening 'the soil ... for the seeds of our analysis to put down roots and grow'. He summarises a number of techniques for 'interactive reading'. Similarly, Layder (1993) also presents guidelines in the 'research map' which can be used 'to prompt various lines of thought' during the research project.

Figure 11.2 integrates some of the key features involved in interactive reading. Techniques such as free association, making comparisons, shifting sequence and focus, interrogation, and transposing are high-lighted. The research map and substantive checklist shown in the figure largely reflect areas of concern to sociologists. A psychologist, for example, might have very different substantive concerns. In a research area such as sexual safety, a psychologist may focus on an individual's knowledge, attitudes, behaviour, personal interactions, and evaluation of social norms regarding safe sex. The checklist (or modification/amalgamation of these) adopted by the researcher will depend on the purpose of the research, the areas of interest of the researcher, the data, and trial and error.

Developing a coding system

The main preoccupation of the researcher when doing data analysis is identifying a coding system. But what do we mean by a coding system? A coding system is a means of reorganising the data according to conceptual themes recognised by the researcher. It is used to further enhance

Free association	Writing down all that comes to mind on a word, phrase or topic in order to question fixed assumptions.
Making comparisons	Compare different interviews, compare data with your own experiences, compare one bit of data with another.
The research map	Self—self-identity, psychobiography, life-career, an individual's social experience. Situated activity—face-to-face activity, focus on emergent meanings, understandings and definitions of situations. Setting—intermediate social organisation, for example bureaucracies, hospitals, domestic labour, social clubs. Context—macro social organisation for example, values, traditions, power relations, social and economic organisation. History (of each of the above factors). Interaction (of each of the above factors).
Shifting focus	Shifting focus between different levels within the data.
Shifting sequence	Reading through the data in different sequences.
The interrogative list	Asking questions of the data—Who? What? When? Where? Why? So What?
The substantive checklist	• Conditions • Interactions • Strategies and tactics • Consequences • Events • Processes
Transposing data	Asking 'What if?' questions in order to develop new perspectives on the data, for example 'What if these men were actors rather than managers?'.

Figure 11.2 Techniques for 'interactive reading'

Source: Modified from Dey, I. 1993, *Qualitative Data Analysis: A User Friendly Guide*, Routledge, London; and Layder, D. *1993, New Strategies in Social Research: An Introduction and a Guide*, Polity Press, Cambridge.

analysis. Codes can be derived from the informant's stories, research questions and theoretical frameworks. For example, if our research question is 'Who are the decision makers behind the institutionalisation decision for older people entering nursing homes?', we might develop the following coding system: decision makers (the coding scheme) and the coding subcategories (could be) older person, family members, friends, doctor, other professionals and so on. Certain theoretical approaches and disciplines suggest particular coding schemes (Bogdan & Biklen 1992). For example, Wiener (1982) was interested in studying the mechanisms which patients develop for the management of pain. Using a symbolic interactionist framework (see chapter 6), Wiener developed a series of concepts which centred around the different mechanisms people use to handle pain. One concept he developed was 'pacing'. The key to developing such a coding system is to create a list of words which can be conceptualised into categories and linked into a general framework.

Why is a coding system important? Any researcher who wishes to do good qualitative research must learn to code well. 'The excellence of the research rests in large part on the excellence of the coding' (Strauss 1987, p. 27). Codes label and reorganise the data according to topics which open the inquiry and permit the researcher to make sense of the thousands of lines of words. They are retrieval and organising devices that cluster the relevant segment of the data relating to a particular theme or proposition (Miles & Huberman 1994). They also play an important role in the process of discovering themes or developing propositions. As you code the data, you may stumble across ideas which bring the material together in a way that you had not previously thought about. For example, you might read the transcript of Mrs Young and decide that she was excluded from the decision to enter a nursing home. However, when you read the transcript of Mrs Baker you decide that she was fully involved in the decision. You write down these two words in your *analytical file*. You develop the coding scheme, 'involvement in the decision-making process', and identify four types of categories, fully involved, excluded, decision-involved and selection-involved in concert with your decision that this coding scheme provides a conceptual model for understanding the processes by which older people enter nursing homes.

When do you develop codes?

An important question you are probably asking yourself is when to start developing codes. The answer is simple. You start developing coding categories the moment you enter the field. We agree with Miles and Huberman (1994) that late coding weakens the analysis. Coding enhances the discovery of concepts and the testing of propositions as you collect the data. As figure 11.1 illustrates, you should always try to code the previous set of fieldnotes before starting the next interview.

Coding is not just something you do to 'get the data ready' for analysis, but something that drives ongoing data collection. It is a form of early (and continuing) analysis. It typically leads to a reshaping of your perspective and of your instrumentation for the next pass. At the same time, ongoing coding uncovers real or potential sources of bias, and surfaces incomplete or equivocal data that can be clarified next time out (Miles & Huberman 1994, p. 65).

The number of codes you develop will depend on the amount of data you have collected and the complexity of your analytical scheme.

There are general principles that you should follow when constructing codes. Codes need to be conceptually based and clearly defined. There is no point developing codes simply for the sake of putting words on your list. The codes you devise should be related to the research questions asked and fit into a conceptual scheme. For example, it is important that we know what is meant by decision makers, and that we can distinguish it from involvement in decision making.

Codes should not be superimposed on the data. Some codes will not work because the way in which they describe the phenomena is not the way these phenomena appear empirically. When this happens you will need to either revise the coding scheme or get rid of it. It is important that you realise that while you might begin with a large number of coding categories, these can be pruned as you refine the focus of your study and propositions (see Appendix).

Strategies for developing codes

A strategy that is commonly used by experienced researchers to develop codes is to ask the question, 'What is this thing (or things) I have before me?' (Lofland & Lofland 1984, p. 93). For example, Goffman (1961) was interested in studying mental institutions. In his attempt to answer the question, 'What is this thing I see before me?', he noted specific features of mental hospitals. By further posing the question, 'What are the general features of mental hospitals?', he developed the concept of 'total institutions'. Let us provide you with another example. Minichiello and his colleagues (1990) were interested in understanding the processes by which older people enter nursing homes. In trying to answer the question, 'How do older people cross the doorsteps of nursing homes?', they developed a scheme of different levels of involvement in the decision to enter a nursing home.

In addition to finding answers to the question, 'What type of unit is it?', the researcher is also searching for the conditions under which a particular type occurs; its underlying features; under what conditions it is present and under what conditions it is absent. For example, Minichiello and his colleagues (1990) were trying to find explanations that accounted for why some older persons were decision makers and others were not. These questions all tend to force the construction of core categories which will be at the centre of knowledge building and its eventual write up (Strauss 1987).

While it is an impossible task to list all the different types of codes you can construct, Bogdan and Biklen (1992) provide a useful list of categories which can be used for developing coding. These include:

1 Setting/content codes—general information on the setting, topic or subjects;
2 Definitions of the situation codes—how informants define the setting or particular topic;
3 Perspectives held by subjects' codes—how informants think about their situation;
4 Process codes—refers to activity over time and perceived change occurring in a sequence, stages, phrases, steps, careers;
5 Event codes—specific activities;
6 Strategies codes—ways people accomplish things;
7 Relationship and social structure codes—regular pattern of behaviour and relationships.

Coding the data

How are the coding categories applied to the data? Coding the data involves learning some basic mechanical skills. This is time consuming and requires patience. To give you an appreciation of the time that it takes to code fieldnotes, Miles and Huberman estimate:

> A single-spaced page of transcribed field notes has about 50 lines. It might contain 5–10 codes. A 2-day field trip usually generates 40–80 such pages, even when the researcher is disciplined. Coding each page might run about 5–10 minutes, once the codes are familiar; in the beginning, you should count 10–15 minutes. So 'inexperienced' coding of a 2-day data set might take up to 3 days; later it could be done in a day and a half or so. Taking more than 2 coding days per contact day is a signal of too-fine units of analysis, too much multiple coding, too many codes, or a weak conceptual (1994, p. 66).

We will briefly discuss the steps involved in coding the data. (For a detailed discussion see Bogdan & Biklen 1992, Miles & Huberman 1994, Strauss 1987 and Strauss & Corbin 1990.)

The first step is probably the most complicated. You need to develop a list of coding categories. Once you have identified the major coding categories (which you will have entered in the analytical file), you revise your list. You may find that some categories overlap one another and can be collapsed. You then assign a number or letter to each coding category contained on the list. Our preference is to give a name to the code, that is closest to the concept it is describing, and to prefix the name with numbers for distinguishing subcategories. For example, decision might refer to decision-making situations, while 'Decision 1' might refer to decisions made by the older person, 'Decision 2' decisions made by doctors and so on. What coding scheme you decide to use is a matter of preference. (For a discussion of the advantages and disadvantages of using number or words see Miles & Huberman 1994.)

The second step involves formatting the transcript file so that you can code the data. You need to make sure that all the pages in the transcript file are numbered sequentially beginning with the first interview. This is important because once you have placed information into a separate sub-file you may want to locate the original source. You should also make sure (as it was discussed in the previous chapter) that the transcript file has large enough margins which can then be used to write down the coding categories.

The third step is to read through the transcript file and code the units of data in the transcript file by placing the relevant letter and/or number corresponding to each category on the margin. By units of data, we mean the sentences or paragraphs in the interview transcript. You will notice that sometimes the same unit of data can be given different codes. This is fine. Double coding occurs when the same data set can be classified under different code categories.

After you have assigned the codes, the next step is to assemble all the data coded to each category and sort it into sub-files. There are computer packages available for this purpose, for example, NUD.IST. These packages include instruction manuals as will be discussed in more detail later in this chapter. Unless you are using a computer which handles the mechanical aspects of qualitative data analysis, you will have to arrange the data manually into separate sub-files. Some researchers use manila folders to sort their files, others use index cards. If you decide to arrange the data manually, we would recommend the use of index cards. (For a discussion of alternative methods of sorting data see Taylor & Bogdan 1984.) You will require some basic tools to sort the data. These include scissors, glue, index cards and filing boxes.

The operation of assembling your data into sub-files is not mechanically complicated. Firstly, you will need to make sure that the top of each index card contains the following information: the identification label for each informant, the coding category, and other analytically relevant information. An example of an index card is shown in figure 11.3. It is important that you include some means to identify where your material came from because this will enable you to go back to the original set of notes if necessary. The coding category tells you that the unit of analysis belongs to a certain coding scheme. Some researchers include relevant conceptual information that assists them in making connections between ideas. In the example reproduced in figure 11.3, the researchers included information on older people's prior living arrangement, marital status and level of involvement in the decision-making process. These factors were identified as influencing the process of entering nursing homes.

Secondly, you cut the relevant units of analysis for each category and paste them on the index cards. (Of course, you should keep a duplicate copy of the transcript file—the original which is filed untouched, and the other for cutting and pasting.) Thirdly, you file the cards in a box. When all the units of data are in the box, you may want to regroup them according to some other part of your conceptual scheme which is relevant for the analysis.

Mrs Vurlow (Informant No. 1; p. 6)

DECISION-MAKING PLAYERS 2 (DOCTORS)

- Widowed
- Living with daughter
- Little say in decision

VM—(When did you first think about moving into a nursing home?)
Mrs Vurlow—Well, it was sprung on me as a sort of surprise. I didn't know I was worrying them so much, so my daughters thought they'd better see where they could get me in, and then when it was raised I cried and I didn't want to come but the doctor explained to me how I was worrying them, you know. And they were afraid to leave me and all this business, so I just took myself in hand and said well, it's the best place for me I guess. (What did the doctor say?) He had a little talk with me and he said it would be more sensible for me to do that because the girls would know I'd be well, there'd always be somebody here and because I used to take those silly old falls, you know, and sometimes, once Patty came home and I was flat out on the bathroom floor. Well, I didn't know I was, you know, and she got me up and got me around, so that really decided things for her.
(See *The Duty Chat* in Analytical File, p. 23).

Mr McAulay (Informant No. 24; p. 241)

DECISION-MAKING PLAYERS 2 (DOCTORS)

- Never married
- Living alone
- Little say in decision

Mr McAulay—I was living on my own after my wife died, and lately I was having blackouts, and the doctor couldn't determine what was wrong with me, but he felt it was best if I didn't stay on my own. I had war injuries and I reached the stage where I needed help and it was really necessary for him to tell me what I should do because I knew myself that I should move into one. He helped me make up my mind sooner.

Figure 11.3 Examples of index cards

Case summaries

Researchers working with qualitative data are often concerned with summarising, collapsing and reorganising data in order to discover concepts and themes contained within it. A transcript file may often be so large and complex that it may be difficult to differentiate between information relevant to the research question and information that is interesting, but peripheral to it. A strategy that is often used by researchers to condense data contained in a transcript file is to produce case summaries of each informant's interview, or to use Taylor and Bogdan's (1984) term, 'develop a storyline'. An example of a case summary is reproduced in figure 11.4.

There are a few general guidelines that we suggest you follow when producing case summaries. Firstly, that you summarise your cases on index cards. Cards can be organised in such a way that comparisons between cases are easily managed. It is less difficult to pull out and sort cards than papers contained in a notebook or folder. Secondly, each card should contain material on the identity of the informant (for example, case number or fictitious name) and some major concepts which are relevant to the research question. For instance, in the example provided in figure 11.4, the researcher included the following concept codes—prior living arrangement, marital status and level of involvement in the decision to move into a nursing home. These factors influenced the pathway residents took to enter nursing homes. Thirdly, the cards should not only contain a summary of the transcript file but also a set of general propositions arising from the researcher's understanding of the data and its relevance to the research question. Of course, these propositions are revised as the researcher collects more data.

The purpose of writing a case summary is to link the material presented in the transcript to conceptual themes and topics relevant to the research questions asked. Perhaps the best way to develop case summaries is to ask the following questions: What is going on? What are the issues raised by the informant? What are some of the possible explanations for why the informant sees the situation in a given way? For example, in writing the case summary for Mrs E, the researcher included basic information about Mrs E; her situation prior to moving into the nursing home; her involvement in the decision; how she felt about moving to a nursing home; and her possible explanations for the move. On the basis of the researcher's analysis of the interview with Mrs E (who was the first informant in the study) the researcher constructed general propositions which related to how married couples entered nursing homes, and how older people decided for themselves to move into a nursing home. The researcher revised and built upon these propositions as he interviewed other residents who found themselves in a similar or different situation to Mrs E (for example, married but not fully involved in the decision, never-married resident).

Case summaries vary in the level of analytical comments they contain. The first few case summaries tend to be written in very general terms;

more as mirror-like summary reports of what was said. Later, as the researcher formulates a better understanding of the topic and develops clearer analytical guidelines for analysing the data, the summary is much more interpretative and integrates knowledge gained from previous cases. As it was explained at the beginning of the chapter, the researcher develops a general picture of the informant's situation and way of seeing the social world. The researcher's understanding of this information is revised as he or she compares individual cases with other cases. This suggests that case summaries are produced not only to sort out information contained within the case but are used to make comparisons and generalisations about propositions. By making comparisons between cases, the researcher is forced into confronting and explaining the similarities, differences and degrees of consistency between informants' accounts. This generates an underlying uniformity which allows for concepts and themes to emerge from the data. It is possible by using this comparative method to move from examining single case studies such as life histories (chapter 6) or clinical case studies (chapter 7) to multi-case studies (chapter 4). Strauss (1987, p. 221) notes that the aim of developing a theoretical commentary in interpreting the case is to give a broadened picture of the particular case: 'The theory puts the case within a more general context of understanding what could have happened under varying conditions, therefore [it explains] why this case happened in this particular way'.

Mrs E (Informant No. 04)—Summary Index Card	• Widowed • Fully involved • Living with husband (1 of 7)

Mrs E is 92 years old and prior to moving to the nursing home, she was living with her frail 95-year-old husband whom she had nursed for the last six years. Although her two daughters helped Mrs E with the housework and cooking 'once a week' and the 'two boys did the other things around the house', it was Mrs E who was solely responsible for bathing, shaving and dressing Mr E.

She and her husband had never once thought about 'ending up in a nursing home' until the accident. Mrs E got up to go to the toilet during the night, slipped and fell. She screamed for help, but without his wife's assistance, Mr E could not get out of bed or to the phone. Unable to lift herself, Mrs E remained on the floor all night long, with her husband lying helpless in bed, both 'shouting for help'. It was not until a neighbour heard their cry for help some hours later that they were rescued and rushed to the hospital.

Upon arriving at the hospital, they jointly decided to move into a nursing home. They had never talked about moving into a home until this crisis. Mrs E did confess to thinking about it but she never mentioned the idea to her husband and children. She kept hoping that they would be able to manage. However, the crisis reminded both of them of how vulnerable they really had become over the years. The horror of both lying helplessly on the ground left its mark. They quickly made the decision to move into a home. (They requested that her niece, a social worker, in consultation with their daughters, search for a nursing home that would 'accept us both'. Both she and her husband were not in a position to visit nursing homes.) They were emotionally very close to one another. When her husband had a stroke six years ago, Mrs E moved into the hospital 'to be near him'. This was no time to be separated. She had to go into a hospital to recover from her fall. They were so dependent on one another that 'if one went, then the other went also'.

The decision was made even before their children arrived at casualty. They [the children] had felt for some time that their parents should not have been living on their own. I was told by Mrs E's eldest daughter during one of her visits at the nursing home, 'We never raised the subject of moving [them] into a nursing home'. As with all of their parents' [other] decisions, 'it was going to be theirs'. However, Mrs E's children did agree with their parents' decision. 'It seemed to be the obvious choice'. Looking after both parents, the daughter explained, would have been impossible 'for any of us to handle'; they [the children] have their own families and work commitments. There was very little family discussion nor the drama of a long and postponed decision. This point was confirmed by the nursing home administrator when I discussed with her the details of Mrs E's admission. 'They realised their situation and made the decision willingly. They simply did not believe in living with their children or in-laws'.

The decision, however, was not without personal troubles. Mrs E blames herself for leaving their home. She explains, 'I had the fall and I couldn't leave him or have him worry my children. So we had to look for a home that would take the two of us and he came with me. It was my fault that we came here really'. When Mrs E recovered from her broken hip, she decided to remain at the nursing home, even though she required no assistance with any of the daily living activities. Her husband's health had deteriorated. Although capable of looking after herself, she was in no position to continue to care for [her] husband at home. Besides, it was he who now needed nursing home care. He moved into the nursing home for her; she was not going to abandon him. Although she would rather be living at home, she is quite happy at the nursing home. She accepts the decision that she will remain at the nursing home until she dies. Her husband died a year ago and although her children tried to persuade her to move in with the family,

---

Mrs E (Informant No. 04) (5 of 7)

Mrs E prefers to live 'in my new home'. Her family consists of two daughters, two sons and a total of eighteen grandchildren. She is very close to them. Mrs E receives a daily visitor; of all her children, her eldest daughter visits most frequently. She spoke very well of her children; how proud she is of them, how close they have always been, and how caring and affectionate they are towards her. Her children also described their mother in such positive terms. Mrs E feels close to the other patients, and in particular to Mrs Vurlow. 'I have found a new family'. As she is getting older and frailer, she does not want to become a burden to her children. She recalls the difficulties (and embarrassments) of going to her children's homes for the day. Both she and her husband have always lived independently. When she was caring for her husband, Mrs E would not use any of the community services. She was aware of their existence, and her entitlement to use them, but she preferred to manage without 'interference from strangers'.

Mrs E (Informant No. 04) (6 of 7)

And she thinks she made a wise decision. She could not have continued to look after her husband for much longer at home. No one was aware of the physical burden she had carried for the last six years. She keeps her affairs private and hidden from the family. Recognising that her independent days are over, she told me, 'When you reach the stage where you feel that you are dependent on other people, the only sensible thing to do is to accept your situation and realise that you have got to be where you are and I've accepted that'. She did have the option of moving in with her eldest daughter, but she chose not to. This was in keeping with her self-image of not being a burden to others. Her health has changed greatly since admission two years ago. She is fully dependent on staff for bathing and requires assistance with going to the toilet and dressing.

Mrs E (Informant No. 04) (7 of 7)

GENERAL PROPOSITIONS
- Married couples who rely on the marital dyad to meet the demands of a disability and maintain an independence from their families may find it difficult to ask or accept help from others.
- Self-images of having lead an independent life and not being a burden to others may be important factors in helping people to make the decision to move into a nursing home.
- The 'fully involved' residents can be people with family support.
- The 'fully involved' residents are not necessarily planners; they may wait until a crisis forces them to think about moving into a nursing home.

Figure 11.4 An example of a summary statement index card

Typologising

Much attention has been focused in this chapter on the importance of identifying themes. This is because the process of reconstructing themes drawn from conversations is the core of the analysis of qualitative data. It is through this process that discrete bits of information came together to make a more economical whole that, analytically speaking, is more than the sum of its parts (Miles & Huberman 1994). But you may well be asking, 'How do we accomplish this?'

Typologising is a method that researchers commonly use to understand phenomena better by grouping ideas and then forming *ideal types* which conceptualise situations that have similar or different characteristics. Ideal types are used to help us make sense of (and visualise) abstract and complex ideas. They are ideal in the sense that they are pure mental constructs which do not exist in reality although they help us interpret and understand reality. Ideal types themselves do not generate knowledge; rather they are a framework or tool which helps researchers to ask particular questions and formulate useful propositions. Let us provide an illustration based on the fieldnotes presented in figure 11.5. In our attempt to make sense of the question, 'How do ministers construct eulogies?', we develop a classification system derived from the minister's personal knowledge of the deceased and the deceased next-of-kin. The classification scheme or typology presented here emerged as the study progressed. It is based on the material collected in the fieldnotes (that is, what the ministers told the interviewer) and how we, as researchers, have conceptualised this information into a paradigmatic form.

You will notice that there are four types of eulogy construction situations. Cell A—a *full-knowledge eulogy* represents an ideal construction of a situation in which the minister develops the eulogy on the basis of both knowledge of the deceased and the deceased's next-of-kin or primary audience. Cell B—an *audience knowledge eulogy* represents an ideal construction of eulogies where the minister develops the eulogy on the basis of knowing the family of the deceased but having had little or no knowledge of the deceased person. Cell C—a *personalised-knowledge eulogy* represents an ideal construction of eulogies given by ministers who knew the deceased but who have had little or no knowledge of their families. Cell D—a *depersonalised-knowledge eulogy* represents an ideal construction of eulogies given by ministers who have had no knowledge of the deceased or their families.

There are three closely interrelated aspects associated with constructing classification schemes such as that presented in figure 11.5. Firstly, the researcher needs to identify two or more categories (for example, knowing the deceased, knowing the next-of-kin). Secondly, these categories need to be identified as distinct and mutually exclusive (for example, Yes/No). Thirdly, these distinct groupings need to be given distinct names (for example, full-knowledge eulogy, depersonalised-knowledge eulogy).

Looking at the data in terms of the influence of the minister's knowledge of the relevant parties at a funeral is, of course, only one way in which this information could have been organised. Any number of alternative classification schemes might have been chosen. For instance, examining the influence of the minister's training and his or her definition of the purpose of eulogies might be another avenue for devising a set of typologies. The point to remember is that whatever scheme you develop, it will allow you to draw on information which you have decided is relevant and allow the data to be categorised in theoretically meaningful ways.

Minister knows the deceased

		Yes	No
Minister knows the deceased's next-of-kin	Yes	Cell A Full-knowledge eulogy	Cell B Audience-knowledge eulogy
	No	Cell C Particularised-knowledge eulogy	Cell D Depersonalised-knowledge eulogy

Figure 11.5 An illustration of typology construction: types of eulogies

The process of developing typologies is a tedious task. It is something that slowly emerges as you read and re-read your fieldnotes. For this reason, it is both a frustrating and exciting task; frustrating when you are trying to develop it, exciting when the data collected begins to make sense in the categories that you have recognised as inherent to it and useful in relation to your research question.

Computers in qualitative research

The option to use computers as an aid in research has been available to researchers using quantitative research designs since computer technology arrived on the market. This has not been the case for those choosing a qualitative data analysis approach. Up until recently, qualitative analysis of data generally relied on researchers manually managing data through the procedures described earlier in the chapter. Not surprisingly, the old-fashioned research tools of typewriters, photocopiers, and pen high-lighters to undertake the clerical tasks of sorting textual material has been seen to be a stumbling block for analysing large qualitative data. This probably explains the regular occurrence of 'single-case' qualitative investigations or studies where there has only been partial qualitative classification of data.

In recent years, a number of computer packages to handle qualitative data have been developed in the USA (see Fielding & Lee 1991, Gerson 1985, Seidel & Clark 1984 and Shelly & Sibert 1986) and in Australia (see Richards & Richards 1987, 1992 and 1993). These include: NUD.IST, ETHNO, Text Analysis Package (TAP), QUALPRO, Ethnograph, TEXT-BASE ALPHA and HyperQual. The use of computers in qualitative research has been reviewed by Fielding and Lee (1991). They discuss the implications of computer-based technology for qualitative research and assess the impact of computing procedures on the formalisation and systematisation of qualitative data. Qualitative computing programs are described, highlighting the strengths and limitations of each program. This is a useful reference for qualitative researchers who may not be familiar with computer programs. It provides information on how to select an appropriate program for various kinds of analysis.

Some of the obvious advantages of qualitative computer software programs to researchers are that they can handle voluminous textual data to facilitate the retrieval of large, relatively unsystematised text material, assist in the task of analysing material which is analytically complex, and 'cut' the data in a number of different ways across a range of cases. Quite clearly, computers can assist in the qualitative analysis of text through their memory-storing capacities, their management and manipulation of data and the managing of the clerical aspects of sorting and retrieval of data. Computers can also allow for greater speed and flexibility in revising codes, adding new codes or for the data to be re-coded in several different ways simultaneously than previous manual clerical procedures.

Word-processing systems and systems for qualitative data analysis

It is important that you not confuse word-processing systems with database management systems. Word-processing systems, such as MacWrite or Microsoft-Word (MS Word), can be used to store quali-tative data. Word processing, with its cut and paste operations, assists in indexing and ordering data. There can be no doubt that word processing is better and quicker than using the old-fashioned typewriter and photocopier. However, word-processing systems do not perform operations which can classify, sort and do sophisticated search and retrieval of data. These tasks can be done by techniques normally associated with database systems. But qualitative researchers need more than databases. Specialist software now available will perform many of the major clerical operations previously undertaken manually by the researcher. It will also do things neither word processors nor databases can do.

Qualitative methods and computer software

With the increasing popularity of analysing qualitative data by computers, this chapter would be incomplete without including a discussion of how computing techniques can be used by the qualitative analyst. It is not, however, the purpose of this chapter to provide a detailed 'hands on' account of how the functions of qualitative softwares can be used to facilitate the mechanical tasks in the analysis process (for such an account see Dey 1993 and Tesch 1990). Rather, this section provides an account of the circumstances where computer analysis may be considered by the researcher and to familiarise you with the fundamental functions of qualitative computer software. We have included in the Appendix a more detailed description of a specific program—Non-numerical Unstructured Data Indexing, Searching and Theorising (NUD.IST).

A word of caution is required before we proceed to discuss the basic purposes and functions of qualitative analysis programs. The computer does not replace the analytical thinking processes underpinning 'interpretative' research as described in the earlier chapters. All forms of artificial intelligence are programmed to assume that the theoretical framework is introduced by the researcher. For example, the coding categories on eulogy construction situations, outlined in the previous section, are embedded within a symbolic interactionist framework, and were not identified by a computer program. Computer programs do not have the capacity to develop propositions from the data—for example, it was the researcher who noticed that the minister's knowledge of the deceased will influence how he constructs the eulogy. Nor does the computer bring to your attention that there are different types of eulogies such as 'celebration', 'pastoral care' and 'gospel'.

Rather, computer software programs have been mostly designed to be an aid for data-retrieval purposes. Computers produce a printout of all text on any topic included in the classification system, with brief descriptions of the content of those passages. It allows the researcher to undertake cross-classification and cross-comparison of text for complex analyses. Tesch (1990, p. 151) describes the basis analysis functions of qualitative softwares as centring around the following features:

- attaching codes to segments of text;
- searching for text segments according to codes and assembling them;

- searching for multiple codes (segments to which more than one code was attached);
- searching for a particular sequence of codes (for segments that follow each other in a certain order);
- searching selectively (through only a specified group of data documents); and
- counting the frequency of the occurrence or co-occurrence of codes in the data.

For example, the programs—AQUAD, ETHNO, QUALOG and NUD.IST—permit the exploration of propositions by examining connections among themes and concepts, including the retrieval of data which allows researchers to confirm or negate emerging ideas from the data. NUD.IST also provides graphic display of connections between the data that can be represented in inverted tree diagrams. More will be said on this topic later in the chapter.

These programs perform basically descriptive functions which complement the interpretative phase of data analysis to the extent that the interpretive phase relies upon the mechanical phase for the presentation of data. In doing so they may facilitate theory building, but they are not specifically designed to undertake the inductive reasoning outlined in chapter 2, such as interpreting the meaning behind words, reading in-between the lines, or building an understanding of people on the basis of what is not said. Stated differently, computers do not contextualise data or recognise the significance of what is being said. Such an analysis has to be constructed by the researcher, whether or not he or she is using a computer:

> If a novice researcher expects the computer to guide her/him through the [analysis] process, the results could be disastrous. The computer is a servant only, not an expert. The expertise has to reside in the researcher (Tesch 1990, p. 302).

It is important to reiterate here that qualitative analysis is more than a mere description of 'facts' (for example, a content analysis of what is said, how often, by whom, when). It involves what Geertz (1973) describes as a 'thick' account of the context of action, the intentions of actors and the process in which action or inaction is embedded. Human behaviour is such that neither motivation nor contexts are self-evident (see chapter 2). The researcher has to allow for the usual mix of ignorance and self-deception, delusions and lies when making sense of, and giving meaning to, his or her data (Dey 1993). This conceptual context provides a guide for understanding the role computers can play in qualitative data analysis. A failure to understand this context can lead to the potential danger of misusing computers. For example, Tesch (1990) points out that some researchers may be tempted to centre their entire analysis process around the functions a computer makes available to them. Every line of text may be coded because the computer favours this form of analysis, whether it is appropriate or not. A more serious problem results if such a coding system is developed without the researcher paying attention to the meaning behind the words spoken, which requires 'in-depth inter-pretation'. Here 'the computer would be allowed to invade the re-searcher's conceptual territory or to influence unduly the direction of the [analysis] process' (Tesch 1990, p. 303).

NUD.IST

The functions of qualitative computer software can be illustrated by describing the NUD.IST program. This program is one of the qualitative data analysis packages discussed by Fielding and Lee (1991). NUD.IST was developed by two Melbourne researchers, Lyn Richards, a soci-ologist, and Tom Richards, a computer scientist. NUD.IST is designed to assist in the handling of non-numerical, unstructured data (text or other) in qualitative analysis. It does this by supporting the processes of indexing data, searching and theorising (Richards & Richards 1992). The program includes operations which clerically manage data and categories, allow the researcher to index data at categories and to apply a set of operations to retrieve relevant sections of the data, or ask complex questions about it, store ideas and develop and explore propositions. Data documents remain intact and can be browsed or explored through indexing. As it will be described below, NUD.IST creates both a document and indexing database, each of which has separate and discrete functions. We have selected this program as an example because it is the most recent and popular Australian package on the market.

When to use qualitative computer software

The decision to use a qualitative computer software package to assist in the management and analysis of data should be based on a number of considerations. The most obvious is that the research project you are designing requires a qualitative analysis. That is, the purpose and overall design of your research project is conducted within the methodological guidelines and theoretical assumptions of qualitative research.

Second, the 'size' and 'complexity' of your study may leave you with little option but to consider the use of computers. On the other hand, if you are conducting a single-case design, a small exploratory study aimed at locating and counting the frequency of individual words and phrases (Tesch 1990), or a qualitative analysis embedded within a larger quantitative program, choosing to use a program, such as NUD.IST, needs to be weighed up against the time, preparation, and cost factors that would necessarily be involved in learning and operating a new computer software program.

The time factor

NUD.IST is available on both MAC and DOS systems as well as mainframes. The more recent version (3.0) has an interactive graphic interface, identical on MAC systems and PC Windows. To use NUD.IST version 3.0 on a MS-DOS system it is necessary for the user to have at least rudimentary skills and knowledge of Microsoft Word for Windows and any compatible word-processing program. For a novice, considerable amount of time needs to be set aside to become fully familiar with this software.

The researcher also needs to set aside additional time to become familiar with the NUD.IST program. Learning any new program has its own in-built frustrations and to master it will require a certain degree of perseverance. NUD.IST is no exception. The development and intro-duction of the new graphic version 3.0 of NUD.IST made learning the program more accessible to those who label themselves 'computer illiterate'. Version 3.0 still has some remnants of the original MS-DOS versions, and so is less user-friendly than other MAC software.

The preparation factor

As with any research project the preparation of material for analysis is time consuming. Whether using a computer software package or not, data needs to be produced in text form. This involves the tasks of recording, transcribing, and editing the material. When using NUD.IST, the transcript material is saved as text-only. In addition, introducing the document into the NUD.IST program also requires time to be set aside.

There are, of course, many ways of limiting the task of analysing large data sets. For example, some researchers suggest transcribing only the segments of data which are relevant to the analysis (Silverman & Perakyla 1990) or selecting database on a particular theme. NUD.IST can quickly search and obtain data which are classified according to a particular theme. NUD.IST can also save time and money with its offline document option. *Offline documents* are documents whose text is not stored in the NUD.IST database. Documents such as books, references, photographs, newspaper cuttings, videos and tapes can all be introduced as offline documents. Documents are identified by names and HEADERS. Headers can contain content information about a document. Documents are divided into *text units* which indicate the researcher's preference for selecting segments of the document. These can be in paragraphs, sentences, lines or words. Researchers can write and edit memos about, or an abstract of, the document. All documents can be indexed and commented on at any time. *Online documents* can have text searched and be retrieved (Richards & Richards 1993).

The cost and accessibility factor

There is, of course, the issue of cost to be considered. The price for purchasing the NUD.IST software will vary for an individual affiliated with an educational institution and someone in a non-educational setting. There may also be some less obvious costs. For example, if your personal computer (PC) does not have all of the necessary specifications to run the program (for example, viz on PCs, at least a 386 enhanced mode and on PCs and Macintoshes at least 4mb of RAM to run NUD.IST) then considerable expense may be incurred to update the equipment.

Some educational and research institutions have NUD.IST available on their network and it will be necessary for you to verify your access to the program. Nothing could be more frustrating than being in the middle of some complex operation and to find that you have to exit from the program because someone else has priority to the equipment or security wants to close the building.

Finally, one last major consideration when deciding on the viability of using a computer data analysis package is whether there are adequate back-up and support services for the software. As NUD.IST becomes more widely used, informal networks can be an invaluable source of information and support. On a more formal level Qualitative Solution and Research (QSR) now market NUD.IST and they offer at a cost consultancy service, which includes trained staff to assist with all stages of setting up and running a NUD.IST project.

Basic concepts and language of NUD.IST

Computer language and software manuals can be a barrier when learning and becoming familiar with a new software package. NUD.IST is no exception. A brief glossary of terms used in the program appears in the Appendix (see Richards & Richards 1993 for further details).

The connection between data analysis and writing up

When one begins the process of 'writing up', the research analysis has not finished. In fact, the analytic and writing-up processes are totally intertwined. Good research depends on the results being communicated clearly and concisely. In this next section, we review the relationship between these processes and how the researcher can go about the writing-up process.

An experienced writer knows that he or she cannot write about everything he or she has seen or heard, and also realises that writing is a multiple-level process that begins the moment the writer enters the field and starts writing fieldnotes. If you have followed our advice and recorded ideas in the personal and analytical files (see chapter 10), you will have started writing your research paper. The files provide a base from which you can select material to write the substantive and methodological sections of the research paper. The rest of the chapter will examine stylistic and content issues in writing qualitative reports.

Playing the writing game

Two important ingredients of good writing are discipline and hard work. Experienced writers would never consider their first draft to be their final product. Becker (1985) has criticised students for being 'one-draft writers'. Many students wait to write their paper the night before the deadline. They may receive a good grade for their efforts. However, as Berg (1989) correctly points out, the submission of first drafts to editors is not likely to get the same results in the academic world. Textbooks and research articles published in journals are not written in this way. The thinking and writing stage spans several months, if not years.

The writer begins with an outline which sketches out the focus of the manuscript and breaks the tasks into manageable parts (Wolcott 1990). Writing seldom comes naturally. The danger of procrastination is always a reality. An outline allows you to focus on particular aspects of the massive information held in your possession. It serves as a starting point that allows you to fill in the skeleton frame of the paper. Once the writer has identified the core elements of the paper, drafts are written and rewritten. The paper is circulated among colleagues for comments. As the writer feels more confident about his or her work, the paper is submitted for publication. At this stage, the paper will go through another round of critical review. Editors and publishers will send the paper or book to anonymous reviewers. The reviewers will be asked to rank the manuscript by checking a list of such phrases as: 'accepted for publication'; 'accepted for publication with minor changes'; 'strongly encourage author to make substantial changes and resubmit paper'; 'paper is not accepted'. The reviewers' report also includes comments on the strengths and weaknesses of the paper and suggestions for improving it. Journals do not accept all submitted papers. In fact, reputable journals only publish between 20–30 per cent of the manuscripts offered. Many are published after the authors make revisions to the original paper.

You may well ask the question, 'What does rewriting entail?'. Does it mean merely editing for typing and spelling errors? Of course, you do not want to submit an article which contains such errors. Editing means much more than correcting typographical errors. It means rewriting substantive portions of the paper. You may decide to further develop or clarify a theme, expand or trim the analysis or reorder the sequence of ideas presented in the paper. Rewriting also involves getting rid of unnecessary 'clutter'. Zinsser (1980, p. 15) uses clutter to mean 'laborious phrases which have pushed out the short word that means the same thing'. When writing you should simplify, prune and strive for order:

> the secret of good writing is to strip every sentence to its cleanest component. Every word that serves no function, every long word that could be a short word, every adverb which carries the same meaning that is already in the verb, every passive construction that leaves the reader unsure of who is doing what—these are the thousand and one adulterants that weaken the strengths of a sentence (Zinsser 1980, p. 7).

A clear and precise sentence is no accident. We seldom get this result on our first attempt. First drafts are often wordy and contain much more than a reader wants to know. Initially, it is important for the author to write everything he or she thinks is important and relevant. It is much harder to get rid of something that you have written than to add something you have not recorded. The first draft should be seen as a starting point, which contains sentences and ideas that are blurry and need to be focused. You should examine your first draft ruthlessly for words that say nothing. A good writer is someone who is persistent, keeps looking, thinking and rewriting until all has been said in the most readable and precise manner. Figure 11.6 shows an example of an early draft of pages 9 and 10 of chapter 1. The main purpose of rewriting is to ensure that what you have written is said more clearly and precisely than in the previous draft. This process is continued until you have a 'clean' copy. When you have reached this stage you go over it once more, reading it aloud. You then ask someone else to read the paper to discover unnoticed clutter and flaws in the argument.

Like writing, editing cannot be completed overnight. It is advisable that you take time to withdraw from your latest draft. A few days of rest from the paper can give you a new outlook. When you return to your paper ask yourself: What am I trying to say? Have I succeeded? Is it clear to someone who has read it for the first time? Have I presented the ideas in a logical order? Is there some other way I can condense my material to make it clearer? Is it wordy? Are my sentences and paragraphs too long? Zinsser (1980) and Becker (1985) provide some helpful suggestions about how to write well. They recommend using active rather than passive verbs. The difference between the two is that active verbs, for instance, carry a clearer and stronger message. As Zinsser illustrates:

> Joe hit him is strong. He was hit by Joe is weak. The first is short and vivid and direct; it leaves no doubt about who did what. The second is necessarily longer and it has an insipid quality; something was done by somebody to someone else. A style which consists of mainly passive constructions, especially if the sentences are long, saps the reader's energy. He is never quite certain of what is being perpetrated by whom and on whom (1980, p. 93).

Adverbs and adjectives clutter ideas and are often unnecessary. Consider the following. Do you think there is a big difference between,

However, a ↑①
✗/number of scholars have argued that whether researchers choose to
[~~ise~~] use

qualitative or quantitative methods is a matter of training, ideology and

the research question asked (Denzin 1989; Sieber 1973; Strauss 1987).

Researchers adopt a given method because they have been trained to

to,   n
believe that their preferred is superior ∕or more scientific tha ∕others (Banks

1979; Goodwin & Goodwin 1984). ∕While there can be no doubt that

training influences our methodological practice, this argument loses sight

of the interrelationship between ⌊method ⌋and theory⌉ As chapter 2 will

, further   s that,
discuss∕ the choice of method is also influenced by the assumption∕the

researcher makes about science, people and the social world. In turn, the

method used will influence what the researcher will see.

As was discussed earlier,   People's
∕ ∅ualitative research attempts to capture ~~the quality of~~meanings,

events
definitions and descriptions of ~~things~~. In contrast, quantitative

research aims to count and measure things (Berg 1989). As shown in

characteristics distinguishing
① figure 1.1, the ~~main differences between~~ qualitative and quantitative

Categories
approaches to research can be divided into two major ~~characteristics~~.

a   and
~~These are: i)~~ conceptual–the nature of the phenomen~~on~~ studied; ~~2)~~
, Coyne & Smith
methodological–the handling of data (Parse ~~et al~~ 1985).

Figure 11.6 An example of editing: an early draft of pages 9 and 10 of chapter 1

'someone clenched his teeth tightly' and 'someone clenched his teeth'?
After all there is no other way to clench one's teeth! Try to avoid using
adverbs unless they serve a purpose. The example cited by Zinsser
illustrates this point:

> If an athlete loses a game because he played badly, 'badly' gives us the helpful
> information that he didn't play well. But spare us the news that he moped
> dejectedly and that the winner grinned widely (1980, pp. 102–3).

Paragraphs should be kept short. It is useful to limit each paragraph to one central theme or point. If you include too many themes or points in the one paragraph you risk damaging the logical flow of ideas (Becker 1985). The advantage of short paragraphs is that they look inviting. Long paragraphs can discourage the reader from starting to read.

You should make it a practice to be concise. Say what you want to say only once and write it clearly. You can master this skill by learning how to choose words that convey what you want to say. The dictionary and thesaurus are invaluable tools in the writing game. Often the difference between being clear or vague lies in the choice of a word. We suggest that you follow the advice of Bogdan and Biklen (1992, p. 182)—'If you feel that you are not saying what you want, look up the words to see if they can be replaced by something more precise'.

A final word of advice. You should avoid using sexist language. Feminist writers have shown us that many writers incorporate a sexist language in their writing. A common issue which confronts many writers today is what to do with the he/she pronoun. In fact, we debated this issue when writing this book. A conventional practice (and the one we decided to use in the book) is to use, that is, to say, he or she. Another common solution is to eliminate the male pronouns and substitute this with the plural pronouns—they, us, we—or recast the sentence to avoid the need for a pronoun altogether.

The less-experienced writer will find it useful to read well-known qualitative research articles and books. Reviewing the manuscripts that others have written may provide you with ideas on how authors present data, how they built their arguments, arrange their sentences and paragraphs, and format their papers. Some classic qualitative works include Whyte's *Street Corner Society* (1955); Thomas and Znaniecki's study of *The Polish Peasant* (1958); and Becker, Geer and Strauss' *Boys in White* (1961).

You may also decide to consult journals which publish qualitative studies. While this is not an exhaustive list, included are *Sociology of Health and Illness*; *Journal of Contemporary Ethnography*; *Qualitative Sociology*; *Urban Life*; *Holistic Nursing Practice*; *Social Problems*.

Structuring the paper

A fundamental question is, 'Who am I writing for?'. You will remember from chapter 10 that fieldnotes are written for yourself. However, this is not the case when writing the results. You are writing for people who will be interested in what you have to say. Understanding your audience is important because this affects what you write about and how you present the information. If you are interested, for example, in writing for other gerontologists, you must address issues and concerns relevant to that particular academic community. If, on the other hand, you wish to reach a more general audience such as consumers, older people, their carers, you must place the issues in a larger and more general context. It is important to realise that the style and presentation of your argument will need to be tailored to the needs of the audience. We suggest that you compare articles which have been written in academic journals with those found in the popular press.

There is another reason for undertaking research—other than satisfying one's thirst for knowledge or furthering career goals. Disseminating the results of your study is an essential feature of research. Researchers have a professional responsibility to share with the scientific community to which they belong the information they have uncovered (Berg 1989). Research without a collective consciousness has little value. Also, as discussed in chapters 8 and 9, the researcher may further acknowledge a responsibility to the individual informant and/or the community to which he or she belongs.

The length and 'surface structure' of the report will vary depending on whether you are writing a book or research article. Surface structure refers to 'the number of major headings that give order to the report' (Berg 1989, p. 146). Books may be several hundred pages in length and may contain several interconnected themes which are organised into chapters. Articles have fewer pages (usually no more than 7000 words) and use subtitles to organise the flow of the argument. However, regardless of whether you are writing a book or a journal article report, the organisation requires a logical sequence. It has a beginning, a middle and an end. The beginning tells the reader what the paper intends to do and lays out the contents. The middle sections tell the story by developing, arguing and presenting the major points. The end summarises what was said and draws the reader's attention to other research questions and the implication of the results for policy and/or professional practice. These sections usually follow the sequence of steps taken in planning the research and in collecting and analysing the data. We suggest that you adopt the format used for research articles in professional journals. This format is summarised on the next page. Obviously, there are alternative organisational strategies depending on the nature of your research and your own personal writing style.

- Introduction (What issue are you investigating and why is this relevant/ important?).
- Method (What procedures did you use to obtain your information?).
- Findings/Results (What did you find? What do your findings mean?).
- Conclusion (What have you said? Why is this important? What are the implications of the study?).
- Abstract (A brief summary of the above points).
- References (A list of sources cited in the report).

The next few pages will consider in more detail the content of each of these sections.

The introduction

The most important sentence in any article is the first one. If it fails to capture the reader's attention, he or she will not bother to read the next sentence. The first few sentences must entice the reader to want to continue reading. You should start the paragraph by presenting an interesting fact or question.

The introduction has to address several issues. First, tell the reader the nature of the problem being investigated. A reader may grow impatient if he or she has to read a few pages before finding out what it is that you are studying. Tell the reader your research question within the first few paragraphs. For example, in the introduction to the research article written by Minichiello and his colleagues (1990), the authors make it clear that they are interested in studying whether involvement in the decision to enter a nursing home influences the quality of life of residents.

Second, place your question in the context of current knowledge on the topic. This means reviewing and summarising previous literature. The analysis of the literature needs to address the following questions: What previous research has been done on this topic? What are the pertinent concepts and theories used to study this question?

You do not need to cite every study written on the topic. Nor should the analysis of the literature read like a string of summary sentences which have been written and incorporated in the introduction section. The literature should be used to substantiate major points and to justify the effort of doing the research. You should cite only those studies which are pertinent to the issues you are addressing and emphasise only their major conclusions, findings or relevant methodological issues (Kidder & Judd 1986). Avoid reporting unnecessary detail.

The cited articles should include the classic and most recent references. If you fail to include relevant studies you leave yourself open to criticism. You can use a number of reference systems for citing the source. We suggest that you consider the commonly used Harvard reference system. References in the text are cited giving the author's last name and the date of publication.

Methodology

This section should provide the reader with considerable detail about how the research was accomplished, what the data consist of and how data were collected, organised and analysed; in other words, details about the informants and data collection and analysis techniques. A reader will carefully evaluate this information when assessing the report. Failure to report this information can weaken the report.

Who were the informants? How many were there? How were they selected? What theoretical sampling model was used? Answers to these questions will assist the reader to draw his or her conclusion on who has been left out and how this influences the conclusions drawn. The information that the researcher provides about the characteristics of informants will vary from study to study. If you were studying nursing-home residents, you may include the following information: age, gender, marital status, prior living arrangement, health status. If you were studying police officers, the following information could be relevant: age, gender, number of years in the police force, education, and social class.

The method section also provides information on how data were collected. This information includes a description of what data-collection technique was used, as well as an account of how the data were recorded and analysed. For example, if you used in-depth interviewing, the reader would like to know if the interviews were taped, the length of the interview, how you stored the data, whether you used a computer package to analyse the data and the coding system developed to classify the data. This information is important for several reasons. First, they place the results in a context that allows the reader to evaluate its merits and credibility. Second, they provide a set of procedures for others who may be interested in replicating the study.

Findings and results

Qualitative reports differ in several ways from quantitative reports in the presentation of findings and results. First, in quantitative reports, the findings are presented in the form of numbers and tables, and these are discussed under the section heading 'Findings and Results'. These two terms, as Berg (1989) points out, although often used synonymously, are quite distinct. Findings refer to what the data say. Results offer interpretations of the meaning of the data. Qualitative reports present the findings in the form of words and are discussed under the headings of narrative labels. While particular schools of thought produce manuscripts with a distinct style (Lofland 1974), most do conform to a general principle. The organisation of findings and results are based on 'analytic logic'. It is common practice for the author to first announce the major conceptual issues or themes and to then develop these, with illustrations from the data. Two examples will be discussed to show this process.

Minichiello and his colleagues (1990) present their general conceptual model in terms of a typology of decision-making situations. The typology contains four different types of decision-making situations. After presenting this general model, the authors proceed to discuss the four types of decision-making situations and use the following subheadings— fully involved, decision-involved, selection-involved and excluded. The findings are the descriptions taken from the transcript to illustrate and substantiate claims made in the text. The results are the propositions put forward to develop an understanding of the decision making to enter nursing homes.

Another example may clarify how qualitative researchers present their findings. Glaser and Strauss (1965) undertook a classic study of the social dimensions of dying. Findings and results are arranged around the core concept of trajectory, outlining its multi-facet phases. Each section focuses on these phases which portray the movement of hospitalised sick persons toward their death and the complex interactions which take place between the sick person, staff and families. For each phase, crucial conditions and strategies associated with the different phases are identified and illustrated with data quoted from informants.

It has been said that presenting the results of qualitative data is like writing a story (Taylor & Bogdan 1984). A good story has to be clearly and logically presented. You should ask yourself: Has the analysis been ordered clearly? Has it been said in its most effective form? Can it be presented more effectively by reordering the flow of ideas?

Conclusion

Having said that the first sentence is the most important line to write, we will now tell you that your last line is just as important. Knowing when to end an article is far more important than most writers realise. Zinsser argues:

> This may seem ridiculous. If the reader has stuck with you from the beginning, trailing you around blind corners and over bumpy terrain, surely he won't leave when the end is in sight. But he will—because the end that is in sight often turns out to be a mirage. Like the minister's sermon that builds to a series of perfect conclusions which never conclude, an article that doesn't stop at its proper place is suddenly a drag and therefore, ultimately, a failure (1980, p. 70).

The conclusion serves two purposes. First, it reviews your argument, highlighting the central themes developed in the paper. You should write this concisely and restrict it to no more than a few paragraphs. But your conclusion should be more than a summary. It should give the reader something to think about. Rather than saying, 'In summary, this paper shows how ...', you can provide interesting interpretations to the summary. For example, you can say that the study has illustrated the process by which older people are excluded from decisions to enter nursing homes. You may add that this provides further evidence of society preventing older people from leading autonomous lives and raises the moral question of the rights of older people.

Second, the conclusion addresses the shortcomings and implications of your study. For example, you may want to draw the reader's attention to conditions which might limit the extent to which your results can be generalised to other populations. Or you may want to discuss the implications of your results for policy development and professional practice. The Minichiello et al. (1990) study discusses, for example, strategies that can be developed to safeguard the voice of the older person in the admission decision. Many writers point out questions which remain unanswered or new questions that have been raised by the study.

Abstract

Most journals require the author to write an *abstract*. An abstract is a brief summary of the research question, methodology, findings and implications of the study. The title of the report is also part of the abstract. The title should convey the content of the paper so that the reader may decide whether or not it is of interest to him or her. A reader will grow impatient if he or she has been deceived into believing that the paper was about something that it is not. Titles can be constructed around major themes of the paper. Abstracts appear at the very beginning of the paper and include no more than 100–150 words. Here is an example of an abstract:

> Theory-generating methodologies can be used to add to our knowledge in areas that are already well researched in addition to areas that have not been extensively studied. The study presented here demonstrates how the grounded-theory method was used to generate a new theory of intergenerational caregiving. Analysis revealed five conceptually distinct, overlapping categories of caregiving. Only one of these includes what is generally considered to be caregiving, that is, hands-on caregiving behaviours or tasks. The other four types are not observable behaviours but are processes crucial to intergenerational caregiving and to an understanding of the experience of intergenerational caregiving (Bowers 1987, p. 20).

Abstracts provide the reader with an opportunity to quickly glance at the major features of the paper and decide if they wish to read the entire report. It is not easy to write an abstract. You cannot summarise everything in an abstract. You must carefully decide what to highlight. For this reason, we suggest that you write your abstract after you have written the paper. You will be in a much better position to decide what is important. Specifically, you should be looking for the key issues addressed in the study; the nature of the data analysed; the major findings; and implications of the findings. These four elements provide a framework which will enable you to produce an abstract. Abstracts are the very first lines that a reader comes across. Therefore, you should write clearly and in a way that encourages the reader to continue reading.

References

The paper needs to acknowledge the use of other people's materials. All sources consulted and used in the text should be properly cited. There are two styles for documenting the books and articles you have cited: superscript numerals or source references. Superscript numbers are sequentially placed after a punctuation mark either at the end of the sentence or quotation. These numbers correspond to reference notes located either at the bottom of the page (footnotes) or at the end of the paper (endnotes).

An alternative method is, as mentioned earlier, to cite the author's name, date of publication, and, in the case of a direct quote, the page(s) from which the quote has been extracted. This brief reference is placed immediately after the point in the text where a quote, paraphrase or statement is made. (This is the Harvard reference system referred to earlier and the style used in this text.) The references cited in the text are listed at the end of the paper under the heading References. They are arranged alphabetically.

Whether you adopt one or the other style will depend on the requirements of the journal to which you are submitting the paper. In the social sciences, source references are more commonly used. Science journals use the superscript numerals style. (For a detailed discussion of rules governing referencing see Gelford & Walker 1991.)

Appendix

How to use qualitative computer software: an application of the NUD.IST program

(With Rosemarie Stynes)

The project—therapeutic counselling and living with HIV/AIDS: infected and affected people's stories and therapeutic counselling

This study examines the therapeutic counselling sessions conducted with people infected and affected by the HIV virus. The analysis pursues two lines of inquiry. Firstly, the content of therapeutic counselling sessions is explored in an attempt to construct an understanding of the impact of the virus on infected and affected individuals' experiences and adjustments to living with the HIV. The focus is on peoples' own accounts of HIV/AIDS, and more specifically their experiences of HIV/AIDS as they are shaped by their interactions with family, friends, partners, and their health care professional. A story metaphor and narrative analysis is used to extract the socially constructed meanings given to the HIV experience (White & Epston 1989).

Secondly, the process of therapy is analysed in order to provide an understanding of the ways in which HIV/AIDS therapeutic stories emerge, develop and are shaped by the therapeutic processes, including issues such as agenda setting, power, trust, who influences who and at what point of the sessions. The NUD.IST program was selected because the data consists of 320 therapeutic interviews (across 32 individual cases) lasting between 60 to 90 minutes. To attempt an analysis of this data without computer assistance would be difficult, if not impossible.

The sample

The informants consist of two groups—a client-group and a therapist-group. The client-group contains 32 cases of 320 transcripts. Contrast is provided along the following dimensions:

1 infected individuals—males, straight and gay;
2 infected/infected couples—gay and straight;
3 infected/affected couples—gay and straight; and
4 affected friends and/or family members attending with and sometimes without the infected person.

The therapist group included six therapists: three heterosexual women and three gay men. The professional training of members of the team are:

1 one female social worker/family therapist;
2 one female social worker/psychologist/family therapist;
3 one female clinical psychologist/family therapist;
4 one male psychiatrist/family therapist;
5 one male psychologist/Gestalt therapist; and
6 one male social worker/therapist.

Data collection and preparation for input into NUD.IST

With informed written consent from clients, therapeutic sessions are recorded on video. The number of interviews per case range from two to twenty-six, with the average being ten per case. The video sessions were copied on to audio tapes and transcribed in their entirety. Therapists' discussions about the case were also taped and transcribed. Transcripts were edited to ensure anonymity and checked for typing, spelling errors and missing data.

Headers (see figure A.1) are typed at the top of each document. A header appears whenever NUD.IST retrieves the text or data units. Its purpose is to identify any context information about the document. A header can be of any length but it is advisable to keep it succinct. In the header below (see figure A.1), the place of the interview (BFTC) is identified along with the case (c35), therapist (t6) and session number (s02), and other information relevant to the research project; for example, who was present at the interview, what sort of data are included and other relevant context comments about the clinical session. Headers are the first text which are prefaced with an asterisk (*). It is useful for clarity purposes to follow a header with a blank space.

Sub-headers can also be added. They help divide a document into meaningful segments, for example, identify who is speaking. Sub-headers are displayed whenever a text unit is retrieved. They are optional and begin with an asterisk and end with a hard carriage return. For example, in the research project being described (see figure A.2) [*Therapist—6] is a sub-header. The header is always printed out with any data or text units, along with the sub-header preceding the text.

HINT:

If a HEADER does not start with an asterisk (*) and you leave a blank line, NUD.IST will not recognise the information as a header.

---

*BFTC-c35t6s02
*SESSION NO, [02] out of how many taped [01] DATE [15/4/92]
*NO. OF PERSONS PRESENT AT INTERVIEW (including therapist—6) [7]
*PERSON/S PRESENT AT INTERVIEW Therapist—6 Therapist—2 Therapist—
      3 INFECTED PERSON [IP—1 MALE] IP—1 MALE (Through Interpreter—
      1) Social Worker—2 Hospital—4
*THERAPIST DISCUSSION [YES]
*NO. BEHIND THE SCREEN [2] WHO? [Therapists 02 & 03]
*DATA SOURCE—THERAPEUTIC INTERVIEWS; THERAPISTS'
      DISCUSSION; MESSAGE
*COMMENTS—Sometimes difficult to hear when many people are talking at
      once.

Figure A.1 An example of a 'header'

---

*IP—1 MALE (through INTERPRETER—1)
Yes. OK he is concerned about {IP—2 WIFE} because he feels she is sick at the moment she's not eating as she's been before and she's very pale and she's very very aggressive ... very aggressive.
*THERAPIST—6
Irritable?
*IP—1 MALE (through INTERPRETER—1)
Yes.

Figure A.2 An example of a 'sub-header'

It is advisable to attach headers at the same time that you are transcribing the interview. However, if you are not clear as to what information you want to include in your header, they can be added later, either when you are editing the document or introducing it into NUD.IST.

Another basic requirement which must be completed at the time of entering the data into NUD.IST is to indicate what segments of data are to be read as text units for indexing. Text units are automatically numbered by NUD.IST from one onwards, and the indexing references you attach to your text use these numbers as descriptors. They include all text between one hard return (HRT) and the next; that is, every time the ENTER or RETURN key is pressed a text unit is defined. HRT can be placed anywhere in a document and a text unit can be a word, sentence, line or paragraph. Paragraphs are automatically read as a text unit because a HRT defines a paragraph. To have a sentence, or even a word, defined as a text unit it is necessary to put the HRT in during transcribing. Alternatively, you can use the 'search and replace' facility on your word processor to insert a HRT after each full-stop, assuming that every full-stop defines a sentence. To have a line defined as a text unit simply save the document as a 'text-only' with lines breaks on a DOC PC. This will automatically save a HRT at the end of each line.

Once the above requirements have been completed, the text document is placed in the RAWFILES directory in NUD.IST. Initially, when starting a new project in NUD.IST, the program automatically sets up four directories. The first is called a DATABASE FOLDER. This directory contains NUD.IST document and index system files. Because these are the programs operating files they should not be touched nor should researchers retain any of their own working project files inside this folder. The other three directories are called *RAW FILES*, COMMANDS and REPORTS. These are for the researcher to use in managing their saved working files. The RAWFILES directory is usually the one where 'text only' transcript documents are stored before being introduced into NUD.IST. The COMMANDS directory is for the researcher's optional customised programs, similar to a macro in a word processor. COMMANDS can be written to automate sixteen of NUD.IST's tasks, such as introducing documents, adding and deleting, indexing. Finally, there is the REPORTS (or RESULTS in version 2.0) FILES directory. Reports about documents, the *indexing system* or a particular node are stored in the REPORTS FILES directory. Reports can be selected and printed from this directory or, alternatively, can be printed from within NUD.IST.

Files can be introduced in two ways: interactively by selecting the 'introduce data documents' and selecting the required document, or non-interactively using the COMMAND FILE option. Interactively, as the name suggests, is when you personally select the particular raw data document you want to introduce into NUD.IST. Working non-interactively with documents means that you are instructing NUD.IST via the COMMAND FILE option to automatically introduce any number of files that are stored in the RAWFILES directory. Interview documents introduced into NUD.IST using both methods will now be described.

> HINT:
>
> The new graphics version 3.0 of NUD.IST makes both of the above procedures for introducing documents into NUD.IST simpler. Have a play! Put a document in both ways.

Introducing a document into NUD.IST (version 3.0)
—interactively

A single interview document (c35t6s02) with a TXT extension is selected from the RAWFILE directory via the Introduce Document menu bar. This online interview document is converted by NUD.IST to a format it recognises. NUD.IST automatically stores the document in one of the sub-directories in the DATABASE FOLDER. The interview document is then retrievable via the Document, Investigate Document, Select Document menu options for editing and indexing. This is a quick, ideal way of introducing documents into NUD.IST when you only have a few to introduce. It allows the researcher close contact with the data at all times.

Introducing a document into NUD.IST (version 3.0)
—non-interactively

When there are a large number of interview documents stored in the RAWFILE directory waiting to be introduced into NUD.IST, the researcher can save time and avoid a tedious and repetitive process by using the COMMAND FILE option. It takes some time and perseverance to write a COMMAND FILE and it is necessary to refer to the relevant formatting instructions in the Users Guide version 3.0 for Macintosh or PCs.

The main shortcoming when using the COMMAND FILE option in version 2.0 of NUD.IST was that any errors made in writing the COMMAND FILE, and it is very easy to make syntax errors (that is, missing brackets, colons), were not detected or reported until the COMMAND FILE completed its run. With the new 3.0 graphics version, NUD.IST checks the COMMAND FILE first before it attempts the run, thereby shortening the process considerably. It reports back on any errors and allows the researcher to correct them while still in the NUD.IST environment. COMMAND FILE options are also available for completing any of the NUD.IST functions that are achieved interactively. COMMAND FILES are written in your word processor or inside NUD.IST version 3.0. To introduce a COMMAND FILE via NUD.IST you select the 'RUN COMMAND FILE' option in the Project menu bar.

The disadvantage of using the COMMAND FILE option is that it can potentially take you away from the raw data because you are not working interactively with the material. Also, if you do not have the time to learn how to write a COMMAND FILE then it is probably just as efficient to work interactively with your material and input manually. It is important to note that the 'entry level' version of NUD.IST does not have the COMMAND FILE option.

Developing and assigning codes

An analytic tool commonly used in qualitative research is that of assigning codes to text material. Codes are kept in NUD.IST at 'nodes' in an index system. The indexing system in NUD.IST can be organised hierarchically in a 'tree structure' of categories and sub-categories. It is this tree structure which is used to explore and analyse the data. NUD,IST does not create codes for you, explain what the data means or point to ways in which it can be interpreted. It simply helps the researcher with the complex clerical task of retrieving and organising the data by the meaningful code created by the researcher, and with the analytical tasks of storing and developing ideas about a category and its links with other categories.

As discussed earlier, codes can be created in a number of ways and from a number of sources. Codes for the project described here were created in the following way. Initially the researcher (Rosemarie Stynes) formalised what she already knew on the topic by recording on paper her thoughts about 'story content' codes. These codes were developed as a result of knowledge gained over six years while working as a clinical psychologist in the area of HIV specifically and in counselling generally. Richards and Richards (1992) describe these initial codes as 'prior categories'. The collection of data further informs and guides the researcher's understanding of the topic, and hence the 'prior categories codes' are continually being developed, modified, extended or deleted. New codes also emerged as the researcher started to work with the data. These are referred to as 'emerging codes' by Richards and Richards (1992). This process is in keeping with the basic principles of the inductive reasoning methods, where there is a co-evolving development of incorporating emerging ideas into the collection and analysis of data.

Creating an indexing system

Step 1: Prior categories codes are defined in terms of key themes that had been informed by clinical practice. Themes such as death of a friend, loss of a lover, notification of diagnosis, receiving AZT, information about the illness, getting on with life, becoming incapacitated/getting well again, dealing with changes in behaviours, living with uncertainty and dealing with issues of disclosure are some of the categories recorded during the early stages of this project.

Step 2: Transcripts for one case are read and indexed according to the content themes of therapy and the therapy process. Linguistically, these codes are initially identified and recorded by the researcher through writing in the margins on the hard copy of the transcripts 'word descriptors' that summarised what client/s and therapist are discussing. Examples of the above themes are found in the transcriptions, labelled and indexed accordingly. As the analysis process went on other themes started to emerge; for example, suicide, social supports, emotional reactions such as guilt, people's reactions to HIV, as well as the original themes being continually refined. For example, under the THEME heading of HIV/AIDS additional sub-themes, such as knowledge about HIV status, length of infection, were identified (see figure A.3. Therapy Talk (Stories) is indexed at node (2), HIV/AIDS is indexed at node (2.1) and the sub-themes are added as the researcher's understanding of the HIV/AIDS theme 'thickens out').

```
NUDIST STAND-ALONE v.2.3.1c FOR IBM PC
This file created on 1993 Apr 29, 19:22:29
******************************************************
(2)       /THERAPY TALK (STORIES)
(2 1)          /HIV-AIDS
(2 1 1)              /KNOWLEDGE ABOUT
(2 1 2)              /REACTIONS TO DIAGNOSIS
(2 2)          /EMOTIONAL REACTIONS TO
(2 3)          /BEHAVIOURAL RESPONSES TO
(2 4)          /RELATIONSHIPS
(2 5)          /HEALTH—ILLNESS
(2 6)          /ECONOMICS
(2 7)          /SOCIAL SUPPORTS
(2 8)          /TIMING
(2 9)          /CONSTRAINTS
(2 10)         /CHANGES
(2 11)         /ABOUT SELF
(2 12)         /FUTURE PLANS
(2 13)         /DECISION-MAKING
```

Figure A.3 A segment of nodes incorporating and refining prior categories codes and emerging codes created in NUD.IST

HINT:

It is extremely important that any codes, existing or new, and any changes or modification need to be documented with a comment that records your reasoning behind the inclusion, exclusion or change. If you are working in NUD.IST it allows you to write a memo at any node. If you are not working in NUD.IST these comments need to be noted somewhere, for example in your analytical file.

In NUD.IST the prior and emerging codes are indexed at NODES. Each node has a reference number and title. As they cluster together into conceptually logical categories a developing indexing system emerges.

Step 3: Constant reading of incoming transcripts resulted in the continued refinement and development of the indexing system until a point of saturation is reached (see figure A.4).

```
NUD.IST IBM-PC Version 3.0 GUI
Licensee: NUDIST Beta Version 3.0.2d
PROJECT: AIDS3-0, User , 11:10 am, 19 Apr, 1994
(3) /TT(content)
(3 1)          /HIV-AIDS
(3 1 1)               /KNOWLEDGE ABOUT
(3 1 1 1)                    /HIV STATUS
(3 1 1 2)                    /LENGTH OF INFECTION
(3 1 1 3)                    /LACK OF KNOWLEDGE
(3 1 2)               /REACTION TO DIAGNOSIS
(3 1 3)               /QUESTIONS
(3 1 3 1)                    /WHO
(3 1 3 2)                    /WHO CAN BE
(3 1 3 3)                    /WHOSE REACTION
(3 1 4)               /COPING
(3 1 4 1)                    /WITH HEALTH PROBLEMS
(3 1 4 2)                    /IN THE FUTURE
(3 1 5)               /IMPACT ON
(3 1 5 1)                    /FAMILY OF ORIGIN MEMBER[S]
(3 1 5 2)                    /PROFESSIONALS
(3 2)          /HEALTH—ILLNESS
(3 3)          /EMOTIONS
(3 3 1)               /SPECIFIED
(3 3 2)               /UNSPECIFIED
(3 4)          /MONEY
(3 5)          (see figure A.5 for details of code (3 5)
(3 6)          /IDENTITY—SEXUALITY & SEXUAL PRACTICES
(3 7)          /BEHAVIOURAL RESPONSES
(3 8)          /DEATH—SUICIDE
(3 9)          /ALTERNATIVE STORIES—CHANGES
(3 10)         /CONSTRAINTS
(3 11)         /SPIRITUALITY—RELIGION
(3 12)         /PLANS—ACTIVITIES
(3 13)         /THERAPY
(3 14)         /POWER—POWERLESSNESS
(3 15)         /METAPHORS
```

Figure A.4 A truncated version of current indexing system for therapy stories

NUD.IST does not require a fixed index system to be entered in the early stages of the research. It allows the researcher to change and improve the index indefinitely. However, this flexibility or openness of entering emerging codes can create some difficulty as one can go on changing and modifying the index system *ad infinitum* without ever having coming to any conclusion. The opposite can also be true, that is, one can move towards a final and fixed index system too early. For example, in her eagerness to 'play' in NUD.IST, the researcher introduced her initial codes, indexed particular segments of the document accordingly and developed the initial indexing as outlined in figure A.3.

In hindsight, the decision to code and index documents turned out to be too soon. As a novice still learning the program (this was version 2.0 of NUD.IST), the researcher found that every time she wanted to reorganise her indexing system, either by adding or subtracting new subcodes, subsuming one code under another or doing any sifting and/or changing of codes, she was spending a great deal of valuable time learning to do these tasks. While this was a useful and invaluable experience, it did succeed in distracting the researcher from the important task of reading, re-reading, thinking and analysing transcripts. In an attempt to become more time effective, the researcher decided to refine the codes using the facilities of the word processor rather than NUD.IST.

The process of establishing a reasonably stable indexing tree can become time consuming. Version 2.0 of the NUD.IST program did not provide an overall display of the indexing picture. However, version 3.0 of NUD.IST does provide a graphic display your indexing, or any part of the tree, while at the same time allowing direct access to the nodes and the ability to reorganise the tree display. This simplifies the processes considerably.

> HINT:
>
> While you are still a 'NUD.IST Novice', hold off putting your codes into the program until you have developed a reasonable and dense indexing system.

It is possible to subsume isolated codes under particular 'logical' headings. For example, conversations about relationships, living situations and economics could all be subsumed under a 'SOCIAL & PERSONAL CONTEXT' node. Figure A.5 shows how many categories can be logically grouped under a common code.

What we see in figure A.5 is the continual refinement of the indexing system as data are further reduced into what the researcher has labelled logical clusters. Keep in mind that if you are using the NUD.IST program for the first time then you are trying to do two new tasks at the same time, that is, analysing and indexing data and learning to use NUD.IST. It is important that not too much time is spent learning the computer program at the expense of data collection and analysis.

```
(3 5)          /SOCIAL PERSONAL CONTEXT
(3 5 1)               /NETWORK—SUPPORTS
(3 5 1 1)                    /of IP
(3 5 1 2)                    /of AP
(3 5 1 3)                    /GENOGRAM INFO
(3 5 1 3 1)                       /FOO
(3 5 1 3 2)                       /FOC
(3 5 2)               /RELATIONSHIPS WITH
(3 5 2 1)                    /LOVER
(3 5 2 1 1)                       /X-LOVER
(3 5 2 2)                    / FOO
(3 5 2 3)                    /WIDER CONTEXT
(3 5 2 3 1)                       /MEDICAL SYSTEM
(3 5 2 3 2)                       /LEGAL—POLITICAL
(3 5 2 3 3)                       /PROFESSIONALS
(3 5 2 4)                    /OTHERS
(3 5 2 4 1)                       /PETS
(3 5 2 4 2)                       /FRIENDSHIPS
(3 5 2 4 3)                       /DOCTORS
(3 5 4)               /LIVING ARRANGEMENTS
(3 5 4 1)                    /LIVING ALONE
(3 5 4 2)                    /SEPARATED
```

Figure A.5 A segment of nodes from the indexing tree of therapy stories at node (3 5) demonstrating the development of a logical cluster

Applying codes for the analysis of data

There are many guidelines about how researchers can conduct the analysis of qualitative data. It is not the purpose here to discuss data analysis issues but rather to show examples of how data can be organised for analysis using NUD.IST. Three indexing trees are illustrated. One tree was for demographic codes (figure A.6), another for story-content themes (shown in figures A.3, A.4 & A.5) and another for story-process codes (figure A.7). These codes were used to assist the researcher to address the following questions: first, what do people living with HIV talk about in therapy? Are there similarities and differences in the stories, and what explains these? And second, how does the therapeutic process shape the HIV discourse?

Once documents are coded, the analysis facilities of NUD.IST can be used to explore and test ideas. For example, links between the coding categories and data can be explored in a number of ways: across and within different client-groups, across and within the therapist-group, within a particular case or even within a particular therapist's client-group. Questions about the interrelationships between any of the coding categories can be examined using the NUD.IST 'Searching and Index System' functions. For example, the computer can be used to address story content questions, such as whether issues associated with depression and suicide are more prevalent in cases where the infected person has experienced multiple losses and social isolation. Likewise, a story process question can be addressed, such as, are therapists more likely to initiate raising issues in the initial stages of therapy than in later stages of therapy? For example, NUD.IST can be asked to search for indexing references using the following nodes: 'negotiating a story' and 'who initiates'. These are only brief examples of some of the simpler forms of analysis which can be performed. The 'Searching Index System' function, with its eighteen options, provides the researcher with a range of ways of asking questions and exploring connections between various segments of the data.

```
NUD.IST IBM-PC Version 3.0 GUI
Licensee: NUDIST Beta Version 3.0.2d
PROJECT: AIDS3-0, User , 12:12 pm, 1 Apr, 1994
(1)      /B-DATA
(1 1)          /IDENTIFIERS
(1 1 1)              /CASE NO.
(1 1 2)              /SESSION NO.
(1 1 3)              /THERAPIST[S]
(1 1 4)              /CLIENT[S]
(1 2)          /THERAPY
(1 2 2)              /TOTAL
(1 2 3)              /NO. TAPED
(1 3)          /DEMOG
(1 3 1)              /GENDER
(1 3 2)              /SEXUAL ORIENT'N
(1 3 3)              /AGE
(1 3 4)              /HEALTH STATUS
(1 3 5)              /OCCUP'N
(1 3 6)              /LOCALITY
```

Figure A.6 A truncated example of demographic codes

```
NUD.IST STAND-ALONE v.2.3.1c FOR IBM PC
This file created on 1993 May 10, 12:56:28
REVISE MAY 20th 93
(4)      /TT(context & process) CO-EVOLUTION OF STORIES
(4 2)          /GETTING STARTED
(4 3)          /NEGOTIATING A STORY
(4 4)          /WHO INITIATES
(4 5)          /HOW DOES IT DEVELOP?
(4 6)          /T-DISCUSSION
(4 7)          /INTERVENTIONS
(4 8)          /TECHNIQUES
(4 9)          /FINISHING
```

Figure A.7 A truncated example of therapy process codes

Glossary

Abstract. Brief summary of the research studies; generally includes the purpose, methods and major findings of the study.

Action research. Research joined with action in order to plan, implement and monitor change. Researchers choose to become participants in planned initiatives and use their knowledge and research expertise to aid their researcher informants or co-researchers to self research.

Aide memoire. Literally, an aid to memory. Here, another term for interview guide or schedule.

Analytical induction method. A method used to make inferences from some specific observations to a more general rule. Used in constructing propositions or theory from data.

Analytical file. Contains a record of reflective notes on the question asked and ideas emerging from the data.

Analytical notes. A term used by Burgess (1982b) for recording ideas which led to the development and revision of themes emerging from the data.

Anonymity. In this context refers to the informant being anonymous or not individually identifiable. This is usually achieved through the use of pseudonyms.

Anti-positivism. An approach that holds that social reality is consciously and actively created by individuals who mean to do things and who attribute meanings to the behaviour of others. *See* Positivism.

Autobiography. Life story written by oneself.

Background demographic questions. Such questions ask the informant to specify their age, sex, education, occupation, place of residence, etc. These questions are a form of descriptive questioning.

Biographical life history. A life history in which information is elicited from the informant detailing his or her individual development.

Broad rationality. Consistency with the goals and beliefs of the surrounding society.

Card catalogue. The main reference source for locating books in the library.

Case history. The history of an individual in which the patient or client provides information about relevant events in his or her past, especially past health.

Case study. The collection of data, both formal and anecdotal, on a single individual or single social unit (for example, a family).

Causal explanation. Explaining events or states in terms of what cause them.

Case summaries. Brief summaries of each interview; generally includes information on themes and topics relevant to the research question.

Clinical interview. An in-depth interview conducted by a clinician to elicit information, to support diagnosis or to provide or support treatment.

Closed-ended questions. Questions in which the informant is asked to respond by choosing between several predetermined answers.

Coding. The general term used for conceptualising and categorising data, including hypothesising relevant categories and their relations (Strauss 1987).

Computer-assisted searches. Used to obtain periodicals and books which are stored in a central data base and are accessible by computer.

Confidentiality. Refers to protecting names of informants, keeping confidences and protecting information about the informant.

Content analysis. A research method applied to texts for purposes of identifying specific characteristics or themes.

Contrast questioning. Questions asking the informant to make comparisons of situations or events in their world and to discuss the meanings of these situations.

Critical reference group. A group, person or collective which is significant for an individual (including a researcher) in determining his or her attitudes and behaviour.

Cross-section. A broad sampling of persons of different ages, income levels and ethnic background.

Cross-sectional study. One that studies a cross-section of the population at a single point in time.

Data analysis. The process of systematically arranging and presenting the data in order to search for ideas and to find meaning in the information collected.

Decentred subject. The person seen as controlled or given meaning by processes outside his or her consciousness.

Descriptive questioning. Questions which ask informants to provide descriptions of events, people, places or experiences. It is often used to start interviews.

Deviant. Not fitting socially acceptable norms.

Devil's advocate question. A form of probing. It is a question which deliberately confronts the informant with the arguments of opponents as abstractions within or outside the 'universe' which is being studied.

Dialectical process. A process resulting from a dialogue or some back-and-forth exchange.

Diary interview method. See log-interview method.

Editing. A form of interpretation and rewriting of given texts, often to make them clearer or more precise.

Establishing rapport. Getting a positive easy-going relationship with the informant.

Ethical absolutist. One who holds that ethical principles are to be adhered to absolutely, regardless of setting or circumstances. For example, a researcher who wants to establish specific principles to guide all social research and who wants to have these principles produced as a code of ethics to be adhered to by all.

Ethics committee. A committee set up by an institution or organisation to act as a moral watchdog on its own members.

Ethics. The study of standards of conduct and moral judgments. In this context, it refers to the system or code of morals we apply to the research process.

Ethnographic context. The everyday activities of the informant, his or her common-sense working knowledge of that cultural milieu or his or her sense of self-identity.

Ethnography. The direct observation of the activity of members of a particular social group, and the description and evaluation of such activity.

Feeling questions. Questions which are aimed at understanding people's emotional responses.

Fieldnotes. A record of conversations the researcher has had with people; observations about their actions, reflections on what happened in the field and interpretations of the data.

Focused or semi-structured interviews. Interviews using an interview guide which simply lists topics to be discussed with no fixed ordering or wording of questions. The content of the interview is focused on the research question.

Front. The actively presented body of information about oneself which is shown to others.

Functionalism. Explaining (usually biological) features by showing their 'purpose' in helping group or species survival.

Funnelling. Starting the interview with broad general questions and continuing by narrowing the discussion using more specific questions which ask directly about the issues that are of interest to the researcher.

Gatekeepers. Those individuals in an organisation that have the power to withhold access to people or situations for the purposes of research.

Grounded theory. The development of a theory by drawing or teasing it from the data gathered. The theory that is developed is then said to be grounded in the data.

Group interview. Interviewing a group of informants for the purpose of research.

Header. A header is used to identify a document in NUD.IST. When any text from the document is retrieved, it is preceded by the document header.

Hermeneutic circle. Oscillating between the whole and the parts in interpreting the meaning of a text.

Hermeneutics. The science of the interpretation of texts.

Hypothesis. A statement of the predicted relationship between two or more variables.

Hypothetical question. A form of probing. The interviewer suggests a possible or plausible number of scenarios, options or occurrences and asks the informant to guess at how he or she would respond to them.

Ideal types. Heuristic aids used in the construction of propositions, especially about kinds of people. They are an exaggeration or idealisation of certain features of reality.

Idiographic approach. Any system for the assessment of behaviour or performance derived from a particular individual rather than from the average of many individuals' performance.

In-depth interviews. Repeated face-to-face encounters between the researcher and informants directed toward understanding informants' perspectives on their lives, experiences or situations as expressed in their own words.

Incidental sampling (judgment and opportunistic sampling). Involves the selection of people, actions or events just as they present themselves. Replication is impossible.

Indexing system. In NUD.IST, it is like a sophisticated catalogue system which stores and locates documents and topics.

Index card system. Classifying and storing on index cards bibliographic and relevant information for each item in the literature review.

Indices. Sources which contain reference material on books and periodicals.

Informal post-interview. The researcher ties up loose ends at the end of the interview by going over some or all of their discussions in an informal manner in an attempt to make some checks on the validity of the account according to the informant's perception.

Informant. The person whose thoughts, words and behaviour are studied in social research. When the person is informing the researcher of his or her views, attitudes and beliefs during in-depth interviews of any kind then the person is called an informant.

Informed consent. Consent being given by an informant or client for research to be carried out, when those requesting this consent have provided the informant with full knowledge of what it is that they are consenting to.

Intentionality. A mental quality of referring outside the self. For instance, beliefs are specified by saying what they are *about*. So are desires. Intentionality lies in the 'aboutness'.

Interpretive approach. An approach that holds that people's individual and collective thinking and action has a meaning which can be made intelligible.

Interpretive research. Based on the interpretive approach.

Interview. A face-to-face verbal interchange in which one person, the interviewer, attempts to elicit information or expressions of opinion or belief from another person or persons, the informants.

Interview guide or schedule (aide memoire). A list of general issues, topics, problems or ideas that the researcher wants to make sure are covered by each informant. It is used to jog the memory of the interviewer and is revised as different informants provide information which indicates the need to do this. Not a standardising instrument unless used in quantitative research.

Interview schedule. Another term for interview guide. *See* above.

Knowledge questions. Aimed at finding out what the informant considers factual.

Legitimation. Being made officially acceptable to social values.

Life-history interview. A sociological autobiography drawn from in-depth interviewing or solicited narratives.

Life history. The history of an individual's life given by the person living it and solicited by the researcher.

Life-grid approach. The researcher provides a means of aiding the informant to write down their life story. This is usually in the form of a diagrammatic representation such as a grid. For example, the grid might have sixty rows representing the informant's years of life, and columns could represent areas of change. It is a diagram version of a diary.

Locale. Regionalisation on a time-space basis. The aspects of settings are normatively implicated in systems of interaction so that in some way they are set apart for certain individuals.

Log interview method. One in which informants keep a running record of their activities for a specified period of time. This is then used to provide a basis for in-depth interviews.

Methodological individualism. Regarding the fundamental unit of explanation in the social sciences as the individual person.

Methodological notes. A term used by Burgess (1982a) for recording reflections on the researcher's field strategies and methods used to collect data.

Methodology. A self-consciously accepted rule-governed procedure or method aiding or guaranteeing scientific discovery.

Militant. Taking an insistent open stance as a member of a stigmatised group.

Mirror or summary question. A variation of the reflective probe. One uses the same strategies but the interviewer also clarifies the informant's comments by summarising them and then reflecting them in the question form.

Mixed strategies. Multiple strategies. *See* triangulation.

Multi-method. *See* triangulation.

Negotiation. Reaching agreement by stages of proposal, rejection and acceptance.

Neurolinguistic programming. It occurs when one purposively matches the perceptual language of another person be it through auditory, visual, olfactory or kinaesthetic processes. When used in interviewing it is a means of gaining rapport and using this rapport to lead the other person into areas of discussion which are significant in terms of the research problem.

Nodes. Are an index record for a particular subject. Any point where a branch on an index tree splits is called a node. In the tree structure of NUD.IST, the node hierarchy is described as root nodes, parent nodes, children nodes. All children of the same node are said to be each other's siblings.

Nomothetic approach. Assessment of thought or action based on the average of many individuals.

NUD.IST. Non-numerical Unstructured Data Indexing, Searching and Theorising. An Australian computer package designed to analyse qualitative data.

Nudging probe. A form of probing in which the interviewer uses verbal cues or body language cues to elicit further information from the informant.

Offline documents. Documents whose text is not stored in the NUD.IST database. Offline documents are introduced into NUD.IST by recording their details. The text unit is any unit chosen by the researcher.

Online documents. Documents whose text is held in the computer. In NUD.IST they are called the DOCFILES folders. These documents can be indexed at nodes; memos can be stored about them and they can be searched for occurrences of particular words or phrases.

Open-ended questions. Also known as free-answer questions. Questions to which there are no sets of predetermined answers for the informant to choose from. Rather, the informant can choose to give any answer he or she wishes.

Opinion/value questions. Aimed at gaining access to or understanding what people think about a particular person, event, issue or experience.

Oral history. The aim in oral history is to gain information about the past from people's spoken testimony, retrospective information, corroborative evidence, and recollection of events, their causes and effects.

Original or primary questions. First questions used to ask an informant about an issue, event, person, place or attitude.

Participant concepts. Ideas, themes, concepts expressed by informants in their own language.

Participant observation. A method of research widely used in sociology and anthropology in which the researcher takes part in the activities of a group or community being studied while also acting as observer.

Passing. Pretending to be a member of a more acceptable social group.

Personal documents. Informant's diaries, photos, letters, formal records, calendars, scrapbooks and all memorabilia which can be used to jog the memory of the informant regarding their life and experiences.

Personal file. An annotated chronological record of the researcher's comments on people, settings and their activities, the social expertise of doing research and methodological issues which arise in the course of the study.

Phenomenology. The study of the forms and varieties of consciousness and the ways in which people can apprehend the world in which they live. It is the study, in depth, of how things appear in human experience. It involves the 'bracketing' or laying aside of preconceptions (including ones derived from science) in order to be able to inspect (one's own) conscious intellectual processes more purely.

Population. Refers to the entire set of people you intend to study.

Posing the ideal. A situation in which either the informant or the interviewer describes and perhaps analyses the most ideal situations they could conceive of in the life of the informant.

Positivism. A doctrine which holds that science or knowledge can only deal with observable entities known directly to experience. The positivist then aims to construct general laws on theories which express relationships between entities.

Probing questions. Questions used to clarify, gain more detail and understand the meanings that informants attach to original or primary questions and answers to them. This is why they are also known as secondary questions.

Productive interpersonal climate. Another term used for establishing rapport.

Proposition. A statement or assertion of the relationship between concepts. Sometimes, a true-or-false sentence which is expressed in a given statement.

Propositional attitude. Mental attributes—beliefs, wishes, desires, decisions and so on—which have to be specified by a proposition. For example, when we say 'John doubts that it is snowing', *doubt* is his attitude and *It is snowing* is the proposition which specifies its content.

Protocol. A standard format for an interview (or more widely, a piece of research).

Qualitative research design. Allows the researcher to observe, discover, describe the themes and underlying dimensions of social life using non-numerical data.

Random sampling. Representative form of sampling where you list all members of the population and using some method such as dice or random number tables, you select your sample from the list of the population.

Rationalisation. A spurious explanation of one's beliefs, feelings or behaviour masking one's real reasons, possibly from oneself.

Raw files. Unprocessed online documents.

Recursive model of interviewing. A form of in-depth interviewing in which the interview follows normal conversational interaction allowing the flow of conversation to direct the research process. It is regarded as the most unstructured form of in-depth interviewing.

Reductionism. For the purposes of this book, replacing mental explanations by would-be equivalent physiological explanations, usually in terms of brain neurones.

Reflective probe. A probing strategy which entails the researcher reflecting the answer given by the informant in order to clarify or verify the information. It is also known as a mirror or summary question.

Reflexivity. Having propositional attitudes *(see above)* towards oneself, especially a desire to understand and improve oneself.

Reliability. The extent to which a method of data collection gives a consistent and reproducible result when used in similar circumstances by different researchers at different times.

Respondent. The person whose thoughts, words and behaviours are studied in social research. When the person is responding to survey interviews and questionnaires, he or she is called a respondent.

Review of literature. The analysis of existing literature pertinent to the area of study.

Sample. A subset of the population which is considered representative in some fashion.

Sampling. The taking of a proportion of individuals or cases from a larger population, studied as representative of that population as a whole.

Saturation. A situation in which no additional data can be found that would add to the categories being developed and examined, that is, you have reached saturation level.

Semi-structured or focused interviewing. Refers to interviews in which there are no fixed wordings of questions or ordering of questions. Rather, the content of the interview is focused on the issues that are central to the research question.

Sensory questions. Those questions asking the informant about what has been seen, heard, touched, tasted and smelled. They are used to induce the informant to describe the stimuli which they have experienced. They are a form of descriptive question.

Signs (natural or social indicators). Clinically (in contrasted to symptoms), indications noticeable to the professional observer, though not necessarily to the client.

Situational relativist. A researcher who holds that there can be no absolute principles of ethical research behaviour or absolute guidelines because ethical decisions are dependent on the individual's interpretation of the particular research situation and the context in which it occurs.

Snowball sampling. Using a group of informants with whom the researcher has made initial contact and asking them to put the researcher in touch with their friends; then asking them about their friends and so on, as long as they fit the criteria for the research project.

Social actionist. An approach to sociology which emphasises how actors perceive a social situation. It emphasises conscious orientation and purposive action.

Solicited narrative. Refers to the interviewer soliciting (asking for) a written narrative (story-like account) from the informant. Researchers often ask for a chronology of the informant's life prior to being interviewed, or the informant is asked to write their own story.

Speaking position. The intentions, social role and relative power of the speaker in relation to the listener.

Splitting. In this book, dividing your stigmatised group into two: the socially acceptable and the socially unacceptable.

Sponsors. In this context refers to those individuals or groups who initiate and/or pay for research to be conducted.

Stereotyping. Assuming that someone with some standard attribute (for example, black skin) will have other standard attributes to match (for example, be an unemployed alcoholic).

Stigmatisation. Making some personal attribute a source of shame.

Story telling. A means of directing interview interaction. The researcher asks the informant questions which requires the telling of a story as part or all of the response.

Stratified random sampling. A variation of random sampling in which quotas are filled rather than just taking a random sample right across the population.

Structural questioning. Questions aimed at finding out how informants organise their knowledge.

Structured, standardised or survey interview. Interview in which the question and answer categories have been predetermined.

Sub-header. In an online document; it is any text unit in the text body (after the header ends) beginning with an asterisk and ending with a hard return.

Subject. The person whose thoughts, words and behaviour are studied in social research.

Substantive notes. A reproduction of the formal interview which took place between the researcher and informant, including a cover sheet that contains relevant information and brief reflective comments on the margin of the transcript.

Symbolic interactionism. A sociological perspective that emphasises the centrality of meaning in symbolic communication between people.

Symptoms. The features of an illness as experienced by the client.

Text unit. The body of data NUD.IST recognises as the one to automatically number.

Theoretical concepts. The ideas, themes and concepts of the informant translated by the researcher using a theoretical scheme.

Theoretical sampling. The process of data collection for generating theory whereby the analyst jointly collects, codes and analyses his or her data and decides what data to collect next and where to find them, in order to develop his or her theory as it emerges.

Thin rationality. Internal mental consistency.

Transcript file. A reproduction of the formal interview.

Transitions. A means of shifting the conversation to another issue or topic by connecting something the informant has said with the topic of interest to the interviewer (even if this connection is a little far-fetched).

Triangulation. The combination of different techniques of collecting data in the study of the same phenomenon. It is also referred to as the use of multiple strategies, mixed strategies or multi-method.

Typologising. The process of understanding phenomena better by grouping ideas and then forming ideal types.

Understanding. The special form of explaining human (and other) minds. The German word for understanding, which is often used in technical discussions of the social sciences, is *Verstehen*.

Unit of analysis. The specific theme, word or concept being used in data analysis.

Unstructured interviews. Interviews in which neither the questions nor the answer categories are predetermined, thus relying on social interaction between researcher and informant to elicit information.

Validity. The extent to which a method of data collection represents or measures the phenomenon which it purports to represent or measure.

Verstehen. *See* understanding.

Wise. Known to understand what it is like to be a member of a stigmatised group.

References

Abercrombie, N., Hill, S. & Turner, B. 1988, *The Penguin Dictionary of Sociology*, Penguin, Harmondsworth.

Abrahamson, M. 1983, *Social Research Methods*, Prentice Hall, Englewood, New Jersey.

Adelman, C. ed. 1981, *Uttering, Muttering: Collecting, Using and Reporting Talk for Social and Educational Research*, Grant McIntyre, London.

Allport, G.W. ed. 1965, *Letters from Jenny*, Harcourt Brace Jovanovich, London.

Altheide, D. 1980, 'Leaving the field', in *Fieldwork Experiences: Qualitative Approaches to Social Research*, eds W. Shaffir, R. Steffins & A. Turowetz, St Martin's Press, New York.

Anderson, H. & Goolishian, H. 1988, 'Human systems as linguistic systems: preliminary and evolving ideas about the implications for clinical theory', *Family Process*, vol. 27, no. 4, December, pp. 371–93.

Anderson, I. 1994, 'Ethics and health research in Aboriginal communities', in *Researching Health Care: Methods, Ethics and Responsibility: Pre-Publication Draft Conference Papers*, St Vincent's Hospital, Melbourne.

Anderson, N. 1961, *The Hobo*, first published 1923, University of Chicago Press, Chicago.

Aroni, R. 1985, *The Effects of Jewish and Non Jewish Day Schools on Jewish Identity and Commitment*, Monash University, Melbourne.

Askham, J. 1982, 'Telling stories', *Sociological Review*, vol. 30, pp. 555–73.

Atkinson, R.L., Atkinson, R.C., Smith, E.E. & Hilgard, E.R. 1987, 'Memory', in *Introduction to Psychology*, Harcourt Brace Jovanovich, London.

Babbie, E. 1979, *The Practice of Social Research*, second edn, Wadsworth, Belmont, California.

Babbie, E. 1989, *The Practice of Social Research*, fifth edn, Wadsworth, Belmont, California.

Bailey, K.D. 1982, *Methods of Social Research*, second edn, The Free Press, New York.

Bailey, K.D. 1989, *Methods of Social Research*, fifth edn, The Free Press, New York.

Baker Miller, J. 1984, 'The effects of inequality on psychology', in *The Gender Gap in Psychotherapy*, eds P. Rieker & E. Carmen, Plenum Press, New York.

Bandler, R. & Grinder, J. 1979, *Frogs with Princes, Neurolinguistic Programming*, Real People Press, Utah.

Banks, F. 1979, 'Sociological theories, methods and research techniques—a personal viewpoint', *Sociological Review*, vol. 27, pp. 561–78.

Barlow, D.H. 1981, 'On the relation of clinical research to clinical practice: current issues, new directions', *Journal of Consulting and Counselling Psychology*, vol. 49, no. 2, pp. 147–55.

Barlow, D., Hayes, S. & Nelson, R. 1984, *The Scientist Practitioner*, Pergamon Press, New York.

Becker, H.S. 1963, *Outsiders: Studies in the Sociology of Deviance*, Free Press, Glencoe, New York.

Becker, H. 1985, *Writing for Social Scientists*, University of California Press, Berkeley, California.

Becker, H., Geer, H. & Strauss, A. 1961, *The Boys in White*, University of Chicago Press, Chicago.

Bell, C. & Encel, S. eds 1978, *Inside the Whale: Ten Personal Accounts of Social Research*, Pergamon, Oxford.

Bell, C. & Newby, H. 1977, *Doing Sociological Research*, Allen & Unwin, Sydney.

Bell, C. & Roberts, H. 1984, *Social Researching: Politics, Problems, Practice*, Routledge & Kegan Paul, London.

Bellow, S. 1973, *Dangling Man*, Penguin, Ringwood.

Benney, M. & Hughes, E.C. 1970, 'Of sociology and the interview', in *Sociological Methods: A Sourcebook*, ed. N.K. Denzin, Butterworth, London.

Berg, B. 1989, *Qualitative Research Methods for the Social Sciences*, Allyn & Bacon, Boston.

Berger, P. & Luckmann, T. 1967, *The Social Constuction of Reality*, Doubleday, New York.

Berlin, I. 1976, *Vico and Herder: Two Studies in the History of Ideas*, Viking, New York.

Bernstein, L. & Bernstein, R.S. 1985, *Interviewing: A Guide For Health Professionals*, fourth edn, Appleton Century Crofts, East Norwalk, Connecticut.

Bertaux, D. & Bertaux-Wiame, I. 1981, 'Life stories in the bakers' trade', in *Biography and Society: The Life History Approach in the Social Sciences*, ed. D. Bertaux, Sage, Beverly Hills.

Bertaux, D. ed. 1981, *Biography and Society: The Life History Approach in the Social Sciences*, Sage, Beverly Hills.

Bilton, T., Bennett, K., Jones, P., Stanworth, M., Sheard, K. & Webster, A. 1981, *Introductory Sociology*, Macmillan, London.

Blaikie, N. 1988, 'Triangulation in social research: origins, use and problems', paper presented at the Conference of the Sociological Association of Australia and New Zealand, Canberra. A revised version was published in 1991, 'A critique of the use of triangulation in social research', *Quality and Quantity*, vol. 25, no. 2, May, pp. 115–36.

Blauner, R. & Wellman, D. 1973, 'Toward the decolonization of social research', in *The Death of White Sociology*, ed. J. Ladner, Vintage Books, New York.

Blumer, H. 1939, *An Appraisal of Thomas and Znaniecki's 'The Polish Peasant in Europe and America'*, Social Science Research Council, New York.

Blythe, R. 1979, *The View in Winter: Reflections on Old Age*, Allen Lane, London.

Bogdan, R. 1974, *Being Different: The Autobiography of Jane Fry*, Wiley, London.

Bogdan, R. & Biklen, S. 1992, *Qualitative Research for Education: An Introduction to Theory and Practice*, second edn, Allyn & Bacon, Boston.

Boudon, R. 1982, *The Unintended Consequences of Social Action*, Macmillan, London.

Bourdieu, P. 1984, *Distinction: A Social Critique of the Judgement of Taste*, Routledge & Kegan Paul, London.

Bourdieu, P. 1990a, *The Logic of Practice*, Polity Press, Cambridge, UK.

Bourdieu, P. 1990b, 'Social space and symbolic power', in *In Other Words*, Stanford University Press, Stanford, California.

Bourdieu, P. 1991, *Language and Symbolic Power*, Polity Press, Cambridge, UK.

Bowers, B. 1987, 'Intergenerational caregiving: adult caregivers and their ageing parents', *Advances in Nursing Research*, vol. 9, pp. 20–31.

Bowers, B. 1988, 'Family perceptions of care in a nursing home', *The Gerontologist*, vol. 28, pp. 361–8.

Bowie, M. 1991, *Lacan*, Fontana Press, London.

Bronfenbrenner, U. 1952, 'Principles of professional ethics: Cornell studies in social growth', *American Psychologist*, vol. 7, pp. 452–5.

Brown, G. 1983, 'Accounts, meaning and causality', in *Account and Action*, eds G. Gilbert & P. Abell, Gower, Hemisphere.

Browne, J. & Minichiello, V. 1994, 'The condom: why more people don't put it on', *Sociology of Health and Illness*, vol. 16, pp. 229–51.

Bruner, J. 1986, *Actual Minds, Possible Worlds*, Harvard University Press, Cambridge, Massachusetts.

Bryman, A. 1988, *Quantity and Quality in Social Research*, Unwin Hyman, London.

Bryson, L. & Thompson, F. 1972, *An Australian Newtown: Life and Leadership in a Working Class Suburb*, Kibble Books, Melbourne.

Bullivant, B. 1975, *The Way of Tradition: Life in an Orthodox Day School*, Australian Council for Educational Research, Canberra.

Bulmer, M. 1979, 'Concepts of the analysis of qualitative data: a symposium', *Sociological Review*, vol. 27, pp. 651–77.

Burgess, R.G. 1982a, *Field Research: Sourcebook and Field Manual*, Allen & Unwin, London.

Burgess, R.G. 1982b, 'Keeping field notes', in *Field Research: Sourcebook and Field Manual*, ed. R.G. Burgess, Allen & Unwin, London.

Burgess, R.G. 1984, *In the Field: An Introduction to Field Research*, Allen & Unwin, London.

Burgess, W. 1925, 'What social case records should contain to be useful for sociological interpretation', *Social Forces*, vol. 6, pp. 524–32.

Burke, P. 1973, *A New Kind of History: From the Writings of Febvre*, Routledge & Kegan Paul, London.

Cameron-Bandler, L. 1985, *Solutions: Practical and Effective Antidotes for Sexual and Relationships Problems*, Future Pace, Ann Arbor, Michigan.

Campbell, D.T. & Fiske, D.W. 1959, 'Convergent and discriminant validation by the multitrait–multimethod matrix', *Psychological Bulletin*, vol. 56, pp. 81–105.

Carmen, E., Russo, N. & Baker Miller, J. 1984, 'Inequality and women's health: an overview', in *The Gender Gap in Psychotherapy*, eds P. Reiker & E. Carmen, Plenum, New York.

Cavan, R.S. 1929, 'Topical summaries of current literature: interviewing for life history material', *American Journal of Sociology*, vol. 15, pp. 100–15.

Chalasinski, J. 1981, 'The life records of the young generation of Polish peasants as a manifestation of contemporary culture', in *Biography and Society*, ed. D. Bertaux, Sage, London.

Cohen, S. & Taylor, L. 1977, 'Talking about prison blues', in *Doing Sociological Research*, eds I.C. Bell & H. Newby, Allen & Unwin, London.

Commonwealth of Australia 1989, *National Aboriginal Health Strategy*, National Aboriginal Health Strategy Working Party, Canberra.

Comte, A. 1864, *Cours de Philosophie Positive*, second edn, Ballière, Paris.

Connell, R.W. 1985, *Teachers' Work*, Allen & Unwin, Sydney.

Connell, R. 1987, *Gender and Power*, Polity Press, Cambridge.

Connell, R. 1992, 'A very straight guy: masculinity, homosexual experience and the dynamics of gender', *American Sociological Review*, vol. 56, pp. 735–51.

Connidis, I. 1989, 'Book review—ageing and the families: a support networks perspective', *Canadian Journal on Ageing*, vol. 8, pp. 187–97.

Cooley, C.H. 1956, *Human Nature and the Social Order*, The Free Press, Glencoe, Illinois.

Corsini, R. 1989, *Current Psychotherapies*, fourth edn, F.E. Peacock Publishers, Ithaca, Illinois.

Cushman, P. 1990, 'Why is the self empty?', *American Psychologist*, vol. 45, pp. 599–611.

Davidson, D. 1980a, *Essays on Actions and Events*, Oxford University Press, Oxford.

Davidson, D. 1980b, 'Mental Events', in *Essays on Actions and Events*, Oxford University Press, Oxford.

Davidson, D. 1984, 'On the very idea of a conceptual scheme', in *Inquiries into Truth and Interpretation*, Oxford University Press, Oxford.

Davies, A.F. 1966, *Private Politics: A Study of Five Political Outlooks*, Melbourne University Press, Melbourne.

Davies, P., Hickson, F., Weatherburn, P. & Hunt, A. 1993, 'Theorising sex', in *Sex, Gay Men and AIDS*, ed. P. Davies, Falmer Press, London.

Day, A. 1985, *We Can Manage: Expectations About Care and Varieties of Family Support Among People 75 Years of Age and Over*, Institute of Family Studies, Melbourne.

de Vaus, D. 1990, *Surveys in Social Research*, second edn, Unwin Hyman, London.

Dennett, D. 1987, *The Intentional Stance*, MIT Press, Cambridge, Massachusetts.

Denzin, N.K. 1968, 'On the ethics of disguised observation', *Social Problems*, vol. 15, no. 4, pp. 502–4.

Denzin, N. 1989, *The Research Act: A Theoretical Introduction to Sociological Methods*, third edn, Prentice Hall, Englewood Cliffs, New Jersey.

Denzin, N. 1992, *Symbolic Interactionism and Cultural Studies: The Politics of Interpretation*, Blackwell, Oxford.

Deutscher, I. 1973, *What We Say/What We Do*, Scott, Foresman & Co, Glenview, Illinois.

Dey, I. 1993, *Qualitative Data Analysis: A User Friendly Guide*, Routledge, London.

Dilthey, W. 1976, *Selected Writings*, Cambridge University Press, London.

Douglas, J.D. 1967, *The Social Meaning of Suicide*, Princeton University Press, Princeton.

Douglas, J.D. 1971, *Understanding Everyday Life*, Routledge & Kegan Paul, London.

Douglas, J.D. 1976, *Investigative Social Research*, Sage, Beverley Hills, California.

Douglas, L., Roberts, A. & Thompson, R. 1988, *Oral History: A Handbook*, Allen & Unwin, Sydney.

Dreyfus, H. & Dreyfus, S. 1986, *Mind Over Machine: The Power of Human Intuition and Expertise in the Era of the Computer*, Basic Books, New York.

Eastop, L.W. 1985, A Study of the Attitudes of People Who Had Been 'Burned Out' in the Ash Wednesday Bushfire, Department of Anthropology and Sociology, Monash University, Melbourne.

Egan, G. 1982, *The Skilled Helper: Models, Skills and Methods for Effective Helping*, second edn, Wadsworth, Belmont, California.

Ellis, W. & Orleans, P. 1971, 'Race research: up against the wall in more ways than one', in *Race, Chains and Urban Affairs Annual Review: 5*, eds P. Orleans & W. Ellis, Sage, Beverly Hills, California.

Elster, J. 1968, *Explaining Technical Change*, Cambridge University Press, Cambridge.

Elster, J. 1983, *Sour Grapes*, Cambridge University Press, Cambridge.

Erikson, E.H. 1958, *Young Man Luther*, Norton, New York.

Erikson, E.H. 1963, *Childhood and Society*, Norton, New York.

Erikson, E.H. 1970, *Gandhi's Truth: On the Origins of Militant Nonviolence*, Faber & Faber, London.

Erikson, K.T. 1968, 'On the ethics of disguised observation: a reply to Denzin', *Social Problems*, vol. 15, no. 4, pp. 505–6.

Fay, B. 1980, *Social Theory and Political Practice*, Allen & Unwin, London.

Fielding, N. & Lee, R. 1991, *Using Computers in Qualitative Research*, Sage, London.

Finch, J. 1984, 'It's great to have someone to talk to: the ethics and politics of interviewing women', in *Social Researching: Politics, Problems, Practice*, eds C. Bell & H. Roberts, Routledge & Kegan Paul, London.

Foddy, W.H. 1988, 'Open Versus Closed Questions: Really a Problem of Communication', Australian Bicentennial Meeting of Social Psychologists, Leura, New South Wales.

Foddy, W.H. 1994, 'Human ethics committee', *University Research News*, vol. 3, pp. 6–7.

Fontana, A. & Frey, J. 1994, 'Interviewing: the art of science', in *Handbook of Qualitative Research*, eds N. Denzin and Y. Lincoln, Sage, Thousand Oaks, California.

Foucault, M. 1970, *The Order of Things*, Tavistock, London.

Foucault, M. 1972, *The Archaeology of Knowledge*, first edn, Tavistock, London.

Foucault, M. 1979, *The History of Sexuality*, Penguin Books, London.

Foucault, M. 1984, 'What is an author?', in *The Foucault Reader*, ed. P. Rabinow, Penguin, London.

Freud, S. 1921, *Group Psychology and the Analysis of the Ego*, Hogarth Press, London.

Freud, S. 1977, 'Case Histories: "Dora" (1905) and "Little Hans" (1909)', in *The Pelican Freud Library, Volume Eight*, Pelican, Harmondsworth.

Freud, S. 1988a, *New Introductory Lectures in Psychoanalysis (1933)*, Pelican, Harmondsworth.

Freud, S. 1988b, 'The Unconscious' (1915), in *Pelican Freud Library*, Pelican, London.

Gadamer, H-G. 1975, *Truth and Method*, Sheed & Ward, London.

Garfinkel, H. 1967, *Studies in Ethnomethodology*, Prentice Hall, Englewood Cliffs, New Jersey.

Geertz, C. 1973, *The Interpretation of Cultures*, Basic Books, New York.

Gelford, H. & Walker, J. 1991, *Mastering APA Style*, American Psychological Association, Washington, DC.

Gerson, E. 1985, 'Computing in qualitative sociology', *Qualitative Sociology*, vol. 7, pp. 194–8.

Giddens, A. 1979, *Central Problems in Social Theory: Action, Structure and Contradiction in Social Analysis*, Macmillan, London.

Giddens, A. 1982, *Profiles and Critiques in Social Theory*, Macmillan, London.

Giddens, A. 1984, *The Constitution of Society*, Polity Press, Cambridge.

Giddens, A. 1990, *The Consequences of Modernity*, Polity Press, Cambridge.

Giorgi, A. 1985, *Phenomenology and Psychological Research*, Duquesne University Press, Pittsburg, Pennsylvania.

Glaser, B. 1992, *Basics of Grounded Theory Analysis*, Sociology Press, Mills Valley, California.

Glaser, B. & Strauss, A. 1965, *Awareness of Dying*, Aldine, Chicago.

Glaser, B. & Strauss, A. 1967, *The Discovery of Grounded Theory: Strategies for Qualitative Research*, Aldine, Chicago.

Goffman, E. 1959, *The Presentation of Self in Everyday Life*, Anchor Books, New York.

Goffman, E. 1961, *Asylums: Essays on the Social Situation of Mental Patients and Other Inmates*, Aldine, Chicago.

Goffman, E. 1963, *Stigma: Notes on the Management of Spoiled Social Identity*, Prentice Hall, Englewood, New Jersey.

Goffman, E. 1967, *Interaction Ritual*, Anchor Books, New York.

Goode, W.J. & Hatt, P.K. 1952, *Methods in Social Research*, McGraw-Hill, New York.

Goodwin, L. & Goodwin, W. 1984, 'Qualitative vs quantitative research or qualitative and quantitative research?', *Nursing Research*, vol. 33, pp. 378–9.

Graff, G. 1979, *Literature Against Itself*, University of Chicago Press, Chicago.

Guba, E. & Lincoln, Y. 1989, *Forced Generation Evaluation*, Sage, Newbury Park, California.

Habermas, J. 1987a, 'Dilthey's theory of understanding expression: ego identity and linguistic communication', in *Knowledge and Human Interests*, Polity Press, Cambridge.

Habermas, J. 1987b, *The Philosophical Discourse of Modernity*, Polity Press, Cambridge.

Hammersley, M. 1989, *The Dilemma of Qualitative Method: Herbert Blumer and the Chicago Tradition*, Routledge, London.

Hammersley, M. & Atkinson, P. 1983, *Ethnography: Principles in Practice*, Tavistock, London.

Harding, S. 1986, *The Science Question in Feminism*, Cornell University Press, Ithaca.

Harding, S. 1991, *Whose Science? Whose Knowledge? Thinking from Women's Lives*, Open University Press, Buckingham.

Haselbauer, K. 1987, *A Research Guide to the Health Sciences*, Greenwood, New York.

Haug, F. 1987, *Female Sexualization*, Verso, London.

Healy, D. 1990, *The Suspended Revolution*, Faber & Faber, London.

Hegel, G. 1931, *The Phenomenology of Mind*, George Allen & Unwin, London.

Heilman, S. 1980, 'Jewish sociologist: native-as-stranger', *The American Sociologist*, vol. 15, pp. 100–08.

Hoffman, J. 1980, 'Problems of access in the study of social elites and boards of directors', in *Fieldwork Experiences: Qualitative Approaches to Social Research*, eds W. Shaffir, R. Stebbins & A. Turowetz, St Martin's Press, New York.

Holland, J., Ramazanoglu, C., Scott, S., Sharpe, S. & Thompson, R. 1992, 'Risk, power and the possibility of pleasure: young women and safer sex', *AIDS Care*, vol. 4, pp. 273–83.

Hollway, W. 1984, 'Gender difference and the production of subjectivity', in *Changing the Subject*, eds J. Henriques, W. Hollway, C. Urwin, C. Venn & V. Walkerdine, Methuen, London.

Hughes, H.M. 1961, *The Fantastic Lodge: The Autobiography of a Girl Drug Addict*, Houghton-Mifflin, Boston.

Humphreys, L. 1970, *Tearoom Trade: Impersonal Sex in Public Places*, Aldine, Chicago.

Husserl, E. 1928, *Logische Untersuchungen*, fourth edn, Neimeyer, Halle, Germany. English synopsis included in Marvin Sarber 1962, *The Foundation of Phenomenology*, Paine Whitman, New York.

Ives, E. 1980, *The Tape Recorded Interview*, University of Tennessee Press, Knoxville.

Ivey, A.E. 1988, *Intentional Interviewing and Counselling: Facilitating Client Development*, Brooks/Cole Publishing Company, Pacific Grove, California.

James, N. 1984, 'A postscript to nursing', in *Social Researching: Politics, Problems, Practice*, eds C. Bell & H. Roberts, Routledge & Kegan Paul, London.

Jick, T. 1979, 'Mixing qualitative and quantitative methods: triangulation in action', *Administration Science Quarterly*, vol. 24, pp. 6002–11.

Jorgensen, D. 1989, *Participant Observation: A Methodology for Human Studies*, Sage, Newbury Park.

Kadushin, A. 1988, *The Social Work Interview*, second edn, Columbia University Press, New York.

Karp, D. 1980, 'Observing behaviour in public places: problems and strategies', in *Fieldwork Experiences: Qualitative Approaches to Social Research*, eds W. Shaffir, R. Stebbins & A. Turowetz, St Martin's Press, New York.

Kaufman, S. 1988, 'Stroke rehabilitation and the negotiation of identity', in *Qualitative Gerontology*, eds S. Reinharz & G. Rowles, Springer, New York.

Kellehear, A. 1993, *The Unobtrusive Researcher: A Guide to Methods*, Allen & Unwin, Sydney.

Kidder, L.H. 1981, *Selltiz, Wrightsman and Cook's Research Methods in Social Relations*, fourth edn, Holt Saunders International Editions, New York.

Kidder, L.H. & Judd, C.M. 1986, *Research Methods in Social Relations*, CBS Publishing Japan, Tokyo.

King, M., Novik, L. & Citrenbaum, C. 1983, *Irresistible Communication: Creative Skills for the Health Professional*, W.B. Saunders, USA.

Kippax, S. 1990, 'Memory-work: a method', in *The Social Sciences and Health Research*, eds J. Daly & E. Willis, Public Health Association Australia Inc., Ballarat, Victoria.

Kippax, S., Connell, R., Dowsett, G. & Crawford, J. 1993, *Sustaining Safe Sex: Gay Communities Respond to AIDS*, Falmer, London.

Kirk, J. & Miller, M. 1986, *Reliability and Validity in Qualitative Research*, Sage, California.

Klockars, C.B. 1977, 'Field ethics for the life history', in *Street Ethnography*, ed. R.S. Weppner, Sage, London.

Komesaroff, P. 1994, 'Medicine and the ethical condition of modernity', in *Researching Health Care: Methods, Ethics and Responsibility: Pre-Publication Draft Conference Papers*, St Vincent's Hospital, Melbourne.

Kuhn, T.S. 1970, *The Structure of Scientific Revolutions*, second edn, University of Chicago Press, Chicago.

Lakatos, I. 1970, 'Falsification and the methodology of scientific research programmes', in *Criticism and the Growth of Knowledge*, eds I. Lakatos & A. Musgrove, Cambridge University Press, Cambridge.

Lake, P. 1992, 'A decade of Aboriginal health research', *Aboriginal Health Information Bulletin*, vol. 17, pp. 12–16.

Layder, D. 1993, *New Strategies in Social Research: An Introduction and a Guide*, Polity, Cambridge.

Leggatt, M. 1981, *Adaption to Psychiatric Disorder and Physical Disability*, vols 1 & 2, Department of Anthropology and Sociology, Monash University, Melbourne.

Liebow, E. 1967, *Tally's Corner*, Little, Brown, Boston.

Lifton, R.J. 1968, *Death in Life*, Random House, New York.

Little, G. 1989, *Speaking For Myself*, McPhee Gribble, Melbourne.

Lofland, J. & Lofland, L. 1984, *Analysing Social Settings: A Guide to Qualitative Observations and Analysis*, second edn, Wadsworth, Belmont, California.

Lopata, H. 1980, 'Interviewing American Widows', in *Fieldwork Experiences: Qualitative Approaches to Social Research*, eds W. Shaffir, R. Stebbins & A. Turowetz, St Martin's Press, New York.

Lynn, J. & Jay, A. 1987, *Yes, Prime Minister: The Honourable James Hacker's Diaries*, BBC Publishing, London.

Lyotard, J-F. 1984, *The Postmodern Condition*, Minnesota University Press, Minn.

Lyotard, J-F. 1989, 'The dream-work does not think', in *The Lyotard Reader*, ed. A. Benjamin, Blackwell, Oxford.

MacIntyre, S. 1979, 'Some issues in the study of pregnancy careers', *Sociological Review*, vol. 27, pp. 755–71.

Maccoby, E. & Maccoby, N. 1954, 'The interview: a tool of social science', in *Handbook of Social Psychology*, ed. G. Lindzey, Addison-Wesley, Cambridge, Massachusetts.

Maddocks, I. 1992, 'Ethics in Aboriginal research', *The Medical Journal of Australia*, vol. 157, pp. 553–5.

Mahew, H. 1985, *London Labour and the London Poor (1851)*, Sage, New York.

Malinowski, B. 1948, *The Sexual Lives of Savages in North-West Melanesia*, Routledge & Kegan Paul, London.

Mandelstam, N. 1970, *Hope Against Hope*, Penguin, London.

Mattingly, C. 1991a, 'What is clinical reasoning?', *American Journal of Occupational Therapy*, vol. 45, no. 11, pp. 979–86.

Mattingly, C. 1991b, 'The narrative nature of clinical reasoning', *American Journal of Occupational Therapy*, vol. 45, no. 11, pp. 998–1005.

Maykovich, M. 1980, *Medical Sociology*, Alfred Publishing, Sherman Oaks, Calif.

McCall, M. 1980, 'Who and where are the artists?', in *Fieldwork Experiences: Qualitative Approaches to Social Research*, eds W. Shaffir, R. Stebbins & A. Turowetz, St Martin's Press, New York.

McDonald, I. 1994, 'Clinicians studying their own practice', *Researching Health Care: Methods, Ethics and Responsibility: Pre-Publication Draft Conference Papers*, St Vincent's Hospital, Melbourne.

McGartland, M. & Polgar, S. 1994, 'Paradigm collapse in psychology: the necessity for a two method approach', *Australian Psychologist*, vol. 29, pp. 21–8.

McGuiness, M. & Wadsworth, Y. 1992, *Understanding, Anytime—A Consumer Evaluation of an Acute Psychiatric Hospital*, Victorian Mental Illness Awareness Council, Melbourne.

McTaggart, R. 1989, 'Principles of participatory action research', *Adult Education Quarterly*, vol. 41, p. 170.

Merton, R.K. 1972, 'Insiders and outsiders: a chapter in the sociology of knowledge', *American Journal of Sociology*, vol. 78, pp. 9–47.

Miles, M. & Huberman, M. 1994, *Qualitative Data Analysis*, second edn, Sage, Thousand Oaks, California.

Miller, B. & Humphreys, L. 1980, 'Keeping in touch: contact with stigmatized subjects', in *Fieldwork Experiences: Qualitative Approaches to Social Research*, eds W. Shaffir, R. Stebbins & A. Turowetz, St Martin's Press, New York.

Mills, C.W. 1959, *The Sociological Imagination*, Oxford University Press, London.

Minichiello, V. 1987, 'Someone's decision: that is how I got here', *Australian Journal of Social Issues*, vol. 22, pp. 345–56.

Minichiello, V., Alexander, L. & Jones, D. 1990, 'A typology of decision-making situations for entry to nursing homes', in *In-depth Interviewing: Researching People*, first edn, Longman Cheshire, Melbourne.

Minichiello, V., Aroni, R., Timewell, E. & Alexander, L. 1990, *In-Depth Interviewing: Researching People*, first edn, Longman Cheshire, Melbourne.

Minichiello, V., Browning, C. & Aroni, R. 1992, 'The challenge of the study of ageing', in *Gerontology: A Multidisciplinary Approach*, eds V. Minichiello, L. Alexander & D. Jones, Prentice Hall, Sydney.

Misch, G. 1951, *A History of Autobiography in Antiquity*, Harvard University Press, Cambridge, Massachusetts.

Moore, J.W. 1973, 'Social constraints on sociological knowledge: academics and research concerning minorities', *Social Problems*, vol. 21, pp. 65–77.

Moore, S. & Rosenthal, D. 1992, 'The social context of adolescent sexuality: safe sex implications', *Journal of Adolescence*, vol. 15, pp. 415–35.

Moustakas, C. 1990, *Heuristic Research: Design, Methodology and Application*, Sage, Newbury Park.

NH&MRC 1991, Guidelines on Ethical Matters in Aboriginal and Torres Strait Islander Health Research Interim Publication, Canberra.

Nieswiadony, R. 1987, *Foundations of Nursing Research,* Appleton & Lange, Norwalk, Connecticut.

O'Shea *v.* Sullivan and other, 6 May 1994, *Australian Tort Reports*, para 81-273.

Oakley, A. 1988, 'Interviewing women: a contradiction in terms', in *Doing Feminist Research*, ed. H. Roberts, Routledge, London.

Park, R.E. 1930, 'Murder and the case study method', *American Journal of Sociology*, vol. 36, pp. 447–54.

Parse, R., Coyne, A. & Smith, M. 1985, *Nursing Research: Qualitative Methods*, Brady Communications Company, Bowie, Maryland.

Patterson, C.H. 1986, *Theories of Counselling and Psychotherapy*, fourth edn, Harper & Row, New York.

Patton, M.Q. 1989, *Qualitative Evaluation Methods*, first edn, Sage, Beverley Hills, California.

Patton, M.Q. 1990, *Qualitative Evaluation and Research Methods*, second edn, Sage, Newbury Park, California.

Pettigrew, J. 1988, 'Reminiscences of fieldwork among the Sikhs', in *Doing Feminist Research*, ed. H. Roberts, Routledge, London.

Phillips, B. 1985, *Sociological Research Methods: An Introduction*, Dorsey, Homewood, Illinois.

Plummer, K. 1983, *Documents of Life: An Introduction to the Problems and Literature of a Humanistic Method*, Allen & Unwin, Sydney.

Polanyi, M. 1967, *The Tacit Dimension*, Routledge & Kegan Paul, London.

Polatajko, H., Miller, J., MacKinnon, J. & Harburn, K. 1989, 'Occupational therapy research in Canada. Report from the Association of Canadian Occupational Therapy University Programs', *Canadian Journal of Occupational Therapy*, vol. 56, no. 5, pp. 257–61.

Polgar, S. & Thomas, S. 1991, *Introduction to Research in the Health Sciences*, second edn, Churchill Livingstone, Melbourne.

Popper, K. 1959, *The Logic of Scientific Discovery*, Hutchinson, London.

Punch, M. 1986, *The Politics and Ethics of Field Work*, Sage, Beverly Hills, California.

Quine, W.V.O. 1960, *Word and Object*, Harvard University Press, Harvard.

Raimy, V. ed. 1985, *Training in Clinical Psychology*, Prentice Hall, Boulder Conf., New York.

Reinharz, S. & Rowles, G. 1988, *Qualitative Gerontology*, Springer, New York.

Richards, L. & Richards, T. 1987, 'Qualitative data analysis: can computers do it?', *Australian and New Zealand Journal of Sociology*, vol. 23, pp. 23–35.

Richards, L. & Richards, T. 1992, 'The transformation of qualitative method: computational paradigms and research processes', in *Using Computers in Qualitative Research*, eds N. Fielding & R. Lee, Sage, London.

Richards, L. & Richards, T. 1993, *NUD.IST User Guide: Version 3.0 Qualitative Data Analysis Solutions for Research Professional Manual*, Qualitative Solutions and Research, La Trobe University, Melbourne.

Ricoeur, P. 1974, *The Conflict of Interpretations: Essays in Hermeneutics*, Northwestern University Press, Evanston.

Ridge, D., Minichiello, V. & Plummer, D. 1994 (in progress), Sexual Identity, Gay Community and Safe Sex Pathways Among Young Gay Men, Sexual Health Research Group, School of Behavioural Health Sciences, La Trobe University, Melbourne.

Roberts, H. 1988, *Doing Feminist Research*, third edn, Routledge & Kegan Paul, London.

Root, M. 1993, *Philosophy of Social Science: The Methods, Ideals and Politics of Social Enquiry*, Blackwell, Oxford.

Rorty, R. 1991, 'Texts and Lumps', in *Objectivity, Relativism and Truth: Philosophical Papers Volume 1*, Cambridge University Press.

Rose, G. 1982, *Deciphering Sociological Research*, Macmillan, London.

Rossi, E.L. 1986, *The Psychobiology of Mind–Body Healing: New Concepts of Therapeutic Hypnosis*, Brunner Mazel, New York.

Said, E.W. 1978, *Orientalism*, Routledge & Kegan Paul, London.

Sanjek, R. 1990, *Fieldnotes: The Making of Anthropology*, Cornell University, New York.

Schatzman, L. & Strauss, A. 1973, *Field Research: Strategies for a Natural Sociology*, Prentice Hall, Englewood Cliffs, New Jersy.

Schein, E. 1987, *The Clinical Perspective in Fieldwork*, Sage, California.

Schlegel, F. 1808, '*Über die Sprache und Weisheit der Indier*, Book II, Chapter 2, translation in eds B.F. Feldman & R.D. Richardson 1979, *The Rise of Modern Mythology*, Indiana University Press, Indianapolis, Indiana.

Schön, D. 1983, *The Reflective Practitioner: How Professionals Think in Action*, Basic Books, New York.

Schön, D. 1987, *Educating the Reflective Practitioner*, Jossey-Bass, San Francisco.

Schopenhauer, A. 1966, *The World as Will and Representation*, Doubleday Anchor, New York.

Schütz, A. 1962, *The Problem of Social Reality*, Martinus Nijhoff, The Hague.

Schwartz, H. & Jacobs, J. 1979, *Qualitative Sociology: A Method to the Madness*, Free Press, New York.

Seaman, C. 1987, *Research Methods: Principles, Practice and Theory for Nursing*, Appleton & Lange, Norwalk, Connecticut.

Searle, J. 1969, *Speech Acts*, Cambridge University Press, Cambridge.

Searle, J. 1983, *Intentionality*, Cambridge University Press, Cambridge.

Seidel, J. & Clark, J. 1984, 'The ETHNOGRAPH: A Computer Program for the Analysis of Qualitative Data', *Qualitative Sociology*, vol. 7, pp. 110–25.

Shaffir, W. & Stebbins, R. 1991, *Experiencing Fieldwork: An Inside View of Qualitative Research*, Sage, Newbury Park.

Shaffir, W., Stebbins, R. & Turowetz, A. 1980, *Fieldwork Experiences: Qualitative Approaches to Social Research*, St Martin's Press, New York.

Shaw, C.R. 1966, *The Jack Roller: A Delinquent Boy's Own Story*, University of Chicago Press, Chicago.

Shelly, A. & Sibert, E. 1986, 'Using logic programming to facilitate qualitative data analysis', *Qualitative Sociology*, vol. 9, pp. 145–61.

Shipman, M.D. 1972, *The Limitations of Social Research*, Longman, London.

Sieber, S. 1973, 'The integration of fieldwork and survey methods', *American Journal of Sociology*, vol. 78, pp. 1335–59.

Silverman, D. 1985, *Qualitative Methodology and Sociology*, Gower Publishing, Aldershot, Hants.

Silverman, D. & Perakyla, A. 1990, 'AIDS counselling: the interactional organisation of talk about "delicate" issues', *Sociology of Health and Illness*, vol. 12, pp. 293–318.

Simmel, G. 1894, 'Das Problem der Soziologie', *Jahrbuch für Gesetzgebung, Verwaltung und Volkwirtschaft*, vol. 16, p. 272.

Smith, B., Johnson, K., Paulsen, D. & Shocket, F. 1976, *Political Research Methods: Foundations and Techniques*, Houghton, Boston.

Spector, M. 1980, 'Learning to study public figures', in *Fieldwork Experiences: Qualitative Approaches to Social Research*, eds W. Shaffir, R. Stebbins & A. Turowetz, St Martin's Press, New York.

Spender, D. 1988, 'The gatekeepers: a feminist critique of academic publishing', in *Doing Feminist Research*, ed. H. Roberts, Routledge, London.

Spradley, J.P. 1979, *The Ethnographic Interview*, Holt, Rinehart & Winston, London.

Sprinivas, M., Shah, A. & Ramaswamy, A. 1979, *The Fieldworker and the Field*, Oxford University Press, Delhi.

Stanfield, J. 1994, 'Ethnic modeling in qualitative research', in *Handbook of Qualitative Research*, eds N. Denzin & Y. Lincoln, Sage, Thousand Oaks, California.

Stanley, L. & Wise, S. 1983, *Breaking Out: Feminist Consciousness and Feminist Research*, Routledge & Kegan Paul, London.

Steiner, G. 1994, 'Trusting in reason', *Times Literary Supplement*, 24 June, pp. 3–4.

Steven, I. & Douglas, R. 1988, 'Dissatisfaction in general practice: what do patients really want?', *Medical Journal of Australia*, vol. 148, no. 6, pp. 280–2.

Stewart, C.J. & Cash, J.W.B. 1988, *Interviewing: Principles and Practices*, William C. Brown, Dubuque, Iowa.

Stewart, D. & Shamdasani, P. 1991, *Focus Groups: Theory and Practice*, Sage, Newbury Park.

Stonequist, E.V. 1961, *The Marginal Man: A Study in Personality and Culture Conflict*, Russell & Russell, New York.

Strauss, A. 1987, *Qualitative Analysis for Social Scientists*, Cambridge University Press, Cambridge.

Strauss, A. & Corbin, J. 1990, *Basics of Qualitative Research: Grounded Theory Procedures and Techniques*, Sage, Newbury Park.

Sullivan, H.S. 1955, *The Interpersonal Theory of Psychiatry*, Tavistock, London.

Sutherland, E.H. 1937, *The Professional Thief by a Professional Thief*, Phoenix Books, Chicago.

Tagg, S.K. 1985, 'Life story interviews and their interpretation', in *The Research Interview: Uses and Approaches*, eds M. Brenner et al., Academic Press, London.

Taylor, C. 1985, *Human Agency and Language*, Cambridge University Press, Cambridge.

Taylor, K. 1988, 'Telling bad news: physicians and the disclosure of undesirable information', *Sociology of Health and Illness*, vol. 10, pp. 109–32.

Taylor, S.J. & Bogdan, R. 1984, *Introduction to Qualitative Research Methods*, second edn, Wiley, New York.

Terkel, S. 1977, *Working*, Penguin, Harmondsworth.

Tesch, R. 1990, *Qualitative Research: Analysis Types and Software Tools*, Falmer Press, New York.

Thomas, S. et al. 1992, 'Focus groups in health research: a methodological review', *Annual Review of Health Social Sciences*, eds J. Daly, A. Kellehear and E. Willis, La Trobe University, Melbourne, vol. 2, pp. 7–20.

Thomas, W.I. & Znaniecki, F. 1958, *The Polish Peasant in Europe and America*, Dover Publications, New York, originally published 1918–20.

Tomm, K. 1989, 'Foreword', in *Literate Means to Therapeutic Ends*, eds M. White & D. Epston, Dulwich Centre Publicity, Adelaide.

Traupmann, J., Eckels, E. & Hatfield, E. 1982, 'Intimacy in older women's lives', *The Gerontologist*, vol. 22, pp. 493–8.

Trost, J. 1986, 'Statistically nonrepresentative stratified sampling: a sampling technique for qualitative studies', *Qualitative Sociology*, vol. 9, pp. 54–7.

Turner, B. & Adams, C. 1988, 'Reported change in preferred sexual activity over the adult years', *Journal of Sex Research*, vol. 25, pp. 289–303.

Valentine, C. & Valentine, V. 1970, *Making the Scene, Digging the Action and Telling it Like it is: Anthropologists and Work in a Dark Ghetto: Contemporary Perspectives*, Free Press, New York.

van Maanen, J. 1988, *Tales of the Field*, University of Chicago Press, Chicago.

Viney, L.L. 1986, 'Assessment of psychological states through content analysis of verbal communications', in *Content Analysis of Verbal Behaviour: Significance in Clinical Medicine and Psychiatry*, eds L.A. Gottschalk, F. Lolas & L.L. Viney, Springer Verlag, Germany.

Wadsworth, Y. 1984, *Do it Yourself Research*, Victorian Council of Social Service, Collingwood, Victoria.

Wadsworth, Y. 1991, *Everyday Evaluation on the Run*, ARIA, Melbourne.

Wakeford, J. 1981, 'From methods to practice: a critical note on the teaching of research practice to undergraduates', *Sociology*, vol. 15, pp. 505–12.

Walker, M. 1987, *Writing Research Papers*, second edn, Norton, New York.

Walker, R. 1989, *Doing Research: A Handbook for Teachers*, Routledge, Cambridge.

Wax, R. 1971, *Doing Field Work: Warnings and Advice*, University of Chicago Press, Chicago.

Webb, B. 1982, 'The art of note-taking', in *Field Research: Sourcebook and Field Manual*, ed. R. Burgess, Allen & Unwin, London.

Webb, E.J., Campbell, D.T., Schwartz, R.D. & Sechvest, L. 1966, *Unobstrusive Measures: Non-Reactive Research in the Social Sciences*, Rand McNally, Chicago.

Weber, M. 1949, *The Methodology of the Social Sciences*, Free Press, Glencoe.

Weber, M. 1958, 'Science as a vocation', in *From Max Weber: Essays in Sociology*, eds H. Gerth & C.W. Mills, Oxford University Press, New York.

White, M. & Epston, D. 1989, *Literate Means to Therapeutic Ends*, Dulwich Centre Publicity, Adelaide.

White, R.W. 1975, *Lives in Progress: A Study of Natural Growth of Personality*, third edn, Holt, Rinehart & Winston, New York.

Whyte, W.F. 1955, *Street Corner Society: The Social Structure of an Italian Slum*, University of Chicago Press, Chicago.

Wiener, C. 1982, 'Tolerating the uncertainty', in *Deciphering Sociological Research*, ed. G. Rose, Macmillan, London.

Wild, R.A. 1974, *Bradstow: A Study of Class Status and Power in a Small Australian Town*, Angus & Robertson, Sydney.

Williams, C. 1981, *Open Cut and the Working Class in an Australian Mining Town*, Allen & Unwin, Sydney.

Wilson, B. & Wynn, J. 1987, *Shaping Futures: Youth Action for Livelihood*, Allen & Unwin, Sydney.

Wolcott, H. 1990, *Writing Up Qualitative Reseach*, Sage, Newbury Park.

Zinn, M. 1979, 'Field research in minority communities: ethnic, methodological and political observations by an insider', *Journal of Social Problems*, vol. 27, no. 2, pp. 208–14.

Zinsser, W. 1980, *On Writing Well: An Informal Guide to Writing Nonfiction*, Harper & Row, New York.

Index